P9-AOL-585

Frederick Rolfe:
Baron Corvo

BY THE SAME AUTHOR

A Bibliography of Ronald Firbank
Ronald Firbank: A Biography

Frederick Rolfe: Baron Corvo

A BIOGRAPHY

Miriam J. Benkovitz

G. P. PUTNAM'S SONS
NEW YORK

DALE H. GRAMLEY LIBRARY
SALEM COLLEGE
WINSTON-SALEM, N. C.

PR
5236
.R27
Z58
1977

First American Edition 1977
First published in Great Britain 1977
Copyright © 1977 by Miriam J. Benkovitz
SBN: 399-12009-2

All rights reserved. No part of this publication
may be reproduced, stored in a retrieval system, or
transmitted in any form or by any means electronic,
mechanical, photocopying, recording or otherwise, without
the prior permission of the Copyright owner.

Library of Congress Cataloging in Publication Data

Benkovitz, Miriam J
Frederick Rolfe, Baron Corvo.

Includes index.
1. Rolfe, Frederick William, 1860-1913 – Biography.
2. Authors, English – 20th century – Biography.
I. Title.
PR5236.R27Z58   823'.8 [B]   77-3671

PRINTED IN THE UNITED STATES OF AMERICA

To my mother and the
memory of my father

Contents

Illustrations

ix

Foreword

FREDERICK WILLIAM ROLFE signed himself from time to time with a variety of names, among them Frederick Austin, Fr. Rolfe, A. W. Riter, Al Siddik, Franz Wilhelm V Bracht, Frederick of Venice, Uriele de Ricordi, and most notably Baron Corvo. 'A wretched impostor', John Lane, the publisher, called him. 'The servant of his poses' was a more tolerant judgement. In either case, his 'tekhnikrym[s]' obscured the man to whom they applied. Baron Corvo is a myth. Behind him is the reality, Frederick Rolfe.

In an attempt to get at the reality, I have depended as much as possible on Rolfe's written word, of course with an eye to its truth or lack of it. Although I have made extensive use of Rolfe's unpublished essays, fiction, and letters, I have consulted the texts of published material with certain exceptions. This biography was written before Cecil Woolf published his editions of the complete, unexpurgated Venice Letters, a number of short stories and essays under the title *The Armed Hands*, and the collected poems. Pieces contained in the last two volumes and previously unpublished, I read in manuscript. The Venice Letters consist of a series which Rolfe wrote from Venice to Masson Fox between October 1909 and August 1910. Excerpts from the Venice Letters had already been printed and, owing to their allegedly scandalous character, several unauthorised and incomplete typed copies have been passed from hand to hand. For the sake of accuracy and completeness, I read Rolfe's holograph letters, now the property of the Humanities Research Library of The University of Texas at Austin. A selection of the letters which Rolfe wrote to Father Charles Sidney de Vere Beauclerk over a period extending from 1897 to 1907 has also been published. But again in the interest of completeness I made use of the letters in manuscript which are a part of the Martyr Worthy Collection. In other instances, I had no choice but to rely on typed copies of letters written by Rolfe, to Rolfe, or about Rolfe. These copies are a part of the Henry W. and Albert A. Berg Collection of The New York Public Library, Astor, Lennox, and Tilden Foundations. Still another body of letters demands comment. Addressed to various correspondents, they are Rolfe's holograph drafts in a letter book which is also in the Martyr Worthy Collection, made by the late David

Roth. There is no certainty that all letters recorded in the letter book were posted. Yet there is evidence from printed sources or from replies to some of the letters that many were mailed, so that to conclude that most or even all were is not unreasonable.

Although the fact will be obvious to every reader, I still wish to state that this is not a critical biography. To write about Frederick Rolfe without writing about his literary output is impossible. But no attempt is made here to examine his literary origins or to place him among his contemporaries, whether in the uncertainties of the 1890s or the burgeoning modernism of the early part of the twentieth century. Nor is there special pleading for Rolfe's idiosyncratic and intensely personal fiction.

For access to the materials referred to above and the help I had with them and with others not already mentioned, I wish to thank the Berg Collection of The New York Public Library, The Bodleian Library of Oxford University, The British Museum, Houghton Library of Harvard University, Humanities Research Library of The University of Texas, National Library of Scotland at Edinburgh, the Public Record Office, Z. Smith Reynolds Library of Wake Forest University, John and Martin Roth, who preserve their father's Martyr Worthy Collection, and the Royal Literary Fund.

Special acknowledgements are owing to Julian Symons, Donald Weeks, and Mary E. Williams. To Julian Symons, executor for his late brother A. J. A. Symons, I am indebted for permission to see and to quote from Rolfe's published and unpublished work. Donald Weeks has invariably proved helpful. My differences with his interpretation of material and his dating of events in Rolfe's life are to be construed only as a part of the progression of biography. Mary E. Williams has acted the thankless part of the critic.

For other especially valuable assistance of several kinds, I wish to thank the late Antonio Arban, Timothy d'Arch Smith, Victor Bonham-Carter, David Farmer, Sally Leach, Winifred A. Myers, George F. Sims, Lola Szladits, and Walter Talevi.

In addition I have incurred obligations to The Armitt Library of Ambleside, The Beinecke Rare Book Room and Manuscript Library of Yale University, Alan Bird, George Bixby, W. H. Bond, Janet Brown, Alan Clodd, The Columbia University Libraries, The Druitt Library of Christchurch, Franca Sacerdoti Fanni, Major Tino Giorgi, Mrs. Gotch, the Gritti Palace Hotel, Carolyn Harris, Mary M. Hirth, Sonja P. Karsen, King's College Library at Aberdeen, C. J. Kitching, Rabbi Bertram Korn, E. S. Leedham Green, Kenneth A. Lohf, Myrtle I. Matthew, Ben Meiselman, Richard Mohr, June Moll, Doris Langley Moore, Gloria Moore, Edwin Moseley, P. S. Moss, Richard J. Murdoch, Henry Pelling, Warren Roberts, Anthony Rota, Irene Roth, S. M. Simpson, Skidmore College Library, Barbara Smith, University Library of the University of Cambridge, the University Registry of Oxford University, Doris Unz,

Arthur Uphill, Lawrence Wallrich, the late Herbert Weinstock, who suggested that I write this book, Eric Weller, the late Herbert West, and Marjorie G. Wynne.

Saratoga Springs, New York MIRIAM J. BENKOVITZ
April 1975

I was made with Job to possess months of vanity, &
heights of weariness were appointed to me.
FREDERICK ROLFE

The pride of the peacock is the glory of God
The lust of the goat is the bounty of God
The wrath of the lion is the wisdom of God.
WILLIAM BLAKE

Prologue

EARLY IN AUGUST 1908, having come first by horse-drawn trap from Langenny in Breconshire to Abergavenny, by train to London, and thence across the Channel to France and Italy, Richard Dawkins and Frederick Rolfe arrived in Venice. They were hardly a more ill-assorted pair than most people who travel together, and the fact that they were conspicuous at all was owing to Rolfe. A former school-master, a failed priest, once an unsuccessful painter, now an unsuccess-ful photographer and writer, Rolfe was in his forty-eighth year. He was a slight but broad-chested man of about average height. He had, he said, 'the very high broad brow of a student and thinker, crowned by short hair of a reddish chestnut slightly silvered'.[1] The *Yellow Book* writer Ella d'Arcy had compared his head with that of King Charles I in his portraits.[2] Rolfe was soberly dressed; but contrary to fashion, he wore no hat and although he acknowledged it as indecorous and very likely to excite '*admiratio*' outside England, Rolfe carried his possessions in a large laundry hamper secured with a padlock. Among them was the manuscript of the book on which he was at work, *Hubert's Arthur*, and a 'sweet little Pindar' which he hoped Dawkins would read aloud.

Rolfe later asserted that Dawkins was incapable of performing 'a noble (i.e. a free) act' and wrote of him as 'repugnant, flabby, carroty, freckled, mug-nosed, bristly . . ., toothed of Singaglia-cheese-colour', and with no chest whatever. His voice, Rolfe said, was the voice of a 'strangulated Punch'.[3] In actuality, Dawkins was a harsh featured, awkward, ungainly man who fidgeted endlessly,[4] but he was also independent, tolerant, iconoclastic, unaffected, kind but prudent, readily amused and amusing. In 1908, at thirty-seven, eleven years Rolfe's junior, Dawkins was already Director of the British School of Archaeology at Athens, a distinguished archaeologist and linguist, and a developing folklorist.

Dawkins had suggested this holiday in Italy and made it possible. As he was most of his life, Rolfe was in real financial difficulties. For much of the past two years he had been dependent on the generosity of a friend, Harry Pirie-Gordon, and his parents, the Edward Pirie-Gordons, for a roof over his head and the food he ate. He owed the elder Pirie-Gordon more than £10. He owed at least one doctor's bill and possibly two, from which in May he had simply walked away. Very likely, Dawkins had sent him money in May; something he did

1

had prevented Rolfe from 'inquiring the way to the nearest work-house'.[5] In any case, Dawkins's idea of a holiday in Italy was a welcome one. It became even more attractive when Dawkins offered to finance the trip with a loan to Rolfe. He planned to repay it with money to be earned in Italy by descriptive writing and two series of artistic photographs, classical and mediaeval Venice, although Dawkins testified later that he expected no repayment and that it did not matter.[6] Owing to the death of John Doyle, his mother's first cousin from whom he inherited considerable property, Dawkins was a man of means. He had not yet grown easy with these circumstances, but he felt able to spend something for the company of a man who shared his faith in ability as the way to success and his distaste for asceticism. Rolfe summed it up for Dawkins and himself in a letter written on the eve of their departure, 'Oh for exercise and slumber, long fasting and full meals. Oh to forget all my scruples and live a while in peace and freedom for the moment only, in a place where all is absent which can stimulate to moral feeling. I am sick of morals.'[7]

The two men set on Venice as their destination almost by chance but only after much discussion. The excursion had been concocted before 9 January 1908, when Rolfe told Dawkins that his 'Italian proposal' was 'too lovely' but that he was unwilling to think of the future. By late February, however, Rolfe was 'saving' himself for Italy in summer and talking about photographic equipment. In April he was explaining that he wanted a few days in Milan so that he could have a look at the current Borgias, Count Francesco and his son Cesare, who, he declared, were 'dying' to be his 'door-mats'. At the same time he wrote of visiting the 'untravelled pseudo-paradise' of the Gargano peninsula with a caravan. He set forth the ideal way of making such a tour, 'with tents and mules and half a dozen young tumblers' giving performances by the way while he and Dawkins posed as 'padroni of the troop'. But Rolfe maintained that anything east and south of Rome was a hazard, what with malaria and hurtling motor cars. He said he thought the 'Heel of Italy' their best 'mark'. Then in a letter of 12 May 1908, although he was quite ready to drive in Calabria (he mentioned Bova) or even go to Rhodes, he declared Dawkins's 'Venice idea' lovely; and thereafter his thoughts turned more and more, with excitement and anticipation, to a 'gorgeous holiday' in Venice.[8]

However light-heartedly the decision was reached, it was one of the most important Rolfe made in his entire life. It is inevitable to wonder whether, like his fictional hero Nicholas Crabbe at a crucial point in his career, Rolfe knew that in going to Venice he was going 'to turn over another book of his life', whether there came upon him the 'delicious feeling . . . which comes upon the swimmer who stands ready to plunge on the brink of a new stream'. Rolfe has described that feeling as 'the grand sensation of inquiry, of experiment, of daring

2

discovery'; and as 'about the most precious sensation which the doctrines of evolution and modernistic and higher criticism have left to us'.[9] When, with Dawkins, Rolfe climbed down from the train in Venice's rail station and prepared to go by ferry and foot to his hotel, the 'underlying fatality of his identity'[10] was at the verge of realisation. He never left Venice except for a few days at a time, and he never wanted to. Indeed, he underwent terrible and killing hardships in order to stay. That Rolfe found particular pleasure in the 'sumptuous bathing and exquisite young persons about' is undeniable. Their beauty provoked a lyrical lament for the lack of someone to fix the beauty and splendour which he saw. He wrote:

> there is not a single painter of young Venetians . . . poised on lofty poops, out on the wide, wide lagoon, at white dawn, when the whole world gleams with the candid iridescence of mother of pearl, glowing white flesh with green-blue eyes & shining hair poised in white air trembling like song in white light reflected in white smooth sea—of young Venetians poised on lofty poops out on the wide lagoon, at high noon, when all the world which is not brilliant is blue, glowing young litheness with its sumptuous breasts poised in air like shadows of lapis-lazuli under a monstrous dome of turquoise—of young Venetians poised on lofty poops out on the wide lagoon, at sunset, glowing magnificent young strength dominantly illumined, poised in an atmosphere of lavender & heliotrope in tremendous stretches of sea & sky all cut out of jewels, limitless amethyst & far-reaching turquoise, or all burnished copper splashed with emeralds and streaked with the blue, the insistent blue of borage.[11]

But Venice was more than a harmony of sea and sky and gleaming young bodies under magical light. Rolfe also relished its teeming streets and alleys through which he threaded his way, always in prayer, as was his habit when he walked alone.[12] At once Venice became what Rolfe had created imaginatively when his experience consisted only of the deprivation and the bitter taste of failure. It answered every fluctuation of his nature, and in it he knew himself endowed with powers as well as lusts and obsessions to some end.

Part I:

1860 – 1890

[1]

FREDERICK WILLIAM ROLFE was born on 22 July 1860 at 61 Cheapside, London. That number marked a building at the corner of Bow Lane and across from the opening into Honey Lane. There and at 112 Cheapside the Rolfe family had manufactured pianofortes since 1784. Members of the family lived on the upper floors.

Frederick Rolfe listed his ancestors as James, son of Nicholas, son of William, son of Robert.[1] No doubt Frederick could have named still more remote lineal ancestors. Robert, his great-great-grandfather, was a maker of musical instruments and clerk of his parish, Eltham, Kent. Kent may well have been the county in which a vast Rolfe clan began and from which it spread throughout Great Britain and America. There are early references to Rolfes in Norfolk, where the most famous Rolfe of all was born, John Rolfe, who sailed for Virginia in June 1606 and on 5 April 1613 married the Indian princess Pocahontas. But the name Rolfe occurred with enough frequency in thirteenth- and fourteenth-century Kentish records and it has persisted significantly so that it is reasonable to designate the point of origin of the Rolfe family as Kent. In Eltham, Kent, Robert's son and Frederick's great-grandfather William was born in 1756.

Eventually William moved to London, where in 1784 he began to make pianofortes at 112 Cheapside. In the early 1790s he was a partner in the firm of Culliford, Rolfe and Barrow, which not only manufactured musical instruments but also published music. In 1797, after he had registered improvements for the pianoforte and secured King George III's 'Royal Letters Patent' for a self-acting pianoforte, William bought out his partners and re-established the firm as a family business, still at Cheapside, with his home on the upper floors. His son Nicholas, who wrote music and one play, a tragedy, also manufactured pianos successfully at both 112 and 61 Cheapside. But in the late 1850s, the Rolfe business began to decline, and James, Frederick's father, was unable to restore its prosperity. While Frederick was still a boy, James was forced to give up the Cheapside location for one in Great Marlborough Street and to move his growing family to Camden Town, where they lived at 17 Hartham Road, Camden Road North. James went from a piano manufacturer to a manufacturer's agent and the number of employees dwindled to one or two workmen and

7

Jenkins, the piano-tuner with a 'weary anxious excruciating asking look in the eyes'.[2]

Frederick Rolfe's mother was Ellen Elizabeth Pilcher, who married James Rolfe, eleven years her senior, in 1859. She was a woman of strong character and understanding with a love for her children which was altered neither by her perception of their differences nor the problems they caused her. According to his brother Herbert, Frederick was 'always eccentric from early youth'; the family could 'do nothing with him ever'.[3] But despite his wilfulness, Ellen Rolfe admired Frederick's intelligence and inventiveness; and she was still defending him long after his death as a 'truly remarkable personality', a man with the 'virtues of a Christian character' in his 'human relationships'.[4]

Not unexpectedly, as the position of the family went steadily downward and its numbers increased, the Rolfe home was more and more cheerless. Such an environment was owing in part to what Rolfe called 'circumstances often cruelly unjust and always rigorously hard'.[5] Perhaps the Rolfe family's austerity and impassiveness rose from their unhappy lot (Frederick maintained that his progenitors and his brothers led 'decent noble lives'), but those qualities were also an inalienable part of the Rolfe heritage. Frederick called the Rolfes puritans and declared that he had a 'thoroughly puritan (but detestable & inefficacious) bringing-up' such as his 'antecessors' had had before him. He described his family as 'typically narrow constricted & entirely insular little family of unadultered blood'.[6]

Despite their hateful puritanism, Frederick was extremely proud of the Rolfes' English heritage and he developed a strong family feeling. He was an affectionate brother to his sisters and the younger Rolfe boys. There were three of them: Herbert, closest in age and always close in sympathy to the eldest son; Percy, 'sensitive and nervous as a girl-child';[7] and Alfred, the youngest and gentlest, an amenable boy. Their father, James Rolfe, whom Frederick characterised as 'that most perfect gentle man', aroused pain and pity in his first born. His heart, as he grew into manhood, was troubled by the sight of James, resigned and aging, and by inability to do anything for his father. Frederick felt a son's love for his mother, overlaid with a sense of accountability which kept her in his thoughts whether he was with her or not. Later he called her a 'very great and wonderful woman'.[8]

But before his boyhood was over, chance and temperament separated Frederick from the Rolfes and their expectations and, knowingly or unknowingly, he was set onto a path he could not leave. At the age of fourteen or fifteen he underwent a momentous religious experience. Rolfe maintained that his vocation for priesthood, a 'Divine Gift', was bestowed on him when he was fifteen. Although it came to him after he had turned whole-heartedly to Christianity, Rolfe was not yet ready to submit to its imperatives. He says that he 'played the fool'

8

from seventeen to twenty, that he neglected his vocation. Nevertheless he marked himself early as belonging to Christ; at about fourteen, he had his breast tattooed with a cross.[9] At this same age or soon thereafter, Rolfe started his unremitting communication with his God and his active reliance on Christ. He explained the procedure in 1906 to a young candidate for the Anglican priesthood. 'My way', Rolfe wrote, 'is to sit or kneel alone in the dark before the Most Holy, and to say quietly and quickly, "Dear Jesus be not to me a Judge but a Saviour," sometimes hundreds of times, until he gives me relief.'[10] Rolfe's simple dependence implies a belief in what he came to term the very satisfying 'narrow way of Christianity', a humble sharing with all men in faith and things, that is, taking Christ seriously, accepting personal responsibility in human affairs, and living one's life as a 'fool for Christ'. The attitude is more joyous, more generous, than the puritanism of his home, although his religious intensity derived logically from his home and his age. Such involvement is a commonplace of puberty.

Adolescence was extremely difficult for Rolfe. Afterward, he characterised as the most awful period in the life of a young boy the point 'when he must watch the death of his own boyhood and assist at the birth of his own youth'. Rolfe's analysis of the pains of puberty emphasised the terror of the 'mind-rending body-tearing pangs' with which 'youth is born'. He told how, after the event, fear increases until the 'palpitating' young man 'braces up every scrap of courage which he can find in every cranny and crevice of himself, and nerves himself to carry the weight of his new self as artfully and as graciously and as unashamedly as possible'. He finds then that the 'bogey (faced) is not so very terrifying or unusual.' He concluded, nevertheless, that 'the shock of the death of boyhood and the horror of the birth of youth is that which marks a man indelibly, as it is borne well or ill'.[11]

During the 'first fierce months of youth' and at much the same time as his religious awakening, Rolfe decided to leave school. Evidence as to his success as a schoolboy is slight, a certificate of honour for proficiency in history, geography, arithmetic, and religion earned at the age of eight and an undated commendation from Charles Wm. Williams, the headmaster of North London Collegiate School.[12] Later, he regretted his lack of education and the quality of the little he had (his brother Herbert declared that Frederick had hardly more than a year at a decent school).[13] But in 1874, when he was fourteen, he acted out of urgency to earn what he could and the discontent of adolescence, and he left school.

These two decisions had long lasting consequences. Rolfe first affirmed his religious enthusiasm by the constant use of the rosary and, for a prayer book, the *Garden of the Soul*.[14] Then slowly he began to examine his faith in the light of his vocation until at last he found his way to Catholicism. His decision to leave school thrust him into

9

adult situations with inadequate preparation, both intellectually and emotionally. Lack of learning as a part of the intellectual side could be remedied, but the more intricate affinities between mind and emotion were another matter, especially when complicated by a difficult adolescence. Rolfe had a boy's yearning for love but only a partially loving nature. His expectations of friendship never outgrew the schoolboy's of popular fiction, and he often concluded his friendships with retaliation for imagined wrongs. Indeed, Rolfe saw human relationships as such absolutes that, as Elizabeth Bowen said of herself, he was 'unrelatable'. In fact, Rolfe passed the rest of his days with a concept of reality no greater than his understanding of it at fourteen or fifteen. That statement does not mean that he was immature. Despite frequent exhibitions of immaturity, to charge him with it is unjust. He simply had an implausible tendency to put Christianity into practice. So much of his religion, such as his reliance on the *Garden of the Soul* at this time and his worship in three or four churches all in one morning later in Venice, can be interpreted as mere ritual or sentiment. The truth is, Rolfe took seriously and literally the precepts of Christ and Christianity. It was one of the illusions by which he lived.

[ii]

As soon as possible after leaving school, Rolfe served first as an apprentice teacher and then as a schoolmaster. He began work at some institution which his brother Herbert referred to only as a 'sort of Dotheboys Hall'.[1] The earliest official record of Rolfe's affiliation with a particular school places him at the Stationers' Company's School, London, in 1879.[2] He was certainly there in 1878, however, when two pupils, Thomas and John Reardon drowned in the Thames on 3 September 1878. For the elder, Thomas, aged sixteen, Rolfe had felt a warm affection which he openly declared afterward. He may have been at the Stationers' School as early as 1875, inasmuch as in that year he was confessing with great zeal to the Reverend Stanton of St. Alban the Martyr's Church, Holborn,[3] a church located in the neighbourhood in which he was born and also in the same district as the School.

On the other hand, so long a stay at the Stationers' School was contrary to Rolfe's practice of leaving after a term or two each of the schools to which he was subsequently attached. In autumn 1880, he began a year's service at King Edward VI Grammar School, Saffron Walden, Essex. The following year, 1881, he moved to the Winchester Modern School, but by Easter 1882 Rolfe was temporarily on the staff of Bartholomew's Grammar School at Newbury. In 1883, Rolfe

10

assisted George Howes at Balsham Manor, Cambridge, before moving once more to Grantham Grammar School.

Yet Rolfe was more than adequate as a schoolmaster. He taught the lower forms, giving instruction in a variety of subjects which included English, Latin, French, history, arithmetic, and divinity. Perhaps he lacked something as a disciplinarian owing to a 'weak subservient aspect'.[4] Nevertheless he worked especially well with the youngest boys. R. M. Luckock, Head Master of King Edward VI School commended Rolfe's teaching, his initiative in offering a class in drawing for beginners, and his help in training a choir of little boys. The choir was quickly brought to the point of taking part in a musical programme at the Saffron Walden Working Men's Club, where in early November 1880 they sang a part song, 'Come Unto These Yellow Sands'. Rolfe was also on the programme as a soloist, singing Sullivan's 'The Chorister'.

During his time at this same school Rolfe's aesthetic bent found considerable expression. His room or 'den', as it was called, was a model of artistic manliness with his six pipes in their rack, a crucifix, a withering relic of Palm Sunday and a skull, several ancient weapons, his motto 'Do ye next thynge' painted on his fireplace and a number of his own drawings on the wall as well as reproductions of one or two by Italian masters of the Renaissance.[5]

Furthermore, in 1880, Rolfe published his long poem *Tarcissus*. Completed by 29 September 1880 and dedicated 'To The Memory of Thomas Reardon R.I.P.' and to twenty other boys, nearly all students, designated only by their initials, *Tarcissus* was printed before Christmas by Boardman of Saffron Walden and bound in decorated, stiff grey wrappers. Rolfe's prize verses in nine stanzas 'Seeking and Finding' had appeared in *School Magazine* for 18 August 1877 and 'The Waits: A Yule Tide Carol' in the issue for February 1878, but *Tarcissus* was his first separate publication. The book was announced by Boardman as 'Suitable for choir boys' and *The Church Times* praised it as 'well written'.

The poem is an account of the eager martyrdom of the 'dear brave Boy' Tarcissus at the time of the Diocletian persecutions. It is also the first of five sets of verses which Rolfe wrote on the subject of boy martyrs. The fact that it was a favourite one of poetic pederasts in Rolfe's time invites speculation, especially in view of the fact that the subject matter of Rolfe's fiction was usually coloured by homosexuality and often it dominated his material. Perhaps Rolfe was a practising homosexual by 1880; he did not lack opportunities even with his pupil-friends. Among them was at least one homosexual, John Gambril Nicholson, a moody, finicky boy whose initials are among the twenty on the dedicatory page of *Tarcissus*. Furthermore Rolfe's confession of having 'sowed wild oats . . . most preciously' a year or two after his fifteenth birthday[6] may refer to aberrant sex practices or the desire for them.

A number of poems which Rolfe wrote at the Winchester Modern

11

DALE H. GRAMLEY LIBRARY
SALEM COLLEGE
WINSTON-SALEM, N. C.

School before Christmas 1881 bolsters this thesis. Indeed, one set of verses called 'Sacrilege' runs:

> What can I do, O heavy heart within,
> That will atone
> For this most sad & sacrilegious sin
> That I have done?
>
> For when my eyes would seek the King alone
> A round bright head
> Lifts up its aureole before the Throne
> And shines instead.
>
> Now jasper lights, now wells of amethyst
> That flash & glow,
> Have grace of colour like the eyes I kissed
> Awhile ago.[7]

Several poems are addressed to boys: Edward Sigurd Allen, Francis Walter Morrison, Robert Clement Austin and a few who are unnamed. Rolfe calls Morrison his 'love' and Austin, his 'heart's darling'. Young Austin captured Rolfe's imagination to such a degree that he added the name Austin to his own, sometimes making it a middle name, sometimes a surname. Rolfe had the wisdom or the good fortune to publish none of these.

The pieces which Rolfe published at this time are well within the sphere of the conventional schoolmaster. Tarcissus made his self-sacrifice according to the very best standards of sportsmanship. Rolfe's prose written during his tenure at Winchester Modern School has no personal reference. Most noteworthy is a piece appearing in the hectographed school magazine, *The Wintonian A Journal of Modern School Life*, for 4 February 1882. It is called 'Leaves from the Diary of Scaraboeus the Upper Dormitory Black Beetle found near his mangled remains and edited by his sorrowful sister Aranea the Lower Dormitory Spider.' This piece runs in part:

Wednesday

I really don't think I can stand it much longer, these boys get more rowdy every night. Now if they would only take a lesson from the boys in the Lower Dormitory, who my sister the spider, used to say, were the most exemplary little dears, who always fold up their clothes & go to bed so quietly & never think of any such things as bolster fights & always get up directly when the bell rings. Poor dear Aranea! I haven't seen her for an age ... I must try to get downstairs tonight to see her when those roughs are asleep. Ah, they're coming upstairs now. I can tell by that lumping noise that almost shakes the pen out of my leg.

* * * * *

11 o'clock

Oh dear! oh! why ever did I venture out tonight before all those monsters were in bed asleep. I'm afraid I shall never get over this. I am writing with my 4th hind leg on the left. As (I shudder to recall it) I was going downstairs to see my dear sister (and I made sure that I had crawled over every boy's face too to see if they were all asleep) a colossal mammoth came gamboling upstairs . . . & stamped on 5 of my 'four' legs and tore them out of the sockets. I have just managed to drag my mangled carcase home again under No. 19's bed. . . .

The poor cockroach was no better off. The next day he lost both horns and in a rush for air then lost his life. The piece ends with a conversation which Aranea reported:

No. 24   loquitor. 'Look there you chaps!'
No. 26   „   'Oh whatever is it!!!'
No. 25   „   'Looks like a nasty squashed black beetle!!!!'
Chorus   „   'Ugh!!!!!!!'

Although flawed by its facetiousness, this story of Scaraboeus is interesting as a forerunner of the method of Rolfe's later fiction. He speaks in the person of his hero, in this case the cockroach, and ends in a different voice which provides a comment on the hero. As a key to Rolfe's career, it shows him exercising imagination and initiative as a schoolmaster. Rolfe may have originated *The Wintonian* and, under the heading 'Sputterings from ye Grey Quill', he wrote numerous items for the paper—nonsense verse, riddles, and comments on the popularity of hockey to the exclusion of 'paperchases Fives and Football'.[8]

Rolfe took an active part in sports, showing his usual energy in organising paper chases, planning sports programmes, cultivating healthy bodies, developing team spirit. His most successful effort was at the Stationers' School where he organised a committee of ten members which in turn arranged for the use of the New Central Bath in Smithfield, beginning on 1 May 1879, and encouraged boys to learn to swim either from members of the committee or from a professional swimming master. Rolfe dispensed at 1s. a pair bathing drawers in colours which he described as 'thunder and lightning, saffron and dragon's blood', and 'rose and azure'. By October, the Stationers' School swimmers numbered eighty. When Rolfe left the school, the swimmers, in appreciation, gave him a silver Maltese cross.

Sporting events, speech days, musical programmes, playing the organ for chapel, or simply giving his time to teaching—none of these meant a permanent post. In 1884, Rolfe moved from Balsham Manor to Grantham Grammar School, where he began his last regular work as a schoolmaster on 22 September 1884.

13

[iii]

Grantham, in Lincolnshire, is a charming, ancient town which was dominated at the turn of the nineteenth century by its ironworks. Some eight miles distant is Woolsthorpe, from which Isaac Newton had set out more than two hundred years before to attend Grantham Grammar School and become its most illustrious 'old boy'. For Frederick Rolfe, Grantham Grammar School was a milepost, because it was during his tenure there that he determined on conversion to Catholicism. That resolution overshadows the fact that at Grantham Rolfe made his only lasting friendship, one with E. G. Hardy, head-master of Grantham Grammar School since 1879. Hardy, born in 1852, was educated at Oxford, where he took a degree in Classics. Figuring in Rolfe's *Hadrian the Seventh* under the name Strong, Hardy is described as strong in mind and body, immensely Rolfe's superior and fully aware of his weaknesses and imperfections. 'It is only grand indulgence and urbanity on his part,' Rolfe as Hadrian wrote, 'which makes him know me.'[1]

Because of Hardy, Rolfe might have led a safe, secure existence at the Grantham Grammar School. Except for rare occasions, it might well have been monotonous and even drudging, as many teachers' lives are. But at Grantham, where he took the lowest form, Rolfe began by earning as much as he had ever earned in any one year of his life, £50 a year. He was a housemaster, a step up in his profession. If his inter-pretation of history was somewhat different from that in Gardiner's *Authors of English History*, especially in the matter of Henry VIII's refor-mation, and his instruction in Scripture was unorthodox from an Anglican point of view, Rolfe was nevertheless a respected teacher.

Conversion to Catholicism meant the end of Rolfe's stay at Grant-ham, only one of many changes to come in his way of life. He was prepared for change and even for sacrifice; he had an especial interest in priests who were martyred for their faith, and in a vague romantic way saw himself as one of them. But Rolfe's heart and soul led him to the Catholic Church. Nothing could have prevented his conversion. On 3 January 1886, a Sunday during the Grantham Grammar School's Christmas recess, which he spent at Oxford, he appealed to Father Parkinson, who received Rolfe into the Church. Here is his own account of it:

At twenty-five I suddenly realized that, if it was 'priesthood' I was after, I was on the wrong road: the Church of England-As-By-Law-Established had nothing of the sort to offer me, for she had nothing

14

to do with Peter, and Peter had the key. Ah well, I realized it one Saturday at Oxford; and on Sunday I made my homage to Peter. It was a Jesuit who received me into the church at 24 hours' notice.[2]

That Rolfe's bent was religious but his conversion unexpected is attested in one instance at least by a gift from an Oxford undergraduate, J. A. Thurstans known as 'Fiffie,' less than two weeks before Rolfe's reception into the Church. It was a parchment bound copy of *A Smaller Biblia Pauperum Conteynynge Thyrtie and Eyghte Wodecuttes . . . With the Proper Descrypciouns thereoff extracted from the Originall Texte off Iohn Wiclif. . . .* On the flyleaf Thurstans wrote, 'Frederick Austin Rolfe from J.A.T. Christmas 1885'.[3] Some years later Rolfe implied considerable intimacy with 'Fiffie' Thurstans by describing a prank the two men and Andrew Ping, another Oxford student, played when Oxford gave a fancy dress ball for the Prince of Wales. Rolfe, costumed as a raven and delivered to the ball in a furniture van, stood at the top of the steps where the Oxford dignitaries formally received the Prince. As he arrived there, Rolfe edged up to the Prince, looked at him first with one eye and then with the other, 'bird fashion', and proceeded to empty 'a pound of whitewash through the hole' in his 'tail'.[4] The story is not true, but it implies that Thurstans should have known whether a book associated with the heretic Wyclif was a suitable gift in 1885. Wyclif's emphasis on simplification of Church practices and a personal involvement for members of the Church was attractive to Rolfe, but Wyclif's book nevertheless seems a strange one for a man on the verge of submitting to the Catholic Church.

Indeed, however precipitate his conversion may appear, Rolfe reached the decision to enter the Catholic Church after long meditation. G. G. Coulton, the eminent historian who acted as examiner at Grantham, says that Rolfe had determined to take orders in the Roman Church early in 1885.[5] He had gone from teaching divinity to young boys to an examination of the relation between the Church of England and the Church of Rome. He had read Littledale's *Plain Reasons Against Joining the Church of Rome* and Father Henry Dudley Ryder's reply in *Catholic Controversy* and, according to Coulton, found Ryder by far the more convincing. Ryder had 'wiped the floor' with Littledale, Rolfe declared. In fact, Ryder had taken shrewd advantage of Littledale's loose arguments. When these were too substantial for easy rebuttal, Ryder's replies were often facile or worse, evasive.[6] That Rolfe took so important a step on so specious a discussion is possible. There is no record of further reading on Rolfe's part, a fact which proves nothing. In any case, by 1885 he had reached the conclusion that Christ had built his church inseparable from Peter and to him and him only had given the keys of the kingdom of heaven. Although Rolfe was too young to feel the impact of the Oxford Movement, he

15

had before him the examples of W. G. Ward, Newman, and Manning as well as friends such as George Benson Tatum. But priesthood was the crucial issue. Confession and the Sacrament of Penance were available to him in the Church of England. Ritualistic splendour was there, too. On the other hand, what he called 'stripping', that is a return to 'apostolic simplicity', is fundamental to non-conformism.[7] Both deny Peter as Christ's key-bearer, however, and neither offers priesthood. Rolfe wanted to satisfy the 'Divine vocation to serve God as a secular priest' which had come to him at fifteen. His whole concept of service was bound up with Holy Orders, historically not recognised in the Anglican Church. Priesthood belonged to the Church of Rome. Fittingly enough, not Newman but Cardinal Manning, clamorous in 1870 in urging the enunciation of the dogma of papal infallibility, administered the Sacrament of Confirmation to Rolfe in the private chapel of the Archbishop's Palace, Westminster, on a Thursday, either 14 January or 21 January.[8]

[iv]

Rolfe was determined now to lead a Catholic life among Catholics. Nothing else would do, a typically Rolfean stand. Not only in his whole-hearted turning to Catholics and Catholicism but also in subsequent convictions—as painter and writer, as resident of Venice—he adhered immovably to his resolutions, and Rolfe's present aim was to achieve priesthood. Until he could find a way to start his training, he meant to immerse himself in Catholicism. First, having discussed his position freely and openly with Hardy, his headmaster and his 'dear and intimate friend', and with Mrs. Hardy, Rolfe resigned his mastership at Grantham Grammar School. He did so not because he must but of his 'own free and unaided will'.[1] On 6 March 1886, he received his final payment from Grantham and moved on to London, with the intention of finding work among Catholics.

In London, Rolfe took lodgings in a narrow, tall, red brick house entered up five or six white stone steps with an iron handrail and a shallow porch off which opened a door ornamented with either crown glass or machine-cut glass. It was hardly distinguishable from the houses standing on each side of it or from other houses in which Rolfe lodged from time to time in London. Sometimes they were in Hampstead and sometimes in Kensington. This one was off the Kilburn High Road on Iverson Road.

From there, Rolfe could walk the short distance, less than a mile, to the Church of the New Priory in Quex Road. He turned at once to the rector at New Priory for help in finding work. This was the first of

16

many occasions on which Rolfe looked directly to his church for assistance. As a Catholic, he thought it his due from other Catholics; it was an exercise of his faith in benignity and spontaneous charity among the elect. And this time, fortunately, the rector could suggest something advantageous.

William Edward Slaughter, a solicitor living in Hampstead, required a tutor for his two younger sons. Edward, who was fifteen, had been two years at St. Mary's College, Oscott, but in 1886 he was at home convalescing after a serious illness. Reginald, a younger brother who had been at St. Augustine's College, Ramsgate, was kept at home as a companion for Edward. Slaughter engaged Rolfe to tutor the two boys. He worked conscientiously with them, giving them instruction in a variety of subjects but emphasising history and Latin because they interested him most. He showed the boys how he painted in oil, entertained them with his talk about the schools where he had taught, and as Edward grew stronger, took them for long walks on the pleasant streets of Hampstead. When he was a grown man, young Slaughter remembered Rolfe as slightly pretentious and thus slightly ridiculous. But most teachers are ludicrous in the eyes of their students, and neither Edward Slaughter nor Rolfe ever forgot the other. They kept in touch by letter and fourteen years later they re-entered each other's lives, again in Hampstead.

The association in 1886, however, was a short one. The position with the Slaughter family ended when Edward was fully recovered so that by early May Rolfe was again looking for suitable work. Before trying to find a position, Rolfe made a week's retreat under the direction of Father Haves at Manresa, a Jesuit House. With more than twenty other men, Rolfe arrived for the retreat late in the afternoon of Monday, 19 April 1886, and on the following Saturday he left after breakfast.[2] Two weeks later, on 8 May 1886, *The Tablet*, a publication for Catholics carried Rolfe's advertisement: 'F. R. experienced in Tuition and school keeping, will be glad to hear of a Vacancy in a Catholic School or Tutorship in a private family.'

In reply to this notice, Rolfe received an offer from the Marquis of Bute to become headmaster of a choir school attached to the Cathedral of St. Columba, then under construction at Oban. John Patrick Crichton Stuart, third Marquis of Bute, envisioned a choir school of a few boys to serve as the nucleus of a group offering daily services in the mediaeval manner at St. Columba. It was an impractical, harebrained scheme for which no one had much enthusiasm except Bute. Oban is a small Scottish community in the county of Argyll at the northern tip of the Firth of Lorne. The island of Mull and a much smaller body of land, Kerrera, protects Oban from the sea, but even so it is bleak and isolated. The cathedral was not yet complete. A cathedral choir school where there was no cathedral and only a few parishioners to hear the choir promised little. But Bute was determined to establish the school. He was a man of great energy in both body and mind with large properties to supervise, numerous projects awaiting his directions, extensive journeys to undertake, and a deep reverence for the church to which he was a convert, the Roman church. Its liturgy was his passion and to that was owing his eagerness for the choir school. He disregarded all objections, including the bishop's, and went ahead with his plans. He hired part of Loyola House, a building belonging to the Jesuits, in which to put the school and its members, and he looked about for a priest to act as head. Efforts in Italy and England were fruitless; no priest of the considerable number interviewed was willing to take so amorphous and bizarre a position. In May, after seeing Rolfe's advertisement in *The Tablet* and communicating with Rolfe, Bute decided that a lay master to head the school and a priest to chant the Mass would answer his requirements. In June, this man of vast enterprises and intense religious ardour met by appointment with Rolfe, no less ardent but a man of no affairs and little experience. Bute offered Rolfe the post of headmaster at the choir school.

Rolfe was dazzled by the Marquis of Bute. His status and his power were outside Rolfe's; his arrogance, tinged with courtesy, was a glorious revelation to Rolfe. Afterwards he spoke of his inexperience, declared he had been 'lured by innumerable false pretences', but at that time, June 1886, Rolfe believed without question what his fellow-convert told him. Although the salary hardly met Rolfe's idea of his own worth, this offer of a headmastership at a Catholic school was too tempting to refuse. Besides, he saw in Bute a potential patron, a man who could surely help him to achieve priesthood and perhaps to the fulfilment of his secret dream, himself as a church dignitary. Bute even hinted at the possibility of minor orders immediately. Rolfe was powerless to do anything but accept Bute's offer.[3]

Although Rolfe began with high hopes and a sense of importance, this new venture brought him only disappointment and failure. Under pressure from Bute to get the school started by early August, late in July, Rolfe packed all his belongings into two boxes and sent them to Oban. He went some sixty miles northeast of Oban to Fort Augustus in order to collect four boys from the Benedictine monastery and take them to Oban. He spent the night of 2 August at the monastery, where he talked eloquently of his prospects and his ambitions for priesthood, implying that he might be an aspirant to the Benedictine Order in the near future.[4] The next day he and his four charges went on to Oban and settled into Loyola House with the caretakers, a French couple named Duhamel, and a fifth chorister. By 4 August, a Wednesday, the school was in session, and Rolfe on his own insistence had become the 'Rev. Fr. Rolfe' to the five boys. From them he demanded absolute adherence to the routine which he established; they had a cold bath each morning at seven and at eleven they chanted the

18

Mass. Despite inadequate recreational facilities and his own uncertainties with the Breviary and his general inexperience with Catholic ritual, Rolfe managed reasonably well for almost a month. Then the unvarying daily round and the isolation began to tell. His painting and a few unsuccessful attempts at verse failed to distract him. He began to issue dinner invitations freely to parishioners. The arrival on 31 August of Father Francis Beurms, a huge red-bearded Belgian, was highly agreeable. Rolfe respected him as a scholar and enjoyed his companionship. But Rolfe still felt unhappy, unsettled. On 13 September, when David Hunter Blair, a Benedictine from Fort Augustus, spent the night at Oban and the evening in Rolfe's company, Rolfe 'poured out a flood of eloquence on the inadequacy of the salary paid him . . . and the utter impossibility of his position . . . as a stepping-stone to any post worthy of his powers and his talents'.[5] Rolfe had been a member of the Catholic Church for less than a year and already he felt abused by one of his fellow Catholics and blamed him for the waste of the ability in which Rolfe had such confidence.

A few days after Hunter Blair's visit, Rolfe's situation worsened. He quarrelled bitterly with the Duhamels; and Mme. Duhamel complained by letter to Bute's marchioness, calling Rolfe a liar and adding that his freedom in extending dinner invitations swelled the school's expenses unnecessarily. The arrival of a French chaplain, the Abbé Bérard, late in September threw the whole school into confusion. Bérard promptly told Beurms that he was no longer needed, but Beurms, having no place to go, stayed on at the choir school. Bérard assumed the mastership, disregarding Rolfe's arrangements and his supposed position and refusing to officiate at Mass at the hour Rolfe designated. Rolfe's resignation from Oban was inevitable. He tells how the two priests 'drank themselves drunk on beer, out of decanters, chased each other round the refectory tables in a tipsy fight', defied Rolfe's authority, and forced the 'ragamuffins of the school' to do the same.[6] Rolfe reported this 'muddle' to Bute, but he ignored it; so, on 10 October, Rolfe resigned, telling Hunter Blair that he did so owing to 'terror of Oban damps'.[7]

The fiasco at Oban left Rolfe with depleted nerves and hopes. To be forced from his position was bad enough. It meant the loss of his only income; however bitterly he may have complained about his salary, it was still all he had. Bérard's appropriation of the headmastership confused him. Added to that was the fact that once Bute, without giving much thought to his words, had suggested that his influence could help Rolfe toward priesthood. Now that possibility was vanishing before his eyes. It was more than he could face. Anxiety invariably affected his health. Under stress, he sometimes merely 'howled' and he sometimes broke out in boils.

Whatever the form of Rolfe's distress in 1886, he felt the need of therapeutic baths. Packing his possessions once more in two boxes, he sent them ahead to the care of Father Parkinson at the Jesuit house attached to the Church of St. Aloysius on Woodstock Road in Oxford. He then took himself to Bristol where, like Fanny Burney's Evelina and a host of others, he could enjoy the benefits of the Hotwells. Only after a series of baths did he feel able to attend to his material needs.

For the second time in less than a year, Rolfe turned to his church for help. Father Parkinson had received him into the church, and Rolfe went back to him, looking for guidance and a new job. When he reached Oxford he learned that only one of his boxes had arrived, and he never saw the second one again. His stay in Oxford was fruitless. Father Parkinson had little direction to offer and nothing in the way of work to suggest. Rolfe's presence in the rectory was inconvenient. Parkinson was overworked and Father Clarke, his assistant, found Rolfe commonplace at best.

Well before the end of 1886, Rolfe went on to London and took lodgings somewhere in Kensington. His efforts to get work were unsuccessful, and his small funds dwindled alarmingly. In December, he once more advertised his availability as a tutor in *The Tablet*,[8] but no one responded. In desperation Rolfe wrote to Bute, reminding that nobleman of his half-promise to use his influence in the matter of orders and at the same time asking for help in getting work. With work, he could simultaneously aid his parents and sister financially and read 'Philosophy & Theology' in his spare time so as to be ready when opportunity offered to 'give himself to the service of the Church'.[9]

So far the Church had brought Rolfe only deprivation and pain. His insistence on limiting himself to employment among Catholics was mainly responsible. Life for Catholics in England in the 1880s was less free than it is today, but Catholicism, increasingly a solace at the end of the century when numerous converts were made, did not demand intellectual or social isolation. In other words, England did not set Rolfe apart as a Catholic; he set himself apart. Furthermore his conversion had not made him a member of a select, saintly brotherhood, so that his expectations of unusual assistance from his fellow-Catholics was unrealistic. Rolfe's misfortunes have been attributed to the fact that he 'imputed to others' his own virtues and 'died of shame when he did not find them'.[10] Less grandly, it can be said that he persisted in imposing his illusions on his environment.

In either event, Rolfe did not die in 1886 and 1887, even in spirit; but he suffered bleak despondency. Of this he has left little record. Whether he took comfort in an awareness of his own worth or despaired at the ugliness and failure which threatened it will very likely never be told. Indeed Rolfe almost recedes into the dingy shadows of the rooming houses in which he lived. All that can be said with certainty about those months in London is that Rolfe began to develop a suspicion of harassment, a conviction that he was the victim of persecution.

Rolfe's mistrust faded when he was offered employment, probably at the end of February 1887, as tutor to Arthur John Riddell, the seventeen-year-old invalid son of Francis Henry Riddell. The Riddells lived in the ancient manor house of Cheeseburn Grange near Newcastle upon Tyne. This pleasant secluded situation and the routine established for the sake of his pupil's health demanded that Rolfe live quietly. Doing so enabled him to refurbish his self-esteem.

Rolfe's new position also contributed to his adoption of certain aristocratic attitudes. The Riddells were a devoutly Catholic family, maintaining at the Grange a private chapel and a resident priest. Their loyalties were Jacobean, a legacy from an ancestor who had fought valiantly as a Colonel with the royalist army in the 1640s. Their cause was compatible with Rolfe's newly acquired Catholicism and his sense of a malign influence at work against him. From his employers he derived his preference, among all Thackeray's works, for *Henry Esmond*, that great novel of English Catholics' misplaced allegiances and lost opportunities. More important, Rolfe learned his reverence for the Stuarts from the Riddells and from them he acquired royalist sympathies which he deliberately opposed to democracy.

Either the Riddell family or the Slaughters, the family of his earlier pupils, created the opportunity for Rolfe to study for the priesthood. One or the other asked the Bishop of Shrewsbury to sponsor Rolfe. Relations of the Slaughter family, the Mostyns, had close ties with an important centre of English Catholicism, St. Mary's College at Oscott, near Birmingham. Through someone's intervention, whether the Slaughters' or the Riddells', Bishop Ambrose agreed to act as Rolfe's financial guarantor at St. Mary's College with the stipulation that he both study and teach—teach the young boys in the lay school and study divinity in the seminary. Rolfe was enrolled as a student on 29 October 1887.

[v]

St. Mary's, in 1887, was under its fourteenth president, Canon Joseph Souter. The college's history went back to May 1794, when as Oscott College it accepted its first student. Before the mid-nineteenth century, when Dr. Nicholas Patrick Stephen Wiseman was its head, Oscott had become the focal point of contemporary England's Catholic history and without question the 'intellectual centre of English Catholicism'.[1] It was at Oscott on the feast of All Saints', 1845, that John Henry Newman was confirmed. By the 1860s, the educational standards had risen enough for Oscott to be described as 'much more like an Oxford College presided over by clergymen'. It was 'as lively as

21

it was varied, cosmopolitan to a high degree'.[2] When Rolfe went to St. Mary's in 1887, it had declined in prestige so that its future was uncertain, and less than two years later it was closed to lay pupils.

At St. Mary's, Rolfe had the opportunity of which he had long dreamed, but unhappily he made little use of it. As a master in the lay school, he was reasonably successful. Rolfe was especially adept at lessening the distance in age and experience between himself and his students by giving boys a very good opinion of themselves. Perhaps this made them 'unable to measure their strength and value afterward',[3] but it eased many an adolescence and prompted boys to make the most of their own interests then and there. In this way he appealed particularly to three lay students at Oscott. One was a senior, James Dey, who planned to study for the priesthood. Another was Mario Sforza-Cesarini, described on the Oscott list, 'dei Conti Santafuora'. Like Rolfe, he came to Oscott in 1887, and it was on him that young Sforza vented his loneliness. The third boy was an Irish-American sent to England for his education, Vincent O'Sullivan. Rolfe preferred Vincent's older brother Percival, whom he described as the 'most exquisitely beautiful boy, body and soul (with the most exquisitely horrible voice)' he ever met.[4] But Vincent (Rolfe later called him that 'silly O'Sullivan'), not Percival, accorded Rolfe the doubtful honour of hero-worship. He admired Rolfe's 'handsome sensitive face', his 'low musical voice' as he spoke with his carefully cultivated Oxford accent, and his 'very charming manners', so apparent when he overcame his natural timidity.[5] 'For almost everyone', Vincent wrote, 'there are some figures of our childhood and youth which have taken an unalterable aspect in memory, like a portrait in a frame. Among these, for me,' he declared, 'was Frederick Rolfe.' As a man, O'Sullivan recalled with nostalgia a tour of cathedrals which he and his brother made with Rolfe during the Christmas holidays of 1887. He remembered in particular emerging from Worcester Cathedral after Evensong, when the choir had sung the hundred and twenty-sixth psalm— 'When the Lord turned the captivity of Zion we were like them that dream'—so evocative of *Henry Esmond*. They talked of that book and of at least two others, *The Channings* and *John Inglesant*; and they parted in the twilight at the railway station, going in different directions after Vincent had quoted from *John Inglesant*, 'The sun has gone down, but it will rise again. It is time to go home.'[6]

That he could talk books with Rolfe made a particular bond for O'Sullivan, even though Rolfe was more likely to recommend to the boys such works as Mrs. Juliana Horatia Ewing's *Jackanapes* or *The Story of a Short Life* than Reade's *The Cloister and the Hearth*, the book about which he was most enthusiastic at that time. O'Sullivan, only fifteen years old, had read with more discrimination than Rolfe and much more modernity (Stevenson, Meredith, Hardy, Henley, William Morris and others). Rolfe recognised Vincent's love of literature and

22

let him talk to his heart's content. Rolfe was also wholly receptive to O'Sullivan's suggestion that he use the 'final k in words ending in ic' and write 'shew for the more usual show', forms which Rolfe retained thereafter. In addition, O'Sullivan supplied him with lists of obsolete words and spellings.[7] Such visual signs of aesthetic inclinations, as O'Sullivan testified, made Rolfe 'prance with delight'.

He learned about these words and forms too late to incorporate them into the first of two poems which he composed at Oscott, 'A Chaunte Royal in Honour of the Most Pure Mother of God'. But when Rolfe next composed a poem he loaded it with obsolete spellings and archaic forms. The poem had this title, 'Sestina yn honour of Lytel Seynt Hew Who Was crucyfyed by ye Jewys atte Lincoln on ye Eve of Seynt Peter ad Vincula yn ye year of oure Lorde MCCLV.'[8]

During his stay at St. Mary's, in any case, Rolfe was much concerned with the visual. His collection of carefully coloured meerschaum pipes, started some years earlier and enlarged during his tenure as tutor to Edward and Reginald Slaughter in imitation of Slaughter senior, was a matter of pride. So was Rolfe's enormous tobacco pouch. The walls of his room at Oscott were papered with his drawings and paintings. According to a clerical contemporary at St. Mary's, he was constantly engaged in 'beating out brasswork' and in painting a picture of 'some historical subject'.[9] James Dey remembered it as a picture showing the corpse of St. William of Norwich carried by a hundred and forty-nine bearers every one of whom, including the dead St. William, had Rolfe's face. Or, and this is more likely, the picture may well have been one of the illustrated initials which Rolfe prepared for the first word of each stanza of 'Lytel Seynt Hew'; the sixth was especially elaborate, showing Hugh's place of burial and a train of mourners numbering fifty-eight.

Having painted his pictures, Rolfe liked to photograph them. For his supplies, he went to a shop owned by William Wort in Sutton Coldfield, some three miles from the hamlet and the college of Oscott. His journeys to Wort's shop were in violation of college rules; St. Mary's students were forbidden to leave the college's grounds more than two days a week, when they were permitted to walk in Sutton Park, a park famous for its hollies and a favourite spot for picnic parties from Birmingham. But Rolfe visited Wort freely, expounding on photography and running up a bill for supplies which was never paid.[10]

Rolfe had little time left for his duties as a seminarian. Had he given them his attention and neglected his gifts, he would doubtless have passed into oblivion. But he had persuaded himself that his gifts justified the attention he gave them. He was convinced that he transcended other men in the discernment with which he 'saw'. This quality, Rolfe said, 'is why some men are artificers or poets, because they have this faculty of extra sight'.[11] Such artificers, he maintained

23

are 'demented, in the sense that they soar above the minds of ordinary men'; and for this cause it is irrational to expect them to comport themselves as 'ordinary men'.[12] If the students 'ruthlessly ragged' him, and if he was considered eccentric, that was all well and good. His answer was to keep much to himself and when he spoke to exercise a 'caustic tongue' on his fellow 'Divines' and in every way to make quite clear his 'unmistakable sense of superiority'.[13] He went on with his poetry, his painting, and his photography.

Yet Rolfe's view of himself as one of the 'artificers of transcendent genius' and his consequent application to the gifts which brought him into prominence—largely posthumous, to be sure—are exactly what prevented Rolfe's getting the one thing in the world he thought he was fit for, the one thing in the world he wanted, priesthood. From the time of his arrival at St. Mary's, Rolfe wore a cassock and biretta, as did all the 'Divines', the candidates for priesthood. On 31 March 1888, from the Bishop of Birmingham, Rolfe received the tonsure which admitted him into the clerical estate, and at once he set about 'acquiring ecclesiastical habits'. He could not forbear voicing his contempt for an occasional 'bit of nasty vulgar Latin' in the Divine Office, but he began at once to say the Office faithfully, using for that purpose a breviary which he had had elegantly bound. Meanwhile he wrote the 'necessary parts of the Liturgy on large sheets of paper, and pinned them' in the place of his own paintings to his bedroom walls, and as he dressed, he learned the liturgy by heart.[14]

But in August 1888, Rolfe was dismissed from St. Mary's College. The Bishop of Shrewsbury wrote to say that he was unable to make further plans for Rolfe because there was no 'unanimous verdict of the superiors in favour' of his vocation.[15] James Dey said that Rolfe had to leave Oscott because the Bishop was 'dissatisfied with the progress of his *protégé*, and not prepared to pay for him to indulge his hobby of painting'.[16] Whatever the cause for it, Rolfe refused to accept the Bishop's decision and he immediately protested it to the president of Oscott, Canon Joseph Souter. According to Rolfe, Souter assured him that his 'talents and energy' would make him a valuable priest and offered to commend him to the Bishop of Southwark. Because the Bishop of Shrewsbury had rejected Rolfe, the Bishop of Southwark could not consider him. And the Bishop of Shrewsbury refused 'to explain, to recede', to afford Rolfe 'satisfaction'. It was Rolfe's introduction to the 'inexorability of the Roman Catholic Machine, inexorable in iniquity as in righteousness,' he said. Rolfe concluded:

that someone carelessly had lied; that someone carelessly had blundered; and that all concerned were determined not to own themselves or anyone else..., to be in the wrong. A mistake had been made; and, by quibbles, by evasions, by threats, by every hole-and-corner means conceivable, the mistake was going to be perpetuated.[17]

The mistake was Rolfe's. It consisted of the unending and incompatible extremes in which Rolfe involved himself by aspiring to priesthood. By temperament he was arrogant, self-willed and sensuous whereas priesthood implies humility, obedience, and carnal discipline. O'Sullivan testified that ugly things pained Rolfe. Yet the cure of souls demands a rational perspective on the ugliness as well as the nobility of men's desires and on the discrepancy of their achievements.

[vi]

When he learned of his discharge from St. Mary's College, Oscott, Rolfe was the guest of Father Angus, a priest resident at St. Andrews. Formerly an officer in the army and once an Anglican minister, Angus was a convert to Catholicism of about fifteen years' standing. He had known Rolfe for little more than a year, that is, since early 1887, when he lodged somewhere in Kensington. Appointed the first priest in more than three hundred years at St. Andrews, the ecclesiastical centre of Scotland, Angus had invited Rolfe, whom both believed to be well on the way to priesthood, for a visit during Oscott's vacation. Rolfe came, proud of his priestly dress and zealous in his clerical offices. He had hardly arrived when he was notified of the action of St. Mary's authorities. He was so distressed that Father Angus began to work in Rolfe's behalf by petitioning the Archbishop of Edinburgh. While these transactions were under way, Rolfe continued as Father Angus's guest over a period of several months.

By 3 February 1889, Rolfe was a guest near Fraserburgh at Boyndlie House, the home of John Mathias Ogilvie-Forbes. No doubt they met through Father Angus. Ogilvie-Forbes, also a former Anglican minister and a missionary in Ceylon, was another convert. Catholics did not abound on this eastern coast of Scotland, and the priest of St. Andrews knew most of them, whether south of Dundee or north of Aberdeen. A meeting between Ogilvie-Forbes and Rolfe was inevitable, and Rolfe's conversational powers did the rest. Very likely Rolfe passed much of 1889 at Boyndlie House, coming and going at will. In late summer, Rolfe went to Christchurch, a quiet, pleasant town not far from Bournemouth. Although, owing to his 'insufferable conceit', he had been estranged from John Gambril Nicholson since 1887,[1] Rolfe was attracted to Christchurch by Nicholson's account of it. During his stay at the seaside town with its ancient Priory Church, Rolfe met Nicholson's friend Joseph William Gleeson White, book collector, owner of a stationery shop and library, editor of *Ballades, Chants Royal, Sestines, Villanelles, Etcetera*, and with his wife the centre of the artistic and intellectual life of Christchurch. According to Rolfe, Gleeson White 'begged' for his acquaintance.[2] Through Gleeson White, Rolfe came to know another of Nicholson's friends, Charles Kains Jackson, a London solicitor and editor of *The Artist and Journal of Home Culture*, who was on holiday at Christchurch with his nephew Cecil Castle. Kains Jackson and Castle, eighteen years old in 1889, maintained a relationship far more intimate than that of uncle and nephew.[3] In early November, Rolfe was at Bristol, probably for thermal baths. On 4 November, he sent a letter from Bristol asking Bute to exert influence in his behalf. Otherwise, throughout most of the rest of that year 1889, including an unfortunate visit at Christmas,[4] Rolfe was probably Ogilvie-Forbes's guest. Yet 3 February is the only date on which Rolfe can be positively fixed at Boyndlie House.

On 3 February 1889, Rolfe wrote from the Fraserburgh address to offer 'Ballade of Boys & in particular of the Percies' to *Blackwood's Magazine*.[5] He wanted *Blackwood's* to print the 'Ballade' as *The Universal Review* had printed 'Lytel Seynt Hew', that is in facsimile with Rolfe's illustrations. *Blackwood's* declined; so Rolfe had the poem reproduced on duplicate sets of cards, one sepia and one blue, with a stanza and illustration on each card.[6]

The 'Ballade of Boys' is only one of a number of pieces which Rolfe wrote in the period following his discharge from St. Mary's. In May 1889 his 'Ballade of the Queen of May', a poem similar to his 'Chaunte Royal' appeared in *The Month*. He was most productive, however, in the late summer months and early autumn, when he was at Christchurch and immediately afterward. He turned out two letters, both originally intended for other periodicals, to *The Tablet*[7] and a flood of verses with accompanying illustrations. Prior to their rift, Nicholson, who then or later wrote 'erotic verse in the old French forms',[8] had called Rolfe's attention to the ballade, the rondeau, and other French forms by means of Gleeson White's book of 1887. Rolfe immediately tried his hand at the chant or hymn and the sestina. Then at St. Mary's Vincent O'Sullivan provided him with ready-made aestheticism by showing him how to convert his words into obsolete and archaic spellings. 'Lytel Seynt Hew' combined the form and the archaic spelling but not very successfully because for Rolfe the form was an ornament and not an integral part of his poem. Nevertheless, 'Lytel Seynt Hew' and its elaborate illustrations got into print, and Rolfe began to work with the ballade, although not always correctly, and to draw pictures appropriate to his compositions. Apparently he did not attempt the rondeau until his visit to Christchurch. There, prompted by Gleeson White, Rolfe composed 'Three Rondeaux (for a picture)'. These include 'Sir Ralph the Page', 'O Glorious Boy!' and 'Arrayed in White'. For them he drew saccharine-faced boys dressed in jerkin and hose. These verses are dated August 1889 in the manuscript.[9] Others of the same period, although they are undated, are 'The Christ Bearer',

'The Boy Martyr of Norwich' and 'Ottava rima: Three Ages of Love'. The most successful piece, like 'Three Rondeaux' dated August 1889 in the manuscript, is 'The Ballade of Boys Bathing'. The second and third stanzas and the Envoy of the ballade run:

> Deep blue water as blue can be
> > Rocks rising high mid the red clouds flare
> Boys of the colour of ivory
> > Breasting the wavelets & diving there
> > White boys, ruddy, & tanned, & bare
> > > With lights & shadows of rose & grey
> > And the sea like pearls in their shining hair
> > > The boys who bathe in Saint Andrews' Bay.

> A summer night on a sapphire sea
> A setting sun & a golden glare
> Hurls from the height where the rugged rocks be
> > Wondrous limbs in the luminous air
> > Fresh as a white flame flushed & fair
> > > Lithe round arms in the salt sea spray
> > And the sea seems alive with them every where
> > > The boys who bathe in Saint Andrews' Bay.

> Envoy

> Andrea! Lay me out tinctures rare
> > Set me a palette & while I may
> I'll fix on my canvas if so I may dare
> > The boys who bathe in Saint Andrews' Bay.[10]

The fact that he wrote 'The Ballade of Boys Bathing', whatever its merit, tells much about Rolfe. The components of his will to write it, the poem itself, and the illustration he made for it expose much of what 'lay in his mind' at Christchurch in 1889. When Rolfe went to Christchurch, his expectation of priesthood was strong. Although Father Angus's negotiations with the Archbishop of Edinburgh for Rolfe's reinstatement as a candidate for the priesthood moved slowly, they were well under way by May, when Rolfe referred to himself in print as a 'young Roman ecclesiastic'.[11] By May, too, he had rejected St. Peter's College, Partickhill, Glasgow, and determined on Scots College, Rome, as the place for his studies and preparation.[12] And if Father Angus's efforts had not entirely succeeded by August, they had progressed far enough to leave Rolfe's confidence unshaken. His mind was free to focus on artistic matters.

Rolfe was also sanguine on that front. He had managed to publish several poems in the months just past, and he was busily sending out the rejected ones as fast as they came back. He made careful lists of the journals which returned his works, noting after each the date of return and 'WT' (declined with thanks).[13] Both in numbers and quality the periodicals which failed to print his work were well ahead of those which accepted it, but he had enough publications to call himself a writer.

At Christchurch and in association with Kains Jackson and Gleeson White, Rolfe once more went at the 'old rhyme-forms', working with enthusiasm and determination to show his mastery of both rondeau and ballade. Far more important than literary talk with these men as a background for Rolfe's 'Ballade of Boys Bathing' was their conversation about *The Bathers*, a painting of three nude boys by Henry Tuke, who had depicted 'the truth and beauty of flesh in sunlight by the sea'.[14] The picture was part of the New English Art Club's exhibition that year, 1889, before it was taken for showings first to Birmingham and then to Leeds. Kains Jackson was especially interested in *The Bathers*. His journal, *The Artist and Journal of Home Culture*, carried announcements of the exhibitions in which the painting was shown and a sonnet which Kains Jackson wrote in praise of Tuke's picture. Furthermore, his beloved nephew may have posed for one of the three boys in the picture.[15] Whether he did or not, the implications of such a possibility account for Kains Jackson's enthusiasm because for him and Gleeson White and in turn for Rolfe, *The Bathers* was a 'passionate statement' about the beauty of the nude adolescent male. It reminded Rolfe of bathers he had observed the year before while staying with Father Angus, boys bathing in St. Andrews Bay. In years to come Grant Richards, the publisher, observed Rolfe indulging himself in the same way at Oxford, where he was 'sitting under the Parson's Pleasure willows on a decrepit chair, rolling cigarette after cigarette in his nicotine stained fingers, and surveying the yellow flesh tints with unbecoming satisfaction'.[16] Rolfe's explanation of such a scene was written in 1906 and rewritten in Venice in a piece called 'Armed Hands', where Rolfe said about Oxford, 'I make a point of being up during Eights Weeks, because (as a physical epicure) I like to see how England's most recent flesh is coming on.'[17] In 1889, he was not bold enough to write those words. But from his association with Kains Jackson and Gleeson White, Rolfe summoned enough courage to tell what he saw. The two men were years older than he, neither was a priest or a schoolmaster and their worldliness was certainly greater than Rolfe's. They were a part of the new aestheticism. Rolfe was gratified by their notice of him and he was downright flattered when Kains Jackson paid him the compliment of imitation by writing 'Ballade of the Serpentine Suggested by some Lines of the Rev. F. W. Rolfe'.[18] Above all, the discreet but undeniable pederasty of both men and their easy acceptance of it was liberating to Rolfe. He was free to set down as painter and poet the 'most recent flesh' he had remarked. He could disclose

28

his own obsessions, as he was convinced Tuke had done, in the name of art. The result was a painting of numerous, almost nude boys at play in the moonlit phosphorescence of St. Andrews Bay and the poem 'Ballade of Boys Bathing'.

[vii]

By the time 'Ballade of Boys Bathing' appeared, without the painting meant to illustrate it, in *The Art Review* for April 1890, Rolfe was nearing the end of his residence as a probationary candidate for the priesthood at Scots College, Rome. Thanks to Father Angus and, through his influence, to Canon Archibald Douglas, Archbishop Smith of St. Andrews and Edinburgh had accepted Rolfe as a 'volunteer' for his diocese and had agreed to sponsor him at the Scots College for a period of theological study and probation. The Archbishop agreed to pay his fees after Rolfe had proved himself and been accepted as a student in preparation for the priesthood on the condition that Rolfe must thereafter serve as a priest in the Archbishop's diocese. The Scots College exists for the purpose of familiarising young Scottish men with Roman ways and 'habits of thought' and preparing them for clerical duties in Scotland. When necessary, their expenses are borne by the diocese. Rolfe believed that he had Archbishop Smith's support, that Father Angus and Canon Douglas had so advised him.[1] Besides, Rolfe had absolute faith in his fitness for priesthood; there was no other 'niche in this world' for him. So with his paintings and poems and his few possessions but without previous communication with the Rector of the College, Monsignor James A. Campbell, Rolfe reached Rome and the Scots College on the Via Quattro Fontane on 7 December 1889. At Christmas, pleading necessity, Rolfe returned briefly to Scotland as a holiday guest of Ogilvie-Forbes at Boyndlie House[2] and then, before the year was out, went back to Scots College to tend his vocation.

At the College, one of Rolfe's first steps was to work out an allotment of his time in a day of sixteen waking hours—so much for chapel, so much for lectures, so much for meals, reading, writing and leisure. Then he set up an 'Horarium' in this way:

5·30   Rise
6·0   Chapel
6·30   Mass
7·15   C & C
8·0   Lectures
10·15 H. M. & B Reading

12·15	Litanies
12·30	Meal (?)
1·0	Pipe & writing
2·0	Reading
4·15	Free Time *VISIT*
6·0	C & C
6·15	Ave Maria & Reading
7·15	De Profundis
7·30	Chapel
8·0	Meal (?) Pipe & writing
9·15	Chapel
9·30	Bed

Pious acts on the floor outside door every now & then.[3]

It was a busy schedule, but unless he used the hour and a quarter designated as free time (which Rome made it difficult to do), Rolfe had little more than two hours a day for writing.

Yet Rolfe managed to carry on his literary efforts without pause. In January 1890, 'Triolet', a New Year's poem composed in the past year as part of his experimentation with poetic forms, was published by *Atalanta* in facsimile with a drawing dated 1890 and signed in the plate. 'Triolet' reads:

> Here's a little New Year pitched out of the sky
> With a great bag of mystery under his arm,
> At the World's street-door, he's beginning to cry,
> (Here's a little New Year pitched out of the sky!)
> Let's take him in out of the cold, and pry
> In the bag while he sits by the fire to warm.
> Here's a little New Year pitched out of the sky
> With a great bag of mystery under his arm![4]

The sentimentality of these verses is equalled only by that of Rolfe's accompanying sketch. But he was gratified by the prestige which he thought he acquired from publication and he liked his tiny fee, his only source of income at this time. He continued to send out his 'Ballade of Boys and In Particular of the Percies' with illustrations, and on 4 February 1890 as 'The Rev. F. W. Rolfe', he offered the poem 'Ottava rima: Three Ages of Love' to *Blackwood's Magazine*. With the manuscript of his poem Rolfe enclosed a circular, a reprint of an article published in the *Whitehall Review* in the previous May. An attempt to call attention to himself, the article spoke of his use of various poetic forms, of his subjects as 'naturally of a religious nature' and then pointed out that 'by the judicious use of the rhyme forms, together with a very musical manner of English', Rolfe contrived to 'give his verses an extremely dainty old-world flavour'. Rolfe listed examples with their places of publication, naming 'Lytel Seynt Hew',

'Chaunte Royal', and the 'Ballade of the Queen of May'.[5] Despite this carefully fabricated advertisement, *Blackwood's* refused Rolfe's verses.

'Ballade of Boys Bathing', published as by The Rev. Frederick Rolfe, was one of the last pieces which constitute Rolfe's effort to be a poet. He continued to write verses and to publish them but he turned increasingly now to prose. For the first time since the days of 'Scaraboeus The Upper Dormitory Black Beetle,' created at the Winchester Modern School in 1882, Rolfe wrote a considerable piece of prose, 'Some Reminiscences of the Late Empress Augusta'.[6] It was published in November after he left Scots College, but one or more of the early versions was set down in the first months of 1890. During that same time, Rolfe made considerable progress with 'The Story of S. William: The Boy Martyr of Norwich', planned as a full length, authoritative book. In October 1890, the London publishers Elkin Mathews of Vigo Street listed such a work by Rolfe in its 'New and Forthcoming Books' and described it in a separately issued four-page prospectus. The book did not appear and no remnant of a prose work on St. William by Rolfe survives.[7] One prose piece which Rolfe concluded while he was still at Scots College is called 'Ghost or Fancy'. In an undated letter written from the College, he offered it to *Blackwood's* and more than a month after leaving the College wrote to ask for a decision on the 'Ghost Story' submitted 'some weeks back'.[8] *Blackwood's Magazine* did not publish.

His attention to his writing was the most important of several ways in which Rolfe aroused the displeasure of Monsignor Campbell, Rector of Scots College. A life lived wholly in common with his fellows was a part of seminary training. That Rolfe spent free time in 'private pursuits' was a breach of discipline. Later he complained that he was forbidden the use of recreational hours for literary work and thus prevented from earning enough to pay his debts, but that statement was sheer self-justification. He had so far earned next to nothing. On the other hand, his debts both in the College and outside it were shocking to the authorities and the students of the seminary. His pension went unpaid because the Archbishop of Edinburgh had agreed to pay it only when Rolfe's probationary period at the College terminated satisfactorily and he was accepted as a candidate for priesthood. Outside the College, his chief creditors were the pharmacy of the British Embassy, operated in the Via Condotti by J. Y. B. Evans, and a tailor, Luigi Giamini. After Rolfe paid no more than L25 on a debt of L513.20, Giamini boldly entered the College and, to the outrage of Rolfe's colleagues, carried off enough of his effects to take care of a large part of the debt. Still another difficulty arose from Rolfe's aversion to the seminary's meals. Convinced that the College served horse meat, he ate only vegetables and those sparingly, until he could get to a restaurant.[10] Fortunately for his purse, Rolfe had at best a meagre interest in food and wine. Besides, most of what he ate away from Scots College was paid for by Duncan MacVarish, an unwilling and unapt seminary student, or 'Fiffie' Thurstans, Rolfe's old play-fellow at Oxford who was presently in Rome as a tutor in an English family.[10]

Such a finicking appetite meant absenting himself from the College often. To the vexation of the seminary, so did the late afternoon hours which Rolfe maintained for visits. Dressed by special permission in a black soutane instead of the student's purple soutane with black soprano,[11] Rolfe was one of the innumerable clerics who hurry, skirts whipping about their legs, through the streets of Rome. He was off sometimes to his appointments with Thurstans, sometimes to a visit with Mario Sforza-Cesarini, a former student at Oscott, sometimes merely to practise his Italian on a shopkeeper. Failing these or another appointment, Rolfe had numerous choices. He might turn left as he emerged from the College and, passing the Church of St. Andrew, plunge downhill to the Piazza Barberini with Bernini's huge Triton and go on by way of the Via Sistina to the Piazza Trinità de Monti or another of several directions. If he turned right as he came from the College, he mounted quickly to the crest of the Quirinal and, having paused at the four fountains, had only to decide which way he preferred. Whatever it might be, he strode on unpaved streets, narrow ways between massive architectural monuments, in which for generations the Orsinis and Borgias and Farneses had walked. The stone façades rose into arches and arches into vaults; noble columns stretched ever upward, and steps invited to another level. Above them all was the sky which had hung over the Orsinis and Sforzas and the Borgias. The streets wound into *piazzas* where he might gaze on a fountain and its pool, an obelisk, the pines of the Pincio at a distance, or a muscular male wrought in stone into every conceivable position. Rolfe's superior manner when he returned from these jaunts in no way endeared him to his fellows or to the Rector.

None of these things in itself, not even erratic attendance at lectures, was enough to cause Rolfe's expulsion from Scots College. Taken together, they generated among his fellow students considerable scorn for Rolfe and worse, a savage annoyance with him. Canon Robert Carmont testified to that fact, and he added that when the seminarians, whom he called a 'set of young cubs, ignorant and opinionated', began to hear from outside gossip which made their College conspicuous, they were so enraged that the end was in sight.[12]

That a man as unobtrusive in appearance as Rolfe—slight, less than average in height, 'pale, rather demure and ascetic in expression'[13] could excite real loathing in his colleagues is unexpected. But his fastidiousness at table and in his dress was an implicit criticism of everything and everyone around him. Being in his thirtieth year, he was older than they. He had special privileges. He had found no 'kindred spirit' in the College; trying to 'contain' himself and 'use' himself in solitude, Rolfe had provoked the charge of sullenness and disobedience. In retaliation, he cultivated singularity and disdain so that he excited more anger among his fellows. The end was indeed in sight.

Rolfe's behaviour and the seminarians' attitude came to the attention of the Rector. On 23 March 1890, not quite four months after Rolfe's first arrival, he told Rolfe to leave the College. Acting instinctively for his own protection, Rolfe at once took up his pen, as he would always do in time of stress. On the same date, 23 March 1890, he wrote to Campbell, commencing with a partial summary of their conversation:

> I understood you to say that you were on the point of writing to the Lord Archbishop of St. Andrews and Edinburgh, my diocesan, to the effect that I was in the habit of breaking the rules of the House by spending the hours of recreation in private pursuits (literary work), that you could not, under the circumstances, permit me to remain a member of this College, nor would you allow the 3 months 16 days I have already spent here to count towards my Ordination.

Rolfe went on to protest that until Monsignor Campbell had spoken to him that morning he had 'not the remotest idea' of 'infringing any rule' when he determined his own 'occupation in recreation hours and during holidays'. He had, he said, 'written frankly' to Dr. Smith his archbishop, telling him how he spent what he considered his 'spare time'. Rolfe went on:

> There was no disguise about it on my part and as other members of this house spent and so spend the time allotted to recreation on their own affairs, I have never had, as I said before, any reason to think that I was meriting such a serious punishment as that with which you are about to visit me.

Having been charged, as well, with asking permission to absent himself from the community during vacations, a reference to his Christmas visit to Boyndlie House, Rolfe declared that he had been unaware that he was 'doing anything unusual'. His letter protested that he was not a child needing supervision but a man who could take care of himself and that he intended to do so both for his own sake and 'for the sake of that ecclesiastical habit' which, he said, he would never 'put off'. To demonstrate that his theological studies had not suffered because of his 'private occupations' and that his study hours had been well spent, he offered to show Monsignor Campbell the 'M.S. work' done since 7 December.[14] Although Rolfe blamed himself for nothing, his letter was reasonable and conciliatory in tone. Whether or not Campbell inspected Rolfe's 'M.S. work' (part of which MacVarish had done for him),[15] the rector rescinded his order, and Rolfe had another chance.

It did not last long. This time the seminarians complained to Campbell, and on 16 April Campbell once more told Rolfe to go, setting the date for his departure as 21 April, a Monday. On the night of 20 April, Rolfe wrote again to the Rector accusing him of unreasonable and unjust treatment. 'You have expelled me', Rolfe wrote, 'for a breach of rules, knowing that it was not in my power to observe them.' He then referred to the injury done him in forbidding him to use his 'recreation hours' for literary work and continued with an account of the hardships his expulsion must bring:

> I have no money at all at present and no friends in Rome who are able to offer me hospitality.
>
> Even supposing I had the means to return to Scotland, I still have no home to go to, nor shall I be able to make any further arrangements by Monday morning.
>
> Having made you aware of these facts, I have nothing to do but leave my effects at the College, to obey your injunctions to the letter, and to turn out into the streets.[16]

At this point Rolfe put the entire responsibility for his situation on Campbell, but even so the rector yielded again and conceded that Rolfe might remain until 3 May. On that day, as he probably already had done and as he was to do in future with irate landladies, Rolfe kept to his bed. At nightfall, when he still had not risen, servants took him up bodily with his mattress, blanket and all, and set him outside the College. His record at the Scots College was marked '*Expulsus e Collegio*'.[17]

More than fifteen years later in *Hubert's Arthur*, a book written partly in collaboration with C. H. C. Pirie-Gordon and then rewritten, Rolfe told how his hero was '*Defiled*' when the Jews of Bristol seized him for ritual crucifixion. He wrote, 'The touch of infamous depraved perfidious hands, pawing and mauling every inch of his flesh, had been as a spear-thrust in his heart nine-times-nine-times repeated, outraging his personal sacrosanctity, violating his regal dignity, defiling the sacred enclosure of his self-repect.'[18] So was Rolfe desecrated when he was forcibly removed from Scots College and in his own case he might have added that his fondest hope was frustrated. There could be no alleviation of his pain, no redress, no restitution because his suffering was not based on error but rather, in the words of Proust, on 'psychological truths, human and emotional truths.' Rolfe's fidelity to his inmost being, ludicrously as it turned out, ended his stay at the College and his opportunity for priesthood. The events which ended in his expulsion were not the cause of it. They were only surface happenings, symptomatic on his side and mere pretext on the side of the authorities.

Men who knew Rolfe at Scots College and men who have written about him since have offered innumerable reasons for his failure. Ambrose Moriarty, later Bishop of Shrewsbury, recurred to non-payment of his pension. Canon Carmont, expressing massive disapproval of Rolfe, saw him as a liar, an ingrate, a *poseur*, a man without piety and affection, and a sufferer from 'a sort of spiritual myopia'. Father John Stuart emphasised Rolfe's irreverence and his eccentricities, giving as corroboration his practice of delivering 'weird sermons in the refectory' and of 'saying his office in his bath'. The Reverend William Rooney, Vice-Rector of Scots College, spoke of 'an element of mystery in and around' Rolfe's 'elusive character'.[19] Others have explained him as lacking a 'natural will-to-community' and thus 'unable to identify himself with the aims of any group on a purely natural level'.[20] More than one writer has put the blame squarely on the College, maintaining that it might have saved Rolfe for the priesthood by means of proper guidance and attention to his spiritual welfare or by means of a rector with greater understanding and fewer limitations than Monsignor Campbell possessed.[21] Monsignor Campbell reported that Rolfe had 'failed egregiously in his trial' and spoke of his 'breaches of discipline', his 'disregard for the duties required of a divinity student, and his debts contracted with the full knowledge that he could not meet them'.[22]

Rolfe, too, had a variety of explanations. He remarked on the character of the rector. As for his debts, Rolfe insisted that they had been contracted owing to promises of the Archbishop of Edinburgh and under the personal supervision of Rooney, Vice-Rector at Scots College. Rolfe mentioned his Jacobite and royalist sympathies, demonstrated by 'praying for the souls of James III, Charles III, & Henry IX at their tomb in St. Peter's', as the cause for severe reprobation 'by some monsignori'.[23] In *The Desire and Pursuit of the Whole*, he expanded this suggestion into the cause for his dismissal. There, speaking of the Sforza-Cesarini family as Attendoli-Cesari and of himself in the third person, Rolfe said:

When he was studying for the priesthood in the Scots College of Rome, he chanced to be of signal service to Mario Attendoli-Cesari, whose princely family shewed due appreciation. The Attendoli-Cesari were of royalist politics, lords-in-waiting and ladies-in-waiting at the Quirinale; and the Black Clericals (following their usual custom of pin-pricking White Monarchist patricians) quickly discovered that the friend of the Attendoli-Cesari had no vocation to the priesthood, and expelled him from college.[24]

Once he facetiously attributed his failure to the colour of his hair. 'Carrots, of course, are admissible,' he wrote, 'but not rutilant auburn . . . the colour of Achilles' hair, the real young nut-colour gleaming like burnished copper in the sun—that's considered unusual and therefore distinct and subtile.'[25] In a letter to Dr. James J. Walsh of New York written on 4 June 1903, Rolfe reaffirmed his vocation, denied that anyone except himself could claim to know about it, and then added:

I believe that somebody carelessly lied, that someone clumsily blundered, and that all concerned were determined not to own themselves or anyone else but me, to be in the wrong. A mistake— a justifiable mistake seeing that I am an abnormal creature and my superiors were about as commonplace a gaggle of fat-witted geese as this hemisphere produced—was made; and by quibble, intimidations, every hole-and-corner means conceivable it has been perpetuated.[26]

Here was the same explanation he had offered after his discharge from Oscott and the same faith in himself. In the letter to Walsh, however, Rolfe uncovered what was at the bottom of his expulsion from Scots College, a profound contempt for his fellow-seminarians and his superiors at the College. To say that he scorned the whole English-Irish membership of the Church is hardly an exaggeration. Even as he turned to the Vice-Rector for support in the last weeks at Scots College, Rolfe described Rooney as a 'mild anemic of thirty with the face of a good young woman'.[27] He charged the Rector with injustice and at last berated him. Still, he told Walsh that his attitude toward Catholics was 'one of severe forbearance'. At the same time, Rolfe declared that he looked on English Catholics as 'physically and mentally hebete, exolete, effete', characteristics which he attributed to the 'effect of . . . exclusion from "that culture which contact with a wider world alone can give". '[28] Although he made that statement in 1903 when, as he wrote *Hadrian the Seventh*, he experienced again the pain and defeat he had known in Rome, nevertheless the gist of it accounts for so much of his behaviour at the College. It explains the 'weird sermons' described by his associate John Stuart as filled with 'stinging hits at our somewhat uncultivated Scottish manners'.[29] It clarifies Rolfe's disdain for young men whose humour rarely went beyond nicknames for prominent churchmen such as Cardinal Merry del Val, known to the theological students as 'Merry Devil'. The statement to Walsh also accounts for the shocking admonition to himself at the end of his 'Horarium', that is, 'Pious acts on the floor outside door every now & then.'[30]

That reminder threatens to confirm Canon Carmont's judgement that Rolfe had 'a very clear and discerning eye for outside values and superficialities—and little else'.[31] Worse, he opens himself to the charge of hypocrisy. Yet from the day of his decision to seek conversion, Rolfe never lost his faith and it never diminished. It was unalterable and unequivocal. 'If I were not a Catholic, I shouldn't be anything at all,' he told his brother Herbert. And to Walsh, Rolfe wrote, 'For in the Faith' was all his 'heart and soul.'[32] Not the faith but the faithful were 'intolerable', and so he declared more than once. They deserved no more than pious acts performed in public. 'Outside values and superficialities' were enough for the 'commonplace,' the 'gaggle of . . . geese' and for his fellow students, 'immature cubs mostly, hybrid larrikins, given to false quantities and nasal cacophonies.' He need not dignify them with his own sincerity, his unwavering belief in 'God, the First, the Last, the Perfect, the Supreme'. He had no respect for them as men or as co-religionists, and he disparaged their perception. They failed to value his individuality or to allow for it in the priesthood. They failed to recognise his vocation. So convinced was Rolfe of its strength that he forgot that 'the Divine Giver' did not 'deign to manifest' his vocation to others as well as to himself.[33]

When servants, following Monsignor Campbell's instructions, set Frederick Rolfe bodily onto the porch of the Scots College on that first Saturday night in May 1890, his every hope for priesthood was at an end. He described the experience as 'one of the many incredibly cruel and unspeakably hideous happenings which marred . . . and soured' him. For the rest of his life he 'cherished with almost super-human pertinacity' a 'bitter corroding grievance'.[34] Yet he refused to acknowledge that the life of a religious was not available to him, and he determined never to 'recede' from the 'grade of tonsured clerk' under any circumstances. To be in readiness for the invitation to priesthood which he asserted would come, he swore celibacy for twenty years. When he was not deluding himself, Rolfe referred to his expulsion from the College as his 'life's great disappointment'.[35] Thereafter, when he recalled his experience at Rome, his pain came back as though 'some kakodaimon rode' his intellect. 'My closed eyes saw myself as I was,' he wrote, 'driven from my road, my life's career wrecked, blocked, checked— . . . thrown out of my stride, thwarted in my sole ambition, utterly useless'.[36] He conceded that he had powers and health and freedom, but he 'craved' bonds.

[viii]

In that May 1890, Rolfe also had the problem of survival with neither farthing nor friend to help him. His friends, by whom he meant the Sforza-Cesarini, were away from Rome, arranging for the 'coming villeggiatura'.[1] He owed money. His tailor had confiscated his goods and, according to the late Bishop of Shrewsbury, Rolfe complained that Monsignor Campbell had seized a meerschaum pipe worth £40. Indeed Rolfe declared that he was 'more than one hundred and twenty pounds out of pocket', expenses which he thought ought rightfully to have been borne by Archbishop Smith. Homeless and almost penniless, Rolfe sought help from Father Peter Paul Mackey, O.P., an editor of the Leonine edition of St. Thomas Aquinas and external confessor to the Scots College. Mackey made clear to Monsignor Campbell that he was not taking up Rolfe's quarrel and that he did not approve of Rolfe or of his 'mode of acting'. On the contrary, as Mackey said in a letter of 4 May 1890, he was much embarrassed by Rolfe and his appeal. Acting only out of compassion for Rolfe's immediate need, Mackey provided him with three days' pension at a perennial and favourite refuge for clerics, the Hotel Minerva, which stands, as it faces Bernini's small marble elephant and obelisk in the Piazza della Minerva, almost in the shadow of the Pantheon.[2]

Whether Rolfe looked for a solution to his problems while he still had shelter or waited until his stay at the Hotel Minerva came to an end is uncertain. More than likely, he immediately denounced Campbell to everyone who would hear him and asked for money wherever he though he might get it. Canon Carmont, recalling Rolfe as a student, commented on his lack of pride, his willingness to beg, his calm assertion of his 'right to expect assistance and favours from those in a position to grant them'.[3] On this occasion he turned to Hartwell de la Gard Grissel, a long-standing Chamberlain of Honour to the Pope. Rolfe who later disparaged him as Sieur Carggontaine de la Gardegrise in *Don Renato* and as Signor Gargouille Grice in *Hadrian the Seventh* and wrote contemptuously about him in a letter to the editor of *The Monthly Review*, had uselessly asked Grissel for help at Oxford immediately after the Oban fiasco. In Rome, Grissel had avoided Rolfe, who nevertheless applied to Grissel for £50 in order to get back to England in style.[4] When nothing could be got there, Rolfe soon put to the proof the few others who might help him, including 'Fiffie' Thurstans, but no one except Father Mackey came to his aid with more than a meal or a night's lodging. Rolfe then appealed to the British Consul for repatriation; the Consul refused to provide the necessary funds and advised him that Monsignor Campbell was 'bound in justice' to restore him to the condition in which he found himself when Smith, Archbishop of Edinburgh, took him as a student.

Making the most of this opportunity to berate Campbell, Rolfe promptly wrote to him again. He first cited three reasons given him for his dismissal from the Scots College: 1 'never observed a single rule. 2 Having contracted unwarrantable debts. 3. Having deceived you about my departure from Oscott.' He then wrote in part:

You have refused to hear the explanations I have to offer which put an entirely different aspect on the case, in short, you and my diocesan have refused me what every Christian principle of justice demands, viz. an unbiased hearing and a fair trial. Moreover, in addition to refusing me what is the right of the lowest felon, you have attempted to besmirch my character, and, as well, to prevent me (and I use the word deliberately) from extricating myself from the predicament to which your tender mercies and *no fault of mine* have consigned me. You must know that charges 1 and 2 are, *as they stand*, absolutely false. You must know that I scrupulously observed *all* the rules of your house which I knew (I never had a copy of them) except when physical incapability prevented me, that you alone are responsible for whatever breach of rule I may have committed. I mean that you knew that I was getting insufficient food for months, you knew the simple fare I needed, you knew that I refused to ask for it because I did not want to bother you, and yet you took no steps to help me ... You knew too that you yourself took away from me the means of paying my necessary debts, by forbidding me what you permitted and do permit to other men in your house, viz. to use my recreation hours as I pleased.

You refused to read the letters which prove how entirely untrue is charge 3 ...

I ask once more, are you going to see me starve in the streets?

You knew that I have not even stamps to communicate with my friends, that I have to go about Rome begging for a meal here and a sofa to sleep on there.

Is such a public scandal to go on indefinitely?

I await your reply which I shall ask your porter for before 9 o'clock tonight.[5]

That Rolfe expected a reply is difficult to credit. Needless to say, the porter had none when Rolfe called for it. Whether the Rector was a liar and a man of narrow capacity or an harassed, scholarly, 'rather choleric, though a generous little man',[6] he could not respond to Rolfe's letter without demeaning himself. Bickering and a continuation of their quarrel or complete agreement with Rolfe's contention that he alone was blameless were the only answers Campbell could give. In other words, Rolfe left Campbell no choice but silence— which, in turn, became another cause for complaint.

Finally Caroline, the Duchess of Sforza-Cesarini, put an end to Rolfe's immediate dilemma by returning to Rome and offering him refuge. The daughter of the English adventurer Robert Sewallis Shirley and Sophia Caroline Curzon, the Duchess was the widow since 1886 of Duke Lorenzo Sforza-Cesarini, member of a collateral branch of that great Italian family descended from the fourteenth century peasant *condottiere* Giacomuzzo Attendolo. Count Mario Sforza-Cesarini dei Santa Fuora, Rolfe's friend of Oscott days, was a relation of the Duchess's husband. Rolfe said that he had been of 'signal service' to Mario and his 'princely family showed appreciation',[7] The Duchess, like Rolfe a convert, said that she took an interest in him because he had told her that 'by having joined the Church of Rome, he had ruined his prospects and his family had discarded him'.[8] Rolfe presented himself to her as an 'expelled Church student with no Vocation' as soon as she returned to Rome from Genzano, where she had gone to prepare her Palazzo Sforza-Cesarini for the summer. She and her family made light of his failure. 'They were disgusted with me', he wrote, 'for making myself ill for what they called a fad.'[9] The Duchess, however, promptly took him into her Palazzo on the Corso Vittorio Emanuele, at the Piazza Sforza, and she offered him hospitality at her Palazzo high on a hill in Genzano, where she was prepared to go to escape the summer heat of Rome. The idea was, Rolfe said, that he should be 'cockered back to health' before making plans for his future. And so, 'all sad with half-shut eyes of a dreaming prisoner',[10] Rolfe went with her.

Afterward, he said that he was happy that summer at Genzano, and he had much to make him happy. He was cared for and briefly he was free from worry. If his own statement can be trusted, he had the freedom of the Sforza-Cesarini family's archives with enough 'chartes, breves, diurnals, accompts, . . . multifarious manuscripts'[11] to keep his mind as active and alive as he wished. Through these records, Rolfe was developing an obsession with Renaissance Italy. He kept at his writing and attempted to place his work, sending off letters and manuscripts to *Blackwood's Magazine* and other periodicals. He renewed his interest in painting, using for his models the same boys whose 'long rose-brown sinuosities of youth'[12] he photographed frequently that summer, often sending prints of their pictures to Kains Jackson. These boys, immortalised in *Stories Toto Told Me* and *In His Own Image*, were doubtless among the 'delightful people of all ages and ranks' who surrounded Rolfe at Genzano and who were, he said, devoted to him.[13] Their simple and intense adoration eased Rolfe's pain at the mockery of his ambitions. He took special comfort from the boys' leader, Toto Ephoros. Toto and his six fellows represented for Rolfe 'singular' perfection with their 'serene reserved nobility of port, their bright gravity of regard and the antick breeding of their mein'.[14] Toto's beauty in particular was extraordinary, and Rolfe was one of the 'brave souls' unafraid to 'honour their Creator by frank admiration of His noblest works'.[15] Rolfe thought Toto as 'divinely smart' in blue livery as he was desirable lying on his back in the woods while 'his arms framed the density of his hair' and his 'head and throat fell back and upward to the sky'.[16] Indeed, Rolfe was enfolded in beauty. His surroundings so impressed him that he could describe them minutely and accurately eight years later when he wrote of the Palazzo Sforza Cesarini as one of the loveliest places in the world:

It stands on the top of a rock amid the hills. Behind it a glorious old garden winds down the crags to the Lago San Giorgio. Before it, the little town ripples to the foot of the rock till it meets the Campagna, and there the broad magnificence of verdant plains lose their outlines in the horizon of a turquoise sea.[17]

As he said, it would have been strange if he had failed to get well and strong in this beautiful spot.

But he also got restless. Rolfe made reasons to go to Rome, travelling with Toto in the Duchess's English dog-cart to Arricia and on past Albano until they reached the Via Appia, which took them in to Rome. He began to wander, he and Toto and the other six boys, in the Alban Mountains, going a half-day's journey, a day's, two at the most when he went as far as Velletri or into the Sabine Mountains. Rolfe bathed in mountain streams and lakes, and slept on wooded slopes or in a hammock slung between the oaks. He spent whole days lazing in the dappled sunlight and he came back to the Palazzo with strawberries from Nemi, memories of the monasteries at Subiaco, of Guido Reni's paintings in the Church of the Santissima Trinita at Marino, of mass in Bernini's Church of San Tommaso da Villanova at Castel Gandolfo. His rambles in the mountains showed Rolfe the road his fictional hero Don Tarquinio would take when he ran from Rome to love and fortune.[18]

More important, from Rolfe's excursions came *Stories Toto Told Me* and its sequel, *In His Own Image*, stories which were first published in 1895[19] but which had their origin in the summer of 1890 in the Alban Mountains. Despite the wealthy Romans' age-long invasion of these mountains, owing to their natural beauty and their coolness in the hot months, the inhabitants preserved their isolation and cultural integrity. Christianity was an ancient heritage, but its orthodox ways and beliefs developed slowly among the people. Even the most faithful in 1890 retained peculiar customs more pagan than Christian, symbolic approaches to the mysteries of luxuriant growth and sudden destruction. They localised their religion. As their ancestors had walked and talked with gods when the world was young, so peasants were familiar with apostles, disciples, saints. While keeping total reverence for Mary, the Holy Father, and their Son, they envisioned his followers as natives of the Alban Mountains and heaven as a wondrous enlarged village inhabited by translated villagers. Here was a simple reflection of Rolfe's attitude in this personally satisfying but personally demanding religion. It neglected dogma and ecclesiastical convention. It ignored the arbitrary, disciplinary limitations of the Church, which Rolfe had unhappily experienced. In fact it not only permitted but actually encouraged individual responsibility in Christ's name. It was a religion vital with the breath of Christ. Both the spirit and the homely localism of the Christianity in these Alban Mountains provided the matter of *Stories Toto Told Me*. In 1890, the stories were 'unworded' but they were a part of Rolfe's awareness, one of the chief literary possibilities he was to take with him when he left Genzano, the Palazzo there of the Duchess of Sforza-Cesarini, and the security which she provided.

As summer faded, Rolfe lingered on at Genzano with the Duchess; but he was increasingly restless and, except momentarily, nothing compensated for the miscarriage of his hopes for priesthood. His hostess made every effort to distract him. According to one account, she 'filled the house all through the summer with the loveliest girls . . . any one of whom would have made him an excellent wife'.[20] Despite his antipathy for women, emphatically stated, Rolfe was well-bred enough to be at ease with them and could even 'in a quiet way pay attentions'.[21] He was polite to the Duchess's young ladies, but he obviously preferred her archives or his expeditions in the mountains with Toto. Possibly the Duchess and Rolfe went to Spezia in October for what he termed 'a little yachting'. In late October or November, when the Duchess returned to Rome, he returned with her. None of this satisfied him. He was without purpose or direction. Throughout his life, Rolfe was invincible in disaster but restive and insecure with conventional ease. As he said, he was a 'man who hates, loves, and excruciates',[22] a man who did not thrive on ease and self-contemplation. The time had come for him to leave the protection of the Sforza-Cesarini household. And so with a financial guarantee of some kind from the Duchess—she described it as 'several presents in money' because she wished to 'start him in some means of getting a living'[23]— Rolfe returned to England.

Part II:

1890 – 1899

[i]

Details of Rolfe's return to England are obscure. Although he once stated that he was in Rome as late as November 1890, Rolfe later said that he was already 'struggling for Life as best he could' in England in November.[1] Lymington, a quiet Hampshire village celebrated for its yacht building, is the first English location at which he can be placed in 1890. His tendency throughout his life to gravitate toward the sea might account for his being there, but that there was some other reason, no doubt quixotic, some association which drew him and which is now lost, is also very likely. Before the year 1890 was out, he moved a few miles westward from Lymington to Christchurch, a place well remembered from the fruitful summer of 1889. It may be, as Mrs. Gleeson White told Kains Jackson, that Rolfe 'made a dead set' at her and her husband, 'thinking Gleeson White would be of use to him from a literary pt. of view—and that he came on from Lymington changing his name with that purpose'.[2]

Certainly Rolfe presented himself in Christchurch with a new name, Frederick, Baron Corvo. The Duchess Sforza-Cesarini may have conferred the title on him without attaching lands; such empty, lifetime gifts are the practice and the right of Italian nobility within their families. She spoke of Rolfe and he spoke of himself as her adopted grandson.[3] Perhaps she merely invented the name after the English Bishop of Emmaus, also Rector of St. Mary's in Chelsea and the Duchess's confessor, facetiously suggested that Rolfe ought to be a baron.[4] Or maybe the Bishop, James Laird Patterson, who had received Rolfe into the Catholic Church, gave him the name when they walked together during the recent days at Scots College.[5] Rolfe explained his title as no more than a pseudonym to protect his baptismal name from any taint of commercialism because he meant to be known by it some day in the priesthood. He said that a priest (by whom he meant Patterson) suggested the use of 'pseudonyms or technikryms' and the Duchess selected the name. That account, he declared, was 'the blind and naked truth on that point'.[6] Yet Mrs. Gleeson White maintained that Rolfe '*never* admitted that he was not the Duchess's grandson', saying when questioned that 'his mother was her daughter'![7] Rolfe's calling cards, which he had made to replace a plain set burned as soon as he settled into Christchurch, showed both his local address and his name, Baron Corvo. Letter paper, similarly giving his address, was engraved with a crest of his own design displaying a raven, that 'grave and noble bird' long since chosen as his sign, and a baronial crown.

Rolfe stayed with the Gleeson Whites at Caxton House, 10 High Street, when he first arrived in Christchurch,[8] but thanks to the Duchess Sforza-Cesarini he had funds and there was no question of his staying long enough to wear out his welcome. His talk about his allowance and his new name were too pretentious for Nancy Gleeson White, but her husband, a hospitable gregarious man, welcomed Rolfe whole-heartedly.

Rolfe quickly engaged lodgings recommended by his hosts at Toinham—now Tyneham—House, in Bridge Street. Christchurch's main thoroughfare is High Street which runs at its top into the close of the beautiful old Priory with its monument to the poet Shelley. The first main turning to the left off High Street is Bridge Street, and half-way along it, on the left, sits Toinham House behind a tall fence with widely spaced iron fence posts and a clanging gate. The house, broad and serene looking, has an entry way recessed between identical wings and a row of second-floor windows, all alike. Charles Carrington Gardner, once butler in the household of Louisa, Marchioness of Waterford, had purchased Toinham House, a private residence, and with his wife Dorothy turned it into a well-appointed rooming house. Kains Jackson's young cousin, Cecil Castle, spent his summer holidays there and Kains Jackson usually joined him in August, as had been the case in 1889, when Rolfe first went to Christchurch, so that he had some familiarity with the place. Toinham House is only a few hundred yards below the river and across the street (named Purwell Road above the point where it crosses the river) from the Church of the Immaculate Conception and Saint Joseph, the only Catholic church in the town. Nearby was the Red Lion pub. In the opposite direction, the walk to 10 High Street and Gleeson White's stationer's shop and lending library, which occupied half of an inherited property, Caxton House (a baker's shop was in the other half), was an easy half-mile at most. Toinham House was ideal for Frederick, Baron Corvo.

Having moved himself and his possessions into his lodgings, Rolfe promptly got to work. His literary efforts went on as usual. *The Paternoster Review* had already accepted for its November 1890 issue, 'Some Reminiscences of the Late Empress Augusta', an uncharacteristic essay signed with the meaningless 'Orthocrates'.[9] He immediately attempted to place three sonnets, presumably brought from Italy inasmuch as all three were written in 1890.[10] Of these, the first is 'Of Gore', described in manuscript as a sonnet 'After the manner of C. J. R. Esquire',[11] by which Rolfe meant C. J. Roope, formerly a student at Saffron Walden and one of the dedicatees of *Tarcissus*. When the poem was published anonymously in March 1891 in *The Anti-Jacobin*, the title read 'Sonnet. (In the Modern Manner.) Of Gore.' The other

46

two were printed in Kains Jackson's periodical, *The Artist and Journal of Home Culture*, in June 1891 under the title 'Two Sonnets, for a Picture of Saint Sebastian the Martyr in the Capitoline Gallery'. One praises the painter Guido Reni for his 'Life, soul and Faith'; the other has to do with Saint Sebastian's martyrdom and his 'stainless soul'. Both are dedicated to the Duchess Sforza-Cesarini. Rolfe had at least one more poem, 'Ballade of The Boy Bishop',[12] a piece owing something to William Dunbar, available for publication. No one wanted it.

Rolfe's zeal went undiminished whether his contributions were accepted or not. In January 1891, he clipped from the paper *Answers* 'A Chat About the Magazines', which provided a list of periodicals with the names of their editors and their rates of payment; of these, Rolfe marked a number as worthy of his attention—*Blackwood's, Cassell's, The Cornhill, Good Words, Temple Bar,* and *Strand Magazine.*[13] It was the *Paternoster Review,* however, which published in its January issue Rolfe's essay 'The General Election of 1890 in Italy' as it had, the previous month, 'Re. Meeting between Caprivi and Crispi', a note signed F.R. Both of these were composed at Toinham House. In the first months there he also worked at some version of a Toto story which waited until 1906 for publication under the title 'The Princess's Shirts',[14] and he began to draft parts of what eventually appeared as *Don Renato.* For immediate publication under the name Bellator Romanus, Rolfe wrote a letter entitled 'The Way the Papists Treat their Converts'. This was an attack on Catholics, Rolfe's first one, not on Catholicism. It had nothing to do with his faith. His belief was unshaken; that same year, 1891, Rolfe stressed his reliance on the evidence of things not seen when he told Kains Jackson in a discussion of agnosticism, 'It does so wreck a man to want to know too much and I think he is far happier who is content to say "There are some things one cannot grasp and I am not going to be bored by worrying about them".'[15] When several 'Papist' newspapers not surprisingly refused his letter, Rolfe sent it to *The Manchester Guardian,* where it appeared on 27 June 1891.

Rolfe soon combined his writing and a developing passion for photography. In July, in response to a note by Kains Jackson in *The Artist* describing photographic effects in colour accidentally got by Baron Corvo, Rolfe wrote about further results with colour photography. What he had to say was printed in *The Artist* for August. Writing in the form of a letter dated 21 July 1891 to Kains Jackson, Rolfe began by stating that since the publication of a notice about his experiments he had carried his 'researches a few steps further'. He then recounted one or two done in the previous summer on the 'terrace of the Sforza-Cesarini Palace at Genzano-di-Roma' and others completed at Christchurch in the past month. He went on to give his conclusions despite the fact that he knew nothing and wished to know nothing of 'formulae', which he labelled a 'stumbling block

47

and a cause of offence' inasmuch as he looked on photography as no more than an amusement.

Photography was a serviceable amusement for Rolfe and his friends. Through it they were never far from the absorbing matter of boys. Three days after writing his remarks for *The Artist*, that is on 24 July 1891, Rolfe sent Kains Jackson a photographic proof of a design for a bookplate and an offer to make a 'neg' of the picture, that of a boy, so that the bookplate might be printed. An accompanying note read, 'The conception is delicious but I don't like the boy. Face is potty and legs (what a poem is a leg!) baggy.'[16] Within the month, Kains Jackson had inquired about Rolfe's relations with boys and been told in reply that Rolfe never made friends with boys now because he was 'too old & uninteresting'; instead he made them his 'bondslaves'. Rolfe continued:

> Then I worship their beauty. When my knees get stiff or I am bored I kick them to Gehenna or Sheol. Then I go on sweet remembrance till I find another idol. But I am not a scrap sentimental about them *to* them (though I often said to Toto 'ah how lovely you are' and he replied 'Eccellenza, si.') & invariably get my self abhorred by them because of my horrid tempers.[17]

Just the same, since picture-taking gave him an excuse to approach boys and to be in their company, he rarely went into the streets without a camera.[18] At the same time, he was extremely careful with his friends, taking pains to get the Gleeson Whites' permission to make camera studies of their thirteen-year-old son Eric, and Kains Jackson's, to photograph Cecil Castle.[19] Because Rolfe was a 'perfectly loyal friend over boys'[20] and never attempted to intrude between lovers, Kains Jackson liked having the boy pose for Rolfe. Thirty years afterward, Kains Jackson recalled how the young man, nude except for a knit cap, assisted Rolfe in getting a 'spontaneous' pose. 'I can recall as though it was yesterday,' Kains Jackson said, 'my enjoyment of the . . . all but realised anticipation of Cecil in his eagerness to run from the sea not stopping in time but upsetting Corvo and his camera. But Cecil was wonderful in those things & stopped dead on the towel laid down as his objective.'[21]

That particular picture—or set of pictures—made while Kains Jackson fondly looked on served Rolfe as background for an arras depicting Saint Michael which he painted for the Church of the Immaculate Conception and Saint Joseph. Painting was Rolfe's chief concern in Christchurch. It was the means by which he intended to make his living and his name. His procedure was to work from the photographs he took so that he was often in need of a photographic model in preparation for a painting. In June he lamented the lack of a photograph of a 'perfectly naked boy floating in mid air perpendicularly, head thrown back & arms up'. Rolfe meant to paint him

48

with a 'gold bow & quiver & call him "Love".'[22] Fortunately Cecil Castle was often available when Rolfe needed him that summer. He depicted Castle in one oil as Saint George, a beautiful, rosy-mouthed blond boy in armour, his bare legs indeed a poem; but he is an unlikely victor over the dragon at his feet, an embodiment of the horror which lurks in man's heart. The dragon, a spiked monster evoked from some primeval darkness of self, was a reality to Rolfe, but Saint George was only a dream and thus far less credible than the dragon.[23] Castle was also the model for a wall hanging which Rolfe entitled 'Canzonata'. He described it to Kains Jackson:

> Inspired by one of the pictures your charming cousin performed for me, I have put a *translation* (mind that word) into an arras of pure flax. At 6 yards it is—hum—ha—well not bad, anyhow Moonlight, Italian, etc. . . . The boy is in white & black . . . on a terrace of red & green tiles with a stone battlement behind him, dark blue sky & black trees in distance. There is a border of black & yellow & the whole thing will hang over a door and be a door curtain.[24]

Designs of a more ecclesiastical character 'translated' like the 'Canzonata' onto an arras of sized linen were the means by which Rolfe attempted to make his way. Because Gardner, his landlord, prohibited the use of oil paints in the rooms at Toinham House, Rolfe hired a small studio from Gleeson White and there produced not only the 'Canzonata' but also the Saint Michael for the church, a Christ in the midst of the heavenly hierarchy, a 'really good St. Edmund', possibly a Saint Martin, at least a rough sketch of the 'five warrior saints of the Catholic Church', and he had in view an Annunciation. To his paintings Rolfe added embroidery, *paillettes*, and other ornamentation surprisingly appropriate to his fixed, almost stylised figures. Kains Jackson's *Artist* reported three times in glowing terms on Baron Corvo as 'a really refined and imaginative artist in decoration for religious edifices', commenting in June on the 'power and originality' of the depiction of Christ 'surrounded by the nine orders of the Celestial Hierarchy' and the importance of the design showing the martyrdom of 'St. Edmund, the English King of East Anglia, murdered by the Danes'. The September issue spoke with admiration of the ' "Corvo" arras representing St. Michael Archangel' and declared that in the central figure the artist had 'succeeded in snatching from nature "a grace beyond the reach of art"'. The article continued with thanksgiving that a 'really respectable piece of work' had found 'a place in a Roman Catholic place of worship'. In November *The Artist* once more spoke of Rolfe's 'good work in church decoration'. Not surprisingly Rolfe turned from asking Kains Jackson's views as to whether there was a living to be had from the wall hangings to a demand for spangles and an introduction to some firm which would 'hang or exhibit' his work.[25]

49

The seaside expeditions with the nude Cecil Castle, whether under the watchful eye of Kains Jackson or not, might be amusing and his writing and the novelty of creating arrasses from linen cloth, absorbing, but Rolfe also relished another side of existence at Christchurch. Intense, opinionated, mysterious as Baron Corvo and apparently affluent owing to his 'Italian grandmother', Rolfe moved about the town and to some degree became a part of its life. For example there was Mrs. Bell, wife of the artist Arthur George Bell, daughter-in-law of the London publisher, and under her own name or a *nom de plume*, N. D'Anvers, a successful writer on all kinds of subjects but especially on art and artists. In 1891, Mrs. Bell was at work on a book having to do with Rome.[26] What was more natural than that Rolfe should spend long nostalgic hours helping her? He said himself that he was thoroughly familiar with the 'Early Renascence' and he had only recently come from modern Rome. He often walked up to the bridge, stopping in good weather to look at the river on the right as it divided before flowing in two arms into the sea. From there he went on to the small church which held his Saint Michael for a talk with its priest, The Reverend Edward G. Swainson, or he stopped at the pub near the church, the Red Lion. On good terms with at least one member of the legal profession, Risdon Sharp, Rolfe sometimes paused to exchange pleasantries with him. With Alfred Mallett, from whom he bought photographic supplies, Rolfe spent hours discussing camera techniques in the shop at 19 Church Street. He admitted that he was a 'good talker'. He had had numerous experiences worth recounting, and he talked of them freely. He liked 'to amuse and to instruct'.[27] Owing to the nearness of his studio and his longer acquaintance with the family, Corvo's social life centred in the Gleeson White home. During most of the early months of Rolfe's stay in Christchurch, Gleeson White was in New York, where he had gone as associate editor of *Art Amateur Magazine*, but Mrs. Gleeson White was at home with their two children and she made the Baron welcome.[28] It was easy to stop for tea with the Gleeson Whites and at the slightest hint stay on for supper. There were often other guests. The Bells came for talk about art. Bell was hardly a vigorous worker, but he had memories of the Slade and of Gerôme at the Beaux Arts in Paris. Henry Tuke, the artist whose flesh tones against the colours of the sea were so stimulating to Rolfe, visited the Gleeson Whites regularly. He very likely gave the Baron a sheaf of drawings to help with the figures he was painting.[29] There was invariably lively talk at these gatherings and thus an opportunity for Rolfe to express his opinions. He was particularly vehement in his loathing of modernity, always a going concern and a matter for definition and discussion with artists and their critics. Worse was 'Modern agnosticism', as he told another artist, Alan Wright. Rolfe thought it 'pitiful and abhorrent'. He could not understand how any man especially Gleeson White could take up 'such an entirely *ugly* and repellent creed', nothing more than a 'pose'.[30] Happier evenings were devoted to music, an enthusiasm of Rolfe and of the Gleeson Whites, including the two children Eric and Cecily. According to Mrs. Gleeson White, the Baron talked more music than he produced. She maintained that he could perform only one piece, Rubinstein's 'Melody in F', and that, 'with one hand on their organ while some one else played a piano accompaniment'.[31]

However well Frederick, Baron Corvo, built his house, he could always bring it down about his ears. However substantial it seemed, he could collapse it into a heap of jackstraws. And this time, as Rolfe well knew, he had built on sand. Although by August 1891 he was in debt and his debts were mounting, no creditor so far saw a reason to question his ability to pay. He spoke often of his allowance from his 'Italian grandmother' and of £100 in his London bank. Only Rolfe knew that neither existed. In the spring of 1891, the Duchess had begun to tell him that she could no longer afford to send him money.[32] Rolfe blamed Patterson, the Bishop of Emmaus, for her decision,[33] alleging that he influenced her out of dislike for Rolfe and a Catholic determination to ruin him. No doubt the Duchess had reached her own decision, governed by her own financial circumstances. Besides, as she said herself, he was 'no relation' of hers, she had 'never seen or heard of him till two years ago', and she had concluded that, although he worked hard, Rolfe could never succeed in making any money.[34] Exactly how much she gave him and at what intervals is uncertain. It may have been as much as £200 a year. Kains Jackson said that he cashed her remittances for £8 per month. She spoke only of 'several presents'.[35] In any case, by later summer, 1891, Rolfe surely knew that he could expect little more from the Duchess.

Meanwhile Baron Corvo had had what for him was an unhappy experience with Nancy Gleeson White, an incident which he said happened during her husband's absence in New York. His account of it runs:

I dined with a woman whose husband was a great friend of mine. Her two children dined with us—a girl of fifteen, a boy of thirteen. . . . Soon after dinner, she sent the children to bed. A few minutes later she went to say good-night to them: she was an excellent mother. I remained in the drawing-room. When she returned, I was standing to take my departure. As she entered, she closed the door and switched off the electric light. I instinctively struck a match. She laughed, apologising for being absent-minded. I said the usual polite idioms and went away. A fortnight later, I dined there again by invitation. All went on as before: but this time, when she came back from saying good-night to the children she was wearing a violet flannel dressing gown. I said nothing at all; and instantly left her.[36]

For Corvo, whose natural bent was homosexual, it was a most distasteful experience which attacked 'some phasma' of his imagination. This was aggravated by the fact that he had to admit that he was 'ridiculously dense' to afford Nancy Gleeson White a second chance at him. The incident remained alive for some years until he converted it to use in *Hadrian the Seventh*. Well before his use of it there, Rolfe had cause to write to the publisher Grant Richards about gossip reported to Richards:

> You have allowed yourself to hear the ridiculous stories which you related to me this morning. . . . All tales of the 'Gleeson White' order are false. *He remained on friendly terms with me for some years after the Episode of the Woman Scorned.*[37]

The statement to Richards is true. His friendship with Gleeson White was unchanged. For a time, too, although Rolfe saw her as 'wickedly ugly', he and Nancy Gleeson White continued in an uneasy relationship. She still made him welcome in her home, and letters which she wrote about him in the next six months are more dispassionate than vindictive.

Then in August, Mrs. Gleeson White and Rolfe quarrelled openly. Gleeson White was almost at the end of his stay in New York. Attracted especially by an opportunity to see Niagara Falls, he was planning a visit to George Herman Ellwanger, a minor writer but a '*delightful* as well as a rich host' living in Rochester, New York; after that he would go home to Christchurch. Before he left New York City, he received a photograph of his son Eric with hair cropped 'horribly (worse than a convict)'. Corvo had shaved the boy's head, much to the annoyance of his mother. She promptly told Rolfe in a note that 'it was a liberty', whereupon, ensued 'paper warfare for a week'. During that week, after urging Eric not to tell his mother, Rolfe made the boy's picture and sent it to Gleeson White in New York with the legend 'The Baron's Crime'.[38] Mrs. Gleeson White and Rolfe were partly reconciled, but they were 'still somewhat on the defensive' as late as August 31. When her husband returned to Christchurch about mid-September, he objected to the 'indignant remonstrance' his wife had sent Rolfe about Eric's hair and urged that matters go on as they had before the stay in New York. Nancy Gleeson White was forced to behave as though no unpleasantness between her and the Baron had occurred, and for once the Baron acted his part too.

That may have been because he owed the Gleeson Whites at least £20. More likely it was because in them Rolfe thought he saw an opportunity to salvage his rapidly deteriorating finances. Soon after his return, Gleeson White disclosed his appointment to a new position in London and his wish to move himself and his family there. Baron Corvo promptly offered to buy Caxton House, Gleeson White's property in Christchurch which contained his residence, his book and stationer's shop, and a next-door bakery, all valued at £11,300.[39]

If Baron Corvo intended to pursue his offer to its logical conclusion, then his behaviour cannot be explained. He knew that he had no way to secure £11,300 and no means of paying for such a purchase. Mrs. Gleeson White eventually accused him of 'subsisting on a concerted plan of *fraud*, even to wresting' their property from them.[40] Rolfe was incompetent, however, to carry out a 'concerted plan' of fraud. His imagination was too fertile. He lost sight of his object in his interest in the fiction he created; he began to elaborate on it and gradually came to believe it. Perhaps this insufficient sense of reality made bearable Rolfe's tragedy, which is one of missed opportunity and of frustration. Within less than five years he had seen his fondest ambition thwarted twice and finally end outside the door of Scots College. Now the chance to prove himself as a creative artist, made possible by the Duchess, was threatened by debt. Both situations had promised fulfilment; both had been nullified. All his ardour, his inventive skill and ingenious effort had earned him nothing but frustration. His suggestion that he buy Caxton House staved off the necessity to recognise another failure and act accordingly. Furthermore he obviously hoped to distract his creditors by means of his offer, to divert them by appearing so affluent in important matters that his credit in lesser ones must go unquestioned or, at worst, his debts be attributed to carelessness.

That his offer was a red herring is the kindest explanation of Rolfe's behaviour in this affair of Caxton House and one for which there is some evidence. Except for summoning John Withers, a young solicitor, from London to prepare for the conveyance, little or nothing was done to bring this transaction to a conclusion. Possibly, too, the Gleeson Whites were unsettled about their projected move until Gleeson White accepted a second London offer, a post as reader with the publishing firm Bell and Sons. There was also some talk between him and his wife of retaining Caxton House and leaving their shop to the management of one of their employees named Galton.[41] Anyway, Rolfe's offer hung fire for several months.

Kains Jackson, Gleeson White's solicitor whose usual August holiday was delayed in 1891 owing to professional obligations in London and who thus came to Christchurch for about a month's stay no earlier than 20 September,[42] learned of Rolfe's offer for Caxton House during the visit. At that time, if he did nothing to encourage Rolfe's scheme, he did not discourage it. By 8 December 1891, Kains Jackson still had no reason to move to protect his client against Rolfe. On that day Rolfe wrote to the solicitor saying that his current legal adviser, probably John J. Withers, was 'rather a fumbler' and that perhaps Kains Jackson would either take over Rolfe's affairs or, if they were too slight—and Kains Jackson must not hesitate to decline on those grounds—suggest another solicitor. Rolfe wanted a lawyer of 'a discreet and able kind', one, he went on to say 'to whom I can unfold all my little secrets and machinations to avoid any jesuitical opponents without any more fear of having them divulged than I have in divulging them to a ghostly father.' He added that he had papers which ought to be safeguarded and, as a master stroke implying financial stability and even considerable means, that it was 'getting about time' to make his will. In the same letter he wrote:

> I see no chance of getting Caxton House and so I am in treaty for the purchase of a similar thing at Dartmouth and another at Plymouth. Heaven send me a settlement soon. I would wait for Caxton if I thought it was any good but Mrs. White has a man named Wilkes and I am naturally not going to enter into competition with any one. I thought that my offer would have been more liberal and that I should have no difficulty.[43]

Rolfe's way out was plain. To keep going in Christchurch, he had only to withdraw from the Caxton House contretemps in disdain of competition with Charles Wilkes (who eventually bought the premises at 10 Broad Street) and rely as long as possible on the prestige earned from his supposed attempt to purchase the property. Such prestige might vanish slowly owing to the impression made by calling himself Baron Corvo. Rolfe believed that the name together with his 'domineering manner', his pedantic diction and his 'austere . . . and exclusive habit' convinced the 'low coarse half-educated and uncultured boors' among whom he lived that he was in fact an exiled nobleman.[44]

His fancy had got astride of his reason. Rolfe had waited too long and he had overplayed his hand, especially where Kains Jackson was concerned. During his month's stay in Christchurch, he had heard murmurs from Rolfe's creditors. Gardner, who was Rolfe's landlord and his chief creditor was also Cecil Castle's and Kains Jackson's landlord. Finally, Gleeson White consulted the solicitor as to the best course to pursue in the matter of Caxton House, and Kains Jackson investigated the various possibilities, among them Rolfe's offer. He soon learned that property which Rolfe had offered as security in the transaction with Gleeson White was non-existent. The Duchess's remittances had stopped. There was nothing behind Rolfe financially.

Rolfe insisted that Kains Jackson had made a 'ghastly blunder', but howl as he might, Rolfe's pathetically contrived existence once more broke into fragments early in 1892. It was still unshaken on 7 January 1892, when, as Baron Corvo, he wrote to the Marquis Ruvigny to declare his loyalty to the memories of James III, Charles III, and Henry IX and to inquire about the British Legitimist League.[45] Shortly thereafter Kains Jackson told Gleeson White what he had learned in his investigation, and one of them informed Mallett, the photographer, and Gardner. Rolfe threatened to 'horsewhip the man' who had 'spread falsehoods about him' and named Gleeson White as the man.[46] Gardner, to whom Rolfe was in debt not only for lodging but also for the frequent hire of a horse and gig, promptly called Rolfe to account. He declared that his allowance was slow in coming from Rome and that he would pay as soon as it arrived. In support of his position he showed affectionate letters received earlier. Gardner was unconvinced; he evicted Baron Corvo. The Baron then managed to beg lodgings for three nights with an unidentified person named Wigham. His creditors began to besiege him—Mallett, who had furnished plates and papers for his camera; the Gleeson Whites, to whom he owed £20 for purchases in their shop plus a loan of £10; and all the tradesmen who had supplied coal, oil, tobacco, minor toiletries, clothing. Rolfe could satisfy none of them, but he vowed that he would not leave Christchurch until every penny was paid.

Truthfully, Rolfe had no other place to go or the means for going. His only chance for help or sympathy was in Christchurch. When his three days at Wigham's terminated, Rolfe approached a man named Daly who lived at the Red Lion pub[47] to ask for shelter there. Daly was forced to refuse, whereupon Rolfe turned to Father Swainson. Again he had no relief. Corvo then tried to borrow from the Bells; but, according to Nancy Gleeson White, Mrs. Bell would not 'allow her husband to lend a 1d',[48] although she admitted that Rolfe had helped her with her book on Rome. She planned instead, she said, to present him with a copy when it appeared. Poor Rolfe never got even that from the Bells. At last, however, he managed to borrow something from Risdon Sharp, the lawyer, in order to go to Bournemouth, where he sold some curios. On his return the same evening, he offered Gardner 5s and begged to be taken in and allowed to stay for as long as that sum warranted, saying honestly enough that no one else would and if Gardner refused there was no alternative but to remain outdoors in the cold winter weather. In that event, Rolfe pointed out, if he did not call for his letters in the morning, he might be presumed dead. Nancy Gleeson White said that 'this touched G. so that he let him in and proposed keeping him' several days.[49]

Gardner had written at least twice to the Duchess Sforza-Cesarini for assurance about Corvo's income. Mrs. Gleeson White wanted her husband to write to the Duchess, too, with 'a very plain and unvarnished statement of facts', but he refused and she did not 'insist on her own way'.[50] When a 'lady friend' came to her bringing the address of a clergyman with 'a handful of Xtian names' who lived in Blackheath, the Reverend John James Fawcett Neville Rolfe, and suggested that he was the Baron's father, she informed Gardner. Hope is indeed livelier than despair. He rushed along Bridge Street to thank Mrs. Gleeson White and rushed back to face Corvo with the information. In reply, he turned 'very white', said 'I have no home' and went off into another room slamming the door'.[51] Gardner thought Rolfe's reaction confirmed the kinship; so a letter went off at once to the

55

clergyman, and briefly Gardner waited to see whether the Reverend Rolfe would come to Christchurch or merely send money. Of course the Reverend Rolfe was a false trail, and when the Duchess Sforza-Cesarini wrote in February she offered Gardner nothing except sympathy for his money lost through Corvo.[52] There was no way to retrieve it.

As his troubles multiplied, Rolfe began to feel oppressed. He lost sight of the fact that he had caused the Gleeson Whites needless delay and anxiety, that his behaviour had at best been ambiguous, and that he owed more money than he could possibly pay. He asked George Lewis, a solicitor, to 'prosecute the persons who were spreading falsehoods about him in the town'.[53] When the few days allowed him at Toinham house ended on a Tuesday, his landlord extended Rolfe's stay until noon on Saturday, swearing that Rolfe would go peaceably then or get turned out and his possessions would be sold the following week. By Saturday Rolfe had neither coals nor oil left and he had long been dependent on others for food. During his stay at Toinham House, Gardner fed him barely enough to keep him alive—'mostly vegetables'. Earlier, Rolfe had begun to 'drop in for supper' at the Bell's home, 'Rastgartt' at Southbourne on Sea. He managed three meals with them before Mrs. Bell refused him admission without giving a reason. Baron Corvo sent her a letter implying that her act was an abdication of a '*grave moral obligation*'. He turned to the Gleeson Whites. Nancy Gleeson White felt sorry for him and because she resented Mrs. Bell's 'I told you so, dear' was sharply critical of Mrs. Bell's behaviour. Rolfe then began to drop in at the Gleeson Whites' for meals, managing to follow this practice for an entire week. Determined at the same time to show how ill-used he was and to what Christchurch had driven him, Rolfe ostentatiously explored the possibilities of enlistment in the army. Then, with a well-displayed consciousness of self-sacrifice, he secured a ticket admitting him to the workhouse; when the time came for him to enter, he tore up the ticket. But no one felt guilty about Rolfe's plight. At noon on Saturday, the deadline Gardner had set for Rolfe's departure, no one opened a door to him. Gardner agreed to wait another two weeks before 'selling up his things' but he refused to allow the Baron to stay on at Toinham House. Corvo, or as Nancy Gleeson White called him, 'the poor crow with stolen draggled feathers', had no choice but to leave Christchurch. Surrendering all his possessions, among them his camera, paints and brushes, and an oak chest filled with papers, and declaring that he would return in a fortnight and '*pay everybody* as he was going to *buy the Turkish Baths* Bristol or Clifton', Rolfe took an afternoon train to London.[54]

[ii]

London was not a refuge for Frederick Rolfe. He had no prospects there, and he took nothing from the miscarriage of his affairs at Christchurch to London. He arrived in London, he said, with a Book of Hours, the clothes on his back, and eight shillings in his pocket.[1] He left everything else behind, even his baronial title, calling himself only Frederick William Rolfe. In London, he had no place to go. The only address he left at Christchurch was that of his solicitor John J. Withers. Believing that Father Patterson, the Bishop of Emmaus, had caused his predicament by turning the Duchess against him, Rolfe thought the Bishop owed him asylum. So he made his way from Waterloo Station to Chelsea, where Patterson was rector at Saint Mary's, Cadogan Street, and, at nearby St. Joseph's Convent, Rolfe asked for a night's shelter. The Convent refused to take him in and Father Patterson suggested that Rolfe go instead to a 'common Lodging-house at four pence'. According to Rolfe, he 'flung back the suggestion in their faces and walked the street all night'.[2]

During that long, cold march through London's streets in early spring 1892, Rolfe consoled himself with his magnanimity, folly though he called it, in trying 'to work with, to live with, to equal' himself in every way with 'verminous persons'. Regrets, even compensatory ones, are bitter. But they were like honey if Rolfe spent that night facing what much of the rest of his life was to be: 'intellectual silence and solitude in an ugly obscene mob, where clean water was a difficulty, food and bed an uncertainty' and the only prospect, 'ceaseless and furious conflict'.[3]

By morning Rolfe had trudged to Holborn, the place of his boyhood. There he attended mass at Saint Ethelreda's, Ely Place, and explained his predicament to its rector Father William Lockhart. Father Lockhart made a practice of opening the house of the Rosminians, the Fathers of Charity, to young Catholic men who had recently come to London and had not yet arranged for permanent quarters. Thus Rolfe found a haven. By early April he had moved to lodgings somewhere in West Hampstead.

Rolfe had hardly got settled in West Hampstead when he instructed the solicitors Withers and Withers to convey an injunction to John Gambril Nicholson, his former friend and pupil, to stop the sale of his recently published book of poems *Love in Earnest* on the grounds that it contained a sonnet, 'St. William of Norwich (Painted by F. W. Rolfe)', belonging to Rolfe and published without his permission. Nicholson received the injunction on the night of 8 April 1892 and immediately asked Kains Jackson for advice after explaining the situation. Nicholson said that prior to 1887, Rolfe had shown him the questionable sonnet 'in rough shape'. With Rolfe's consent, Nicholson had made it 'fully Petrarchan' by reworking ten lines of Rolfe's original and completely rewriting four. Rolfe was scornful. 'I send you an uncut diamond,' he said; 'you send me back a polished crystal. No thank you!'[4] But Nicholson liked the 'fully Petrarchan' version and published it as his own. The sale of *Love in Earnest* was suspended and briefly there was a flurry of letters and telegrams not only between Nicholson and Kains Jackson but also between Nicholson and Gleeson White (who insisted on keeping his name out of all negotiations) and between Nicholson and his publisher Elliot Stock. Nicholson wondered how Rolfe dared turn on him in view of the rumours about Rolfe, and Kains Jackson gave it as his opinion that he could frighten Rolfe if he actually brought suit and that he probably meant only to get money from Nicholson.[5] The affair was settled when the questionable poem was cancelled and a sonnet by Nicholson called 'St. William of Norwich' substituted.

Little else about Rolfe's life in London during these few months in 1892 can be told in such detail. His precise address in West Hampstead is unknown. How he managed to clothe himself is a mystery. Whether he paid his rent and, if he did, where he secured the necessary funds are also mysteries. Neither how deeply he fell into despair at the difficulties he faced nor how high his prayers and his imagination lifted him above the pity of his lot can be gauged.

Yet, there can be no question that at this time Rolfe associated with two of London's most prominent and interesting men, Herbert Alford Vaughan, appointed on 29 March 1892 to succeed Manning as Archbishop of Westminster, and William T. Stead, advocate of the 'new journalism' and editor of *Review of Reviews*. Rolfe tried to interest Stead in some sort of scheme involving photography, possibly one having to do with the preparation of slides for illustrated lectures, made either from his own drawings or from photographs of other people's drawings. Once Rolfe informed Stead of an opportunity to make photographic copies of Gustave Doré's engravings which had appeared in Doré's and Blanchard Jerrold's *London*.[6] But he also sent Stead a preliminary design representing a funeral procession in the catacombs for a magic lantern slide and told him about an 'awfully good' drawing in progress, 'Felicitas and Her Seven Sons Before the Prefect'. In connection with some such project, shortly before 9 April, Stead authorised Rolfe to purchase various supplies from the Stereoscopic Company—a Kodak, developing dishes, a dark-room lamp, drawing pins, India and Chinese inks, brushes, paper blocks, and other things. Meanwhile, encouraged by Rolfe's extravagant admiration for Vaughan and his own editorial interests, Stead proposed to the Archbishop a 'journalistic notion' in which Rolfe was somehow involved. But Vaughan did not respond favourably. Meanwhile Stead's manager, Carter Paterson, was outraged by the bills which Corvo had run up with the Stereoscopic Company and on 14 April Stead's medium, Julia, after handling an amulet which Rolfe had brought to Stead in a 'little brown bag' declared Rolfe untrustworthy. Accordingly, fearing that Rolfe had 'disappeared into space', Stead asked twice for the return of the materials. Rolfe regretted their loss to him; but because he could not afford to buy them, he sent everything back to Stead by way of his manager, Paterson, on 26 April.

Stead's withdrawal of support following close on Vaughan's lack of interest in the 'journalistic notion' reduced Rolfe's chances of survival in London on his own terms to almost nothing. Urged by Father Lockhart, who had written a letter of recommendation for him, Rolfe tried to get advice or help toward employment of a literary kind through Wilfrid Meynell. Lockhart had given Meynell lodging in the priests' house on Ely Place when he first came to London. That Meynell was editor of The Weekly Review, a Catholic publication, was owing in large part to Lockhart's intimacy with Cardinal Manning. Meynell was the logical person for Lockhart to ask to help Rolfe. He called on Meynell eight times without seeing him.[8] The literary world in London was inaccessible. As long as he persisted in seeking his living from photography or from drawing and painting, Rolfe had no future in London or, for that matter, anywhere else. He had no equipment with which to work, no reputation, no commissions. Apparently the thought of getting employment as a clerk, a teacher, or in any of the innumerable jobs, menial or not, which every large city offers never occurred to him. If it did, he dismissed it.

But Rolfe had enormous resilience. His perennial failures nurtured it; otherwise blow after blow must have driven him into apathy until he expired in his own woes. Maybe his salvation was that he 'very imperfectly realised his own life,' that 'while he deceived others, he deceived none so much as himself'.[9] His steadfast faith in himself and his belief that someone—any one—else was accountable for his difficulties helped him persevere. He refused to allow his co-religionists any justification for their failure to do their duty to their neighbour.[10] To his determination, Rolfe added resourcefulness. He endured hardships or he found solutions. He was accustomed to both.

[iii]

Rolfe's last security in Great Britain had been in Scotland; so he resolved to go back there. Calling to mind how, in 1889, he had moved in and out of Boyndlie House and in again as the guest of its owner,

John M. Ogilvie-Forbes, Rolfe travelled to Fraserburgh and once more established himself at Boyndlie House.

His host saw to it that Rolfe did not stay long. Ogilvie-Forbes's kinswoman Miss Georgina Hay wanted a tutor-companion for her orphaned nephews Cuthbert and Malcolm Hay. Their father, James Gordon Hay of Seaton, had been dead for nine years; their fragile mother had died in 1891, confiding her two boys, aged ten and eleven, to the care of Miss Hay. She required a young man, Catholic and severely moral, to take over the welfare of the boys during their summer holiday. Ogilvie-Forbes recommended Rolfe. Miss Hay was not enthusiastic about him, but he was difficult to refuse. From the sanctuary of Boyndlie House, Rolfe had once more renewed his attempts to enter the priesthood. He had appealed to Hugh Macdonald, Bishop of Aberdeen, and, as Rolfe made clear to Miss Hay, he was only awaiting some positive action from the Bishop in order to fulfil what he called his 'ecclesiastical aspirations'. The commendation from Ogilvie-Forbes, a most 'ultra Catholic' Catholic, plus Rolfe's expectations could hardly be ignored. When Cuthbert and Malcolm, back from school, visited Boyndlie House in July, they returned to their home, Seaton House, Old Aberdeen, with Rolfe.[1]

Scottish summers are short, and this one passed all too quickly for Rolfe and the Hay boys. Malcolm Hay long afterwards testified that he and his brother had 'nothing but the pleasantest memories of their tutor', that he was 'as kind as possible', and in every way a delightful companion.[2] Whether they had much besides companionship from their tutor is doubtful. He encouraged them to smoke cigars, entertained them for hours at a time with what eventually appeared in print as Stories Toto Told Me, and when these paled, he gave his attention to carving a likeness of Hugh Macdonald, Bishop of Aberdeen, in the bark of a tree on the grounds of Seaton House.[3] Rolfe enjoyed this exercising of his gifts for the Hay boys, and his pleasure was enhanced by the presence of five neighbours, the Burnett brothers. He enjoyed the comforts of Seaton with clean quarters, numerous servants, and well-prepared meals (for which he said grace as often as Miss Hay allowed).

It was such a comfortable assignment that Rolfe offered his services as tutor on a permanent basis, but Miss Hay developed a serious objection to Rolfe. What it was, she failed to disclose. She did not approve of photographing one of the Burnetts, Robin, dressed in only a loin cloth and posed as St. Sebastian. She was shocked by volumes of Rousseau and Voltaire in Rolfe's possession but the Bishop assured her no harm would come from them as long as they were kept out of Malcolm's and Cuthbert's way. Something more damning than either of these came to her attention; so Miss Hay sent her nephews back to school and saw to it that they received no letters from their tutor. Both she and Ogilvie-Forbes evaded Malcolm's questions as to

Rolfe's address. Miss Hay dismissed Rolfe and when he asked to stay for a time after his charges had gone back to school, she refused. Rolfe left Seaton on 19 September 1892.[4]

Almost from that day until a meeting late in 1893 with H. H. Champion, the Socialist leader, Rolfe's life was a series of follies, deceptions, frustrations, and hardships. He began well enough when he left Seaton House with a visit to Father Alexander Gerrie, priest of the tiny parish of Strichen. It might have been a vantage point from which to cultivate the Ogilvie-Forbes connection, but that had been damped by Miss Hay so that Ogilvie-Forbes showed himself courteous but cool. Apparently indifferent to the 'Pictish lairdie', Rolfe was busy preparing photographs for Aberdeen's Home Industries Exhibition, an event on 13 and 14 October. He expected to win awards in the photographic section and thus get his 'secular work known to the public'.[5]

All in all, Father Gerrie's house suited Rolfe exactly. He had time for his work, and he found most congenial the 'ecclesiastical atmosphere'. Indeed he declared that it was impossible for him to live outside a priestly environment with his 'mental constitution'.[6] And for once he could pay for the privilege, having saved something from his summer's earnings. He established himself as a paying lodger with Gerrie, who found his lodger's money 'serviceable'; the arrangement suited both Gerrie and Rolfe.

The Bishop of Aberdeen, however, objected to Gerrie's having a lodger, and Rolfe, as he put it, 'was hunted out of the priest's house at Strichen'.[7] For what happened to him thereafter in Aberdeen, Rolfe held the Bishop responsible. He made no such accusation, but his behaviour each time he was faced with a new crisis was a constant reminder that Rolfe thought something was due him from the Bishop. Of necessity, Rolfe left Strichen and moved into Aberdeen shortly before the opening date of the Home Industries Exhibition.

[iv]

After consulting a number of advertisements, Rolfe settled himself as a boarder in a lodging house operated by a Mr. and Mrs. Lamb at 162 Skene Street, Aberdeen. In doing so, Rolfe talked of special dietary needs, for which he supplied recipes cut from a penny-weekly, of an allowance from the Duchess of Sforza, and of income property in Ireland. He also paid a fortnight's lodging and maintenance. Except for a few shilling presented with the excuse that he had failed to get to his bank for more, that fortnight's payment was the only one he made at 162 Skene Street.[1]

Some two weeks later, Rolfe applied to the firm of one of the judges for the photographic division of the Home Industries Exhibition, Messrs. G. W. Wilson & Co. of St. Swithin's Street, for a position on their staff. He was willing, he said, to work for little or nothing. The photographs which he had entered in the Exhibition had received none of the seventeen awards so that all he wanted now, he said, was 'to improve himself in the photographic art'. Owing to his persistence, Messrs. Wilson gave him a 'boy's place', subject to the 'ordinary rules of the works', at a weekly wage of 12s. 6d.

The venture was not a success. After more than two months of his 'messing about, coming and going when he liked, pretty much doing what he liked' and telling 'enormous yarns' to support condescension toward his fellow-employees, Rolfe was dismissed. He refused to be dismissed and returned for work each day. Wilson & Co. then put in writing the fact that he was no longer wanted on their premises. Rolfe replied by letter on 24 January 1893:

> It is a curious thing that at the moment I received your note I was about to carry out an intention I have been forming for some time —viz. to ask whether one would be allowed to invest a small sum say £1,000, in your business, and so secure a permanent and congenial appointment suited to my capacities. Perhaps it is inopportune now, but I think I had better mention it.[2]

He continued to go to his job until he was threatened with ejection by the police. Rolfe then wanted to sue Wilson & Co. for breach of contract, but he could find no solicitor to take the case.

Because the Bishop of Aberdeen had made clear that he had no intention of sponsoring Rolfe in a renewed attempt at priesthood, by January 1893 Rolfe knew that he must earn his way. He meant to do it largely by photography. Messrs. Wilson's insistence on getting rid of him did not deter Rolfe. He was unsuited to a 'boy's place' and he knew it. The economic wisdom of adapting himself, even temporarily, to such a job never occurred to him. His conviction that he had unusual talents and his assumption that they must be used at whatever cost stood between him and an ordinary day's work. Yet Rolfe was not lazy; in his own way he was indefatigable and his 'messing about' at Wilson & Co. was with a purpose. He took advantage of the firm's facilities to experiment with flashlight and submarine photography. It was not all done on Wilson's time or premises, but these two advances in technique occupied him throughout much of his stay in Aberdeen.

Occasionally Rolfe had some encouragement in his work. The Bishop of Aberdeen allowed himself to be photographed 'in various attitudes' (five, to be exact); and Rolfe with another photographer named Geering made enlargements and prints, secured copyright, and prepared for sale through canvassers and shops. Geering assured Rolfe he could expect sales amounting to £100.[3] In the third issue of

The Studio, its editor Gleeson White published two pictures 'from photographs by Baron Corvo'. These accompanied an article on the nude which commenced with an initial C imposed on another of Rolfe's photographs.[4] In its next issue, *The Studio* reproduced a picture Rolfe had made of Gleeson White's son Eric, again with a superimposed initial, to demonstrate the artistic possibilities of flashlight photography. For a time Commander Littlewood, in charge of H.M.S. *Clyde*, stationed off Aberdeen, urged Rolfe to photograph the Royal Navy Reserve drilling on board the ship and tried to bring his submarine photography to the attention of the United Services Institution. Rolfe himself had written about experiments with submarine photography to Lord Charles Beresford, whose fortunes in another way were almost as mercurial as Rolfe's. When Beresford showed enough interest to suggest that Rolfe come to Chatham House and discuss the matter, Rolfe declared that his experiments were sure to 'mean two if not three fortunes to him'.[6]

Although the British Admiralty two years later credited Rolfe with the invention of submarine photography and although he twisted and turned in a dozen different directions, he made nothing from his photography or from much else in 1893. One scheme involved the reproduction of already existing pictures as illustrations for lantern lectures, but no one required such services. In even such small transactions as having his old camera repaired and purchasing a few inexpensive supplies, he ran into difficulties, generated no doubt by foolish boasts which served only to undermine his plausibility. While buying several items from James Henderson, who sold photographic supplies at 168 Union Street, Rolfe talked about his preparations for photographing the Pope at the Vatican in his jubilee year. Later, under pressure from the same shopkeeper to pay an indebtedness of £2 10s., he offered his cheque for £5 and asked for the difference in sterling. Henderson, unimpressed by Rolfe's attempts to impress, quickly ascertained that he had no bank balance to back up his cheque and, according to one report, forced Rolfe to sign a statement admitting his attempted fraud.[7] On a larger scale, too, he was unsuccessful. Repeatedly Rolfe tried to get financial support for his flashlight photography, writing for £2,000 to William Waldorf Astor, who had recently inherited $100,000,000; to Sir Henry Ponsonby, by whom he wished to transmit a picture made by flashlight to Queen Victoria; and to the Duke of Norfolk, to whom Rolfe complained of hunger. As for the submarine photography, he saw an opportunity to put it to practical use when H.M.S. *Victoria* was rammed and sank off Tripoli in June 1893. He wrote at once to the *Illustrated London News* and *The Graphic*, suggesting that he be commissioned to proceed to Tripoli at once and photograph the sunken ship. Neither paper hired him. To demonstrate under-water camera work, he required machinery of his own design. When he attempted to have ironwork done by Messrs. M'Kinnon, Spring-garden, and fittings installed by an electrical engineer with the appropriate name of Spark at a cost of some £70, Rolfe's order was refused because he lacked funds. He tried then to interest two local businessmen in forming a joint stock company to launch his underwater photography, but his plans were too grandiose and too impractical for the gentlemen, Hay and Rae. Letters to W. T. Stead, Gleeson White, and again to the Duke of Norfolk were not productive.

The only help Rolfe had came from the Association for Improving the Condition of the Poor in Aberdeen. Earlier, in London, he had appealed for help from the Charity Organisation Society. His statements to them were forwarded to the Association in Aberdeen, who agreed to help him. They secured the necessary chemicals and working facilities for his experiments and over a period of ten weeks, commencing on 2 September 1893, gave him £5 19s. That sum was paid out to him in sixteen instalments, a number of them amounting to 10s. each, but one as small as 1s. In mid-November, George Milne, secretary of the Association, investigated Rolfe's progress and found it disappointing. When Rolfe requested further assistance on 18 November, the Association, which had increasing obligations in a time of rising unemployment in Aberdeen, could offer him nothing more except refuge in the workhouse. Rolfe had thought of himself as earning by his 'undoubted powers' the payments made him. The workhouse spelled alms, and he refused to accept what he called 'that deridable futility now masquerading as charity'.[8] Rolfe's relations with the Association for Improving the Condition of the Poor in Aberdeen came to an end.

Everything had come to an end. Everything had failed. Although Rolfe had considered photography his main stock in trade, he had been active in other directions too. When the post of librarian at Aberdeen University fell vacant, Rolfe applied for it, asking the Bishop of Aberdeen to support his application. The Bishop refused, and someone else was named to the position. In late March, thanks to the interest of Father Lockhart, once rector of Saint Ethelreda's in London, Wilfrid Meynell wrote to Rolfe, offering him help of some unspecified kind. The letter also contained a gift of money. Rolfe took the money, applied it to his photography, and then tried to make something of Meynell's offer of help. Meynell had in mind the kind of paternalism he and his wife, Alice Meynell, had provided Francis Thompson, whose first volume of poems had appeared that year. But Rolfe had none of the humility or frailty of spirit which characterised Thompson. Rolfe protested that he wanted 'no one's alms', and he refused such help. As he told John Comper, rector of Saint Margaret's Episcopal Church, Aberdeen, he asked only for an 'opportunity of making use of the powers . . . entrusted' to him; so to Meynell, Rolfe wrote, 'I have goods to sell & the money I shall make by them will secure the capital on which I can do all that is necessary for myself & by myself'.[9] He proposed that Burns & Oates, a firm for which Meynell was literary adviser, take him on their staff and let him put to use the 'originality and versatility' of his mind. As an alternative, Rolfe suggested that *The Weekly Register*, which Meynell edited, publish a series of letters already in manuscript. Rolfe described them as illustrating his 'wants & the easy thing it would be to correct them'. He was sure these letters having to do with 'the condition of converts' must be interesting to Catholics. Instead Meynell made arrangements for a Mr. Thomson, an Aberdeen printer, to interview Rolfe and find a way to help him. Rolfe reluctantly agreed to visit Thomson. 'I shall let him know', Rolfe wrote to Meynell about Thomson, 'what I can do and what is necessary to enable me to do it,' even though he expected nothing to come from the visit. 'A shabby, badly-dressed person with a wan face haggard with the worry of 7 years torment & insufficient food,' Rolfe declared, 'stands no chance in this world.' Still, he went to Thomson, taking along a 'set of capital letters'. Thomson was impressed enough with Rolfe's 'power of design' as shown in the letters to lend him £5.[10] In time, according to Rolfe, the printer offered to provide him with a new suit of clothes and to teach him the business of a printer's reader and then, at the end of three months, recommend him for employment elsewhere. Rolfe refused, saying he already had too many trades; and when he did, Thomson told him to go and take his drawings, by then spoiled from lying on Thomson's dirty office floor. 'I am too wearied with my struggles & starvations to give my attention at 33 to a new and *uncertain* occupation,' he explained to Meynell.[11] Meynell made no reply to Rolfe's letter. Careful not to neglect his art work during this year, Rolfe offered for sale at seventy guineas each three paintings 'in monochrome', one of Saint Michael and the Dragon, and the others of Saint Edmond and of Saint Gregory. These were prominently displayed in a window of Gifford's, a highly respected gallery, and meanwhile Rolfe wrote to anyone whom he considered a likely buyer. His letters went to the Marquis of Huntly, Sir Walter Dalrymple, the Duke of Norfolk, Sir Stuart Knill, Sir David Stewart, and one or two more. The Marquis of Huntly showed enough interest to have the pictures inspected, but no one bought. Rolfe was particularly insistent that Hugh Macdonald, Bishop of Aberdeen, purchase the paintings. The Bishop refused even to look at them. He 'stamped his foot' at Rolfe, told him there was 'no room for "high art" in Aberdeen', and offered him a one way ticket to London. At last a chance acquaintance made at Archibald Duff's baths, frequented by Rolfe when he could pay his way, enabled him to give the three pictures to a local lawyer as security for a loan of £20.[12] Rolfe failed to redeem his paintings for the simple reason that he at no time had the necessary £20.

Indeed, well before his relations with the Association for Improving the Condition of the Poor terminated, Rolfe was homeless and penniless. By the beginning of August 1893, he owed the Lambs

£37 2s. 9½d. for meals and his room at 162 Skene Street. It was a top floor room, often damp from his laundry—he washed all his clothing, even jackets and trousers—and increasingly impersonal as he pawned his few possessions. From there had gone out his letters soliciting help and funds, and there he had waited for replies which did not come. That a local medical student named Cruickshank, whose father Rolfe had known as a factor at Boyndlie House, thought him hardly normal is not surprising. The tale that Rolfe stuck his head from the window of his room at Skene Street in the dead of night and screamed into the darkness in despair and loneliness may well be true.[13] But it was the sum of £37 2s. 9½d. which brought matters to a head with the Lambs at Skene Street. The landlord's duns grew more and more insistent so that Rolfe was afraid to leave his room lest he be locked out, and in the end he stayed in bed for fear he might be 'thrust forth'. Then Lamb took action. *The Daily Free Press* of Aberdeen carried an account of what happened:

> One evening, about six o'clock, the landlord besought the aid of a fellow-workman. They entered the Baron's bedroom, and the Baron was given ten minutes to dress and clear out. He refused to move, and when the ten minutes were up he seized hold of the iron bedstead and clung for dear life. He was dragged forth, wearing only his 'pyjamas', out to the staircase, where he caught hold of the balustrade, and another struggle ensued. Thence he was carried down the long staircase and was shot onto the pavement as he stood . . . His clothing was thrown after him, which he ultimately donned—and that was the last of Baron Corvo in that particular locality.[14]

Rolfe obtained another night's shelter at once. As usual, he turned to the Bishop of Aberdeen for help. And the Bishop, long-suffering with Rolfe, responded by providing food and a bed at the house of the Poor Sister of Nazareth. But provision was made for only one night, and thereafter Rolfe was without resources.

Rolfe's next moves were desperate ones. He asked an Aberdeen doctor, possibly a Doctor Thompson of the Royal Infirmary, to certify him as insane so that he might have the Asylum's roof over his head.[15] The doctor refused. Thanks, then, to contributions of the Poor Association, Rolfe obtained lodgings with people named Wade who lived in King Street. His stay there ended in November, when the funds from the Association ended so that, as the cold of Aberdeen intensified, Rolfe was forced onto the streets and eventually, according to some reports, into a sand dune on Aberdeen's shore, where only 'the wind and the spray gave life'.[16] In his misery and isolation, Rolfe then sought out Henry Hyde Champion at his apartments in Union Street.

Champion had come to Aberdeen from London to conduct his campaign as Labour candidate for Parliament in the General Election of 1893. Once a lieutenant in the Royal Artillery, he had developed profound Socialist convictions from his reading while he convalesced after typhoid fever in 1881. The next year he resigned his commission in order to give his time to publishing and Socialist agitation. In that connection, with funds provided by his father, Champion had founded three journals: *Today* in 1883, *Common Sense* in 1887, and *Labour Elector* in 1888. Owing to various aspects of his personality and powerful Tory associations, however, Champion's political career had been disappointing. He was accused of betraying his own movement with 'Tory Gold', and in 1890 he had gone to Australia. Nevertheless his belief in Socialism and in the cause of the labouring man was unshaken. After a few months in Australia, Champion returned to England in 1891, secured an appointment as assistant editor of the influential review *Nineteenth Century*, and then arranged his candidacy for Parliament at Aberdeen. Both family alliances with the Scottish Urquharts and friendly, personal ones with leaders of the local Labour Party made his chances for election favourable. Meanwhile he had started a weekly paper with a Socialist slant, *The Aberdeen Standard*. Despite subsequent defeat at the polls, estrangement from Labour's emerging leader Keir Hardie, and a rapidly deteriorating position with the Party, Champion stayed on in Aberdeen. The city was his headquarters from which he went to several Socialist and Labour congresses, promoted various Labour causes, and published his paper.[17]

It was at this time that Rolfe approached Champion and managed to excite his interest. Ignoring Nancy Gleeson White's advice that the use of his foreign title generated suspicion,[18] he introduced himself to Champion as Baron Corvo and, with his defiant account of his situation and how he came to it, caught the liking and sympathy of Champion. The very characteristics which had contributed to Rolfe's undoing with others appealed to Champion. He knew what it meant to be an outcast and to scorn one's detractors. Furthermore his Urquhart forebears had no doubt accustomed him to individuality. One, David Urquhart, alive in Champion's time, was notable for convincing Karl Marx that Palmerston, twice England's Prime Minister, was in fact a Russian agent. Another, John Urquhart, had commanded a privateer in the service of the king of Spain when she was England's chief enemy. Sir Thomas Urquhart, translator of Rabelais, is reputed to have died of laughter when he learned of the restoration of the Stuarts in the person of Charles II.[19] Rolfe, by comparison with Champion's relations could hardly hold his own for eccentricity. Champion took him into his apartments, provided him with food and new clothing, and gave him employment as his own secretary and as a member of the staff of *The Aberdeen Standard*.

In 1893 and throughout his life, Rolfe was neither a Labour sympathiser nor a Socialist. He once sent a subscription of 5s. to the Fabians because George Bernard Shaw, writing in the *Clarion*, had criticised the

67

Labour Party and apologised 'to the Universe' for his connection with such a party.[20] Rolfe's reasons for avoiding militant Socialism, as he gave them in 1907 to Hubert Bland, a Socialist with a Tory taint, are largely expedient. 'The only Socialists I have ever met (excepting one family and one man),' Rolfe wrote, 'are people who make me sick.' He took for granted that Bland would understand the one family to be his own and the one man, Champion. Rolfe went on to say that if he became a Socialist, he would lose his 'means of livelihood', an event which by 1907 had occurred too often to be risked again. He concluded:

> You see it is not that I am difficult, not a matter of my personal pleasure, not by any means that I'm violently addicted to the 'place to which it has pleased God to call me'. Oh no. It's just simply that I do what I do & live as I live because I know no better way. If I did, I should leap at it.[21]

Actually Rolfe's position was shaped less by self-interest or necessity than by intellectual persuasion. He caused Nicholas Crabbe, his fictional spokesman of the early 1900s, to say, 'There's . . . an aristocratic catholic conviction in my brain which I don't practise.'[22] Rolfe long contemplated a reply to Edward Carpenter's *Towards Democracy* and eventually undertook one entitled 'Toward Aristocracy'.[23] Furthermore, from his brief observation of the politics of Socialism and the Labour movement, especially as they pertained to Champion's enemies, Keir Hardie and others, Rolfe derived the characterisation of Jerry Sant, the craven, blustering assassin of *Hadrian the Seventh*.

Whatever his politics, Rolfe was glad of the opportunities Champion offered him. Although he was distracted with poor health and his rapidly deteriorating political status and 'driven almost crazy by taking other people's troubles on his own shoulders',[24] Champion found time to attempt to promote Rolfe's colour photography. His efforts came to nothing, but Rolfe was still in a more favourable position than he had been since leaving Father Gerrie's house at Strichen. He knew where he would sleep at night, he had food, and he could keep clean, a matter of at least as much concern to him as food. For the first time in his life, he was in close touch with a working journalist who could bring intelligence and purpose to bear on what he had to say and then say it with clarity. Rolfe once more began to publish, fashioning at least one article after Champion's models by presenting his own controvertible opinion in 'The Architecture of Aberdeen'. There he described the houses of Aberdeen, generally noted for their stability and beauty and often regarded as among the handsomest in the United Kingdom as 'granite rabbit hutches'. The article, signed 'Corvo', appeared in *The Aberdeen Standard* for 30 November. His name is attached to no other piece published in *The Standard*, but several others can be attributed to Rolfe. 'A New Local Industry'

68

offers a singular possibility for relieving Aberdeen's unemployment, that is, that the unemployed act as artist's models and for that purpose start a register of those suitable for such work.[25] Two letters in the issue for 13 January 1894, one called 'Catholic Criticism' and the other, 'A Roman Catholic Replies' with the signature 'A Worshipper', may both be Rolfe's. Another piece, 'One Shilling to Kneel Here', published two weeks later, is also very likely his.[26]

Still one more piece composed about this same time or shortly thereafter owes something of another kind to Champion. Entitled 'An Unforgettable Experience', it is placed in early 1892, when Rolfe stayed at the house of the Fathers of Charity in Ely Place, London. The tale is an account of a woman pronounced dead from puerperal fever by a workhouse doctor and returned to her home for burial with her dead child. Because her interment is to take place in a Protestant cemetery, a priest, Father Serafico starts to read the burial service over her open coffin in her slum rooms. But when he observes the woman, he pauses because he cannot believe that she is dead. After a series of frantic efforts in which the narrator who calls himself Baron Corvo is involved, she is demonstrated to be very much alive and subsequently visible any day at early mass at Father Serafico's church. The ambience of this tale comes directly from Rolfe's association with Champion, that of a slum dwelling where the old and young alike live in crowded acceptance of human suffering. The woman in the coffin with the dead infant at her side, her other children writhing on a dirty bed 'like maggots in cheese', her 'tipsy' husband, a barrow boy, and his speech are elements of Rolfe's attempt to portray an environment about which he had not written before and would not write again. That he himself had been reduced to similar circumstances or worse, and that at intervals he continued to be throughout his life, hardly affected his literary output. Each such episode was for Rolfe a nightmare better forgotten in the light of deserved prosperity, an accident to be overcome by the exercise of imagination and will. His depiction in 'An Unforgettable Experience' of so sordid an environment was owing to Champion's work, his attempts at betterment of the poor through political manoeuvre. Even so, Rolfe's interest is less in the poor than in the priest, Father Serafico. After Champion had called it to the attention of Jerome K. Jerome, the editor of *To-Day*, 'An Unforgettable Experience' was accepted for publication in that weekly, and it appeared in the issue of 21 April 1894.

His intervention with Jerome was the fulfilment of a small part of the promise Champion had given Rolfe to make him known to photographers, editors, and publishers, people who might assist him in getting work in London.[27] By late November Champion's position in Labour politics was steadily deteriorating, and he could find little support among dissidents like himself. Keir Hardie, a leader in the movement, and Champion were avowed enemies. He was further

69

hampered by scarcity of money and ill-health. Almost forced by his circumstances to return to Australia as an emigrant, Champion left Aberdeen well before Christmas and went to London to settle his affairs. Rolfe remained in Champion's apartments for a time and then either immediately after Christmas or early in the next year, 1894, he too went to London, where, by invitation, he joined Champion at 37 Greville Road, Kilburn. At least one other person belonged to this household, someone identifiable only by the initial R, who was closely associated with Champion. In January and February 1894, Champion had no time for furthering Rolfe's photographic schemes or literary status and almost none for anything else. He was extremely busy winding up the affairs of a lifetime (even though it spanned only thirty-five years), preparing for his departure, and attending one last Labour conference at Manchester. There, from the visitors' gallery, on 3 February 1894, he heard himself censured to the enthusiastic applause of the delegates. Three weeks later, that is, on 23 February 1894, Champion sailed from Liverpool for Australia, leaving Rolfe with R at 37 Greville Road.

[v]

Before his departure, Champion had provided for Rolfe. R had agreed to make the round of photographic studios and attend to the introductions to editors and publishers for which Rolfe was so eager. His maintenance was also turned over to R, who owed Champion £40; against that, R was instructed to charge Rolfe's expenses, whether Rolfe stayed at 37 Greville Road or not. The plan was, however, that he remain there until R completed plans for going to New York. Further, Champion had authorised R to give Rolfe £10 3s. in three payments plus two payments of £10 each, one on 4 March and the other on 15 April. Rolfe was then to hold the entire sum until Champion sent for him to come to Australia, when he was to spend it for 'clothes and things'.

These arrangements failed. Both men remained at 37 Greville Road until the time of R's departure for New York, but they did not get on. R found Rolfe a 'drag' on his movements and said so plainly. Rolfe found R extremely selfish. On 19 March 1894, he gave Rolfe £1 5s. to start on his 'own hook', but made no further disposition for Rolfe's maintenance. After they left Greville Road, R sent Rolfe a post-dated cheque for £4, urging that Rolfe spend it as he saw fit. R arranged for another £6 3s. to be paid in several small amounts by a man named Best, who was R's debtor to that extent. Rolfe had difficulty cashing the cheque for £4. That he received the £6 3s. from Best is most unlikely. According to Rolfe, the payments scheduled for 4 March and 15 April were never made, although R told Champion that five cheques were sent to Rolfe in care of Colles, a literary agent; the value of the cheques was not specified. That Champion sent for Rolfe to join him is improbable. Certainly Rolfe never lamented Australia as a lost opportunity as he did so much else.

Once more Rolfe found himself in London and short of funds. His anxiety over the fact was complicated first by guilt at having 'played the goat' with Champion's money. Instead of saving it to equip himself for the proposed journey to Australia, Rolfe had spent it. He was also heart-struck that R had betrayed Champion in respect to the money and betrayed him, Rolfe, by failure to make the promised introductions. Rolfe's last words to R were contained in a letter written on March 1894 and sent to await R in New York. Actuated by a real regard for Champion and an unusual trace of self-pity, Rolfe wrote in reply to R's insistence that he was too sensitive about the miscarriage of Champion's financial arrangements:

> What is the good of saying that if I come to grief because I would not spend money that I imagined was Champion's (you know it is his and not mine as well as I do) I couldn't hurt him worse or help to [make] him miserable in a worse way? I am not quite so fatuously conceited as to believe that anybody cares more than two twos what happens to me.

The letter concluded with this thrust at R:

> And now you are free to think even more of your own affairs, nor will you be worried about the different promises voluntarily made to me . . . there is nothing to prevent your whole attention being devoted to the contemplation of your own navel, and no doubt you will henceforth be perfectly happy. Well, and why shouldn't you? Ad multos annos.[1]

But Rolfe was indomitable. Before writing that letter he had found lodgings at 7 Beaufort Street, Chelsea, and set about the business of surviving. It was not easy. From the time of his boyhood, London had proved to be a harsh, tough city for Rolfe; and this stay which had commenced with contentment and even bright prospects owing to Champion turned out to be as difficult as any. His removal in mid-March from Greville Road to Beaufort Street marked almost the last security Rolfe was to know in 1894 and the early months of 1895. Adversity dogged his every effort. 'People never stop to think', he wrote '. . . that men of parts become rakes, or scoundrels, or paupers, for lack of opportunity to live decently and cleanly.'[2] The first obstacle to opportunity for Rolfe came from Hubert Vaughan, Archbishop of Canterbury. Later, Rolfe wrote about a commission obtained from a 'certain prelate' for a set of pictures 'to illustrate a scheme which he had conceived for confounding the Anglicans'.[3] The prelate was Vaughan.[4] By some means, Rolfe managed to interest the Archbishop in ecclesiastical wall hangings such as he had painted and otherwise adorned at Christchurch. Vaughan provided a 'disused skittles-alley for a studio' and enough materials for Rolfe to begin his work. But Vaughan soon changed his mind. From the time of his elevation to the archbishopric, he had determined to build Westminster Cathedral, and preferred to turn all available funds to that purpose. Only a few weeks after Rolfe had started his work, Vaughan's secretary terminated it.[5] Rolfe felt that because he had been 'deemed void of Divine vocation' he was fair game for misuse and harassment by clerics[6] and the archbishop was no exception. He declared that Vaughan had defrauded him.

Certainly the loss of Vaughan's patronage meant hardships. Of that, there is ample evidence. In *Hadrian the Seventh*, Rolfe has his fictional counterpart, Rose, add after his account of Vaughan's defection, 'I don't know how I kept alive until I got my next commission.' Rose tells how he 'laboured like a driven slave', how he 'designed furniture and fire-irons', made negatives for lantern-slides of the Holy Land', painted 'saints and seraphim and sinners', and worked as a journalist reporting inquests at eighteen pence a time.[7] He might have added that he kept on doggedly at the development of his photography, that he tried over and over to sell what he called his 'Catholic stories', the tales of Toto, that he sought patronage from Bute and Gleeson White among others, that he sold everything he possessed except the clothes he wore, and that it all added up to near-starvation.

None of these, in any case, was how Rolfe kept alive. He did that by believing invincibly, incontrovertibly in his unrecognised gifts. In a story called 'Temptation' written in 1897 in collaboration with John Holden, the hero, who is another version of Rolfe, comments on himself as 'an artist of temperament'. He admitted that he 'lacked technique, the conventional *technique* of the schools, or'—in contrast with Aubrey Beardsley—'the blatant impertinence of the nineteenth-century black and white work'. Thus he was appreciated not by the general but by 'two widely-divided classes, the *cognoscenti* and the utterly uncultured'.[8] Some of this was arrant exaggeration and some, self-delusion. Yet to give way was a contradiction of his ability, an assent to mediocrity. Even when his health was threatened and he was told that he was at the edge of nervous collapse, he persevered. On that occasion, he maintained, a Jesuit offered him admission to a certain House of Rest and he was ready to accept when he remembered that it was a 'licensed madhouse where they imprisoned you by force and tortured you'. Rolfe reported that by an 'effort of will' he escaped that danger; he 'contrived to recover' his nerves and to continue his battle.[9]

His battle was all too often against hunger and cold. He had only light summer clothes which he wore unchanged much of that winter of 1894-5. Often he had no place to sleep, and he was hungry enough once or twice to pick food from the gutter. Tobacco was scarce and a visit to a bath house, rare.

At the end of 1894 there was a respite in Rolfe's discomfort. He and his well-nigh perfected colour photography caught the interest of a member of the Redmayne family, a cotton-waste merchant from Blackburn, near Manchester, who had established a business in London some ten years earlier. Brathay Hall, the Redmayne summer home at Ambleside in Westmorland, was the residence of Hugh Redmayne, who lived there the life of a country gentleman. A part of Brathay Hall was set aside for Rolfe and equipment provided for him to make further experiments with photography. And so in late December 1894, Rolfe set off by train for Ambleside. But like every attempt to aid Rolfe, this one came to nothing. The problem was the discrepancy between the amount of money Rolfe wanted to promote his colour photography and the amount the man of business was willing to spend. Although Redmayne liked Rolfe personally and believed in the value of his inventions,[10] £1,500 was too much to risk. In the new year, possibly in January, Rolfe moved on.

Rolfe's existence in the next few months was as precarious as ever, but most of the time he had a roof to cover him and something to eat. Instead of returning to London when he left Brathay Hall, Rolfe kept to the western part of England and travelled south, going to Colwyn Bay. Nearby was Arnold House School, where his former student and sometime friend John Gambril Nicholson was a schoolmaster. The two men had been on anything but good terms since 1887, and Rolfe had hardly improved his position with Nicholson more recently by threatening a law-suit over the use of Rolfe's sonnet in *Love in Earnest*.[11] Nevertheless Rolfe offered himself as a guest to Nicholson, who took Rolfe into his small quarters and made him as comfortable as possible. But their relationship was, at best, an uneasy one, and at the end of the month or at the beginning of February Rolfe once more set out, this time going on foot toward Holywell, Flintshire, in his light-weight clothing and 'ventilated boots'.[12]

[vi]

Rolfe's next stop was a dozen or so miles west of Chester at the monastery of the Capuchin brothers of Pantasaph. There he presented himself as Frederick Austin, an artisan who could clean and restore a 'large Calvary of Bronze' set at the top of a 'little hill behind the convent'. In return he asked not for money but for 'food and lodging

73

and spiritual direction as long as he should be employed by the convent.'[1] Father Sebastian, the superior, welcomed the application and instructed Rolfe to come to the convent 'at Ave Maria the next day', when he would be given lodging in a guest house. By the next day, however, Father Sebastian had thought better of his bargain. Austin, the superior said, might provide him with directions for making the restorative lotion for the crucifix so that a novice at the convent could take care of it. Acting in what he was sure was a 'Christain spirit', although with the awareness that he could use Father Sebastian's faithless behaviour as material 'for literature afterwards',[2] Rolfe—or Austin—wrote out instructions for preparing the lotion. But he wrote them in Greek, a language not one among the Capuchin brothers at Pantasaph could read.[3] They were all, he concluded, 'lumps of clown' only less despicable than the superior, whom he characterised as a 'hard mean vulgar bit of dirt'.[4] Having given away his secret, he parted from Father Sebastian without spending a single night with the Capuchin brotherhood.[5]

Rolfe went in dejection. His own predicament was no worse than he was used to, but his treatment at the hands of Father Sebastian rankled. Rolfe stated firmly that he was not pious. 'My worst enemy', he said, 'can't accuse me of that.'[6] He believed that scheduled acts of piety and formal concentration on spiritual matters belonged to the Pharisees. But if he could not look among the religious for charity, honour, and conscience, where could he look?

As far as Pantasaph was concerned, Rolfe found charity and conscience for the time being at least with Mrs. Victoria Morris, whose address was St. Clare's Cottage. She said of him, 'He came without luggage of any description at night' and of herself, 'I gave him home and shelter when I saw he was in distress, as few others would have done.'[7] Whether Rolfe first went to Mrs. Morris on the evening of his application to Father Sebastian or on the next, after Ave Maria and after the priest had secured the recipe for the metal polish, is uncertain. In either case, from an undetermined date in February until early August 1895, Rolfe lived at Pantasaph as Mrs. Morris's lodger.[8] He introduced himself as Frederick Austin, but he soon let her know that he might properly be called Baron Corvo. His arrangements with her were for a bedroom in St. Clare's Cottage, meals, and the use of a washhouse in which to paint. Throughout his stay with Mrs. Morris, Rolfe-Austin-Corvo was engaged in a series of paintings. When his landlady had an opportunity to let the bedroom which Rolfe occupied to someone who would pay more and more regularly, a Mrs. Knight, he willingly moved to an unoccupied cottage, St. Elizabeth's, where he both worked and slept. He had the key to the cottage and allowed no one to enter, no room to be dusted, for fear of spoiling the paintings.[9] The result was frequent bickering between Rolfe and his landlady. She could not enter her own premises except with Rolfe's leave. On the other hand, he accused her of expecting him to do 'housemaid's work at St. Elizabeth's for weeks together' unless he was willing to 'pig' in the 'disgusting conditions' of the cottage,[10] conditions which she herself described as 'filth and squalor'. Repeatedly Mrs. Morris gave him notice, repeatedly she exhibited what he called her 'very naughty temper,' and he answered with 'polished sarcasms', until at last she rid herself of him.

Of course the dusting at St. Elizabeth's was not the only cause of the continuing quarrel between Mrs. Morris and Rolfe. Another was his meals. 'He declined roast on Sundays and other times', but on Fridays he demanded meat. Contrary to Catholic practice, Rolfe ate no fish on Friday or on any other day. It was a food, he said, which his 'gorge' rejected 'without even trying it'.[11] He maintained that Mrs. Morris had agreed to provide the simple food he could eat but that, near the end of his stay, she refused simply in order to gratify her 'private spite'. Forcing him to endure near-starvation as well as squalor and discomfort, Rolfe said, was plainly a contradiction of her 'ostentation & noisy proclamation' of 'Franciscan & Catholic unworldliness'.[12] Most important however, was their quarrel about money. When Mrs. Morris took him in, Rolfe agreed to pay 21s. a week, but after the first week he 'did not offer more than 15s., saying he would have to tramp his way to Cornwall'. Mrs. Morris felt sorry for this shabby, stray painter and she believed, then, what he told her. As she said later of herself, she was 'foolish enough to allow him to remain and try to get work'.[13] After a time Rolfe stopped paying altogether.

Whom Rolfe had to thank for the little which he paid to Mrs. Morris or, for that matter, for the money with which he first bought paints and brushes is open to conjecture. That he reached Pantasaph entirely penniless is improbable. Surely Redmayne and possibly Nicholson had given him a few pounds. By the time that was spent, Rolfe was very likely in the care of Father Charles Sidney de Vere Beauclerk and Saint Winefride of nearby Holywell. While Rolfe was still in Aberdeen, it had been his practice (or so Aberdeen's *Daily Free Press* declared) 'to register a vow—duly attested and subscribed—to Our Lady of Lourdes, or to Our Lady of Eternal Hope, or some other benevolent saint' that if, in a set period of time from offering the vow, he was given property which would provide him with 'at least £10,000 a year', he would have a daily Mass said and build a church to honour the saint.[14] Now, although he set his sights much lower, he appealed to the saint whose well at the Welsh village Holywell, some three miles from Pantasaph, had effected a number of miraculous cures in the past year or so, Saint Winefride. Rolfe had read of the remarkable incidents of healing in the February 1894 issue of *The Month*, where his old friend W. T. Stead was quoted in support of the miracles of the Well. Indeed the article in *The Month* had prompted Rolfe to take the direction of Saint Winefride when he left Nicholson. Rolfe sought no cure for ill health but an opportunity to participate in vigorous faith at work and to have the protection of Saint Winefride, whom he was ready to serve. The stop at Pantasaph put him next door to Holywell and so to Saint Winefride's Well.

The Well was England's answer to Fatima and Lourdes. It had gushed forth instantaneously from the ground on the very spot where Winefride, a postulant of the seventh century, had been cut to death when she repulsed the advances of a princely and excitable young man named Caradoc. Around it grew Holywell, by 1895 still only a 'petty town' in Flintshire of about 3,000 inhabitants. It was a stronghold of Calvinistic Methodism, although the aristocrats attended Anglican services and other religions survived, among them Roman Catholicism. According to Rolfe, there was a flock of exactly sixty-seven Catholics, all 'persons of no importance, well known to the police'.[15] The shepherd of this flock was Father Charles Sidney de Vere Beauclerk, a Jesuit. Until Beauclerk's arrival, Holywell had been a 'very sleepy place'. He began regular services at Saint Winefride's Well and processions every Sunday evening which terminated with veneration of the relics of Saint Winefride; on special occasions there were special processions throughout the town. The priest was a man of energy and passionate determination. When his processions were slow to start or ill-formed, he grew angry, even violent—violent enough, Rolfe said, to knock a man down. [16] But owing to Beauclerk's efforts, Saint Winefride's became an English shrine of increasing importance so that more than 35,000 people visited Holywell in 1895.[17]

The work which Mrs. Morris made it possible for Rolfe to obtain was from Father Beauclerk in the service of Saint Winefride. Father Beauclerk commissioned him to paint ecclesiastical wall hangings or banners suitable for use in the frequent processions. These required the same techniques as he had practised at Christchurch. Rolfe must have impressed Beauclerk very favourably, since there were already two painters of banners in the vicinity, a Mr. Park at Preston and a Mr. N. J. Hamner from another nearby village. Obviously Father Beauclerk felt the need for his own painter. So he made some arrangement whereby Rolfe could pay Mrs. Morris and provided brushes and paints and blessed the brushes for the glory of Saint Winefride. On his part, Rolfe forgot that priests are 'black, small, silly, selfish, slippery',[18] and he set to work to produce a series of saints: Saint Ignatius Loyola, founder of Beauclerk's Jesuit order; Saint David; Saint Augustine; Saint Gregory; and of course Saint George, whose dragons were Rolfe's own; and Saint Winefride, shown in flight from Caradoc, her would-be molester. Needless to say, these and other banners were not done all at once or indeed in a year. But first in Mrs. Morris's washhouse and then at her cottage called St. Elizabeth's, he began his work.

Rolfe's work and his mode of life suffered almost no interruption from his rupture with Mrs. Morris and his removal in August from Pantasaph to Holywell, only three miles distant. He had little to take from one village to another except his paints and brushes. He had one suit, shabby and 'fearfully and wonderfully common and stained',[1] and he wore it. Father Beauclerk helped him find quarters at Loyola House in Well Street, one of two lodging houses operated by Mrs. Richardson; later he went to live in her Greyhound Inn. From the beginning, she made special terms for Rolfe because Father Beauclerk intervened in his behalf. The priest provided him with an unused schoolroom as a studio, and Rolfe went on with his banners.

Within a month after his establishment in Holywell, Rolfe had a quarrel by letter with Mrs. Morris. She presented him with a bill for the amount he had left unpaid on his departure from Pantasaph, charging him at the rate of 21s. a week. He refused to pay, disavowing any such arrangement for the 'dirty squalor, discomfort, and starvation' he had 'particularly endured so long at St. Elizabeth's'.[2] Further, he declared that he had not yet got back the washing given her at her request six weeks earlier and that his toothbrush and soap were nowhere to be found. Rolfe's letter upbraided his former landlady for her injustice, her temper, her housekeeping, and her sanctimonious pretensions to naïveté. Mrs. Morris made no reply to Rolfe. Instead she appealed to Father Beauclerk and asked him to get the matter settled. She sent Rolfe's letter to the priest so that he could judge Rolfe's 'spirit of justice and kindliness by the language of his letter' and offered to take as payment what either Beauclerk thought fair or 'Mr. Austin alias Baron Corvo or what ever else his name may be'[3] considered due her. He thought nothing due her so that anything she received came from Father Beauclerk. He did not know that Rolfe's actions were part of a pattern which he had already formed and to which he would adhere over and over again, or Beauclerk might well and rightly have repented sponsoring Rolfe, who went on with his banners and his life in Holywell.

Within two months after Rolfe's establishment in the Flintshire market town, two of the tales with the general heading Stories Toto Told Me appeared in the October issue of The Yellow Book. They are 'About San Pietro and San Paolo' and 'About the Lilies of San Luigi'.[4] These were the first of six stories, all signed by Baron Corvo, which appeared in The Yellow Book between October 1895 and October 1896.[5] One of

Toto's stories, not among these six and not published until 1906, Rolfe had written as early as 1890. He had had them all at his tongue's end when he used them to amuse Malcolm Hay of Seaton and his brother Cuthbert in 1892. More than likely these six and possibly others were completed by the time Rolfe went to stay with Champion in Aberdeen or shortly thereafter. Champion read the Toto stories either then or later in London, as did the member of his household designated as R. It was because of the Toto tales that Rolfe had sought introductions from Champion and R to Colles, the literary agent, and to Jerome K. Jerome.[6] But neither introduction was effected, and Rolfe had sent his stories to one editor after another without arousing the slightest interest. Exactly how many editors saw them is uncertain. He said that 'the first Toto set', that is the first six, were refused by 'more than a score before Messrs. Lane & Harland' of *The Yellow Book* 'sniffed their merits'.[7]

The Toto stories have decided merits. The first six in revised versions were eventually collected into a volume, *Stories Toto Told Me*,[8] and at the suggestion of Rolfe's publisher, John Lane, these six, a story printed in *The Butterfly* for August 1899,[9] and some two dozen others were published in 1901 with the title *In His Own Image*. Predictably, with so many stories in the same form, they are uneven and at their worst mere vehicles for Rolfe's spleen as, for example, 'About the Cheek of Fra Sebastiano'.[10] But on the whole, the Toto stories are rich in invention and in the sophistication of primitive myth without loss of power or lyric quality.

Furthermore, the Toto stories are significant in any consideration of Rolfe. They had their origin in that summer of 1890 spent wandering from the Sforza Palazzo, at Genzano, into the Alban Mountains. The adventures in the mountains are enriched with Rolfe's listening and looking as he walked between the dark beehives of houses on the cobbled streets—narrow steep passages—which wind off from the rear of the Palazzo. Actual events in Rolfe's life, whether in 1890 or later, are evident in the tales. Indeed, little though Rolfe wrote, even the autobiographical trilogy (*Hadrian the Seventh, Nicholas Crabbe*, and *The Desire and Pursuit of the Whole*) is more self-expository than the entire group of tales told by Toto. Their narrator Toto Maidalchini was the passionate, 'ripe', and beautiful leader of the corps of boys with whom Rolfe passed most of that bitter-sweet summer.[11] The nuances of his relationship with them are inescapable. They serve him without question not from necessity but from adoration. Taken together they constitute an ideal of friendship, long desired and long pursued, with himself at its heart. The relationship is more explicitly stated in his descriptions of the boys but especially of Toto. In one tale, he looks 'divinely smart'; in another, he is said to have 'undulated deliciously'; in a third, he is called 'a slim faun of the forest'.[12] Once Toto is described as having brown skin 'with real red blood under it, smooth as a peach'.[12]

78

He is also an example of simple, unquestioning faith. He is, 'thank God & all His Saints,' Rolfe declared, 'an uneducated peasant. No school board had ever defiled him; and hence his exquisiteness.' For Rolfe, Toto was the 'triumph of tradition over litera scripta',[13] and this was at the centre of faith. Rolfe maintained that the English Catholic practised 'Puritanism with a veneer of Catholicism,'[14] but Toto's devotion, like his heart, was simple, natural, diurnal. Thus, in his characterisation and in his tales, Toto combines the complexities of Rolfe's personal tensions, his hostilities, his longing for what he termed 'tender puerice', and his fidelity to a benign and humble Christianity based on spontaneous charity. The harsh facts of survival blurred his morality, as in his dealings with Mrs. Morris, but his faith was firm. It was not as sober as it sounds. Instead, although as Rolfe observed, the 'humour of seculars' has a 'narrow range', he thought it undeniable that the 'very funniest tales in all the world should be those which concern holy persons and holy things'. Thus gentle wry amusement is the net which holds together the strange blend of the later twenty-five Toto stories as well as the first set of six published in *The Yellow Book*.

The Yellow Book had commenced publication in the spring of 1894 with John Lane as publisher and Henry Harland as editor. They opened its pages to modern writers and artists such as Max Beerbohm, Will Rothenstein, George Egerton, Harland, and above all Aubrey Beardsley. With these were mixed more traditional contributors, including George Saintsbury, William Watson, and Sir Frederic Leighton. Henry James, a particular enthusiasm of Harland but too majestic to belong to either camp, also appeared in the new periodical. In other words, *The Yellow Book* was comprehensive enough and *avant garde* enough not to be frightened, as Rolfe said, 'of strange things';[15] so it accepted the Toto stories. The issue of *The Yellow Book* in which these stories first appeared, October 1895, was not particularly distinguished. Only a fraction of the forty or so contributors, apart from Baron Corvo, are remembered at all: Richard LeGalliene, Kenneth Graham, Richard Garnett, Olive Custance, Ella d'Arcy, Hubert Crackanthorpe. Most of even these few are special and, when they are considered in a literary way, a subject for special pleading. Some, such as Olive Custance, who married Alfred Douglas, are remembered for non-literary reasons. But *The Yellow Book* was new and very much in vogue. To appear in print there meant a certain amount of *éclat*, and without doubt the Toto stories brought that to Baron Corvo.

Rolfe-Corvo-Austin did not, however, regard the publication of his stories as an opening to a literary career. Books and writing belonged to his leisure time. John Holden, the twenty-one-year-old nephew of Rolfe's landlady, had come to Holywell to convalesce from a serious illness a month or so after Rolfe arrived, and the two soon struck up a friendship. Holden observed that Rolfe subscribed to

Pearson's Weekly and the *Daily Mail* when it was first published in May 1896. Holden thought both contemptible, but many nights he and Rolfe read books together which Holden had brought with him. Although they chose from a variety of authors and titles—Marlowe, Chaucer, poems selected by Gleeson White, Pepys's *Diary*, the Bible, *The Cloister and The Hearth*—their favourites were the Book of Proverbs, the *Mikado* and *Patience*, and above all Cellini's *Memoirs*. Holden said that Corvo 'soaked' himself in Cellini.[16] Occasionally they stopped early enough to talk about their reading and these, Holden said, were memorable discussions, some of the most pleasant of his life.

Prompted by Holden's 'wondrous beauty', which gratified his 'sensuous palate', and the need for an *alter ego*, Rolfe soon suggested that he and Holden form a partnership. 'You are the man I have been waiting for,' he told Holden. 'We are flint and steel to each other. I need you and you need me.'[17] When Rolfe had Henry Harland's letter accepting the Toto tales, he announced it to Holden and told him that they now had much to do to compose other pieces for publication. Their procedure was to pin sheets of foolscap to the studio walls and jot down on them ideas as they occurred. Words or phrases which either found displeasing were circled in red and others put down in their place. Saturday night was 'revision night', when the two went over the week's work. In case of disagreement as to how a thing should be said, Corvo had the final word. Pieces almost finished were brought to a conclusion. Then they were signed. The better ones received Corvo's signature; the others bore the name Holden had chosen as a *nom de plume*, John Blount. In this way they completed prose pieces meant for publication and all kinds of verses—sestinas, triolets, rondeaux, and limericks (Holden's speciality)—for their own pleasure.[18] These activities were hardly more than pastimes.

Meanwhile Rolfe was still dabbling with colour photography. According to Holden, Rolfe was always 'experimenting with toning solutions, his theory being that he could obtain the original colours of the subject by submitting the print to a series or a mixture of toning solutions'.[19] Holden thought it all a waste of time, but then, as he said, he had 'no great idea' of Rolfe's knowledge of chemistry. Rolfe had lost heart when he found no one willing to take the risk of financing his photographic experiments. Nevertheless he made his achievements in that field known to Holywell and especially to Mrs. Tennant, who operated a studio on High Street. Mrs. Tennant advertised 'Attendance at the Well Daily to take Photos' . . . and, after hearing from Rolfe about his ability with the camera, Mrs. Tennant asked him 'to attend at the Well' in order to pose a Miss Parry Jones 'artistically'. Mrs. Tennant was prepared to exchange the supplies he had bought from her for this service. Rolfe refused, saying that he did not 'care to try to perform the impossible' and that her request was a 'gross & unladylike impertinence'.[20] In time their differences enlarged to include Rolfe's ridicule of Mrs. Tennant's 'vow of holy widowhood' and his accusation that she refused to sell pictures he had taken and that she unlawfully detained his darkroom lamp. Mrs. Tennant replied with a letter worthy of Rolfe; the mildest term she applied to him was 'viper' and she ended by telling him that if he continued to 'molest' her, she would summon her 'stalwart country friends' to deal with him.[21] Thereafter, although his ability as a photographer was to serve him well in 1908, Rolfe's interest in it as a possible source of income dwindled. In 1898, when two of his photographs from *The Studio* were reproduced in a chapter of Lincoln Adams's *In Nature's Image*, 'The Nude in Photography',[22] Rolfe made no mention of it. Probably he never saw the book.

Rolfe's real business during the first eighteen or twenty months of his stay in Holywell was to paint Father Beauclerk's banners. They provided his livelihood. According to John Holden, who by the terms of their partnership helped paint borders and occasionally cleaned the brushes, Rolfe had difficulty with his drawing. So, when he found in an illustrated paper, a magazine, or an advertisement, a figure which suited his needs, Rolfe pasted it on cardboard and cut around it. Then by means of a strong light, Holden cast a shadow of the figure on a sheet of white paper and Rolfe outlined it with a pencil. Figures in the foreground of one banner came directly from an advertisement for Scotch Whisky; others, with 'hands uplifted in supplication', were traced from eighteen photographs, each from a different perspective, of a statue called 'Youth Supplanted'.[23] To Holden, Rolfe talked grandly of his work and of what Father Beauclerk and he could do for the greater glory of Saint Winefride and the greater prosperity of Holywell. Within a few months he spoke confidently of the basilica they would build; he had already chosen a site and soon he meant to draw designs for it.[24]

Rolfe's tone with Father Beauclerk was totally different. He made every effort to convince the priest that he worked tirelessly out of concern for his soul's salvation and devotion to Saint Winefride and to Beauclerk's churchly efforts. Once, Rolfe composed a litany and sent it to Beauclerk with the suggestion that it be used for a procession accompanied by six small harps or a theorbo.[25] But what Father Beauclerk wanted was the banners, and Rolfe was eager to please him. In mid-March 1896, when the priest found fault with the faces represented on banners Rolfe had proudly shown him, Rolfe was quick to apologise. 'If I have been unduly elated, forgive me. I will try not to do it again,' he wrote. He explained that he could not help feeling pleased because he had contended successfully against numerous difficulties and thus 'gone up *one* little step' towards an unattainable goal. He was quick to credit any achievement to the saints who had 'deigned to impart some modicum of their radiance'. Rolfe added, 'As I correspond more closely with the graces they impart, so much the more beautiful will my work become.' He then promised Beauclerk that he would take care not to show him 'ugly or hurried faces again', that he would 'stick and pray at them' until they were right. In the same letter, Rolfe wrote, 'Nor is it for want of diligence that I fail if continuous work is diligence. But I do not concentrate all the time & so I fail. Faces? Yes they are only the shadow of what I have seen. And I fail to reach the reality for the reason of hurry & human respect & worry.'[26] He spoke of making a retreat in Holy Week. Five days later, Rolfe regretted having nothing more to show because he had been busy with borders and retouching. He assured Beauclerk of a welcome at any time and promised to have something worth seeing by 23 April if he could meanwhile 'keep up to the mark'.[27] On 3 April, after a few days in Manchester, Rolfe wrote again to declare that he was 'attacking his work with renewed vigour, being purged and happier'.[28]

Rolfe had made that particular visit to Manchester to offer himself and his partner John Holden as secretaries to Redmayne, the cotton merchant who had arranged the stay in 1893 at Brathay Hall in Ambleside. Redmayne and several other men in the cotton trade were planning a 'Commercial Mission' to China, Persia, and Japan. Rolfe was eager to accompany them. Holden said Rolfe's attempt to get them positions as secretaries had commenced in February. At first Holden had been enthusiastic. Then after a 'tiff' with Rolfe and a 'few hours spitting at each other like two wild cats', Holden had decided he would not go under any circumstances. Rolfe, however, made several trips to Manchester to further the scheme and once urged his partner to come there to meet Redmayne, but Holden was adamant. That there was any possibility of Rolfe's accompanying the Mission with or without Holden is unlikely, but he told Holden that Redmayne persisted in wanting them and that his refusal of both was owing to Holden. Rolfe reproached Holden with attempting to ruin him and added that Holden must 'rejoice at the miserable existence' he caused Rolfe, forced as he was 'to put up with . . . unreasonable tantrums' from Holden's relative, Mrs. Richardson.[29]

Rolfe was already unhappy and restless in Holywell, when he had been there less than a year. In a letter to Father Beauclerk dated 15 March 1896, Rolfe declared that lately he had felt that he must 'shriek or burst'. He continued, 'I have developed a violent & raging temper, blazing out at what I suppose are small annoyances, & overwhelming people with a torrent of scathing & multilingual fury. I make amends for it afterwards but it leaves me weak in mind & body. It's the Mr. Hyde surging up.'[30] He attributed his rages to 'worldly worries', but he was also the victim of 'chained impotence', the inability to achieve what he aimed for. His failure, he complained, made him seethe inwardly while outwardly he insisted on keeping a 'demeanour most marble' which was unfortunately mistaken for pride and cynicism. He saw himself as inscrutable to the people of

Holywell, a mystery. In a tale written the following year, called 'The Saint, The Priest, The Nowt, The Devil', his description of the Nowt by whom he meant himself reads, 'No one knew from whence he came, nor what, nor who he was. He dropped down . . . from "the back of beyond", settled there, worked like a slave, spoke to few, and made no friends.'[31]

Certainly that last statement is correct. Rolfe had no friends except Beauclerk, Holden, and a boy named Leo Schwarz. The son of a German optician who had emigrated to England and established his family at Holywell, young Schwarz was one of several altar boys whom Beauclerk had sent to Rolfe's studio to do odd jobs. The others came once or twice, but Leo remained to run errands, mix paints for the banners, and listen to Holden and Rolfe talk.

Rolfe's description of himself refers also to his ability to hold a roomful attentive when he chose to speak, the 'meticulous delicacy' of his habits, and the fact that these together with his voice and accent 'stamped him as a person of culture and consideration'. Holywell, he said, invented romances about him, spoke of him as a gentleman who had fallen on hard times, and refused to believe the truths which he had told to a few.

Holden affirmed a part of this from observation. He called Rolfe's manner impressive, his speech deliberate and his face, because of his immobile mouth and the powerful glasses which hid his eyes, 'almost inscrutable'. Most people, Holden said, were awestruck and Mrs. Richardson's servants were terrified by Rolfe. Yet, he could be a pleasant dinner table companion.[32] On the whole, however, Holden's view of Rolfe accorded ill with Rolfe's view of himself. Holden discredited the 'truths' Rolfe confided. These included the disclosure that he was Baron Corvo, partly Italian and related to the Sforzas and other important families of Italy, where he had passed much of his life. His denial of ordination, he attributed to a conspiracy of English bishops, and his subsequent sufferings, to church dignitaries; he said that even then he was in hiding from powerful enemies. He talked of his own ability as sculptor, painter, writer, and linguist, stating that he had mastered five languages.[33] Furthermore, Holden's description of Rolfe's person is hardly that of a figure about whom romantic legends grow:

He was a little below the average height, with fairly broad shoulders and decidedly bandy legs. . . . He had a smooth high forehead, a rather pointed nose, and a somewhat aggressive chin; his hair was of a faded light brown, and he was bald over the temples and the crown; he was clean-shaven, and I think that if he had let his beard grow it would have been reddish brown; his mouth was small, and his lips, particularly the upper lip, were thin; he was very short-sighted and wore a pair of extraordinarily powerful glasses. He was very shabbily dressed. I was most struck by the mouth, it looked so hard and cruel.[34]

Holden supported his implication of toughness and cruelty in Rolfe by saying that Rolfe often proclaimed contentment, humility, and forgiveness as 'three nasty, mean little virtues'. Throughout their long acquaintance Holden never once heard Rolfe express sympathy with or pity for anyone. On the other hand, Holden admitted that despite the 'wretched time' Rolfe was having in Holywell, he never once indulged in self-pity. As Holden put it, *'It was Corvo against the world, and the odds on Corvo.'*[35]

Such arrogance and self-satisfaction are always only a breadth from the ridiculous. Holden's reaction to Rolfe was often one of derision. His characteristic snort expressing almost anything, his delight in a chance to exercise his powers of invective, his habit of writing letters to Holden, although they were in the same house, were absurd. After Rolfe suggested their partnership, Holden had a good laugh about it with Mrs. Richardson, his aunt. He thought it nonsense when Rolfe refused to burn his letter books on the grounds that they would be useful when his biography came to be written, that everything relating to him would be of interest some day.[36]

To Holden the most ludicrous aspect of Rolfe was his sex life, the fact that he saw 'nothing incongruous in his going to Rhyl in search of inspiration for a sacred banner' and a chance sexual encounter. He went frequently to Chester and Manchester as well to see whether he could find 'anything at all possible'. Once he had picked up a girl on Manchester's Oxford street and gone with her to her room, but when she grew maudlin after three bottles of stout, he left her. Another time a bath-chair attendant on the front at Rhyl had 'acted as his pimp and procured him a servant girl'. Still another time, he told how he first had a Turkish bath and luncheon at Rhyl before enjoying a casual romance.[37] Once he talked of several unsatisfactory excursions and worried that he might be impotent. Holden suggested that he smoked too much and had better give up either smoking or women. At that, Holden said, Rolfe 'very deliberately plugged and lit his pipe and began to puff at it furiously'.

This account of Rolfe in search of women in no way corresponds with his known homosexuality, his protestations of purity, or indeed with what Holden knew about Rolfe. He lost no opportunity to denigrate women to Holden: that they are usually superfluous, that they always expect to be made love to, that they are fit only for breeding and their 'curves and protruberances' demonstrated the fact.[38] In any case, Rolfe freely admitted that he was terrified of women. Besides, he maintained that when he was driven from the Scots College, he had taken a vow of chastity and observed it to help show his suitability for priesthood. Once Rolfe declared that he had 'delighted in impure thoughts', all aroused by his reading, less than a dozen times in his life, but after having 'dallied with them he dismissed them'.[39] Nearly every statement here is contradictory of the other inasmuch as Rolfe's homosexual inclinations were apparent when he was little more than a boy, and eventually he proclaimed them in letter after letter. Very likely what he told Holden was a camouflage for his real activities at Rhyl or Manchester or wherever he sought a companion for sexual purposes. Although arguing from such flimsy evidence is self-indulgent, Rolfe's reference to the Turkish bath at Rhyl is particularly suspect, inasmuch as public baths have been notorious meeting places with elaborate rituals for homosexuals at least since the days of Caracalla.

Whether his reports of his sexual activities were bravado or subterfuge and whether he was a tragic or farcical figure, Rolfe's life at Holywell was a meagre one and unlikely to improve. What Beauclerk paid him was a pittance, enough to cover his lodging and little more. When his one suit got past wearing, the priest provided another, a blue cover-all. Payment for the Toto stories was slight, £5 5s. for each of the first two pairs of stories, and that was slow in coming. On 4 June 1896, he was still attempting to collect for the third and fourth stories which had appeared in the April issue of *The Yellow Book*[40] and he did not receive a cheque until July after he had written both to Henry Harland, its editor, and John Lane, its publisher.[41] For the fifth and sixth stories Harland promised £10, but Rolfe received only £7.

Many a man has endured worse, accepting his condition as God-given or fated or the result of whatever he believes in, even if it is only himself. For some men such circumstances are an invitation to overcome. As for Rolfe, his reaction was neither of these; as he had feared, he 'burst'. Perhaps he was weary of the role of humility which he assumed for Father Beauclerk; it was hardly consistent with Rolfe's character. Or he may have acted out of misplaced opportunism. Rolfe had delivered an especially fine banner for display on 22 June 1896, Saint Winefride's feast day, when it was first blessed by the Vicar Apostolic of Wales and then paraded from the Church along Well Street and through the town. It was used again on 24 August, when a large procession (some 1,000 persons) formed to remove a new statue of the Sacred Heart, a copy of the one which stands in Montmartre, from the railway station into Holywell. In addition, there was a huge banner representing the 'archangel slaying the red dragon' and another portraying St. George. These and other banners created much comment and admiration, and during that summer of 1896 'lady visitors' backed a number of them with 'liberty art velvet, suitably bordered with embroidery and fringe'. They were steadily in use in Beauclerk's processions or in the Church, where they were placed around the walls.[42] At the peak of his career as a painter of banners, Rolfe was confident that Beauclerk needed him. What followed was a quarrel between Rolfe and his patron so monumental that it altered Beauclerk's pastoral career and, after eighteen months of stubborn suffering, turned Rolfe against his will into a writer but also helped send him to the workhouse.

The quarrel began slowly. Holden says that early in 1897 relations between Beauclerk and Rolfe began to cool, and the priest seemed eager to be rid of Rolfe, his 'Old Man of the Sea'. Rolfe was an expense justifiable only in terms of the banners and there is a limit to the number of banners a small church in a small town can absorb. One day, as John Holden tells it, Father Beauclerk came to Rolfe's studio for a private talk. Holden said that immediately afterwards he could see that something was wrong. His account continues in part:

> Corvo was thinking hard. At last he looked at me in a very strange manner and said slowly: 'You have often been here when Fr. Beauclerk has called, and you have heard him say that I was to have £– (I have forgotten the amount) for each banner I painted?' I replied: 'I have often been here when Fr. Beauclerk has dropped in, but never once have I heard him speak of paying a penny for one of your banners. I have always understood that he was finding you work until you got on your feet again. And this is the first time', I continued, 'that you have ever told me that you expected to be paid.'[43]

Certainly Rolfe wanted payment for the banners. No later than 8 April 1897, he asked for payment without setting an exact price. On that date he listed the banners for Beauclerk, and apparently Beauclerk responded by calling to Rolfe's attention a 'document' in which Rolfe had stated his willingness to 'work hard & have patience' and trust to 'the hopes of a bright future' which Beauclerk had held out to him. The document spoke of Rolfe's 'great respect' for Beauclerk, a respect 'tinged, as far as possible, with personal friendship', but no remuneration was mentioned. Believing that Beauclerk had burned the document, Rolfe was indignant that the priest used it against him. Rolfe posted the list of paintings and a detailed account of the situation to the Provincial and to the Vicar Apostolic of Wales, offering however to be absolutely silent if the Vicar Apostolic so decreed. This was 'open revolt' on the part of Rolfe, for which he blamed Beauclerk's 'injustice and duplicity'.

The Vicar Apostolic, Frank Mostyn, ignored Rolfe's communication, and the quarrel was on in earnest. Father Flynn, also a Jesuit who had come to Holywell the previous May to assist Beauclerk, intervened and on 9 April, when he wrote to thank Flynn, Rolfe stated that he 'truly regretted that neither his own forbearance and plainness' nor Flynn's 'reasoning' could make Beauclerk 'act, for a change, in an honourable manner'. Rolfe added, 'I cannot imagine what Father Beauclerk hopes to gain by his obstinate persistence in his attitude. In any case I have well earned double any amount he will pay by the piles of literature he has squeezed out of me by his evil deeds.'[44]

The 'piles of literature' to which Rolfe referred were eleven contributions, made since November 1896, to *The Holywell Record*. Frank W. Hocheimer, its editor-publisher, had come to Holywell as an advertising canvasser. He had stayed at Mrs. Richarson's Greyhound Inn on his arrival, but after deciding to settle in Holywell, Hocheimer had moved to 3 Bank Place. There, in May 1896, he had issued the first number of the paper which he represented as his wife's property but the offspring of his own 'Catholic spirit, business experience, brain-power and capital'.[45] At the same time he emphasised that he had commenced the *Record* at the 'direct stimulation, incitement, and encouragement' of Father Beauclerk.[46] Because it was the 'greatest pleasure and aim' of his life to help others—or so Rolfe said—Rolfe had given several pieces to the paper.[47] None was signed as by Rolfe, Baron Corvo, or Frederick Austin. The first two, 'The Solitary Soul' and 'Purgatory' appeared in the number for November 1896. Four more were in the March 1897 *Record* and five in the April issue. Of all these pieces, only one is noteworthy. Each has a distinctly Rolfean or Corvine flavour, particularly when invective or ridicule is employed, but many of the pieces such as 'An Open Letter to the Editor', signed by 'Al Siddik' and presented as a feature in March and April,[48] and 'A typical Case from Life'[49] are arguments in the unending, petty differences between Protestants and Catholics. 'The Breastplate of St. Patrick (Lorica Sanctii Patricii)' is a litany for St. Patrick's Day. 'Little Petronilla in Paradise', supposedly translated from the Italian of 'Vincenza, Duchess of Deira', is a sentimental tale of a mischievous innocent at the gates of heaven in conversation with Saint Peter. 'Purgatory' is a meditation related in subject matter to 'A Solitary Soul';[50] but 'A Solitary Soul' is a dark, imaginative impression of purgatory narrated by the lone soul. The concept is hardly new, but the presentation is strong and individual. If the editor benefited at that time from the fact that he could partly fill the columns of *The Holywell Record* with these pieces which Beauclerk extracted, free, from Rolfe, Hocheimer was soon to pay more dearly for them than he could have thought possible. He was soon to be deeply involved in Rolfe's quarrel with Beauclerk.

The question of the value of Rolfe's banners was still unsettled in late April. Park, the banner painter from Preston, was asked to estimate their value, but he resolved nothing. Rolfe protested that his differed from the 'Preston banners' in that they were 'absolutely original unique designs'. On the same day, 20 April 1897, at Father Beauclerk's 'command' that he set a price on the banners listed in his letter of 8 April and 'demand' payment, he said that for his 'incessant and very painful labours' since coming to Holywell, he 'would humbly entreat' the priest to give him only what appeared pleasing to his profound and discreet judgment. Rolfe assured Beauclerk that whatever the amount, it would be held 'amply liberal' and much more satisfactory than any sum he might name as long as it came with 'gracious good wishes'. Rolfe declared that he named any amount only at Father Beauclerk's insistence. He went on to say that he would do the banners for no one else for 1,500 gold sovereigns. By comparison with Mr. Hamner's, they must be valued at £1,102 10s. Rolfe then said that he would accept £700 and from that make an offering to Saint Winefride, inasmuch as he was resolved to spend the rest of his life in the service of the saint and of Father Beauclerk. Rolfe urged Beauclerk to take care of the affair at once and thus relieve Rolfe from the 'horrible torture and suspense' he had so long suffered and could no longer endure. He ended: 'I would rather receive a single six shilling and eight-pence at the hands of your reverence than a whole fortune from any other patron; and am, at the same time, ever worrying Heaven with prayers for your reverence's preservation.'[51]

Prayers and unction notwithstanding, only legal measures put an end to the question of payment for the banners. In late April or early May, Rolfe turned his claims over to F. Llewellyn Jones, a solicitor, maintaining that payment for his paintings was long past due and that his health had suffered from overwork and anxiety. By 16 May, he had directed his solicitor to add to the writ against Beauclerk the charge of 'libel and deprivation of employment by slanderous threats'.[52] Rolfe contended that in early May, Beauclerk had put a boycott on him, had told the Catholics of Holywell that he was a dangerous man, that persons who did business with him would be 'hounded out of town and made to suffer'.[53] Rolfe described the boycott as originating when his solicitor attempted to serve a writ against the priest. As soon as he learned of it, he rushed to Rolfe, shook him by the shoulder, put a curse on him and swore a great oath, 'by God and St. Scioquio'. The oath included burning Rolfe's works in order to wreck his 'chance of winning fame and credit', ruining him, making him suffer, preventing him from earning a living, and having him 'hounded out of the town'. After a correspondence of 'appalling dimensions' with Father Beauclerk's solicitor, Augustine Watts of Watts & Carr, Liverpool, and a conference in Holywell on 27 May between Watts and F. Llewellyn Jones, Rolfe's solicitor, Jones accepted £50 for Rolfe and £10 15s. in costs and agreed to withhold the £50 from Rolfe until he surrendered the key to the studio and Jones in turn delivered it to Beauclerk.[54]

Rolfe had been living in his studio, the unused school room, since 11 May, when Mrs. Richardson succeeded in getting him out of the Greyhound Inn. John Holden said that when his aunt attempted to rid herself of Rolfe, he fell ill and that Mrs. Richardson and her mother nursed him for a period of three weeks before he left. When he did, he owed £7 16s. for board, £2 17s. 6d. for beer, and £1 14s. 6d. for laundry.[55] But the studio was a hazardous refuge. Much of its furniture belonged to Mrs. Richardson, hired by Beauclerk for Rolfe's use, and she soon reclaimed it.

Although he was willing to concede that Mrs. Richardson might be suffering from 'May Madness' and assured her that when she came to feel sorry for what she had done to him, she must not be afraid to say so, Rolfe bitterly resented his former landlady. She had failed to provide him with clean linen at the studio so that he had had to endure 'disgusting piggery' while 'straining every power' to satisfy Beauclerk. Rolfe failed to understand her devotion to her 'beloved rector'. Rolfe told her vehemently that the priest was a liar, a thief, a bully, a slanderer, a 'vilely criminal priest' who had cursed Holywell and begged Saint Winefride 'to stop all the works & let the grass grow in the streets'.[56] He was convinced that Mrs. Richardson had turned him out of the Greyhound Inn at the instigation of Father Beauclerk and that she, like all Holywell's Catholics, must rejoice at the spectacle of his 'camping out in the parish somewhere', when he came to that. Furthermore, he attributed Holden's defection to Mrs. Richardson.

The loss of Holden as follower and friend was a sharp blow. Friendly relations between Holden and Rolfe had ended after Rolfe first broached the subject of payment from Beauclerk and Holden declared himself neutral in the contest he could foresee.[57] Rolfe wanted an ally and finding none in Holden made an enemy of him. From that time, there were no more literary talks at the studio, no work together on banners, no more references to Holden as Giovanni. Rolfe accused the young man of threatening him with assault and with destroying notes for the material which eventually went into a revision of the Toto story 'How Christians Love One Another'.[58] Rolfe demanded an abject apology for that deed as well as for other misdemeanours on Holden's part; these included the 'breach of his engagement' with Rolfe and cursing him 'by the mouth of Leo.' The matter of Leo—Leo Schwarz—was another affront to Rolfe. He insisted that Beauclerk had forbidden the boy to accept help in his lessons or even to speak to Rolfe, threatening to turn the child off the altar if he disobeyed. On 11 May, anticipating some such thing as the priest's threat, Leo and Rolfe had agreed to speak only in the street. But even after Beauclerk relented, Leo's father forbade the boy to see Rolfe.[59] This he could not lay at the door of Mrs. Richardson, but it added to his unhappiness at Holden's desertion and to ease it, he blamed her rather than himself that his partnership with Holden had collapsed. Rolfe wrote to her, 'Your nephew came to my studio after you made him break his engagement & spoilt his life for him, to fetch his books. I suppose he fetched them all. And that is that.'[60]

Rolfe was at odds not only with his former landlady and her nephew, but he quarrelled also with nearly all Catholic Holywell and one or two people outside it. As with Mrs. Richardson and Holden, where there was no enmity, Rolfe created it. He had already quarrelled with Mrs. Tennant, the photographer. To his insistence that she retained his property unlawfully, he added the charge, in time, that she collected for subscriptions to The Holywell Record and kept the money. Rolfe was disgusted by her femininity and her talk of being a 'sister' to him.[61] A squabble with Mrs. Thomas Corrigan, who lived at Ransom Cottage on Well Street and kept a stand near Saint Winefride's Church for the sale of newspapers and holy objects, widened to include a woman named Rachel Holmes, who sold statues opposite the Church, and Mr. Corrigan. Numerous letters passed between Thomas Corrigan and Rolfe as to whether or not he had spread in 'mere wanton malice' a 'vile report' that Corrigan's wife had had twins.[62] There was a difference with C. W. Bell, Solicitor, over advertisements in The Holywell Record.[63] Thomas White of Accrington, a nearby village, was called an emissary of Beauclerk and charged with plotting against The Holywell Record.[64] In a letter dated 21 August 1897, Rolfe set down his opinion of Beauclerk—an 'habitual wanton and malignant liar, a calumniator, a curser, a thief'—and invited E. J. Catherwood, who kept the Antelope Hotel in Holywell, to take sides.[65] Rolfe even dragged in his London friend and former pupil Eddie Slaughter because he was a cousin of Mostyn, Vicar Apostolic of Wales. Slaughter was questioned about a statement from Beauclerk that Mostyn had remarked on the 'beastly clothes' Rolfe wore and on the naked figures in his banners. When Slaughter transmitted Mostyn's denial, Rolfe faced Beauclerk and Father Flynn with it and reminded Flynn that his superior was a confessed liar. Nevertheless Rolfe found Mostyn's answers evasive, attributable, he thought, to the two priests' wish to conceal the truth, and by November he declared that Slaughter had turned against him.[66]

The only ally Rolfe had was Frank W. Hocheimer, owner and editor of The Holywell Record. This man, whom Rolfe later described as a Prussian and a 'drunken sot' with a 'pretty Protestant wife',[67] willingly joined Rolfe in his battle against Father Beauclerk. A statement which Rolfe composed and Hocheimer signed and directed to The Reverend Father General of the Jesuits asserted that Hocheimer had asked Rolfe to contribute occasional pieces to The Holywell Record. Then, well before the breach with Rolfe, Beauclerk had commanded him to make no more contributions to the paper, accompanying this command with a threat against The Record and its owner. The priest soon forbade Hocheimer to hire Rolfe-Austin but relented, and Hocheimer offered him employment.[68] According to Rolfe, this occurred 'about the time when Fr. Beauclerk began to show the cloven hoof'; so Rolfe refused. Knowing, he said, 'the contemptible deceitful nature of the Spaniard' (Father Beauclerk), he feared the priest's 'ignoble and savage revenge' on any one with whom he was connected.[69] Within the next two weeks, however, Rolfe was forced to surrender the key to his studio, and for forty-five hours he was without food or drink or shelter.

Even the £50 got from Beauclerk for the banners was gone; Rolfe had changed it into gold and made of it a 'deodand by offering it up as charity just as it was'.[70] Although he 'supported life' with cigarettes during those hours, he faced once again the acute uncertainty of his existence. He quickly reached an understanding with Hocheimer whereby Rolfe went to live with the Hocheimers at 3 Bank Place and on 24 July 1897 took up the editorship of *The Holywell Record*.[71]

[viii]

Rolfe's grand gesture with his £50 had settled the matter for him. The money might have taken him elsewhere and helped him start again. Instead he chose to demonstrate that he was not a recipient of charity but a donor from his own earnings. By so doing, he lost the choice of staying at Holywell or leaving. He had to stay.

Rolfe turned necessity into a virtue and vowed he would not leave Holywell until every restitution—financial, personal, spiritual—was made to him. Only when that had happened, he said, would he 'rest content' and prepare to leave. 'But until then,' he declared, 'here I am; and here I stay.' He told Mrs. Richardson that in the interests of the Church in Wales, the 'starved half-civilised Catholics of Holywell', and in his own interest he was prepared to make 'a fierce fight to the death with this worldly divine', Beauclerk. To the priest, whom he accused of denying him the sacraments and thus inflicting a curse on him, Rolfe said, 'I spit upon it, and defy you; and you may rest assured that I shall fight against it as long as I can hold a pen.'[1]

Yet, in almost the same breath, Rolfe was seeking some way out of Holywell, which he characterised as 'the most bestially disagreeable place I ever saw'. On 29 November 1897, he wrote to John Lane, the publisher, asking to be taken on as a reader or as an editor of *The Yellow Book*. He went on to tell what an awful time he had had and was having and added, 'All I want is to be picked out of this hole where I am buried, and to be given a chance to use myself.'[2]

Certainly Rolfe had little reason to want to remain in Holywell. With the Hocheimers he lived in 'humble poverty'. They hired necessities such as beds and basins, and used packing cases for most of their furniture. More disturbing than the furnishings was Beauclerk's refusal to perform the 'Rite of Benediction' on their house, thus condemning them, as Rolfe put it, 'to live on the territory of daemons'. Having been denied that rite, both men thought themselves forbidden the sacraments as well so that they considered themselves excommunicated without formal sentence.[3]

There was much work to do. For the next year and more, Rolfe devoted his energy and his talents to *The Holywell Record*. He designed an elaborate letter-head for the Record Publishing Company, signing it with the drawing of a raven, his talisman associated in its Latin form *corvus* with Corvo. He filled the columns of *The Record*, his contributions to each issue never numbering less than five and once, in May, running to nine items. Indeed, from the time he moved to 3 Bank Street, Rolfe wrote nearly the whole of every issue which survives. Nothing was signed as by Rolfe or Frederick Austin. Many pieces were published anonymously, but many had pseudonyms such as Franz Wilhelm V. Bracht, Al Siddik, John Blount (a name used earlier with John Holden), May Chester, Vincenza, Duchess of Deira, Baron Corvo of course, and others. No signature was needed for the regular features, 'Local Notes etc.', 'Worth Reading', and 'Answers to Correspondents', but Rolfe was the author of all these. The demands on his imagination were as constant as the drudgery.

Whatever he did, Rolfe's efforts came to nothing. *The Record* was a Catholic sheet aimed at Catholics, but the Catholic advertisers, aware of the quarrel between its editor and their priest, withdrew their advertisements and refused to make use of the 'Visitors List' in the paper or to supply a full list of visitors to it. Father Beauclerk withheld information from *The Record* which he gave to Protestant papers. Printers accepted copy reluctantly and allowed no credit. Subscriptions went unpaid. Sales fell off. According to the complaint to the Father General of the Jesuits, the responsibility was Beauclerk's; the priest stated in other local papers and at services held at Saint Winefride's Well that he was no longer answerable for the contents of *The Record*, thus '*implying* a former official connection'.[4] Pilgrims to the Well then thought the paper heretical and refused to buy it. With each issue, publication became more difficult.

Aware in September that the end of the paper might come any day and hoping to help the Hocheimers by conciliating this priest who was 'persuaded that his celluloid collar was a halo, and his Roman stock the Divine Aureola',[5] Rolfe voluntarily went into 'exile'. By that time, in any case, life at 3 Bank Place had become 'a horror'. Rolfe analysed it: 'Pen three people in one little house, render all their labour void, deny them the company of their species, and the distraction of religion, and what can you expect?' Hocheimer took to drink and neglected his work. Mrs. Hocheimer 'nagged and grizzled and grew ugly' and cursed all Catholics.[6] So Rolfe left. In a letter to Beauclerk dated 3 January 1899, Rolfe recalled his voluntary absence from Holywell between 13 September and 4 December. Elsewhere, Rolfe says, that during that time he went into another country. If he did, he left no account of it. On 24 November 1897, he wrote from his place of exile to Beauclerk deploring the continuance of the boycott against the Hocheimers and giving notice that he intended to return to Holywell at his own convenience to help his friends; but he wrote on *The Record's* letterhead. Letters sent to John Lane on 25 November and 29 gave Rolfe's address as 3 Bank Place, Holywell.[7] In his second letter, he asked Lane to keep to himself both the address and the knowledge of his 'miserable existence'. *The Daily Free Press* of Aberdeen mentions a visit to that city which Rolfe made in the summer of 1897,[8] but even if Rolfe thought of Scotland as 'another country', the summer was not the time of his exile.

Wherever Rolfe passed the period, 13 September to 4 December 1897, he maintained his association with *The Record*. He had six separate pieces in the October issue, and he knew that thereafter there was not 'a farthing' for the printers, that *The Holywell Record* was in a perilous state, and that his removal from Holywell had not helped it or the Hocheimers. Rolfe went back to Holywell and to 3 Bank Place and to the relentless pursuit of his quarrel with Beauclerk. On the very day of his return, he composed for Hocheimer's signature a vindictive letter to Beauclerk, warning him of the scandal sure to come from imminent proceedings in bankruptcy since Hocheimer could not meet his creditors' demands. The letter went on to say that the Vicar Apostolic, the Father General of the Jesuits, and the Cardinal Prefect of Propaganda would have details of Beauclerk's 'immorality of behaviour'.[9] There was a temporary cessation of hostilities at Christmas when Mostyn, the Vicar Apostolic, intervened and Beauclerk sent Father Flynn to bless 3 Bank Place. Beauclerk also heard Rolfe's confession, thus allowing him to conclude that the excommunication, never passed, was in abeyance. Afterwards, Rolfe insisted that in the confessional, when he was 'shriven,' the priest urged him to leave town and swore he would not let Rolfe 'get on' unless he did.[10] The threat seems not to have troubled Rolfe at the time. He was more impressed that on that Christmas Eve, outside the confessional, Beauclerk 'offered' him conversation, assured him of good will, and gave him hope that 'Peace was on the wing'. But Christmas passed and 'not a soul in the town, not a single Catholic in the world . . . dared a syllable of friendship' to the Hocheimers or to him.[11] On 4 January 1898, Rolfe wrote to tell Beauclerk that a bailiff was in possession at 3 Bank Place and had seized and taken away their goods. The day before had marked what Rolfe described as the 'twelfth year of the anguish of being a Catholic'[12] and the prospect of lessening the pain was grim. Shortly before Easter 1898, because he was anxious about his 'Easter duties', Rolfe made overtures once more, asking, 'Is it to be peace or war?' Beauclerk's only reply was a reference to Psalm 139.[13] It commences with these lines:

> Deliver me, O Lord, from the evil man: preserve
> me from the violent man;
> Which imagine mischiefs in their heart, continually
> are they gathered together for war.
> They have sharpened their tongues like a serpent;
> adders' poison is under their lips.

Rolfe retaliated and so the letters went on condemning Beauclerk as a vicious and criminal priest and above all as a liar. The letters repeated over and over the charges of boycott, calumny, attempts at 'hounding them out of town', and starvation. They made much of Mrs. Hocheimer's Protestantism and her sufferings from hunger.

All three had too little to eat. As early as July their hunger was apparent enough to N. J. Hamner, the banner painter, to send them a gift of food.[14] According to Rolfe, they lived on bits of bread, potatoes, and tea-leaves stewed over and over again until they lost their colour. When the season permitted they 'took a country walk' to get blackberries, nuts, mushrooms, whatever grew wild and was edible. Early in June, Rolfe had inherited the sum of 19s. 6d., with which he was directed to buy a mourning ring. Instead he bought a store of stamps, tobacco, Hovis loaves, and cocoa so that they all might live a little longer.[15] Sometimes they had nothing to eat and then Rolfe informed Beauclerk to what condition they were reduced and asked whether he wanted the scandal very likely to follow to result from the parade of their starvation.

With this threat of scandal Rolfe made one more effort to lessen Beauclerk's animosity toward Hocheimer and thus save *The Record*. Rolfe had composed every letter Hocheimer had written in this endless quarrel with the priest, and it is reasonable to assume that he wrote the letter to Beauclerk dated 18 June 1898, a Saturday, and signed by Hocheimer. It began with Hocheimer's dissociating himself from Rolfe—or Austin, as he was known in Holywell. Hocheimer explained that he had been compelled to resume the editorship of *The Record* because 'Mr Austin's troubles have been quite too much for him', and he was no longer competent 'to reply to letters addressed to him in such a capacity.' The letter went on about Rolfe,

He has chosen to go without food since Wednesday morning, solely for the purpose, I believe, of dropping down and creating a scene and a scandal, a mode of proceeding which I strongly disfavour.

We are not without food in the house, at present, as we have several times been during the 13 months you have boycotted us, and therefore I, finding no excuse for such conduct, dissent from it and wish to dissociate myself from any evil effects which may be caused by it.

The conclusion of this document reads, 'I would ask you to make a pastoral visit to him but could not guarantee you ordinary decent treatment.'[16] Hocheimer was penniless; his health and his wife's health had suffered. No doubt he had had enough of Rolfe's feud and Rolfe's histrionics. No doubt he would have welcomed peace. But he did not matter in this quarrel. It belonged to Beauclerk and Rolfe. Furthermore, the tone of tolerance for Rolfe and complicity with Beauclerk in that last sentence bred no good will for Hocheimer. The

priest offered peace not to Hocheimer but to Rolfe so that on 19 June
Rolfe replied with thanks and the suggestion that the priest draw up
the 'terms of the Treaty in accordance with precedent'.[17]

[ix]

Less than a month after that letter to Beauclerk offering him the
privilege of dictating the terms of peace, Rolfe had moved from 3
Bank Place, where a bailiff was 'making himself objectionable', to the
Hotel Victoria, 13 Victoria Square, Holywell. How he managed to find
a hotel keeper who would take him in is miraculous. He had had
money from time to time that spring. In April, he had offered payment
to Mrs. Richardson, who had refused it. On 2 May, Lane sent £10 for
the copyright of the six Toto tales, due to come out in book form in
September. But by late May, Rolfe was writing urgently to Frederic
Chapman, Lane's manager and literary consultant, for an advance on
a second lot of Toto stories. He was by then frantic for money which
was not forthcoming.[1] Yet Rolfe remained at the Hotel Victoria from
some time in July until the end of that year 1898, desperate and hungry.

At the Victoria, Rolfe anticipated nothing better than he had already
had in Holywell. Nor did he have it. On 24 June he had described his
existence of the past ten days to Chapman as one made up of 'tea, 4
lemons, one Hovis loaf', cigarettes, and complete silence. It was
typical, he told Chapman, of his way of life for the past fourteen
months,[2] as it would be for the next six. Rolfe did not tell Chapman
for obvious reasons that his cheerlessness was increased by the fact that
he was engaged in an occupation which he abhorred, what he called
the 'loathsome occupation of writing'.[3] Rolfe made clear that his
preference was art; but when he could not buy paints, then he wrote.
Of course, he laid the necessity for this hateful work at the door of
Father Beauclerk. 'You will not let me . . . earn my living in my own
way, persist in making me a writer against my will,' he told Beauclerk;
'you . . . have forced me into a position which I hate, and loathe, e.g.
Literature.'[4]

In spite of his distaste for authorship, calling himself as a writer a
monster created by Beauclerk, and in spite of every handicap and
hardship, the Holywell years forced Rolfe against his own judgement,
always poor in any case, to do what he did best. They made a writer of
him. He had come to Holywell with his Toto stories, six on paper and
ready for *The Yellow Book*, and ideas or plans in the form of notes,
abandoned to Lamb in Aberdeen to be sure, for forty-three others.[5] On
5 February 1898, Rolfe agreed to the publication of his six *Yellow Book*
stories as a Bodley Booklet; and four days later he directed John Lane,
the publisher of Bodley Head books, how to pay him the £10 offered

95

for all rights in the stories. On 29 May, Rolfe asked that his 'Toto Booklet' carry a dedication to the Earl of Rosebery, a request which was not carried out. Earlier that month, that is by 5 May, Rolfe had revised his six tales and started preparations for a second booklet. On that date he told Lane that, although he had been ill from hunger, he had completed a second series of seven Toto stories. Among them he valued most highly one which he designated as the 'Epic of Saint George', a tale published with the title 'Being a Rehabilitation of San Giorgio'. The longest of all Toto tales, Rolfe liked it particularly for the way in which Toto had commingled 'the complete Perseus myth, Danae, Our Lady of Wisdom, & the Casa Santa Croce'.[6] Lane and his adviser Chapman were less enthusiastic than Rolfe, but they refused to let him offer his new work to another publisher and they still planned to issue a second book of the Toto stories.[7] By 23 August, Rolfe had composed another series of five, although he had no paper on which to make fair copies and asked Lane to provide it. In less than a month the new manuscript was ready, written in a copy book which Lane had sent with a dozen penny stamps, all for Rolfe's use. A few days later he had his six author's copies of Stories Toto Told Me, the first collection of the tales, published 27 September 1898. On 11 October, Rolfe sent seventeen more stories, all for the second collection and all composed rapidly and under difficulties in his drab room at the Hotel Victoria.

Rolfe next produced a pamphlet called The Attack on St. Winefride's Well or Holywell Gone Mad. This pamphlet points out the folly of selling bottling rights to the water from the Saint's Well. Using statistics and thoughtful argument presented with his characteristic nervous vigour, Rolfe contends that Holywell's interest is best served by leaving Saint Winefride's Well to the Catholic mercy of Father Beauclerk. A first reading gives the impression that Rolfe's enmity toward Beauclerk must have abated, that he is defending Beauclerk. In fact the pamphlet reduces the priest in his exploitation of the Well to the level of a bottling works promoter. It attacks Holywell's Urban Council and Father Beauclerk equally for their commercialisation of the holy Well. In effect, it asks why Holywell cannot be satisfied with the profitable scheme it has, why it requires another merchandiser for the Well. The Attack on St. Winefride's Well, priced at 1d., was advertised as available from Hocheimer and the priest late in October or early in November.

Although he had started it earlier, Rolfe was also at work throughout the period in which he drudged to turn out The Holywell Record each month, on a book which in the 1890s he called 'Dom Gheraldo' but which he eventually gave the title Don Renato An Ideal Content. He first referred to it on 1 September 1897 as a translation which he had almost completed.[8] That is what the book purports to be, a translation of the recently discovered journal of an Italian priest Dom Gheraldo Pinarj in the service of a great Renaissance family of Rome. This

96

journal or 'diurnal' ends suddenly with an account of the marriage of the heir of the family, Don Renato, performed clandestinely by Dom Gheraldo. The narrative then proceeds through a letter from Don Renato to his father, whom he addresses as 'a Sacrilegious Murtherer and my most dear Father'. The last part is an epilogue supposedly from the pen of the translator; it tells of his discovery of an *oubliette* containing the skeleton of a priest with a gold-hilted dagger embedded in its skull. Later Rolfe described it as a 'book in XVI Century macaronics, Italian and English, amazing, pathetic, terrible, nonsensical, noble, real people and real events'.[9]

Rolfe's preoccupation in early 1897 with simulated translations is evident in three pieces which appeared in *The Holywell Record* that year, 'Little Petronilla in Paradise', 'Why the Ass Has Long Ears', and 'The Simplicity of Fra Innocent of the Nine Choirs'.[10] All are presented as translations from Italian by Vincenza, Duchess of Deira. The Duchess had no essential function, however, in the three tales. At most she enlivens *The Record*, so often dreary in its appeal to middle-class religiosity. Her practical use was to serve Rolfe as one of several pen names so that his authorship of so many pieces in so many issues of the periodical need not be oppressive. But as early as 1882, when he wrote the diary of a beetle for schoolboys, Rolfe had experimented in a crude way with writing in someone else's skin, relying solely on the narrator to tell his story and thereby expose his own character. The Toto stories are not told by Toto but by a narrator who describes Toto and repeats what the boy has to say. The narrator characterises himself as the Duchess of Deira does not, but his characterisation serves little purpose except shaping a frame for Toto's tales. In *Don Renato*, Rolfe returned to his earlier method, fully developed by 1897. The priest Dom Gheraldo gives an account of what happens as it happens to him; in doing so he demonstrates that he is vain, proud, a pedant in love with language. The shift to Don Renato is less successful, although it strikes a sombre tone suited to the contents. The Corvine spelling and contrived language make the book difficult to read, but they are a part of Rolfe's setting as well as of his characterisation of Dom Gheraldo.

That Rolfe was enlarging his capacity to look inward is nowhere more apparent than in another piece which he offered Lane for publication shortly before moving from Bank Place to Victoria Square. That is 'How I Was Buried Alive'. In it, Rolfe tells how he was buried alive after falling into a death-like trance and how he rescued himself from his coffin. He attributes this unlikely experience to a state induced when a small, grey lizard jumped into his jacket sleeve as he walked one morning near the Sforza Palazzo in Genzano. Acute sensitivity to reptiles was characteristic of Rolfe, who described himself as 'cataleptic in the presence of a snake'. John Holden testified to observing Rolfe in an encounter with a toad, when his reactions were

97

similar to those described in 'Buried Alive'.[11] Regardless of the truth behind the tale, it shows marked improvement over 'An Unforgettable Experience', his earlier piece having to do with premature burial. In 'An Unforgettable Experience' the question of mistaken certification of death is only one of ritual, of what priestly functions Father Serafico of that story can rightly perform. Premature burial is no more than a possibility and the whole series of events is observed from outside by Baron Corvo, who narrates them. In 'The Solitary Soul', written for *The Holywell Record*, Rolfe has moved from outside to inside experience. He makes no attempt in either of these pieces to investigate what death is, what it means. He is concerned with how it feels. In 'How I Was Buried Alive' he presents the sensations of collapse, coma, and interment. They are his own, and because they are they become harrowing adventures.

On 4 June 1898, saying that he had recently found it, Rolfe sent 'How I was Buried Alive' to Frederic Chapman of John Lane's Bodley Head. On 22 June, Rolfe wrote asking for a definite refusal or acceptance because the editor of *The Wide World Magazine* wanted the piece. Every article published in that magazine purported to recount an actual happening; so Rolfe also asked whether it was advisable to publish in a way which might make people stare at him. 'I mean', he wrote, 'is it advisable to get oneself known as a man who had been buried alive?'[12] That Chapman said publication in *The Wide World Magazine* would do no harm to his reputation as a man of letters, Rolfe communicated to Lane on 9 December 1898, adding about his piece that he thought its style, 'abominable'.[13] When he wrote that letter, 'How I Was Buried Alive' signed by Baron Corvo was already in print, having appeared in the November issue of *The Wide World Magazine*, and the last ordeal in Holywell for both Father Beauclerk and Rolfe had begun.

On 8 November 1898 the *Daily Free Press* of Aberdeen printed the first of three anonymous attacks on Rolfe in response to 'How I Was Buried Alive'. The two subsequent articles appeared on 12 November and 26 November. The first attack began by questioning the reliability of Louis de Rougemont's adventures, which had started as a serial in the August issue of *Wide World*. The attack then commented on 'another remarkable personage' and went on, 'The new writer tells a story of his experience with great minuteness but there are many experiences of his much more striking than the statements in the "Wide World Magazine," which it would be as well for the world to know.'[14] This article and the two which followed proceeded gleefully and scathingly to ridicule the title of Baron Corvo and to expose every aspect of Rolfe's shabby, unfortunate life. By the time the third instalment had appeared, his departure from Grantham Grammar School, his failure in Rome, his life at Christchurch, in London and in Aberdeen, including his stay with the Hays of Seaton, had been reviewed. Anecdotes from his residence in Aberdeen were set down;

letters written to Rolfe and letters written by him were quoted. There was enough truth in each article to give credence to its context, biased and libellous as it was. The last article quoted part of another account of Rolfe's vagaries from *To-Day*.[15] By Rolfe's count, the three pieces contained sixty libels.[16]

As the articles appeared, they were reprinted word for word in Aberdeen's *Evening Gazette*. On 18 November 1898, *The Catholic Times and Catholic Opinion* reprinted much of the attack made in the first two of the *Daily Free Press*'s articles. According to Rolfe, fifty-one 'false and malicious' libels were present and the total effect was to make him seem, as he said, a 'wastrel who hangs on to the skirts of religion or any thing else' by which he could get an easy living and his 'struggle with adversity as "piquant and amusing".'[17]

Who was responsible for the attack in the *Daily Free Press* which in turn provided impetus for the article in *To-Day* and the material for the article in *The Catholic Times*? The author or authors are still unknown. Various people have been named, such as the mysterious R of Champion's London household or some other member of his Aberdeen staff; Father David Hunter Blair, whom Rolfe first met en route to Oban; Father Patrick Green, whom Rolfe had known at the Scots College and in Aberdeen. Both Nancy Gleeson White, owing to Rolfe's rejections of her advances, and Miss Georgina Hay, aunt of Malcolm and Cuthbert Hay of Seaton, owing to her intense dislike of Rolfe, have been suggested. Either would answer Rolfe's statement that he detected in the articles the 'obscene touch of the female'.[18] Rolfe referred as well to a 'letter-thief' who engaged in 'job-journalism' and to the 'fine Roman hand of a pseudonymous editor', one of his own contemporaries at the Scots College, on whom he had bestowed a 'harmless jibe simply composed of the man's own initial and surname joined together'.[19] That description points to Patrick Green inasmuch as Rolfe had called him 'Peagreen' when they were both students in Rome. Nowhere else is there a description or allusion to any participants in the attacks which warrant even a tentative identification. Whoever the author of the three pieces may have been, he got most of his material for them from Rolfe's papers left in Christchurch and Aberdeen. Rolfe listed the abandoned papers in a letter to Edward Slaughter written from Holywell on 1 September 1897: 'an oak chest filled with papers' left with Gardner at Christchurch, 'a pocket book of papers' left with Wade at Aberdeen, and 'a dressing bag filled with papers' left with Lamb at Aberdeen.[20] That the author of the articles was in communication with the Lambs of 162 Skene Street, where Rolfe first lodged in Aberdeen, is apparent from the 12 November issue of the *Daily Free Press*. The article about Rolfe tells how its author showed Rolfe's picture, a photograph reproduced in *Wide World Magazine*, to Mrs. Lamb and how she exclaimed, 'Oh, the villain,' and dashed the periodical to the floor. In the same letter to

Slaughter, Rolfe had demonstrated that he needed £100 to redeem his goods. Shortly after the attack was concluded, that is on 10 December 1898, Rolfe reproached Beauclerk for denying him £100 in settlement for the painted banners. With £100, Rolfe said, he could have repossessed the three lots of abandoned papers and thus made impossible 'all the outrages' which had defiled him since. At the same time he referred to the persons behind the attack as 'criminals, clerical and lay', and declared that he could 'convict' them.[21] He mentioned no names.

Rolfe's letter of 10 December 1898 to Beauclerk was written in response to one from the priest which accompanied a copy of *The Catholic Times* for 12 November 1898. Beauclerk had evaded Rolfe's suggestion that he name the terms of their peace, made first on 18 June of that year and repeated on 25 July and 6 August. So Rolfe wrote on 17 August that he must conclude that peace negotiations had fallen through and that their relations were once more what they had been before 18 June. He offered Beauclerk the 'privilege of perusing' a manuscript copy of five new Toto stories in September; but by 7 October, Rolfe was again at war with Beauclerk, calling him a liar and renewing his accusations that the priest had barred him from the sacraments and wanted Rolfe's ruin. The insult of *The Attack on St. Winefride's Well* came next. This state of affairs, continuing throughout the autumn, was aggravated (if that was possible) by the fact that on 2 December Rolfe received a Judgment Summons for a bill owed to P. M. Evans for supplies bought toward the banners. Rolfe denied responsibility for the indebtedness. He said that he had incurred it on the priest's authorization and that he was prepared to spend his thirteenth Christmas as a Catholic in prison to 'slake' Beauclerk's 'thirst for revenge'.[22] Rolfe was therefore surprised and moved when he received a letter from Beauclerk on the morning of 10 December urging him to defend himself against the Aberdeen attacks. 'I beg it' and 'expect it', Beauclerk wrote, and he insisted that Rolfe's 'better self assert itself and this time never to go down'.

Rolfe at once sat down to write his answer. He stated first that illness and agitation prevented his giving Beauclerk's 'most affecting letter' the reply it merited, that he could speak only with 'unreserved plainness'. He admitted that he had considered legal action as a defence against the articles in the *Daily Free Press* but that he dreaded the 'hideous and most disgraceful scandal' which must follow his exposure of the Monsignori, Bishops, Archbishop, a Cardinal Archbishop, and Father Beauclerk, who had dragged him down and made him what he was. He declared his blamelessness before saying with eloquent and perfect truth:

> You (I use the plural) call me mad, rash incorrigible, proud, irreconcileable, deluded, and all the rest. But you must allow me to

100

lead my life upon that higher, and uncrowded plane where super-natural influences work unchecked, and where the aegis of the gods and the angels overshadows and protects the soul who wholly, purely, and always, trusts.

Rolfe's reply to Beauclerk's insistence that he 'put' himself 'straight with the world' ran:

What do I care for the world, that I should plane my prominences down to fit its narrow groove? Have you not realized yet that it is not an ordinary, but an extra-ordinary, man with whom you have to deal; and with whom not ordinary, but extra-ordinary methods must be used? Why assert myself before a mob which will not understand? Why waste my valuable time, like that; when I must slave, in body and mind, to win my daily bread?

Rolfe was back on familiar ground once more. Even in this letter he could not forbear castigating Father Beauclerk, and at last he came to the point where he laid all responsibility for his defence on Beauclerk. 'I shall take things as they come,' Rolfe wrote. 'I do not doubt that justice will be offered me, some day: and in the meantime, I shall remain the beastly spectacle I am, and do as I am doing now. I *under-go* that I may *over-come*.' Rolfe went on:

This is my mind at present. I think it is *your* duty to defend *me*. I am your black sheep. (You shall have the humour, as well as the pathos, of the situation.) You (plural), who have dragged me crooked, must put me straight with the world. I think, sadly and honestly, that you, Fr. Beauclerk, have been the chiefest sinner against me: and I think that if the expressions with which you have afflicted me today, are really and truly genuine, you will exert your-self with the other sinners to win me the honourable justice which you admit to be my due.

The letter assured Beauclerk that Rolfe prayed for him, his 'shepherd' who had trampled him 'in the mire'. And it ended with the statement that if he was forced to appear in court in the matter of indebtedness to Evans, he would not 'hesitate to court imprisonment', he would 'stick at no suffering now'.[23]

Only Monsignor James Dey came to Rolfe's defence. His letter protesting the injustice and inhumanity of attacking a man with his outworn follies, a man who was working against adversity to support himself as a writer, was printed in *The Catholic Times* of 16 December 1898, but it was mutilated to suit the paper's purposes. Printed with Dey's letter was another distorted letter, one which Rolfe had written to Beauclerk on 20 November. Rolfe accused the priest of making it available to *The Catholic Times* even as he was insisting that Rolfe deny its allegations.[24] Certainly as soon as he had the paper, Beauclerk sent it to Rolfe, urging him to defend himself. He replied at once with a prolonged defence of his own integrity, which he was determined to keep at any cost. He wrote that his vocation to the priesthood, which he still meant to follow, demanded it of him. He reproved Beauclerk for allowing their feud to thrive for nineteen months, for the 'outrages' done him in Beauclerk's 'secular character' and for charging him with an attack on Saint Winefride. Furthermore Rolfe disclaimed what Beauclerk wrote to him about the 'Catholic stand-point'. In his letter of 10 December addressed to the priest, Rolfe had maintained that he was a 'loyal son of Holy Mother Church'. He had recorded his 'perfect confidence in the judgment of the Church; and none whatever in judgments of individuals'. Now Rolfe made clear what was for him the Catholic standpoint and would be as long as he lived and as long as he had breath to declare that he found the 'Faith comfortable and eximious' but its 'professors utterly intolerable'. Rolfe wrote to Beauclerk,

> Where is the 'Catholic stand-point'? On those shifting sands where a venal mob thinks one thing and says another, and fears to act according to its conscience? Well, you may call that the 'Catholic standpoint'; but I never will.
>
> Holy Mother Church has given us rulers and governors who are invested with authority; and to that authority I will bow.

He ended with reiteration of what he had implied in his letter and said more than once to Beauclerk, 'You (plural) have made me what I am; and you can make another man of me whenever you please.'[25]

Rolfe was exhausted and beaten. The suit against him had been adjourned on 13 December, probably owing to Beauclerk.[26] Thanks to Rolfe's charges in the letter signed by Hocheimer and sent to the Father General of the Jesuits, Father Beauclerk was removed from his parish at Holywell at the end of 1898.[27] Rolfe maintained that the priest had 'competed for defeat' and lost.

If Rolfe won, it was at a terrible cost. Christmas brought no happiness or good will. Only two days before it, he asked W. E. Scott-Hall to visit him at Holywell, explaining that he was boycotted and excommunicated since May 1897, that he wanted a friend.[28] When the New Year came, Rolfe was penniless and in debt for his room at the Hotel Victoria. On 9 January 1899, Rolfe entered the Holywell workhouse. When John Holden saw a notice to that effect in some small journal, he thought that Rolfe was 'showing once more to what a miserable condition his enemies had brought him'.[29] Rolfe later confirmed Holden's opinion when he spoke of the workhouse as a desperate method of calling attention to Beauclerk's 'tyranny',[30] but he also said that he was 'stranded, naked, exhausted',[31] as indeed he was. Aberdeen had been transformed for Rolfe into a vast sounding board from which his ill-doing and ill deserts reverberated inexorably throughout England. He was broken in spirit and numbed in mind and body. The workhouse was the acme of his pain.

[x]

By his own request, Frederick Rolfe, Baron Corvo, was discharged from the Holywell workhouse on 3 February 1899. After breakfast he set out on foot. Over his blue cotton workman's suit, he wore a threadbare coat; his cap was pieced together from corduroy scraps, and on his feet he wore rope-soled canvas shoes.[1] These were poor protection against the winter weather of Northern Wales, and he had little relief as he trudged south. He was bound for Oxford and for the man who had come forward after the Aberdeen attack to assure him of friendship, Dr. E. G. Hardy, a former headmaster of Grantham Grammar School and in 1899 Tutor at Jesus College, Oxford.

Rolfe was also bound for a new career. He had, he said, drawn a 'sharp line' across his life owing to the 'series of libels' directed against him in the newspapers.[2] Forced to abandon his painting, his experiments with colour photography, and the invention of submarine photography, he was going on to something else. He meant now to devote himself to letters, to be a 'Romancer'. However much he hated writing, he meant now to write fiction within the definition of Charles Reade (Rolfe called him a 'master-romancer'), who had discussed fiction as 'a thing done, being merely another word for Fact'.[3]

Sharp line across his life or not, Rolfe still harboured resentment against Father Beauclerk. Beauclerk was responsible, Rolfe charged, for his 'acerbity' to Roman Catholics. Rolfe forgot that he had long held the 'Faith comfortable and the Faithful intolerable', that he had had only contempt for his 'invidious brothers in the Faith' at least since 1889, before he was dismissed from the Scots College. Thus he accused Beauclerk of souring the milk of human kindness in him and forcing him into the workhouse. Whether Rolfe had invited the difficulties with the priest, whether he had forced the priest into 'an attitude of antagonism' by demanding the impossible from him, or whether Beauclerk actually made 'certain conditional promises' and when Rolfe fulfilled the conditions and asked Beauclerk to honour his promises, he refused, Rolfe believed he had been betrayed. He may have brought himself to believe it, an easy procedure for Rolfe. His conviction that Beauclerk had acted against him never diminished. As late as 1905, Rolfe told Beauclerk,

You certainly did say very often, 'Your talent with pencil & pen will lift you out of your difficulties: all that is needed is a shelter

103

where you can work in peace.' But yet, you who were well-fed, well-clothed, well-housed, well-supported, unscrupulously abused your strength & your advantages to drive me, starving, naked, homeless, lonely, into the workhouse.[4]

Although he was willing, even eager, for Beauclerk to make amends, Rolfe was not moved to forgiveness. 'If my garden produces wormwood,' he told Beauclerk, 'it is because an enemy sowed the seeds among my lavender'.[5] Indeed, Rolfe's brooding on his wrongs at the hands of the priest nowhere fits with his concept of what is 'profitable' as well as comfortable to the soul; and that, he declared, was the only thing that mattered. He failed to follow his own precept: not to make 'one's wormishness a perennial and paramount consideration—and to take one's modern critical habit with one into sacred shrines, is to court . . . pain and dissatisfaction'.[6]

And so, after trudging the approximately one hundred and fifty miles from Holywell, Rolfe reached Oxford. He was too numb to feel that 'undying adoration of the sacred exuberant exquisite place'[7] which usually overcame him at Oxford. He was cold, dirty, hungry in body and spirit. But life was strong in him and he meant to do 'Ye nexte thynge'. From Hardy, Rolfe got a calm acceptance of his circumstances, a suit, and railway fare to London.

Part III
1899 – 1904

[i]

Rolfe went to London late in February. The first address he is known to have had there in 1899 for more than a few days was 69 Broadhurst Gardens, South Hampstead. He occupied an attic room eleven feet square under a slanting roof. The chief furnishings were a wooden washstand, a chest of drawers, a campbed, and a low shabbily upholstered armchair which was placed directly in front of the iron fireplace. Rolfe worked in the armchair. Wearing an eye-shade and large-lensed, silver spectacles, he sat there with his pen, 'the largest Waterman Ideal in the world',[1] poised over a supply of paper held at the top with a metal clip and placed on an old drawing-board which in turn was placed on his knees. When he raised his eyes, he had before him pictures of what he regarded as the most beautiful of God's creations, the nude young male. He had tacked a piece of brown wrapping paper over his mantel and on the paper pinned photographs of the Hermes of Herculaneum, Sebastian of South Kensington, two Davids, Donatello's and Verocchio's, 'Cellini's Perseys', and an unknown 'Rugger XV'. Stuck under the edges of the pictures were a cheap chromo of an 'olive-skinned black-haired cornflower crowned Pancratius',[2] and postcards and pages torn from magazines showing, among others, Andrea del Sarto's Saint John, Boucher's runners, and Friant's wrestlers.

Rolfe had come to these quarters thanks to Harry Bainbridge and Edward Slaughter. Rolfe's private pupil in 1886, Slaughter was now a solicitor with chambers in Arundel Street and rooms of his own at 69 Broadhurst Gardens. One August evening, having an errand to do when Rolfe visited him, Slaughter introduced Rolfe to Bainbridge, also a lodger at the same address, and asked him to look after Rolfe for an hour or so. Bainbridge, who worked with Dr. Ludwig at his White Lead Works, was playing Tchaikovsky on the piano, and at Rolfe's request he continued. Then, without knowing his guest as the author, Bainbridge talked enthusiastically about something he was reading, 'How I Was Buried Alive'. Rolfe confessed that he had written it. He was grateful to have the piece which had brought him so much pain valued by anyone, and he felt a warm liking for Bainbridge at once. In September, finding himself faced with homelessness and with Slaughter away from London, Rolfe wrote desperately to ask Bainbridge to take him in. The two men had already established some

107

sort of social exchange. They had in common a friend, William Henry Davis, a chartered accountant living at 2ᴬ Marlborough Road, Bedford Park, and Rolfe asked Bainbridge to send him there a pair of trousers. 'Man without trousers', Rolfe declared, 'is, after all, but a poor class of thing.' Besides, he had left a rosary with 'at least 5,000 years of indulgence attached to every bead' in a pocket of the trousers. As soon as Rolfe's plea for shelter reached him, Bainbridge arranged with his landlady, Mrs. Isabelle Griffiths, for Rolfe to occupy the attic room at 69 Broadhurst Gardens, and Rolfe moved in on 23 September 1899 as Bainbridge's guest.³ That he stayed was owing in part to the fact that Slaughter provided him with a small but regular sum to be returned as Rolfe was paid by his publishers.⁴ This was an arrangement reached no later than 5 March 1899, when Rolfe assigned £8 19s. due him from John Lane to Slaughter.

Nothing exists to show where or how Rolfe lived before going to Hampstead. In April he looked to Slaughter for money to 'satiate a ravening landlord',⁵ but he failed to identify the landlord. Rolfe's letters bear no address or else they show that they were written from the Reading Room of the British Museum, where he sometimes occupied seat B4. He asked for replies either to Slaughter or to John Lane. Perhaps Ella d'Arcy, a sub-editor of *The Yellow Book* whom Rolfe described as an 'intellectual mouse-mannered piece of sex', was correct when she said that he slept in doss houses or on the embankment and carried about with him his worldly possessions and his manuscripts in a portfolio.⁶ John Lane spoke of him as dirty when they first met and recalled Rolfe's carrying his possessions tied up in a coloured handkerchief.⁷ Rolfe pictured himself as shabby in an old brown-checked mackintosh which 'covered deficiencies' and concealed admirably a haversack containing his worldly goods, 'soap in a box, nail-brush, tooth-brush, sponge, a large Selvyt duster, three classics, and a MS. book'.⁸ On 13 March, not surprisingly, Rolfe said that he had been very ill. Surely by that time he had found some sanctuary in which to suffer, a place 'where he could agonise in secret anyhow',⁹ although it was no more than a decaying lodging house. He doubtless went from one to another, unnoticed unless he owed money.

Almost the first step Rolfe took in London, well before he moved in at 69 Broadhurst Gardens, was to visit John Lane, his publisher. Rolfe had contemplated this meeting for some time. In March 1898, he had written to say that he might be in London shortly and to ask whether Lane was 'visible anywhere'. Meanwhile, in September 1898, *Stories Toto Told Me* had appeared, and in October Rolfe had sent from Holywell a final lot of stories for a second Toto book. The fate of that book as well as the fact that he hoped to secure some kind of literary employment or a commission for another book were both an excuse and a reason for calling on Lane. The visit occurred on the morning of 27 February 1899, a Monday. Rolfe said that Lane, knowing his recent past and having published his first book, was curious about him. Rolfe declared that he, however, took no more interest in Lane than 'one takes in the chopper which one seizes at random for hewing out steps to fortune'.[10] Actually Rolfe was pleased to have found a man with enough critical sense to recognise genius when he saw it, and he was hopeful that in Lane he might also find an adviser, almost a collaborator, in the business of getting on. At the same time, he was wary of Lane; Rolfe was wary of anyone on whom he was dependent and to whom he had confessed that he needed money. He was conscious, too, of his worn shoes and his old macintosh, especially when he looked at Lane and saw a 'tubby little potbellied bantam, scrupulously attired and looking as though he had been suckled on bad beer'.[11] In his carefully modulated speech (he was proud of his speech and his voice, which was 'low and minor, sometimes E♭ minor'), Rolfe explained his purpose and his predicament and attempted to get a commitment from Lane for the new Toto stories. Lane was reluctant to come to terms for the book, but he finally agreed to do so the next day. He had nothing to offer in the way of employment. After suggesting other publishers from whom Rolfe might seek work, Lane sent him on his way with a sovereign to put in his pocket. Lane always regretted that sovereign; he called himself a fool, long after Rolfe was dead, for giving it. As for Rolfe, frustrated and enraged, his first impulse as he came onto the street was to fling the coin into the gutter. But he remembered that he had been paid less than he was promised for a piece in Lane's *Yellow Book*, and he pocketed the sovereign.[12]

At Lane's urging, Rolfe went at once from the office on Vigo Street, 'bus-wise', to call on Henry Harland, who had been the literary editor of *The Yellow Book*, at his flat in Cromwell Road. Harland claimed to have been born in St. Petersburg and to have been educated in Rome and Paris. Eventually he gave himself aristocratic English parents. In fact he was born in New York of parents from Connecticut. He studied briefly in Paris and at the Harvard Divinity School. Then he turned to authorship, and in America he had considerable success as a novelist writing under the pseudonym Sidney Luska about the life of poor Jewish immigrants in New York City. These novels were applauded as realistic depictions written by a Jew. When Harland's pretence was exposed, he moved to Paris and in 1889 to London, arriving with an impeccable introduction to Henry James. Harland thereafter became a Jamesian stylist and a part of the aesthetic movement. With Aubrey Beardsley, he had planned some version of *The Yellow Book*, and those two with John Lane had produced the 'small square lemon-coloured quarterly' from 1894 to 1897, publishing some of the best prose, poetry, and graphic art than current in England. As 'The Yellow Dwarf', Harland had published comments in it on writers and writing, among them Rolfe and his stories. Although in 1899, Harland was already ill with the tuberculosis which was to end his life in 1905 at the age of forty-four, he was a man of great energy, great editorial ability and real charm, especially for women. Rolfe, who had read Harland's novels of New York and his latest book, *A Latin Quarter Courtship and Other Stories*, regarded him with anti-Semitic disdain, thinking Harland an apostate Jew; but Rolfe went to meet him willingly because he intended for Harland to help fulfil his literary ambitions. At this first meeting, Harland was elegantly dressed, and both he and Rolfe were aware of the contrast with the visitor's soiled and frayed clothing and his thin, unkempt beard and hair. Rolfe talked matter-of-factly about his recent stay in the Holywell workhouse and he listened to Harland's 'amazingly witty, pleasant, ephemeral, and insincere'[13] conversation and he ate Harland's eggs and bacon for his lunch and after some protests he accepted a sovereign from Harland against the same sum owed him for a Toto story. Rolfe admitted that he enjoyed the visit, especially when Harland remarked that the new Toto stories would bring him £700 in six months.

The next morning Lane and Rolfe concluded arrangements for the second collection of Toto's tales. Although he had written and re-written that book in order to make it a 'perfect work of art', he agreed to further revision and some additions. Lane then offered Rolfe £20, £10 at once and £10 less the sovereign given him the day before and the twelve penny stamps sent him in Holywell on publication. It was a mean, bitterly disappointing offer. Of course Lane was an imaginative, innovative, courageous publisher. He recognised ability where no other publisher could see it so that his Bodley Head had on its lists at one time or another nearly every writer and illustrator of importance in the decade of the nineties. He made or helped make reputations for Kenneth Grahame, Arnold Bennett, Max Beerbohm, Aubrey Beardsley, Will Rothenstein, and William Strang to name a very few. Lane seemed an ideal publisher to many, but others, Gertrude Atherton and Alfred Douglas among them, despised him. Rolfe knew that Lane was taking advantage of him, but he had no alternative but to accept, although he insisted on being paid in guineas. He needed the £10 and he could assign the amount still owing to Slaughter in return for immediate cash. Furthermore his gifts of which he was 'by no means unconscious' impelled him to accept Lane's offer; it meant to Rolfe that even with such a 'snivelling little swindler' for a publisher[14] he was getting on with his literary career.

Rolfe now had a contract with Lane and he had decided to let Harland be useful. That was progress. Rolfe hoped he was enlarging his prospects when he made the acquaintance of Grant Richards, a publisher younger than Lane but certainly as energetic and as reluctant as Lane to pay for what he got. Alfred Douglas maintained that Rolfe could not have found any two publishers who were less likely to treat him fairly. He characterised Lane as a 'mean little brute' and declared that Richards, although 'personally a decent fellow' was hopeless as a publisher.[15] Rolfe's connection with Richards began badly. At first sight, Rolfe thought Richards ludicrous, a 'scorbutic hobbledehoy', a 'strenuous stripling in a spotty plush waistcoat' who conscientiously split his infinitives. Richards had heard gossip about Rolfe, especially in respect to Nancy Gleeson White, now living with her husband in London. Richards had the talk from Isaac Henry Soloman Isaacs, Richard's manager who later changed his name to Temple Scott. He was an ugly man—Rolfe described him as a 'broad-nosed dough-faced dwarf' whose large head was thinly covered with 'woolly hair'—but he was an astute publisher and Richards thought him a genius.[16] Before coming to Richards, Isaacs had worked for George Bell & Son, and there he had heard from Mrs. Arthur Bell about Baron Corvo's progression through Christchurch. Out of loyalty to his friend Gleeson White, Richards confronted Rolfe with what he had been told and Rolfe, on 6 April 1899, wrote a 'Categorical denial' of the 'ridiculous stories' and urged Richards to give 'unprejudiced consideration' to his literary productions as became a publisher.[17]

Rolfe was contriving articles and stories and proposals for articles which he offered first to Lane and usually, when Lane proved disinterested, to Richards. Before 5 March, Rolfe offered to translate a work of 'Cheiromancy' and the commentaries of the fifteenth-century pope Pius II or Enea Silvio de' Piccolomini for Lane to publish.[18] Rolfe sent a number of manuscripts to Richards, asking him to place them wherever he could. None was printed. But on 2 April 1899, Rolfe's article entitled 'When the Pope Dies: Marvellous Description Written . . . from Intimate Knowledge of the Proceedings, by a High Catholic Authority' appeared in the Sunday magazine section of Joseph Pulitzer's New York World. Rolfe produced six or more special articles for the World, including one on the Dreyfus affair, a timely subject in the year of Dreyfus's second court martial. Only the article on the Papal Conclaves was published.[19] On the strength of its appearance, he asked Grant Richards to make the editor of The St. James's Gazette aware that Rolfe could supply endless comments 'De Papismo'.[20] From Lane, Rolfe tried to get a travelling commission which would take him for a year to Persia or Sicily or Calabria or the East Coast of Italy; wherever he went, Rolfe promised to find much to photograph and to write about from a 'richly interesting point of view',[21] all to Lane's profit.

Rolfe was still reworking the book sent incomplete to Lane the year before, Don Renato, and sending it to one publisher after another, but his only success seemed to come from the Toto stories. By mid-June, he had finished three more. On the basis of these three, he managed to sell a set of seven to Grant Richards for his recently acquired Butterfly Magazine.[22] On June 19, Rolfe offered the book rights for the seven—four were still unwritten—to John Lane, asking for an immediate

111

reply to the Hogarth Club on Bond Street. 'Being rather pressed for cash', Rolfe wanted to take them back to Richards at once if Lane was not interested. The first of these stories, 'About What is Due to Repentance', appeared in the August issue of *The Butterfly*, which paid Rolfe £3 10s. and then changed hands without publishing another of his pieces. That one tale with the title 'About What is Due to Contrition' was added to the second Toto book.

That book was Rolfe's main consideration. From the time of his first meeting with Lane, Rolfe had been revising and rewriting the twenty-four stories which make it up. He worked on them in the 'green glades' of Kensington Gardens in summer. But by 19 September, he still had three stories to prepare and he was frantic because he had no place in which to work or even to sleep. He was briefly the guest of William Henry Davis in his flat at 2ᴬ Marlborough Road; but Davis expected other visitors in a few days. With Slaughter away from London, Rolfe asked Bainbridge to invite him to 69 Broadhurst Gardens. Rolfe explained that he was 'stony broke' and thus could go nowhere and that he must finish his book without delay. 'I only want to shut myself up in a bedroom and write AND WRITE, eating bread and butter and drinking milk' because he could do more work that way, Rolfe said.[23] And so, on 23 September, he went to live at Hampstead and thus he was at last enabled to deliver his finished Toto stories to Lane six days later.

[ii]

Although Rolfe complained of being 'shabby, nervous, and flabby', he could not, for once, complain of lacking an arm to lean on when he needed it, of going in terror that he could not manage to live without such support. Bainbridge had given him prompt and friendly help. More important, within the next few weeks Rolfe had the offer of a commission; Grant Richards asked him to write a book on the House of Borgia. Rolfe preferred the thirteenth century, the 'greatest Century'—or so he said and pointed to his 'Sestina yn Honour of Lytel Seynt Hew' as proof—but he recognised that the fifteenth had more in it and that it contained 'mines of the most delicious stories in the world'.[1] On 20 November 1899, Rolfe agreed to write the history of the Borgias on Richards's terms, £1 a week while he wrote the book which was due, completed, in July. On publication Rolfe was to receive an additional £10.[2]

Rolfe immediately began research for the book, spending day after day from early morning until the hour of closing at the British Museum. By 9 December, he could promise that if he survived the

Borgia book would be a great one. Survival was not easy. As he told Richards, he 'could die but not live'[3] on £1 a week. Rolfe got through the first week by ignoring dinner, but by the end of February, he was forced to ask Richards to increase the weekly allotment to 30s., the additional 10s. to come from the amount payable on publication.[4] Meanwhile, although he missed the help of 'an interchange of conversation' with Richards, Rolfe reported on 27 February from Oxford that the Borgias' history was progressing. He gave much care to making a genealogical tree of the Borgias, choosing illustrations, and arrang-- ing for casts of medals; but he was also busily writing the history, which he likened to 'swimming in strange waters'.[5] In mid-May, he assured his publisher that 'La Borgiada' would be ready at the time stipulated, the end of July. At the same time, Rolfe outlined the book:

Book I The Kindling of the Fire (Calixtus), Book II The Furious Flame (Alexander), Book III The Steady Light (St. Francis) . . . with their accessories of *Fuel, Sparks,* and *Embers* . . . and Book IIII The Final Flicker (Stefano) with its *Ashes.*[6]

Six weeks later, again in Oxford, Rolfe called the book 'a bit of a wonder' but thought he might want it published without his name. He explained that his long seclusion had affected his nerves so that he shunned publicity; he was 'sick of the world and tired out'.[7]

Certainly from November, when he began the Borgia book, Rolfe had a grim lonely life. He was a member, as John Lane was, of the Hogarth Club at 175 Bond Street, a meeting place for the aesthetes of the nineties, whether writers, painters, or publishers. But Rolfe had no associations with them. He used the club for letter writing and for collecting letters sent to him there. At no time did he participate in the conviviality of those who gathered at 'Jimmy's'—the St. James Restaurant—for oysters (which he loathed) and kidneys or in the late night talk and exchange of ideas over hot gin and water which took place on the settees of The Crown, a pub in Charing Cross Road near Cranbourn Street. In 1899 and thereabouts, it was a favourite of Richards and Lane and a number of other men with whom Rolfe might have had much in common: Hubert Crackanthorpe, Beardsley, Robbie Ross, John Gray, Beerbohm, Rothenstein and Conder, Theodore Wratislaw, and even Baron Corvo's old friend Kains Jackson. But Rolfe was not a companionable man. He took friendship too seriously to show himself friendly or to indulge in the easy give and take of joviality. He was shabby and suspicious and demanding. No one invited him to join such a circle.

Rolfe was welcome, however, at Henry and Aline Harland's parties at their flat in Cromwell Road. Ella d'Arcy relegated him solely to the afternoon receptions which, she said, were 'to the evenings what the Luxembourg is to the Louvre', and she recalled him as a 'disquieting creature who wrote disquieting tales' and left 'singularly lively traces

113

of his presence in Harland's armchairs'.[8] Rolfe describes one such party with significant differences. He tells how Harland 'skipped and hovered and sat on his hind leg everywhere, like a cricket, a bluebottle, a toad clickety-clacking, buzzing, and rarely dumb'. Rolfe, on the other hand, was silent but watchful as he drank his tea and ate his farthing bun. At length he brought out the manuscript of 'About What is Due to Repentance', and Harland read it aloud to his guests. An American visitor, Arthur Stedman, was as much impressed with the story as Rolfe, who particularly admired his own description of a storm at the start of the tale. Stedman, a literary agent, asked for a copy to take back to New York, and Mrs. Harland detained Rolfe at the end of the party when both she and her husband offered him encouragement and sympathy. But Rolfe felt uneasy with the Harlands and most of their friends. And before long he offended W. J. Fisher, editor of the *Daily Chronicle*, by inquiring whether 'historical accuracy came within the scope of a Radical periodical' and offering to correct the *Chronicle's* account of the 'case of the Dreyfus Parallel'.[9] In any event, nothing came of the Harlands' gestures except poor advice and empty promises.

What Rolfe wanted was work of a literary kind. Instead he got an active social life. There were invitations to dinners with the Harlands and with James Hannay, editor of the *Daily Telegraph*, and his wife, Margaret. Ethel Reid's mother had him to dine and then took him to her Chelsea flat, where he saw Miss Reid's work in *art nouveau*. Rolfe had tea at least once with John Lane at 37 Southwick Street in 'barbaric Bayswater', having first had 'his head and hands groomed and his face made by Clarkson', theatrical costumier, in order to simulate 'elegant negligence'.[10] Occasionally, Rolfe invaded the Queen's Theatre, a favourite of London homosexuals whose preferred ticket was for standing room in the balcony.

Most of that social activity stopped when Rolfe undertook the Borgia book in November. He became a recluse, shutting up his 'grim air and sensitive longing soul' in his room at 69 Broadhurst Gardens. In February 1900, he began a long series of twice-yearly journeys to Oxford, where he stayed at Jesus College with Hardy, once Rolfe's headmaster at Grantham Grammar School. In return for room and board and a modest fee, Rolfe read papers for Hardy, who suffered from glaucoma. But even there, Rolfe devoted nearly every minute not given to Hardy to his own work. In London, except for visits to the British Museum and the Victoria and Albert, Rolfe rarely left his attic room. He sat smoking his pipe or innumerable long, fat cigarettes which he made himself and he worked. Almost his only recreation was exercising with dumbbells. His custom was to strip (he admired his body for its boyish slenderness, its firm muscular whiteness) and, taking a pair of ten-pound dumbbells, to sweep them overhead with both arms together or to swing them right and left as he swayed from the hips.[11] He was too busy to go to Vigo Street to confer with John

Lane about the production of the second Toto book. Although he had one or two ideas about the colour of the cloth for the binding and the style of lettering on the cover, he declared himself willing to leave all technical matters to Lane's 'good taste'. Rolfe was unable to call or to undergo the 'ordeal of a discussion', he told Lane, because he was 'engaged all day on some special work'.[12] He stopped it only long enough to send drawings to Lane intended for the title page and colophon and to agree that Lane might include the first six Toto stories in the new book as long as those six were 'incommunicably separated from the Twenty-six'.[13]

To add to his enforced isolation and his demanding work, Rolfe accepted a commission from Lane to translate the *Rubáiyát* from the French of J. B. Nicolas. Isaac Isaacs, now calling himself Temple Scott by deed poll, had moved from Grant Richards to Lane's Bodley Head, and Scott suggested the translation to his new employer. When Harland and Kenneth Grahame supported the suggestion,[14] Lane made an offer of £25 for the translation to be delivered in May for July publication. The project seemed impracticable in view of the earlier commitment to Richards, but Rolfe accepted. His French, self-taught, was adequate; he needed the £25, and Lane had said in a hearty and unguarded moment that he intended to make Rolfe a 'commercial success' as he was already an 'artistic success'.

Rolfe somehow found time to get to his new task at once. He began with almost a literal translation lacking grace in both language and rhythm. Nicolas's first quatrain reads:

Un matin, j'entendis venir de notre taverne une voix qui disait: A moi, joyeux buveurs, jeunes fous! levez vous, et venez remplir encore une coupe de vin, avant que le destin vienne remplir celle de notre existence.

An early version of Rolfe's translation, since discarded, runs:

One morning, I heard issuant from a tavern a Voice which cried: Hither joyous sots and merry youths! awake, and fill yet one new cup of wine, before that fate shall cause life's cup to brim.

Rolfe had placed the translation of each quatrain, carefully numbered, on a separate sheet of paper about 4½ by 5½ inches; working with each sheet without regard to numerical order, he polished and ornamented his flat, 'too bald' rendering of Nicolas first by using words of his own invention, eventually described as 'Greek idioms'. It was a predilection which Rolfe indulged in the composition of *Don Renato* as he revised and extended it over and over. A comparable vocabulary might be expected in the book on the Borgias since its composition occurred at the same time. To what extent his publisher was responsible for the absence of such language in that book is impossible to ascertain. Richards' reader objected to the style and Rolfe objected to

115

the reader; nevertheless Rolfe revised as he was asked to do.[15] But Rolfe took seriously his obligation of 'inherent probability' as an historian and sooner or later suited his language to it rather than to a 'kopriematose imagination'. In his translation of 'Umar, however, he relied heavily on such constructions as occur in the opening lines, 'philopots' and 'hybrist'. Furthermore, he took much pride in them. He wrote to Temple Scott:

> I have invented a new set of English words expressing the Persian idea *via* the Greek language, strictly following philological rule, so that, though these words hit you in the eye, they strike a spark of intelligence in the brain *instanter*. Anyone can see the meaning of Hybristick... the epithet applied by Homer to the suitors of Penelope —rude and tipsy and libidinous and gay and young—wanton, but a much more pregnant word.[16]

In Rolfe's view, such inventions served perfectly to condense his early version and to concentrate his meaning without diminishing the metaphorical possibilities. His final version of that first stanza runs:

> Lo, Phosphor! And a Voice from the Tavern crieth, Enter, hilarious Philopots, hybrist Youths; enter and fill yet one more Cup of Wine, before that Fate shall fill brimful your Cup of Life.[17]

Of the two possibilities, that 'Umar was a philosopher and mystic or a voluptuary, Rolfe chose the second. Nicolas insisted that 'Umar was god-intoxicated and added a note to say so where his translation could not bear him out. Rolfe, in love with language and ornament, infused eager sensuality into his translation, making it to a large extent a paean to wine and homosexuality. He completed the translation, as agreed, in May. On 22 May, he asked for payment of £13 still owed him, and the next day he acknowledged receipt of that amount and sent his manuscript to Frederic Chapman, Lane's associate.[18]

While Rolfe was putting the final touches to his translation of 'Umar's quatrains and preparing a fair copy, he experienced the one real happiness of this desolate time. His misconception of excommunication was corrected and the religious rites restored to him. His distress at his supposed state was so patent that Edward Slaughter make it known to his cousin Dr. Mostyn, in 1900 Bishop of Menevia, and arranged a meeting late in April between him and Rolfe. Rolfe wrote a detailed account of it in a letter to Temple Scott in which he described Mostyn as 'too fat to be a wicked man, and just fat enough to be stolid'. The Bishop came to 69 Broadhurst Gardens and received Rolfe in the parlour, allowing him to kiss the apostolic ring. Apparently Mostyn had no idea of the 'wrong' from which Rolfe suffered; his letters sent over a three-year period had made no impression on the Bishop. But when Rolfe made his distress plain to Mostyn, he was horrified and quickly declared that he had pronounced no sentence

116

of excommunication nor had Rolfe incurred 'the excommunication *latae sententiae.*' Mostyn offered to restore the Sacraments. Rolfe said he wanted no fuss but since he had been degraded publicly he wanted the Bishop to restore them and tell the Cardinal, after arranging the matter with the Archbishop. The next morning, Mostyn heard Rolfe's confession for three years and set him 'straight again'.[19] He wrote soon after to tell Grant Richards that the Bishop of Menevia had acted of his 'own volition'.[20] Almost as satisfying was his conviction that his campaign against Beauclerk had good and sufficient cause; during their talk, Mostyn had spoken of Rolfe as 'really very good' and 'hideously maligned'. He reported the fact with great pride to Chapman.[21]

As he wrote that letter to Chapman, Rolfe was within a day or two of ending his second stay in 1900 with Hardy at Jesus College, Oxford. He told Chapman that no one but a fool could be anything but happy at Oxford 'when the weather is weather'. But Rolfe had no time for happiness. At seven each morning he swam 'coldly' at Parson's Pleasure to be fresh for his work. From 9·30 in the morning until 11·30 at night he was occupied with Hardy's examination papers and his Borgiada. 'After that,' he declared, 'I am as limp as any rag and fall on sleep.'

Rolfe was also within less than three weeks of ending his work on his chronicles of the Borgias for Grant Richards and much concerned about his future. 'You may take it', Rolfe wrote to Chapman in the same letter, one dated 12 July 1900, 'that at the end of the week I shall be homeless and penniless again.' A week later, he told Richards much the same thing. 'I have nothing else in the way of income save this,' he wrote in reference to the Borgia book and said that when he delivered the manuscript he would be without home or income unless, he added, he could be 'started on fresh work immediately'.[22] Temple Scott, in New York as the representative of Lane's Bodley Head, had given Rolfe an order for a story, but he said that with no place to work, he could hardly write it.[23] Rolfe's complaint about lack of a home was untrue; he could go back to 69 Broadhurst Gardens. In any case his attempt to elicit sympathy or help from Richards or Lane was unrealistic. He had already tried to interest first one and then the other in a translation he proposed to make of a book encountered in working on the Borgias, a 'wondrous little treatise in French' *La Procès des Borgias* by René, Conte de Maricourt. Rolfe declared that the publication of his own book must create a 'Borgia Boom' which the translation would intensify.[24] Failing that and still in Oxford, Rolfe thought he would like to stay and enlarge 'Don Gheraldo'—later *Don Renato*—to four times its present bulk with the idea that Doubleday in America might take it. Then Rolfe presented a number of new subjects to Grant Richards, hoping that one of these might secure another commission. 'I quite understand', he wrote, 'that I am on my

Trial with the Borgiada.' He said that it could not have been done better under the circumstances, but that he could and would do better with better things. He was anxious to hear favourably from Richards as quickly as possible to avoid having 'to be recovered from ills due to delay'.[25]

By August, Rolfe was looking elsewhere. Kenneth Grahame had read the manuscript of 'Toto Maidalchini's Folklore' and praised it. Having heard this fact, Rolfe asked for Grahame's influence to get permanent literary work, a post as reader, reviewer, literary adviser, or descriptive reporter in a place such as Persia—anything which would provide a regular income while he wrote long works. Rolfe had in mind critical and standard histories of several Italian families based on their archives, another set of seventeen stories from Toto, and the book of Don Gheraldo Pinarii. He was still in correspondence with Grahame after an interview with the firm of Smith Elder in late December. Rolfe wrote to say that at Smith Elder's suggestion he was asking Richards to lend them the manuscript of the Borgias' history although he was sure Richards would refuse. Rolfe could only conclude, 'And so the matter stands.'[26]

[iii]

By December 1900, Rolfe was on the verge of a number of quarrels. Rolfe had not yet met two of his antagonists and one was inconsequential, but by December he was none too happy with John Lane and Eddie Slaughter, and he was moving rapidly towards a dispute with Grant Richards. No later than 1900, Rolfe had come to live his life in predictable patterns. Perhaps all men do. In Rolfe's case, he had made the two enduring changes from Protestant to Catholic and from painter to writer; little more in the way of change could fairly be expected of him. His behaviour in certain given situations, no matter how often they recurred, was almost invariable by 1900. One had to do with his demands and expectations from whoever kept the house in which he lodged. Whether it was Gardner in Christchurch, the Lambs in Aberdeen, Mrs. Griffiths now in Hampstead, or several hotel keepers later in Venice, Rolfe varied his actions hardly at all. Another was the inevitability and progression of his quarrels. They were so nearly a part of his personal and professional relations that they could be charted well in advance. 'I am clever, I am charming,' he said of himself, 'but I can't make friends or keep them because I have not the means to show myself friendly.'[1] He might more accurately have said because his notion of friendship and the claims he made on it on any level of intimacy were preposterous in an adult world. Rolfe began

118

each one more or less with a manly, reciprocal association. He soon confessed his problems and gradually expected to be the focus of the relationship because of them and to have sympathetic help in dealing with them. The help had to be on his own terms; if it deviated one iota, he found insult, neglect, enmity, or all three. He then retaliated in the form of letters filled with his masterly invective. Of course, Rolfe was not always at fault, nor was he always faultless. He was simply unwise and impractical and thus unfortunate. His retaliatory letters, so lethal in his view, devastated only himself and advanced his cause not at all.

Rolfe's difficulties with Richards began with the first reader's report on the Borgia book, made in September. Rolfe was already disturbed that Richards had not even acknowledged receipt of the subjects submitted to him for another commission. When Rolfe had the first report, he was ill with a 'violent lung-attack'; but the next day he conferred with Richards and went back to Broadhurst Gardens to tell Richards by letter that only Richard Garnett and Mandell Creighton were fit judges of *Chronicles of The House of Borgia*. 'It is crammed with items to make to think,' he wrote. 'It is a book from which one can *learn*, not an Aunt Sally.' He went on to express his fear of reducing the book to mediocrity and thus ensuring its failure. His evaluation of his book continued: 'As it stands, it is striking, fresh, original in point of view, with a touch of satire, but inspired with the highest broadest and noblest morality.'[2] Within two days, he had the second report and at once was writing to protest that he had taken care in planning 'a method, & a style of writing'. He assumed that he had got the commission because Richards liked his previous work and now could not understand why the publisher endorsed the reader's description of the style as loose and clumsy and the spelling, incorrect. Rolfe promised, however, that the entire book would be 'recopied, revised, and gelded' on condition that it be published without his name. He was willing to be held responsible only for works of which he approved, 'things quaint or curious, and distinguishable from the works of the million'.[3]

As he had promised, Rolfe revised *Chronicles of The House of Borgia*, condensing some parts and expanding others, modernising the spelling and expurgating everything ' "lewd," "improper," and "frank".' One section of that nature which caused considerable animosity between publisher and author was a passage quoted from Benedetto Varchi, a sixteenth-century Florentine, contained in the third of Rolfe's seven appendices. Appendix III, entitled 'A Suggested Criterion of the Credibility of Historians', refuted charges of homosexuality made against various Borgias by several historians of the Renaissance, among them Varchi. The question at first was only 'the tearing-out' of Varchi's statement, quoted in Italian. Rolfe urged that it be kept, but he left the final decision to Richards, who decided to omit not only Varchi but the entire Appendix III as well. Rolfe knew that Richards could not read Varchi and accused him of accepting a faulty translation and then charging Rolfe with lewdness in a 'graphic account of a bishop raping a boy'.[4]

The revisions were done by 12 November 1900, and by that date Rolfe's resentment vanished briefly. Only that week he had got in touch with Count Cesare Borgia and as a result had access to new and unexpected materials which he was eager to add to the book. Rolfe could now correct a number of errors, add documents heretofore unpublished, reconstitute the genealogy of the Borgias, and increase the last part of the book by 10,000 words. This he would do for 260 guineas and allow the name Frederick Baron Corvo to appear as author.[5]

When Richards failed to take up his offer, Rolfe attempted to borrow the manuscript and arrange publication elsewhere. If he could do so, he promised to give back to Richards the amount already paid for the book. Rolfe appealed to Mostyn, Bishop of Menevia, and he in turn asked David Hunter-Blair to help. In 1901, Hunter-Blair was Master of the Benedictine Hall at Oxford University. He arranged for the Royal Historical Society to consider the Borgia book; but something about the proceedings aroused Rolfe's rancour, and he began to hurl his finest invective at Hunter-Blair.[6] Meanwhile, Rolfe had managed to interest Smith Elder in the Borgias.[7]

Richards, however, was unwilling to let Rolfe peddle the manuscript about; and so the bickering and wrangling went on while *Chronicles of The House of Borgia* was prepared for publication. Richards preferred to discuss problems at his office as they arose, and Rolfe preferred to resort to letters. Richards, the epicure, invited Rolfe to lunch at Romano's. Rolfe refused the invitation; he had given up lunches so that they could not 'clog his mental machinery'. Rolfe had lent Richards a coin, a rose-giulio, in order to include a picture of it in the Borgia book, and Rolfe was annoyed at not getting it back promptly. The date for publication was another bone of contention. The two men quarrelled about literary agents, advertisements, money, and proof-reading. But at last, in October 1901, Richards published *Chronicles of The House of Borgia* with the name of the author, Frederick Baron Corvo, on the title page. E. P. Dutton & Co. issued the book in New York on 23 November 1901.

Rolfe continued to find fault with Grant Richards. His delay in sending the author's copies was a cause for displeasure. When they reached him, Rolfe complained that they were mutilated and too few in number.[8] Particularly exasperating to Rolfe were letters sent to him in care of Richards. Rolfe had given instructions that the publisher's office was to forward no letters to him under any circumstances; everything addressed to him was to be returned to the post office. Yet Richards's office refused some letters and sent others on to Rolfe. He protested with increasing vehemence, but still the letters came. Finally, when his patience was at an end and his sufferance of all things tried by the fact that his father lay fatally ill at 5 Highbury Hill, Rolfe received another letter, a message urging him to hurry to Highbury Hill, forwarded from Richards's office. He then turned his fury on Grant Richards; writing from Hampstead on 4 March 1902, Rolfe said:

> Now that fate has given you an insight into my private affairs, let me tell you that it is your malfeasance which has added two years to the seven during which I have been exiled from my parents; and, if the summons which you now send is from my father's death-bed, I intend to hold you personally responsible for his death and my own despair.
>
> By all, to whom I name your name, you are despised and hated: but I doubt whether you ever have made a more ruthless or persequent enemy.[9]

In the midst of his difficulties with Richards, Rolfe's arrangements with Edward Slaughter came to an end. During his stay in Oxford in July 1900, Rolfe had questioned their disorder. Apparently that problem was resolved because in August Rolfe gave his address as care of Slaughter at Broadhurst Gardens and in October he consulted a doctor, Hugh H. Roger-Smith of 1 Cottage Terrace, Hampstead, recommended by Slaughter. As Rolfe's adviser, he participated in the skirmishes with Richards, but Slaughter had his feelings hurt by an anonymous letter from the publisher's office and he tired of the long wrangle. Thereupon Rolfe denounced Slaughter as a false friend 'unable to stand through storm' and 'stripped his selfishness naked',[10] and months later Rolfe was still watching for an 'opportunity to smash him'.[11] Almost immediately after their quarrel, Slaughter left Broadhurst Gardens and England, sailing for South Africa as an Imperial Yeoman in the Boer War. He had not gone when Rolfe gave an account of their conflict to Richards in a letter dated 6 March 1901. Rolfe wrote of Slaughter's 'perridiculous mismanagement' and the abuse of confidence by a 'stupid and dishonourable Roman Catholic'. He blamed Richards's inclination to negotiate through Slaughter and 'that pious deceiver's perfervid protestations' that Rolfe was a 'promising speculation' for submitting, against his own judgement, to Slaughter. Rolfe compared himself with wheat between two grindstones and finished by saying that he had had his last transaction with the 'Slaughter gang' and with Roman Catholics generally and that henceforth he was managing his own affairs.[12]

On the day before Rolfe wrote the letter disavowing Slaughter, that is on 5 March 1901, Lane published the second book of Toto's tales under the title *In His Own Image*. It was not the title Rolfe wanted, and he persisted in thinking it meaningless and blasphemous. Rolfe preferred 'A Sensational Atomist', a term in logic meaning 'one to whom all knowledge is atoms received by the senses'; he considered it 'catchy'

121

and exactly descriptive and he opposed it to Lane's suggestions, 'Mortal Immortals' and 'All the Company.' For a time Rolfe deliberated over withholding his name from this book to which he was not allowed to give a title. At last, however, he was forced to yield to his circumstances and accept Lane's 'In His Own Image'. He consoled himself with the notion that the title was a quasi-guarantee of the publisher's intent to make him *'not only an artistic success but a commercial success as well'*.[13]

Rolfe had expected his 'tralation,' as he called it, of 'Umar Khaiyam to appear before the Italian stories. That plan had been Lane's reason for hurrying Rolfe with the translation, but the publisher changed his mind without informing Rolfe. He had corrected the proofs for most of *In His Own Image* before he learned that it would precede the *Rubáiyát*. He was angry and suspicious of Lane's motives but he managed, barely, to control his spleen. It was already near explosion at the delay in the publication of *In His Own Image*, a period of eighteen months. He forced himself to look on the slow appearance of both books, however, as the price the unknown author pays for publication.

Still, *In His Own Image* did not get published without offence and bitterness. The book carried a dedication to Henry and Aline Harland and James and Margaret Hannay 'in acknowledgement of hospitality'. As Rolfe tells it, *In His Own Image* was still in manuscript when Harland unexpectedly urged him to remove a certain 'flavour' from the book. At Rolfe's insistence, Harland named it, pederasty. According to one account, the episode occurred during a discussion in which Rolfe was openly critical of Lane, Harland's business partner, and resentful of Harland's seeming indifference to Rolfe's financial dilemma. Each man was annoyed with the other owing to Rolfe's tactlessness and the demands he made. Harland's accusation, however, was a considered one. When Rolfe heard it, he 'flamed in the face' and then answered coldly and incisively, 'That's quite gratuitous. What a frightfully degenerate imagination you must have. Now mark me: I won't make or permit to be made, a single alteration—'. Harland called Rolfe a fool and told him that if he persisted with *In His Own Image*, he would no longer be welcome at Harland's home or the homes of Harland's friends. The word friend was bandied about and Rolfe questioned Harland's sincerity. They parted, both men hurt and indignant, and Rolfe was convinced that the Harlands were enemies who meant to keep him in the 'mire of poverty'. Rolfe wrote to Hannay, allowing him to refuse the dedication, an opportunity which Hannay welcomed.[14] When Harland praised the Borgia book after its publication, Rolfe sent the letter to Richards, but Rolfe never forgave Harland.

Resentful and angry and eager to underscore Harland's defection, Rolfe changed the dedication of *In His Own Image* to read, 'To the Divine Friend Most Desired', expressed in Latin. Because the book was printed in New York, Temple Scott, Lane's manager there, saw the new phrase as it went to press and asked that the book be dedicated to him instead. Rolfe chose to retain 'Divo Amico Desideratissimo. D. D. D. Fredericus'.

The divine friend was Rolfe's impossible dream. The desire for it was one of his strongest emotions. Because it was, it provided a theme, whether central or peripheral, for much that he wrote. *Nicholas Crabbe* tells of the search for the friend and its failure. *The Desire and Pursuit of the Whole* tells of its success. *Hubert's Arthur* is narrated by such a friend and his attitude controls the book. In *Hadrian the Seventh*, friendship determines the fictitious pope's appointments; the theme finds further expression in the discussion of love and Hadrian's inability to love. Yet Rolfe's unending quest and unending failure demonstrate what Thomas Hardy called the 'theory of the transmigration of the ideal loved one, who only exists in the lover . . .' Hardy's reference is to relations between a man and a woman. Rolfe, on the other hand, freely confessed that he had no sympathy for such a relationship. In a letter sent to Temple Scott in New York probably before September 1901, Rolfe wrote at length about his estimate of human passion and love:

> I am struck aghast every now and then by the strange thing people call Love. One would be silly to deny it—because every now and then an example crops up of a sensible man or woman having their life tangled up with the life of another in blind mystery. They actually support each the continual presence of the other. Oh, there must be something in it.
>
> But it seems so excessively funny to me. Carnal pleasure I thoroughly appreciate, but I like a change sometimes. Even partridges get tiresome after many days. Only besotted ignorance or hypocrisy demurs to carnal lust, but I meet people who call that holy which is purely natural, and I am stupefied. I suppose we all deceive ourselves. To blow one's nose (I never learned to do it) is a natural relief. So is coition. Yet the last is called holy, and the first passes without epithets. Why should one attach more importance to one than to the other? I don't think that I want to know. . . .
>
> So that, except carnally—I fail to understand the love of man for maid. But carnally—well, of course. Extra-carnally, there is a perfectly possible relation of taste, of admiration of soul, of body.[15]

The fact that Nicholas Crabbe in *The Desire and Pursuit of the Whole* finds completeness with Gilda does not contradict Rolfe's letter. Rolfe said that the way to his heart was through his 'more than acute' sense of beauty; and although he spoke of 'innate delicate modesty in the female', he admitted that he knew nothing of women and denied that men and women could know each other or that he had ever wanted a woman. He asserted that the 'form and ornament of them made him simply sick . . . by reason of its vapid bunchiness and vacuous inconsequent patchworkiness'.[16] Rolfe's idea of beauty, according to John Holden, was contained in a verse from 'Samuel' descriptive of the boy David, 'Now he was ruddy, and withal of a beautiful countenance and goodly to look to.'[17] Rolfe repeatedly defined physical beauty in terms of boys. His first sight of Kemp, the beloved of Nicholas Crabbe, is that of a 'very slim boy', whom he called the 'most vivid and most dainty personality' he had ever seen. The beauty of Gilda in *The Desire and Pursuit of the Whole* is described as an interruption of nature which had made a 'grand broad-chested thin-flanked waistless boy by intention but a girl by defect'.[18] Indeed, Rolfe's ideal was a large boy of sixteen to eighteen years clothed with 'most lovely pads of muscular sweet flesh', whose skin was of a 'rosy satin fineness and softness'. Such a boy was at his prime before 'some great fat slow cow of a girl' had an opportunity to 'open herself wide and lie quite still & drain him dry', before he had got 'hard and hairy' with a moustache, 'brushes in his milky armpits' and 'brooms on his splendid young thighs'.[19]

Thus the divine friend much desired must be male, preferably young, and, according to Rolfe's demands, he must exhibit those qualities of which Rolfe believed himself capable, self-sacrifice, honour, and unflinching fidelity. Of course Rolfe was doomed to disappointment. No friend proved to be quite what he seemed and even at his most devoted, if he failed in judgement or achievement, Rolfe suspected him of malice. When Rolfe dedicated *In His Own Image* to 'the divine friend much desired', he let Harland and Hannay know that they had failed him, but he had little hope of finding the ideal. He had 'flung the thing at random to the Gods (who dwell in Olympian mansions), naming one, without the slightest belief in His Divinity's existence'.[20]

When he received a letter on 4 April 1901 purporting to come from the 'divine friend', Rolfe was too surprised and alarmed to respond at once. The letter was signed by Trevor Haddon, an artist who had studied at the Slade and who achieved considerable success with Spanish and Venetian subjects and with portraits. Haddon had lately come back to London from six months in Rome; he was still homesick for Rome, so that he immediately fell under the spell of the tales in *In His Own Image*. Its picture of life in the Alban Mountains enchanted him, and his sympathy was awakened by the dedication and the appeal for affection from a man who lamented in the opening paragraph of the tale 'About Some Friends' the 'impenetrable mail of ice about himself because no one bothered to melt it'. Feeling a similar need, Haddon impulsively wrote to Rolfe to tell something about himself and his Catholic connections and to offer 'his hand with his heart in it'.[21] Rolfe was puzzled by the 'rather tackily' written letter filled with discriminating praise and sympathy. Had he found the 'Much Desired, always young, always lovely, always faithful'? Because he was fearful of Haddon's acquaintance with enemies, especially Father Beauclerk,

Rolfe hesitated a week before replying. At last he wrote, 'I do not know whether to thank you for Hope: or to execrate you for another illusion dispelled; for additional matter for Despair.' He confessed his terror of the Catholics they both knew and listed thirteen enemies whom Haddon might question in order to learn the worst. Rolfe closed his letter: 'In secret I am fled away; and I will live alone, until—. I dedicated my book to the Divine Friend Much Desired. I do not know whether you are he—or another'.[22] Haddon refused to question the thirteen enemies and again he offered his friendship with a pledge of loyalty to the death. This was a highly decorative exchange highly appropriate to the situation. Still Rolfe hesitated.

When he had cast lots by opening a Book of Hours at random and reading first, 'Behold, I send Mine Angel' and then, 'for the mouths of those speaking iniquity have been obstructed', Rolfe felt safe in proceeding with Haddon. He accepted Haddon's invitation to visit his studio at Westminster and there he found the painter, a man four years his junior, the painter's wife, and three children. Mrs. Haddon instinctively loathed Rolfe, 'short and spare' and wearing strong glasses which accentuated a 'myopic expression'. She disliked his cold reserve and she called him a 'liar, a sponger', and a sexual deviant.[23] But Haddon invited Rolfe to their home in Elms Road, Clapham Common. They talked. Rolfe played the piano, including among his selections a hymn to William of Norwich of his own composition, and he lavished on Haddon 'illimitable confidence' as to his 'frightful (but not abnormally blameful) past' and his current difficulties.[24] Rolfe borrowed small sums of money from Haddon and allowed himself to be known. Always eager for an audience, he showed the painter an early draft of the piece eventually published as *Don Tarquinio*. He was more reticent about the book called 'Dom Gheraldo' in 1897 and in 1902, 'An Ideal Content'. But after tantalising Haddon with amusing quotations and frequent allusions, Rolfe showed the book to Haddon. When Haddon had read it with due appreciation and remarked on its authenticity of detail, Rolfe announced his wish to dedicate 'An Ideal Content' to the painter.

For this dedication Rolfe wrote a series of five letters, all addressed to Haddon. The first, the true 'epistle dedicatory', makes clear that the entire prefatory material is in response to a favourite subject for discussion on Haddon's part, the 'how' of making beautiful objects, the 'rationale of creative art'. As a painter Haddon was concerned with the aesthetics of his own craft, and he was curious about Rolfe's, especially as to the transfiguration of fact into fiction. Haddon had asked where Rolfe got his material, how much was 'invention, how much divination, how much a systematic "culture" of such fragments and unconsidered trifles as his reading and research enabled him to pick up'.[25] The next four letters set out to answer the painter's questions, as indicated in the 'epistle dedicatory'. In it Rolfe said:

Because you, o painter incessantly perturb me with inquisitions concerning the sources of my curious knowledge of matters archaick and abnormal, because you . . . molest me with entreaties that I, as man to man or (at times) as artificer to artificer, should demonstrate to you the four causes of my gests, especially that I should tell you how I do my deeds (and you know how many and how rare these be)—I will give you this book.[26]

In fact the last three letters, those having to do with the material cause and the formal cause (there are two letters 'Of the Formal Cause', one for each part of the book), are largely specific as to the matter of the book. Only 'Of the Efficient Cause' attempts to answer Haddon, inasmuch as it is a meditation on historical fiction. That, Rolfe believed, was his métier; he thought that if he must write, he had better devote himself to 'rather solid and very brilliant and picturesque historical fiction based on unusually extensive researches in historical fact'.[27] Thus 'Of the Efficient Cause' indicates his concern with the relation between literary sources and form, subject matter and form, realism and form. There Rolfe says:

historick romance must be true, apparently if not actually, accidentally if not essentially, implicitly if not explicitly. I had learned that the Form of it must be appropriate to the Matter in order to give it individual existence; and that with these must be included Potentiality and Actuality, all in a most correct Aristotelian formula.[28]

In the final analysis Rolfe begs the question he had set out to answer, that is, 'How the Thing is Done'. Haddon says that in reply to a letter in which he suggested the 'idea of mediumship', Rolfe admitted that he relied partly on 'divination' and that the 'divination had to wait on favourable conjunctions'.[29] In 'Of the Efficient Cause', Rolfe speaks of Mark Twain's *Joan of Arc* as an 'absolute' work, one in which the elements are totally integrated and says that he suspects it 'of being the result of occession'. Rolfe had confessed that he could supply no 'apophthegm' for creativity. By attributing it to 'occession', he implies something less occult than mediumship and closer to inspiration in a Platonic sense. The result may be, as he says, 'An Ideal Content', but he has given no fixed answer to the 'how' of creativity.

That discussion was one of Rolfe's few excursions into aesthetics. It was made at the challenge of Trevor Haddon and in deference to him. It was Rolfe's way of thanking Haddon for small loans and for reviving his hope of making a living from his writing. Without telling Rolfe anything about it, Haddon had written to Stanhope Sprigge, a recently established literary agent, and invited him to associate himself with Rolfe's 'rising name'. Sprigge promptly communicated with Rolfe, sending him brochures which made authorship sound exclusive, painless, and financially rewarding. He asked for a copy of *In His Own Image* and a visit from Rolfe. When he went to call a few days later, Rolfe was impressed with little except the agent's china teeth. He was frightened by the fact that Sprigge, like Haddon, had associations with Father Beauclerk. But Haddon urged Rolfe to be sensible, and so in May 1901 Rolfe committed his literary career to Sprigge and for a short time believed that he was on the brink of success after all the 'frightful years'. He showed 'An Ideal Content' and a sixty page sketch of *Don Tarquinio* to Sprigge. He handed over a number of short stories and essays for immediate sale. He described his problems with Grant Richards. Assuring Rolfe that his worries in that direction were at an end, Sprigge injected himself into the quarrel with Richards. From that time until the end of the year, Sprigge's advice in the Borgia-Richards affair was often vacillating and invariably poor. Sprigge helped only to worsen matters. Furthermore, Sprigge sold exactly one of Rolfe's short pieces, 'The Cardinal Prefect of Propaganda', the only signed publication which Rolfe had in the latter half of 1901. It tells how the Abbatino William Jameson, by whom Rolfe designated himself, forced his rector, the writer's variant of Father Beauclerk, to eat a 'bellyful of humble pie'. Rolfe had composed it not long after the commencement of his quarrel with the priest to show the form his retaliation would take for the wrongs he said Beauclerk had done. The tale appeared in *The Candid Friend* on 22 June 1901. A second piece, 'Begging Letters: With Facsimiles and Fancy Sketches of their Writers', published in the August number of *The Harmsworth London Magazine* as by Frank Holmfield, is attributed to Rolfe. At the top of the article is a line drawing of a man wearing an eye shade and writing at a table. John Holden identified the picture as a self-portrait of Rolfe.[30] Neither the manner of the article nor its subject matter suggests Rolfe. Indeed the subject matter was repugnant to him after the *Daily Free Press* of Aberdeen accused him of trying to keep himself by means of begging letters, a common enough practice then as now. In any case, Rolfe had difficulty in getting paid. Sprigge at last collected from *The Candid Friend*, but Rolfe received only 30s., having offered Sprigge a commission of 25 per cent instead of the usual 10 per cent as an inducement to greater effort.

Always mistrustful after having trusted too expansively, Rolfe revived his suspicions of both Haddon and Sprigge. Rolfe decided they were in collusion with Beauclerk to prevent his earning a living. When Sprigge wrote on 1 January 1902 to say that the manuscript of one of Rolfe's stories had been lost and, what was worse, lost by an inferior periodical, Rolfe was convinced of their villainy. He struck at Sprigge by a letter which terminated their connection. On 10 January, Rolfe notified Richards that Sprigge, 'agent and Roman Catholic' no longer represented him; three months later a similar letter went to Lane saying that Rolfe had dismissed Sprigge on account of his Roman

Catholicism.[31] For Rolfe that was tantamount to saying that Sprigge had proved himself a liar and a thief. Trevor Haddon fell into the same category. Early in January, Rolfe asked Haddon to list the various sums of money still owing. As soon as Haddon complied, Rolfe wrote to him, 'When the manuscript which was purloined by your accomplice Sprigge has been returned to me, it will be time enough for me to consider the settling of your bill.'[32] In Rolfe's eyes Trevor Haddon had proved himself not a gift of the gods but the 'Demon False Friend'.[33] Although Rolfe retained the prefatory letters of 'An Ideal Content', they were thereafter addressed to *Apistophilos Echis* or 'untruth loving viper'.

By March 1902, Rolfe had another candidate for the 'Divine Amicus, Much Desired' and for what he desired as much as the friend, a collaborator. That was a part of his yearning for wholeness through complete identity between himself and another. At Holywell, he had proposed partnership with John Holden and, although the translation of 'Umar's *Rubáiyát* was entirely his own, Rolfe had wanted Edward Slaughter's name on the title-page as collaborator in gratitude for financial help, but Lane removed it.[34] The new relationship, like that with Haddon, came about through *In His Own Image*. In early March 1902, Rolfe received a letter which ran in part: 'Your kindness to me and all other readers of the stories of Toto has made me bold. I want to hear the story of Fioravanti. My Toto—I say it humbly—is called Fioravanti.'[35] Written from Southsea in Hampshire, the letter was signed with the name Sholto Douglas.

Obviously Douglas had seen in *In His Own Image* the same flavour as Harland and Hannay; but far from objecting, as they had, Douglas welcomed it. According to his own statement, Douglas was a homosexual. Among his miscellaneous papers are numbers of unpublished compositions both in prose and verse celebrating what he termed 'amorous enthusiasm or platonic love, which in the true sense of the phrase is the affection of a man for a youth'.[36]

Rolfe had seen none of these pieces in March and many he very likely never saw. They had no influence on the fact or the nature of his correspondence with Douglas. It began with a flurry of linguistic exhibitionism on both sides. Rolfe replied to Douglas's first letter in Italian, and Douglas countered with French; Rolfe then wrote in Latin, and Douglas answered in Greek. After that the exchange settled down to English. Rolfe learned from Douglas that he had a degree from Oxford, that he worked as a private tutor in order to reduce his poverty to a 'tolerable minimum', that he had spent short periods in Italy and Southern France, and that he dabbled in woodcarving and writing. By that time, Rolfe had recognised a fellowpederast in the other man's allusions, however evasive, to boy-lovers and especially to 'one' other than Fioravanti in whom Douglas was both 'blessed' and 'content'. Everything Douglas told him interested

128

Rolfe. He wanted a picture of Fioravanti; he discussed the eroticism of colours, and both men wrote of their mothers. Rolfe was quick to confide his despair and his yearnings and the nature of his work. As he had warned Haddon by naming thirteen enemies for investigation, so he sent a copy of *The Catholic Times* containing much of the Aberdeen attack to Douglas. Rolfe offered to send 'An Ideal Content' in its current form, but Douglas was reluctant and coy. No other word, unless it is coquettish, applies so well to a man who ends a letter as Douglas did his of 21 March:

> *Ave valeque*
> One other word
> And yet . . .
> No, not another word,
> Who am I that should say another word, the other word?[37]

Douglas was hesitant about meeting Rolfe. In a letter dated 28 March 1902, Douglas insisted that the decision as to whether or not the two men met must be Rolfe's, but he closed this letter 'doubtfully' and then asked how to find Rolfe. He sent Rolfe a photograph of a carving, one of his 'neo-Assyrian barbarous monsters' and wanted to hear Rolfe talk about it. Some two weeks later when Rolfe extended an invitation, Douglas thought him unwise but made an appointment for 12 April 1902 at 4·30. On that date he visited Rolfe at 69 Broadhurst Gardens in his 'commonplace little room with a few shelves and photographs about, mostly his own handiwork'.[38]

The meeting went well because the next day Douglas addressed Rolfe as 'Dear Man' in a letter which remarked on the 'very human kindness' which twinkled 'so charmingly' behind Rolfe's spectacles. Douglas also invited Rolfe to tea at the London flat on Margaret Street, Cavendish Square, of Arthur Smith Graham, Douglas's host and his dearest friend; this time he ended his letter 'Delightedly'. By early May, Douglas was reading the Borgia book and accepting Rolfe's recommendation that he read *The Lady Paramount*, a new novel by Henry Harland which Rolfe compared to an 'intagliate sea-blue beryl'. Douglas was moved now to close at least one letter, 'Good-bye, good-night good love.'[39] It was a comfort, he said, to have Rolfe to 'write at'.

Rolfe had learned from Douglas that his 'scribbling' had produced a small cache of manuscripts which included a translation of *The Songs of Meleager*, several 'Studies in Unwritten Literature', and one piece of a series later referred to as 'Thirty Naughty Emperors'. Rolfe could hardly wait to see them, but Douglas, on 21 May, sent him only one manuscript, 'The Goat in Priest's Clothing', a piece which used Heliogobalus to discuss the question of godhead and sin. Although Douglas sent the essay with the comment that it was 'enough to make a cow scoff: my soul must have been made of shoe-leather',[40] Rolfe, as soon as he had read it, suggested that Douglas and he collaborate. He proposed that Douglas as an 'imaginary historian' write several such pieces; Rolfe meant to revise and prepare them for publication. After he had made them saleable, Rolfe proposed that they be published as jointly written for Douglas's sole profit. Douglas objected to benefiting from Rolfe's fame, but he was dazzled by the possibility of publication. He sent off his translation of Meleager to Rolfe. Rolfe responded with a photograph of himself in priest's dress and a manuscript copy of the still unpublished translation of the *Rubáiyát*.

Doubtless inspired, Douglas turned out imaginary historical accounts of Commodus, Lampridius, Caracalla, and others to a total of eight before he grew sick of writing and convinced that he tortured 'every thought into lupinarian phrases' or they remained 'flat balderdash'. Rolfe applied to each piece his 'wondrous Attick talent' and returned it to Douglas, who was instructed to 'bombard a magazine'. Douglas obeyed, but he was unwilling to write anything more until these were printed. He thought it impossible to compose enough for a book Rolfe wanted to call 'Thirty Naughty Emperors'. Douglas suggested a book of twenty emperors and ten 'naughty popes'. Rolfe vetoed the popes, and eventually he took over Douglas's studies, rewrote them, and proposed to write others so as to have a book containing essays about '30 Caesars from Hadrian to Diocletian'.[41]

At the same time, Rolfe insisted that 'Studies in Unwritten Literature', which had such titles as 'On Plato's Dialogue Concerning the Music of Wagner' and 'On Shakespeare's Tragedy of King Charles', must be developed. He was sure that these studies, renamed first 'Notes on Posthumous Literature' and then 'Reviews of Unwritten Books', would keep any reader 'in a simmer of giggles and guffaws till Finis'.[42] Douglas wrote the original drafts of at least fifteen such reviews and Rolfe revised them. Douglas was not always pleased with Rolfe's editing. He thought that Rolfe damaged the 'Reviews' although he sold twenty-four, of which nine were actually published, to *The Monthly Review*.

Even so, Rolfe thought the collaboration ideal. According to Rolfe, the two turned out 'stuff' which was 'as rich and as pregnant and as aromatic as a Christmas pudding'. They might disagree, but neither grew angry, neither refused to learn. [43] At some point they decided to publish with both names on the title-pages and two thirds of royalties assigned to Douglas. Again he protested that Rolfe was foolish to mix his name with such 'poor stuff', but Rolfe was adamant.

Rolfe's refusal to yield on any question which the collaboration on the translation of Meleager provoked brought to an end the relationship between Douglas and Rolfe. Sholto Douglas had made his translation only with a view to enabling others to read the original. Because he could not be both graceful and exact, he chose to be exact.

But he consented to revise and on 22 May 1902 he began work on a freer version. Three days later, he jubilantly posted the first half to Rolfe with a list of things which he wanted Rolfe to observe. Rolfe's reception of the new version was too dogmatic for Douglas; so, on 5 June, Douglas wrote to Rolfe, 'You annoy me about Meleager.' Calling Rolfe a 'dear orangeado-pie', Douglas said that each had been attempting to force his own version on the other. He added accusingly, 'You wave your hot luxurious quill and jet sugared words: I with adulterate complexion heave hecatombs of sighs and submit.' Douglas then asserted one use of collaboration to be squabbling and declared that he meant to 'squabble all the time'.[44] The next day he was again at work revising the second section of Meleager, 'Songs of Love of Women', and in good faith advocating that royalties be shared equally in the event of publication. Rolfe once said that 'all his life long he had yearned to be giving',[45] but in this case he gave without generosity and Douglas resented it. 'Are you really girding at Meleager only to please me?' he asked and said that if that was the case, his pleasure was 'bitter-sweet'. Rolfe's reply was a denial of 'personal swagger or even dignity' and an admission of his scholarly limitations. Douglas thought his 'pose of a modest ignoramus' absurd in the face of his easy display of pedantry, of 'the learning of . . . Notes and Queries'.[46] In fact Douglas was a better and better educated classicist than Rolfe, but Rolfe had no intention of being put in second place. Neither had Douglas. He acknowledged that Rolfe had 'dragged' Meleager out of its 'obscure grave in a cupboard' and put it into 'acceptable shape'. Nevertheless Douglas declared that Rolfe had 'failed to find the soul of Meleager' and that his own version as a whole was better than Rolfe's. Douglas objected to Rolfe's remoteness from the Greek text, his repetitions, and his spelling of proper names. Rolfe, determined to impose his version on Douglas, charged him with bad temper. Douglas admitted that he was angry, but justifiably so. He asked about the manuscript, 'Do you trust yourself so firmly that I am to send it back to you un-touched and leave everything in your hands?' Yet he tried to keep peace. He urged Rolfe to publish his own translation under his own name and sent 10s. so that Rolfe could 'push Meleager'. When Rolfe persisted in their joint effort, Douglas told Rolfe to keep the manu-script. Rolfe sent it back to Douglas anyway with instructions as to how he was to proceed. Indignant, Douglas then wrote, 'Under no circumstances will I ever collaborate in a tralation again with you. You are fascinating as an original writer, but you are a most un-sympathetic tralator: you put too much of yourself into it.'[47] With a further discussion of split infinitives, the collaboration and the friendship came to an end.

Rolfe's dream of collaboration and of the Divine Friend had proved illusory. In this instance Rolfe pictured himself as less angry than be-reft at Douglas's defection. Later Rolfe made every effort to copyright

131

'Reviews of Unwritten Books' in Douglas's name, and long after Rolfe's death Douglas recalled mistakenly that Rolfe had paid over to him all money received for the 'Reviews'.[48] Yet a few months after the break with Douglas, Rolfe lumped him with Trevor Haddon in a comment on *In His Own Image*:

> It brought me two devils. One, of course, was a Catholic. He deluded me with false promises to help me to a happy issue out of all my afflictions. He delayed my work for eleven months, made himself cognizant of all my plans and prospects; and he threw me into the gutter. The other of course was a Kelt. He robbed me of six months' work at 18 hours a day 7 days a week. They both of course pretended to be the Divine Amicus, Much-desired.[49]

[iv]

Whatever his expenditure of emotion on Haddon and Douglas and the abrasions to his ego in the case of Douglas, both episodes were of little consequence to Rolfe. He regretted the break with Douglas to a greater degree because it spoiled his image of himself as the mentor of a young man with literary possibilities, but after a time Rolfe began to speak of Douglas as a young Oxford man whom he was trying to ' "place" in literature'.[1] The breach with Haddon was unavoidable because Rolfe thought his potential income threatened. His economic survival, never very sure, was his most serious concern and a motive for unremitting effort throughout the period of his association with both Haddon and Douglas and long afterward. Rolfe freely confessed that he wanted literary success less than commercial success. From 1901, the year in which he met Haddon, to 1905, Rolfe slaved to produce one composition after another simply to keep alive. He concocted project after project and he looked for help in the most unlikely places, and nothing succeeded.

Economic necessity governed Rolfe's relations with Temple Scott. In 1901, Rolfe still hoped for unusual sales of his work in America through Scott, working in New York as John Lane's agent. In July of the previous year, Rolfe had sent a manuscript copy of the *Rubáiyát* as a gift to Scott, who 'howled with delight across the ocean at so dainty an attention'. In return he commissioned Rolfe to write a story on the fashionable life of Italy in the fifteenth century, a tale 'embodying every act of a man of fashion of that era during a certain four-and-twenty consecutive hours'.[2] Rolfe was elated until Edward Slaughter, encountered unexpectedly on a Baker Street bus at Piccadilly Circus, gave an off-hand opinion that there was nothing legal about the commission; it was merely a promise to pay from 'one man of honour to another'.[3] Rolfe had no great faith in Scott's honour; but he was determined to believe in Scott, who dangled more commissions and begged Rolfe to come to his 'Future' in America.

Rolfe's faith was strained when he had an objectionable letter from Scott. It was too personal, a 'Marcus-aurelian letter' dealing with 'all the mumbo-jumbo of the Pseudo-theological sophist', the kind of thing to be expected from an 'emancipated Jew' such as Scott. Rolfe wrote in June 1900 to refute the 'divers damnable heresies' contained in it: that Scott knew him who did not know himself; that Scott (whose letter was 'all imagination') had nothing to do with imagination; that Rolfe was content with his Borgia book, which he called a 'poor starved pretentious thing'; and that Rolfe was a sybarite. The last charge was the most offensive, one which Rolfe was sure derived from the 'insidious calumnies' of the Aberdeen *Free Press*. 'It is such a common thing', he wrote, 'to say that one uncommon is luxurious,' and he insisted that he was not, that he loathed strawberries and merely tolerated asparagus. He went on:

> I do pride myself on being dainty, but my daintiness is for the little and the simple. Food doth not worry me, nor clothes. I prefer omelettes, green things, and a gown, to unnatural and splendid opulence. I crave of the unhearing gods a climate, books, precious stone, baths, five slaves, and my naked soul. But strawberries and asparagus forced—*Anathema sint*![4]

Despite his pique at the letter and his disdain for Scott, Rolfe talked over his problems with Scott on his return to London, showed him current work, and allowed Scott to take several manuscripts back to New York. Silence followed; so, in February 1901, Rolfe called himself to Scott's remembrance by sending to him as a letter a masterly essay on kingliness and kingship after standing ankle-deep in a horse-trough at the Marble Arch to watch Queen Victoria's funeral procession go by.[5] In the same letter he offered the dedication of the *Rubáiyát* to Scott, hoping for 'paying work' in return. Scott was wildly enthusiastic, but the only offer he made was that Rolfe do some kind of research at the British Museum at the rate of a pound a week. Rolfe refused. He asked for payment for the work he had already done. But no cash for Rolfe's manuscripts was forthcoming nor were the manuscripts returned.[6]

Now Scott had become a false friend and a 'despoiler'. Rolfe did what he could to make Temple Scott pay. First, Rolfe cancelled the dedication of the *Rubáiyát*. Within a month or so when he composed the prefatory letters for 'An Ideal Content', he made Scott his antagonist in the letter 'Of the Efficient Cause'. The letter tells of a symposium consisting of an unidentified Cockney, Frederic Chapman of the

Bodley Head, Scott, and Rolfe. Their discussion of historical romance ends when Scott, who is called only 'the Israelite,' declared that 'the day was gone in which writers might have consumed the sweat of their brains in elaborating masterpieces'. He denigrated the quality of popular demand and elevated the publisher who kept 'one eye on the Publick's whimseys, the other eye on his bagmen and advertisements, and a score of threadbare specialists at a pound a week in his back office to whom he himself would adumbrate matter, form, and all things connected with the confection of books which could be sold in demimillions'. The Israelite, 'this publisher's manager of the Twentieth Century, this "bleating echo of the far away past", ' sought to 'reconstitute Grub Street'. Rolfe objected, saying he preferred a 'dignified death by hunger' rather than to be made a machine which, 'when filled by a pig, would produce literature paragonable only to sausages, flabby, flaccid, enervate and obscene'.[7] He then upset his tea, fell over the dog, and went away in a rage. After meditating on their discussion over a 'chop and a pint of sherry wine' at the Spaniard's Inn on Hampstead Heath, he concluded that the public, especially the English public, admires individuality and distinction and he resolved to do 'historick romance of such a quality as would controvert the abjectly imbecile thesis of that Israelite'.[8]

Although Rolfe was confident that he had soundly admonished Scott, Scott never saw this prefatory letter because *Don Renato An Ideal Content*, as the book was finally entitled, was not published in his lifetime. But Rolfe had no hesitation in disclaiming all friendship with Scott when he was arrested the following year on charges of forgery and of misappropriating the funds of John Lane's New York office. The court dismissed the charges, but while he was awaiting trial in New York, Rolfe, in a conversation with Lane, said of Scott, 'He was ... perspicacious enough to recognize the value of my work. It would have suited him to be intimate with me: but I had little or no intimacy to give him. ... Privately, he has not treated me any better than he has treated you.' Had Rolfe forgotten the evenings when he had his meal with Scott's family, still the Isaacs family at that time, and then read aloud the tales he was writing for *In His Own Image*? He even allied himself with Lane in a letter of April 1902 where Rolfe said about Scott, 'You as well as I have been the victims of gross mismanagement in America; and, I suppose we must put up with the annoyance.'[9]

Because a quarrel with Lane about his delay in the publication of the *Rubáiyát* seemed inevitable and as recently as 31 January 1902, Rolfe had told Lane, 'I like frankness; and I don't like the way you have treated me at all,' Rolfe was happy to blame Scott for frustrations and delays experienced with Lane. He could still hope that Lane meant well by him and honestly intended to make him a commercial success. His eagerness to be on good terms with Lane is apparent in his response to the publisher's explanations:

As long as a good understanding exists between us, and you treat me with frankness and consideration, you will find me perfectly willing to oblige you to the utmost of my power. I am glad you have given me an opportunity of trying sincerely to make you understand this.[10]

This harmonious state lasted from April to mid-November although Rolfe maintained that he never lost sight of the fact that for eighteen months Lane was 'playing the fool' with the *Rubáiyát*. Rolfe had received proofs, a few at a time, commencing in January 1901, but none was sent him between April 1901 and late March 1902. By April 16, he could report to Lane that even though it had been a 'difficult and intricate piece of work to pick up the threads which were dropped in April 1901, and to weave them aright',[11] he had little more to do. Lane had secured Nathan Haskell Dole, a noted American scholar, to write the introduction for Rolfe's translation. Rolfe was delighted at the 'novel and very grateful experience' of being 'joined in literature with "a gentleman and a scholar" such as Mr. Dole'.[12] Rolfe was singularly docile in accepting some of Dole's suggestions and extremely polite in rejecting others. He was due in Oxford in late May, but he put off going until he could see Lane, who had asked for a meeting. Rolfe first ascribed Lane's request to a suspicion on the part of Lane that Scott and Rolfe had conspired against him. Then Rolfe decided that Lane was apprehensive lest Rolfe attack him in print as he had Grant Richards in the matter of the Borgia book, and thus lessen the sale of the *Rubáiyát*.[13] For almost a week, Rolfe expected Lane to come to 69 Broadhurst Gardens at tea-time. Instead, on 28 May, he went to tea with Lane and found that he had something else in mind. He wanted Rolfe to facilitate immediate publication of the *Rubáiyát* by waiving his right to a revised proof. Rolfe did so only after Lane had promised that the book, when published, would be one of which Rolfe need not be ashamed or which he would be 'compelled to disown'. Lane further declared that Rolfe would 'net four figures' from the book. And back Rolfe went to Hampstead to write a letter confirming the conversation. He ended by saying, 'I hope you will make a *great success* with your Rubai'yat: indeed in view of your notorious talent for making very great successes of very slight things, I EXPECT you to make a very great success now.'[14]

But Lane did nothing to speed publication of the *Rubáiyát*. By the end of October Rolfe was once more driven to the wearisome task of prodding Lane. He assured Rolfe that every mail might bring word that the sheets, printed in the United States for economy's sake, had been shipped. In November, however, he informed Rolfe that publication had been put off until the spring of 1903. Rolfe was aghast and incredulous. He recalled the years which had elapsed since the commencement of the work, how he had rushed to finish it, and the fact that he had agreed to forgo his rights to revised proofs; he pointed out the damage done to his literary reputation by repeated announcements of the book followed by its 'continued non-appearance', and he told Lane he must be joking. Rolfe reminded Lane that he had made an enemy of Maurice Hewlett by a 'similar course of neglect'. Adding that Hewlett's affairs were not his, Rolfe said that he wanted only to have his relations to Lane and the *Rubáiyát* clearly defined. 'It is my pose, and has been since July to make friends and not enemies,' Rolfe wrote. 'But I like to know where to draw the line.'[15] When he asked at Christmas for his copies in advance of publication in order to give one to his mother, Lane answered that none had yet come from America and explained that they were in the process of being bound there, although in fact the five hundred copies issued in England were bound in England. But he assured Rolfe that the book would be out in early January.[16]

When the book failed to appear by 16 January 1903, Rolfe asked for a copy of his contract in case he turned to the Society of Authors for help. He had become a member four days earlier. He accused Lane of having taken a 'rather dirty advantage' of his misfortunes by underpaying and deceiving him, that so many broken promises had strained Rolfe's 'indulgence to the point of rupture', and that now he meant to 'follow other counsels'. Finally, after Rolfe had threatened Lane only once more with the Society of Authors, the translation of the *Rubáiyát* appeared on 27 February 1903, almost three years after Rolfe had delivered the manuscript.[17] It had been published in the United States on 26 January.

In keeping with his pose of making friends and not enemies, Rolfe had been singularly mild throughout his dealings with Lane. There was always the chance, however slim, that Lane would carry out his casually pronounced intention to make Rolfe a 'commercial success as he was an artistick success'. Although his efforts were unremitting, his manoeuvres and schemes ingenious and his productivity impressive in a craft for which he had no love, Rolfe could not achieve commercial success for himself. His financial situation in London was little different from his situation in Holywell; and as it had in Holywell, it went from bad to worse.

By his own account, Rolfe earned about £70 in 1899, the year he came to London,[18] but what he is known to have earned and to have received in addition to earnings does not add up to £70. That he was penniless apart from the amount E. G. Hardy gave him when he left Oxford in 1899 may be inferred from that fact that he overcame his distaste and kept the sovereigns given him by both Lane and Henry Harland at their first meetings with him. Rolfe borrowed at least £8 19s. from Slaughter and repaid it in March when Lane, carefully deducting the sovereign and the cost of a dozen penny stamps, paid the £10 due for *In His Own Image*. Rolfe earned £3 10s. from *The Butterfly* and £6 which Grant Richards paid for the Borgia book at the rate of £1 a week from 20 November to the end of the year. Slaughter contributed a regular amount to his support; Harry Bainbridge, his fellow-lodger at 69 Broadhurst Gardens that year, helped him over some bad times, and at Christmas Rolfe had a gift of £2 2s. from Henry Harland.

The next year, 1900, was better. Rolfe said that he earned about £90 that year, and he felt cheated of another £25. Temple Scott had promised him that amount for the serial rights to some version of *Don Tarquinio*; but Scott refused to pay although he 'alleged nothing against the story'.[19] The £1 a week received from Richards was increased after 16 May to £1 10s. and continued until 26 July, making a total in 1900 of £42 10s. For the translation of the *Rubáiyát*, Rolfe received £25. He had some kind of payment for one or more articles published by the New York *World*; he earned a part of £25, the total amount paid him in 1900 and 1901 for reading examination papers at Oxford for Hardy; and at Christmas once more Harland sent him £2 2s.

That year, 1900, represented the peak of Rolfe's income during his London years. The remainder of his stay was increasingly difficult; he lived from crisis to crisis without funds and almost without hope. The next fifteen months were especially lean. In that time he published no more than two short pieces, 'The Cardinal Prefect of Propaganda' and possibly 'Begging Letters: With Facsimiles and Fancy Short Sketches of their Writers'. If he wrote the second piece and was paid for it, he failed to acknowledge the fact. He said that his income from writing in 1901 amounted to 30s., exactly what Sprigge paid him.[20] In addition, Rolfe had some part of £25 for work at Oxford and £2 2s. from Harland at Christmas. On Christmas Eve he posted Harland's cheque to Harry Bainbridge for cashing and four days later was awaiting the money with impatience; he was 'dying for a Turkish Bath'.[21] It had been a bleak Christmas. On the day after it, he told Bainbridge, 'I got rather wretched on Christmas Day, and went for a little walk which made me worse. I even envied the happy fools behind the window curtains lighted up.'[22] An opportunity to help Bainbridge with a report on the effect of lead fumes on vegetation which he was preparing for his employer Dr. Ludwig Mond was a godsend for Rolfe. It gave him something to do, and he plunged into research at the British Museum. The result was a considerable summary 'in re Lead Fume'.[23] Bainbridge may have paid for the report, but if he did not, it was little enough return for the loans and gifts he made to Rolfe from time to time.

On 17 March 1902, Rolfe described his circumstances to Maurice Hewlett, whose *Richard Yea-and-Nay* had been most successful two years earlier, and asked for his interest in securing a grant from the Royal Literary Fund. Rolfe attributed his situation to his publishers, Lane and Richards, with a larger share of animosity directed at Richards for having mutilated the manuscript of the book about the Borgias, thus making it 'futile', and for having issued it contrary to Rolfe's explicit prohibition as by Frederick Baron Corvo. Rolfe had felt strongly enough about the matter in January to send *The Athenaeum* a letter remonstrating against a criticism of *Chronicles of the House of Borgia* and defending himself, but the letter was so garbled in publication that it failed in its purpose, and Rolfe's subsequent attempts to steer the periodical 'back into the path of truth' accomplished nothing.[24] When Rolfe wrote to Hewlett, he had succeeded, however, in attacking the book in *Notes and Queries* and he was awaiting the appearance in America of a 'ferocious denunciation' of both book and publisher.[25] At the same time, Rolfe indicated enough work 'on the stocks', enough ideas and articles, and enough distress at his inability to write 'at full power' to elicit Hewlett's intervention. Hewlett wrote sympathetically to A. Llewelyn Roberts, Secretary of the Royal Literary Fund, and to its committee, of which Hewlett was a member. Rolfe made a formal application supported by E. G. Hardy of Oxford, and on 2 April 1902, Rolfe was granted £50, which was paid to him on 10 April.[26]

The next day Rolfe thanked Roberts effusively for the 'succour' which made it possible to 'subsist'. Yet, except for a good supply of tobacco, Rolfe was little better off than he had been before receiving the £50. His clothes were threadbare and his boots needed mending. He was hopelessly in debt to Mrs. Griffiths, to whom he had not paid the weekly guinea for his room and board in about two years. He had no immediate income from writing. His 'Ideal Content' with its new prefatory material had gone to Heinemann on 17 March, but it was refused and the manuscript was waiting for him to fetch it by 31 May. Meanwhile bailiffs had been at 69 Broadhurst Gardens, and by mid-July Rolfe was reduced to accepting 10s. from Sholto Douglas while looking for something or someone to alter his fortunes for the better.[27]

Briefly his literary prospects improved. In October 1902, Rolfe had two book reviews in *The Outlook* and, at the end of the next month, a poem celebrating Queen Alexandra's birthday.[28] At the end of that month, November, in view of his difficulties with Richards and Lane, Rolfe decided that the 'intervention of an agent' might be profitable. He turned to James Pinker, already experienced with publishing when he began to operate as an agent in 1897. Before his death in 1922, he had represented a number of prominent authors, among them Henry James, Joseph Conrad, D. H. Lawrence, and John Galsworthy. Rolfe approached Pinker by sending to him at his office in Effingham House, Arundel Street, Strand, two 'Reviews of Unwritten Books' and a note dated 30 November 1902 asking whether he could do anything with 'things of this sort'. The note was signed with the name Frank English. Pinker wrote on it, 'Return—scarcely important enough' and his staff acted accordingly. But Rolfe persisted with the information that he had twenty-two others of the same series, two complete books, and 'a heap of miscellaneous stuff'. Within the week, he could tell Pinker that Henry Newbolt of the *Monthly Review* had made an offer for the entire series of the 'Reviews of Unwritten Books'. Still as Frank English, he continued to send manuscripts to Pinker, who continued to regard them as insufficient evidence of the writer's ability to warrant his acting for Rolfe. Pinker finally suggested that they meet, but Rolfe wrote that he was going to Oxford to read examination papers and thus could not have 'the pleasure' of Pinker's acquaintance before Christmas.[29]

Rolfe was going to Oxford for a roof over his head as well as to read papers for Hardy. In the midst of his display of confidence and his attempt to entice Pinker, Rolfe was in despair. As she did periodically, his landlady had put her foot down and ordered that he pay or leave, and he had less than 10s. On 11 December, the same day on which he wrote to delay meeting Pinker, Rolfe also wrote to explain to Harry Bainbridge his 'distrait air' of the night before. 'I am quite done now,' Rolfe said and gave an account of his position: the *Rubáiyát* due early in the new year, the twenty-four articles accepted by *The Monthly Review*, two completed books. 'But I have no means of living and no place to live in till I get payment for this work,' Rolfe added. 'I have just 8s. left, no prospect of more, and not a soul in the world to help me.' He admitted that it would be a 'big job' to help him now, that anything 'going to be done must be done without a moment's delay', because his ship was 'sinking fast'. He pointed out that he could show praises of his work from 'experts, such as Dr. Garnett of Brit. Mus. & people at Oxford', and he ended, 'Think as kindly as you can of me, whatever you may hear said of me in the future. I have tried my best and I have failed.'[30] This letter was either a blunt attack on Bainbridge's purse or an exercise in self-pity. Yet every word of it was true. Rolfe had worked endlessly, sitting in his attic room writing himself 'blind and vertiginous', all to no purpose. He had neither recognition nor reward, both promised and both denied. He had failed.

But Rolfe was indomitable. By 23 December, he had been to Oxford and come back to London with three guineas in his pocket and a manuscript, 'Live Pork and a Peall'. He posted it to Pinker at once and followed it with a telegram the next day to call attention to the manuscript's connection with news of the final illness of Pope Leo XIII.[31] Although on 26 December, Rolfe stated as '*literally* true' that unless he could get a 'lump of money soon i.e. at once', he and his landlady would be 'sold up' and forced into the workhouse, he was sanguine enough to have a plan which, with someone else's money, must rescue him from disaster and make 'several fortunes' for everyone involved. For *Chronicles of the House of Borgia*, Rolfe had prepared a genealogy, which Richards had deleted. Meanwhile Count Cesare

139

Borgia had enabled Rolfe to add to it. He had then devised an elaborate, ornamented document, nine feet by sixteen feet in size, containing 293 names, some 210 more than in any previous genealogy of the Borgias. He fixed his hope on this document. He wrote to tell Bainbridge about it, emphasising its unique quality. He offered to sell the document outright or, if Bainbridge would 'join forces' with him, by which he meant house and feed him, until he could turn his genealogy and the knowledge it indicated into a standard history of the Borgias, he was sure of success; and he promised Bainbridge that he 'should know how to reward' those who had 'enabled' him.[32]

This scheme for the Borgia genealogy appealed so strongly to Rolfe that he began to promote it everywhere, beginning with Pinker. Still as Frank English, Rolfe had suggested a meeting with Pinker immediately after returning from Oxford, but this time Pinker held off and the meeting did not take place until Friday, 9 January 1903. Rolfe's eagerness for it can be inferred from the fact that he agreed to go to Pinker's office between 4.30 and 5, an hour on Fridays usually devoted to Rolfe's mother. When he got there, Rolfe cast off his pseudonym Frank English and made himself known as Frederick Rolfe, author as Baron Corvo of *Stories Toto Told Me, In His Own Image, Chronicles of the House of Borgia*, and translator of the still unpublished *Rubáiyát*. He talked with enthusiasm and confidence of his plans as a writer. As soon as he could afterward, and still on 9 January, he sat down to review their meeting in a letter to Pinker. 'I hope I clearly impressed upon you,' Rolfe wrote, 'my firm intention to succeed in literature.' He affirmed that the measure of his success was financial. He acknowledged that his 'Historical romance, "An Ideal Content",' would hardly make money but it would introduce him to the public. He described other 'less academick, deliberately "popular"' books and told Pinker 'You will see that you have the chance of "making" a writer, and I hope that our connection will be for our mutual advantage.'[33] On 17 January, Rolfe offered the Borgia genealogy to his agent, assuring him that with his 'enterprize and initiative', he might be able to make something of it.

Rolfe was not willing, however, to rely wholly on Pinker's enterprise or initiative. A week later he told his agent that he had carried out a suggestion from Richard Garnett that the Borgiada be put before the Italian Government and that Alberto Pansa, the Italian ambassador, had granted an audience for the next Tuesday, 27 January. Rolfe asked Pinker to accompany him in order to explain the genealogy and 'to manage any business details' which might evolve. On the appointed day, Signor Pansa offered Rolfe credentials to Alfredo Baccelli, Under-Secretary of State, with a view to bringing the matter before the King of Italy and her government. Pinker was not present to hear Pansa's offer; he had suffered a sudden 'indisposition'.[34] The next day, Rolfe outlined to Pinker a number of other possibilities for his Borgiada: the Bodleian Library, the Royal Historical Society, the Society of Arts in England and museums, libraries, and universities in America. He was entirely willing to have any of these or 'Mr. W. W. Astor', who had been United States Minister to Italy and who had written about Cesare Borgia, as his patron. Rolfe defined his idea of patronage as 'a sum sufficient to enable' him to give his 'time and trouble to a Standard History of Borgia, i.e. a collection of all documents connected with that House'. He was more explicit as he went on, saying that he estimated the sum at £1,000; Rolfe was willing to accept a smaller sum such as £500, but he could not then guarantee to complete the work.[35]

Rolfe's grandiose scheme and his impatience for it to be put into effect prompted him to write for himself to Astor on 30 January 1903 with an offer to exhibit the genealogy. Pinker had it delivered, and when Astor's secretary G. T. Maquay wrote to say that Astor had seen the 'Borgia Pedigree' but did not want to buy it, Rolfe was sure that Pinker had bungled the transaction.[36] Without any one's help, Rolfe continued his search for a patron in Joseph Gilder of Dodd Mead, Courtney of Constable, Sir Arthur Balfour, and Horace Hart, Comptroller of Oxford University Press. Hart saw the Borgiada the latter part of March, when Rolfe had shown it to everyone he could induce to see it, and his energies had begun to sag. But he never admitted that his prospects with the Borgiada were hopeless. In May he told Maquay that he was 'not neglecting Borgia' because he wanted to but only because he was forced to. 'If one can not go on living one must put one's idea aside,' he said, but that did not mean giving it up.[37]

Despite his conviction as to the great value of the Borgiada—a view supported, he usually added, by Dr. Richard Garnett—Rolfe bombarded his agent with letters and manuscripts, trying in every way he knew to whet Pinker's interest and suggesting one thing after another to attract editors and publishers. Early in January, while Pinker still knew him as Frank English, Rolfe gave Pinker leave to negotiate for the American serial rights and all book rights in the twenty-four 'Reviews of Unwritten Books'.[38] He began delivering proofs of each one to Pinker as it came from *The Monthly Review*. On 9 January, by then as Frederick William Rolfe, he was making suggestions for the publication of the translation of Meleager and advocating that some 'enterprising publisher might create for him a vogue verisimilar to that at present enjoyed by '*Umar Khaiyam*.' He asked Pinker to note that he reviewed for *The Outlook* and was 'open to undertake "specials" in Journalism'. The next day, Rolfe telegraphed to call the agent's attention to a review in the current *Outlook*, 'All Glorious Without', pertaining to Meleager. Ten days later, he sent Pinker the appendix which Grant Richards had eliminated from *Chronicles of the House of Borgia*, now revised and called 'Suggestion for a Criterion of the Credibility of Certain Historians'. He spoke of the subject as a

141

'delicate and recondite one, treated in a delicate but daring and entirely novel manner', and said that 'properly placed' this essay must 'cause a storm of controversy'. In fact, he said, 'it's a bombshell'.[39] On 22 January, he provided Pinker with a key to the tin box containing 'An Ideal Content', already delivered to his office; with the key went the recommendation of a publisher, the little known firm of Hurst & Blackett. A mutual friend had promised to tell Blackett that Rolfe was a writer 'well worth cultivating'.

The next month, February 1903, was better. *The Monthly Review* began publication of 'Reviews of Unwritten Books' with 'Machiavelli's Despatches From the South African Campaign'. It was unsigned. Two more of Rolfe's reviews, also published anonymously, appeared on 21 February in *The Outlook*.[40] Before February had advanced very far, Rolfe had notified his agent of something sure to produce £200. Through W. T. Mainprize, a member of the staff of *The Morning Post*, Rolfe had offered its editor 'secret information . . . concerning a discovery . . . of inexhaustible petroleum in Zanti.' If the report was accepted and paid for, Rolfe was sure he would get £200.[41]

Meanwhile the campaign for recognition went on. In early March 'Notes on the Conclave' went to Pinker; although Rolfe suggested 'the Pall Mall Gazette, Pall Mall Magazine, and Mr. Stead', the piece was destined for *The Monthly Review* in August. At the end of April, Rolfe sent 'A Goat in Priest's Clothing' as a 'specimen of the series called "Thirty Naughty Emperors", ' which he declared would make a 'not invaluable book'.[42] An article, 'Excommunicate' by Frank English, went at the same time. Rolfe discussed with Pinker the possibilities of vanity publishing through the Grafton Press, proposing that an expert 'switch their noses round from the direction in which they would to the direction in which they *should* go'. Because he feared to miss a chance, he decided to write to the Grafton Press himself. When Pinker returned 'A Goat in Priest's Clothing' at the end of April and dismissed the entire series, Rolfe tried to stimulate his agent by raising the usual 10 per cent commission to 20 per cent, and on 5 May he had enough misguided courtesy to thank Pinker for accepting the offer.[43]

Groping for some way to earn his 20 per cent, Pinker arranged for Rolfe to confer with Arthur Henry Bullen, who, with Frank Sidgwick, had issued the poets of the Muses Library. Rolfe agreed to call on Bullen only if Pinker thought it essential. 'I would rather you did all talk,' he told Pinker, 'for you have seen what a fool my solitary life makes me at that—' While Pinker at Rolfe's urging tried to 'push Bullen . . . one way or an other' about the 'Meleagros', Rolfe advanced the merits of 'An Ideal Content'. He described it as an 'amazing book which would pay anyone who knows how to deal with an amazing book'.[44] Rolfe went to see Bullen, and they discussed Rolfe's translation of Meleager. Rolfe followed his visit with a letter outlining the book which could be made of 'Reviews of Unwritten Books' and listing thirty separate titles for essays, six more than the twenty-four already written. But Bullen showed no interest in such a book and preferred a translation of something other than Meleager, especially in Rolfe's version.[45]

Not content with giving Pinker instruction, Rolfe simultaneously repeated or expanded them in letters to Leonard Moore, a man commencing his career as literary agent with Pinker. Throughout 1903 and well into 1904, Rolfe wrote to Moore about the prospects of the 'Meleagros', 'An Ideal Content', and 'Reviews of Unwritten Books' with explicit directions as to how to conduct business relating to them. Rolfe tried, too, to tempt Moore with the implication that unusual exertion on his part would produce an unusual commission. At length Rolfe began to distinguish his transactions with Moore from those with Pinker, and to Moore Rolfe confided his mounting disenchantment with Pinker. 'Why', Rolfe asked Moore in October, 'has Pinker never asked me to dine at the Whitefriars, both in order to talk things over . . . and to introduce me to likely people through whom he might be able to make something out of me? Is he taking a bit of trouble or interest . . . ?'[46] At least twice Rolfe approached a social meeting with Moore, obliquely and crab-like in conformity with his astrological sign. He asked whether Moore ever listened to Hyde Park orators on Sunday afternoons before going to the nearby Express Dairy for his tea, as Rolfe did. On 5 December, a Saturday, the two men had a tentative appointment to meet at the door of the British Museum. Rolfe waited for forty minutes, but Moore was prevented from coming.[47]

During this year, however, Moore visited Rolfe at 69 Broadhurst Gardens. Contrary to many who knew him, Moore gave a sympathetic account of Rolfe, how he spread out the great Borgia genealogy on the floor and explained its details, how he offered his guest extra-long cigarettes while puffing at a meerschaum pipe, how he selected a 'delightful little chased patch-box from his choice collection of Georgian silver' to give to Moore, and how Rolfe put on both his eyeshade and his grandfather's large silver spectacles to read aloud a part of his work. Rolfe was almost genial that evening, without 'vituperation of anyone'. He was a 'good host' who displayed the 'Borgia Tree' enthusiastically and spoke proudly of his family and his ' "vigorous untainted English blood".' Moore said:

> Conversing with Rolfe (it was *listening* to Rolfe that evening) was an unusual pleasure. His quiet conversational manner contrasted oddly with his style, but the matter was what one would expect—and desire—from the author of *Stories Toto Told Me* and the *Chronicles of the House of Borgia*.[48]

Obviously there was no hint throughout the visit of the painful financial straits which existed then and in 1904 at 69 Broadhurst

143

Gardens. Long before Moore's visit, that is on 13 February 1903, Rolfe wrote to Bainbridge about another 'violent nerve-shattering scene' that morning. 'Summonses keep pouring in,' he went on; 'God knows what will be the next move. The suspense is horrible.' Bainbridge had invited Rolfe to take refuge with him at Shapwick, Bushy Heath, but Rolfe refused. 'That is quite impossible,' he said. First was the question of his clothes; during the years in London, he had worn out his underclothes, shirts, socks, boots, handkerchiefs. Everything was in such 'rags and tatters' that he could present a decent appearance only 'outwardly', and that, about once a week. He dared not visit a 'decent house' and expose his nakedness. Then, if he was to continue his work, his 'books, papers, & tools of trade' must be moved and that would require several pounds. 'No. Leave things as they are,' Rolfe told Bainbridge. 'When the worst comes, it must be faced. That's all.'[49]

To avoid the worst, Rolfe had been all over London the day before trying to get an advance on his work 'without damaging his prospects by disclosing the real state of affairs'. Where he had gone, to whom he had made his appeal unless it was to Henry Newbolt, is impossible to conjecture. It was not to Lane or Pinker. Rolfe had written to Pinker on Wednesday, 11 February, asking him to advance £100 on the manuscripts in his possession, since in Rolfe's view that was 'one of the functions of a literary agent'. Although Rolfe described himself to another correspondent a month later as 'well and vivid and vigorous, altogether wholesome and natural (except 2 artificial teeth) at 42',[50] he pleaded ill health to Pinker, saying that his doctor had advised a 'change of air'. He continued to play the part, for Pinker, of a man trying hard to avert a 'break-down of eyes' and nerves.[51] Nevertheless, when Pinker proved unwilling to supply the £100, Rolfe was able to recommend asking several publishers, among them John Murray, Smith Elder, and Longmans, for an advance on the basis of a synopsis and two chapters of an incomplete book called Hadrian the Seventh.[52] Meanwhile he interrupted the deterioration of his relations with John Lane to say, 'If you are anxious to do me a favour, the loan or advance of a hundred pounds would be very convenient to me at the present moment.'[53]

On the very day on which he acknowledged Pinker's refusal, 18 February, Rolfe wrote to Bainbridge to say that his landlady had 'got the tax people to refrain from putting in a distress till the end of the week'. As for himself, he could get hold of no 'ready money' and the effort of keeping up appearances before the tax men was killing his will to write. 'I'm sure,' he said, 'I shall go cranky all of a sudden.' The next day, a Thursday, he sent a hasty note to ask Bainbridge to lend him £10 at once. Rolfe offered as collateral 'Reviews of Unwritten Books', from which he expected about £15 in March. His urgency, he explained was owing to the fact that Mrs. Griffiths, his

144

I Frederick Rolfe, 1883

II Reproduction of a painting of Saint Aloysius made by Rolfe c.1885 and
used as a bookplate by John Gambril Nicholson in his copy of *Stories Toto
Told Me* by Baron Corvo

III Frederick Rolfe c.1889

IV(a) Toto

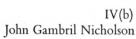

IV(b)
John Gambril Nicholson

V(a)
Henry Harland as seen
by Max Beerbohm, 1896

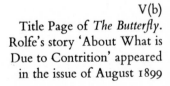

V(b)
Title Page of *The Butterfly*.
Rolfe's story 'About What is
Due to Contrition' appeared
in the issue of August 1899

VI Frederick Rolfe, 1898

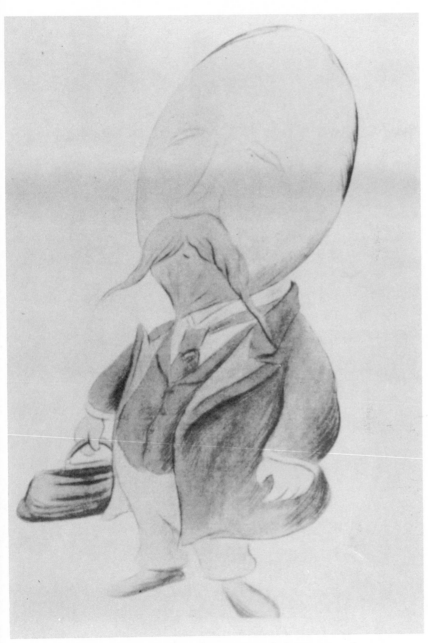

VII John Lane as seen by Max Beerbohm, c.1901

VIII(a) Self portrait of Frederick Rolfe, 1903, at work in his attic room at
69 Broadhurst Gardens

VIII(b)
E. Nesbit
(Mrs Hubert Bland),
1905

IX(a)
Rolfe's work sheet for the
dedication of *Innocent the Great* by
C. H. C. Pirie-Gordon

IX(b)
Robert Hugh Benson,
1907

STATION.
ABERGAVENNY.

GWERNVALE,
CRICKHOWEL.

XXV May 1907

Dear Mr Bland:

Now that is good of you.
If you can't fix Lane with N.C., do speak
to Lawrie. I'm not at all anxious for
a "sum down". If I can meet a publisher
who will do his work properly (i.e.
issue me in decent shape & advertise
me like a patent pill.) I should be
quite content with a share in the profits,
ie. a Royalty.
As for the Times, I have described N.C.

X(a)
Facsimile of a
letter from Rolfe
to Hubert Bland

X(b)
Proof of a bookplate
which Rolfe made for
Edward Pirie-Gordon, c.1907

XI C. H. C. (Harry) Pirie-Gordon in the Robes of
the Grandmagistracy of the Order of Sanctissima
Sophia

XII(a)
Frederick Rolfe,
c.1908

XII(b)
Charles Masson Fox

XIII Binding cover of Rolfe's first published work, his long poem
Tarcissus, which appeared in 1880

Stories Toto Told Me

BY

BARON CORVO

JOHN LANE: THE BODLEY HEAD
LONDON AND NEW YORK
1898

XIV Title page from *Stories Toto Told Me,* Rolfe's second published work

XV Binding cover of the first edition of Rolfe's *Hadrian the Seventh*

HADRIAN THE SEVENTH

A ROMANCE

BY

FR. ROLFE

LONDON
CHATTO & WINDUS
1904

XVI Title page of *Hadrian the Seventh*

landlady, said that three judgment summonses to the amount of £10 must be paid the next day. Bainbridge did not respond, but Mrs. Griffiths kept the bailiffs out with a post-dated cheque. Immediately after it was due, according to Rolfe, he received an instalment from *The Monthly Review*, which met the cheque but left him 'naked'.[54]

Rolfe's statement about the use of the fee from *The Monthly Review* for Mrs. Griffiths is puzzling. Sholto Douglas said that he got it all, that Rolfe took nothing from 'Reviews of Unwritten Books'. About that, Douglas was either mistaken or misinformed. Rolfe took at least half of the amount paid by *The Monthly Review*, in accordance with his agreement with Douglas. Rolfe's report of his earnings between April 1902 and May 1903, made to the Royal Literary Fund on 6 May 1903, included £13 6s. 8d. from 'Reviews of Unwritten Books'. His use of £10 of that amount to cover Mrs. Griffiths's cheque was at least unexpected even though he owed her close to £160. Rolfe was usually at variance with his landladies and landlords, who harried and hunted him for their rightful charges. Mrs. Griffiths was no exception. In September, she threatened to keep his few possessions when, having only 6d. to his name, he thought once more of going to Bainbridge at Bushy Heath.[55] Yet Rolfe insisted that she trusted him and excused her demands for what was due to her on the grounds of necessity, adding in a letter to Henry Newbolt about Mrs. Griffiths, 'That of course is not all,' and then denied the 'ordinary liaisons or vices'.[56] In the case of her cheque, Rolfe acted largely in self-interest, convinced as he said that a woman cannot understand anything but 'cash down'. Despite his disastrous relations with John Lane and Grant Richards, Rolfe had managed to secure Mrs. Griffiths's 'perfect confidence' and her promise to help him until he could 'recover' his losses. To make good Mrs. Griffiths's indebtedness with the payment from *The Monthly Review* could only bolster her faith in his prospects, especially if she thought there was a possibility of more to come from the 'Reviews'.[57] In this way he once more escaped the nightmare of homelessness.

[v]

Rolfe's need was intensified in several ways in 1903. That fact was partly owing to the circumstances of his sister and recently widowed mother. After seven years of alienation from his parents and almost no communication with any member of his family except his brother Herbert, Rolfe was reunited with his family in 1901 or early 1902, when his father fell ill. For a few weeks he went each Friday to his father at 5 Highbury Hill.[1] On 30 July 1902, the elder Rolfe died and thereafter the Friday engagement was transferred to the mother.

Rolfe knew that his father had been unable to provide for her. Rolfe could give her little more than sympathy; neither could his brothers, who were all fighting a 'desperate battle' for survival.

Yet Rolfe felt his 'duty' to his mother and his sister.[2] He attempted to keep alive what little business William Rolfe & Sons, the family firm, still had. It was mostly piano tuning performed by Jenkins, a 'drudge' who had learned his 'art' from Rolfe's grandfather, Nicholas. Rolfe got out circulars announcing his father's death and the continuance of the business. Transacting business on the letterhead of what he called 'my firm', he managed to clear 17s. in the next twelve months by selling two Kemmler pianos.[3] One of these went to Harry Bainbridge, who paid £20 in cash and £3 quarterly thereafter until he had made up the total price of thirty-three guineas. Rolfe was diligent in collecting the payments, often overdue, for his sister. To Bainbridge, he reported the 'dreadful state' of his mother and sister in March 1903.[4] His mother had collapsed and nothing but months of rest and absence of worry would restore her. There was nothing Rolfe could do; he did not have the one thing which would relieve his mother, money. He could only rage helplessly at his inability 'to put things right a bit . . . to straighten out tangled lives'.[5]

Rolfe's sense of helplessness grew more insistent when the Royal Literary Fund refused his application for a second grant on 14 May 1903. At the end of March, in accordance with instructions from Roberts, the Fund's secretary, Rolfe described his circumstances, asserting that he was 'worse off' than he had been a year ago. He blamed John Lane and his delay in bringing out the *Rubáiyát*. The result, Rolfe said, was an inability to place three other books and a difficulty in concentrating on the work-in-hand. He explained the discrepancy between his income and his expenses and debts. He was fearful that unless he had assistance soon, his health would not allow him to go on. Rolfe added, 'I detest the making another application for pecuniary help; and venture to ask you to lay this before Dr. Gosse and Mr. Barrie personally hoping that they will put in my way some of that literary work over which they have so much influence.'[6] Roberts answered the next day, regretting Rolfe's circumstance but rightly saying that his official position prevented his doing what Rolfe asked, that he must write for himself.[7] Rolfe promptly sent letters to Edmund Gosse and James M. Barrie, both members of the Committee of the Royal Literary Fund; he asked for their influence in securing work. In each letter Rolfe enclosed one of the circulars offering pianos for sale from the remnants of William Rolfe and Sons Pianoforte Manufacturers.[8] Neither man replied. A week later, that is on 31 March, Rolfe reported the fact to Roberts and stated the necessity for making application to the Royal Literary Fund in May. In due course he proceeded with his application, securing a testimonial letter from Henry Newbolt, whose *Monthly Review* was then publishing the 'Reviews of

Unwritten Books', and a re-affirmation of his testimony of the previous year from E. G. Hardy at Oxford.[9] Shortly after submitting his formal application, Rolfe wrote two letters on his own behalf. One explained his lack of success despite his energy and ability as owing to his 'disposition' to let others take advantage of him and the 'malignance or imbecility of Barrabas', Rolfe's term for publishers. Two of these, Richards and Lane had tarnished his pseudonym and thus forced him to begin his writing career again under his own name. After a lament for his health, his debts, and his wardrobe, Rolfe mentioned his willingness to teach, frustrated by the impossibility of getting pupils because he was a Roman Catholic, although Catholics shunned him because as a student in 1890, he had 'capped the King of Italy in the Corso of Rome'. Rolfe's second letter accompanied his genealogy of the House of Borgia, which he explained as a 'skeleton or ground plan' of a history of the Borgias. He 'most earnestly' wanted to write this history. 'My scheme', he said, 'is to produce such a history as will be popular with the intellectual public which loves (like a plucky boy) to be taken a little bit out of its depth (because it can swim), and useful to the historian from the complete collection of historical documents which I shall append to it.[10] He proposed to write in English, Latin, Italian, and French, all to be published simultaneously. In support of his plan, Rolfe submitted a letter from Richard Garnett.[11]

The failure of Rolfe's application was inevitable. As soon as Barrie had Rolfe's letter asking for his influence, he wrote to Roberts about Rolfe, 'He says that he can't wait until the next meeting of the Council —and that you suggested his appealing to me, but I can't think you did anything of the kind.' On 28 March 1903, only two days later, Barrie praised Roberts for acting 'judiciously', thanked him for his explanation and added that it bore out what he had just learned 'from other sources about Mr Rolfe'.[12] Whatever Barrie had learned, it had to do with the fliers offering pianos for sale, and it cast doubt on Rolfe's integrity. The circulars had implied to the members of the Committee, which included in addition to Barrie and Gosse, Julian Sturgis and Maurice Hewlett, that Rolfe had income from his family's once prosperous and well-known factory. Edmund Gosse said as much. On the day before the Committee met, he wrote to Newbolt and, like Barrie, questioned Rolfe's representations. Gosse called Rolfe a 'sturdy beggar', asserted that if the truth were known it would doubtless show him to have a comfortable roof over his head. Gosse gave it as his opinion that Rolfe was very likely mad.[13] Furthermore, the members of the Committee thought his application 'clever silly'.[14] When the Committee met on 13 May, its members refused to make a grant to Rolfe, and on the next day Roberts wrote without explanation to inform Rolfe.

Rolfe was numbed. He sent Roberts's letter to Newbolt, admitted that it struck him flat, and asked for an appointment. Rolfe delayed fetching his books and the Borgiada from the offices of the Royal Literary Fund until he had mastered his gloom. At the end of the month he was still bewildered. 'I am working through a desperately bad time,' he said and resolved to use all his energy to get him through.[15] He began to think once more about the possibilities in the Borgias and the materials Count Cesare Borgia could provide from Milan; but he concentrated on writing 'eight-and-sixpenny reviews for *The Outlook* and 'anonymous absurdities' for *The Monthly Review*, fearing that if he did not, he might 'die of inanition'.[16] Almost three weeks after the fiasco with the Royal Literary Fund, Rolfe had had no word from Newbolt, who, with the members of the Committee, suspected him of attempted fraud. On 5 June, he wrote again to Newbolt first about literary matters and then to ask whether he had offended in some way.

Rolfe was now able to face his predicament. He declared that if he stopped working for even two days, he would be penniless and homeless. He was determined not to stop until he had the means or collapsed, and collapse was a distinct threat. His doctor, Roger-Smith, warned him that he must have a long rest and freedom from worry or expect a serious break-down. And Rolfe talked of counting the pulsations of his heart as he lay in bed at night: 'fourteen-am-I-going-to-say-fifteen ... ninety-seven-shall-I-be-here-to-say ninety-eight, and so on to thousands.'[17] Then his natural buoyancy reasserted itself. 'I (metaphorically) took my doctor by the throat', Rolfe said, 'and told him he *must* keep me going. So he applied blisters on the back of my ears. I am all raw and quite unpresentable: but I'm still here and still slaving and when the booming in my head gets unbearable I just clap on another blister.'[18]

On 3 July, Rolfe learned from Henry Newbolt that *The Monthly Review* would publish no more 'Reviews of Unwritten Books'. By that time nine had appeared, the first in the February 1903 issue and two thereafter in subsequent issues, March through June. Newbolt had in hand another fifteen which Rolfe expected him to publish. He held John Murray, the publisher of *The Monthly Review*, responsible for the cancellation.[19] Because the 'Reviews' had been very well received and seemed very likely to be a fixture in *The Monthly Review*, Rolfe had asked for an increase in fee. Murray refused and they stopped altogether. Rolfe was still ignorant, of course, of the accusations which had led the Royal Literary Fund to refuse him aid, and he had no idea that Newbolt shared the suspicions and was glad to be rid of him. In any case, the cessation of the 'Reviews' was a blow. Rolfe particularly regretted that he had not signed at least the last two and thereby acquired a little prestige. Now he had nothing. As usual, all his efforts, his ingenuity, his scheming, his endless work in the attic room at 69 Broadhurst Gardens had come to nothing. By his own count, he had endured '7½ years [of] incessant work . . . in beastly conditions, and without a single holiday and with interminable difficulty—and with no tangible success'.[20]

Still Rolfe persevered. He urged Pinker to serialise the fifteen unpublished 'Reviews of Unwritten Books', to 'stir up' Bullen, to circulate 'Live Pork and a Peall'. He had already asked to be made sub-editor of *The Monthly Review*, and once he asked Newbolt whether he knew a bear which needed a leader. Then by a macabre piece of luck, Pope Leo XIII died on 20 July, and Rolfe's article 'Notes on the Conclave' was timely all of a sudden, especially with its minute particulars (acquired by occult means, Rolfe said). Newbolt, who had held 'Notes' for some time without making a decision about it, sent him payment early in August, and the piece, signed Fred. Will. Rolfe, appeared in *The Monthly Review*. Another essay, the suppressed appendix from *Chronicles of The House of Borgia* went to Brimley Johnson for *The Westminster Review*.[21] Although neither sale owed much to Pinker, he was careful to collect his commission at 20 per cent, and Rolfe was careful to pay it and to report that Newbolt had called his article 'the most adequate a/c of the Conclave the public have had'.[22]

Payment for both articles amounted to so little that Rolfe tried again to promote the 'Borgia subject'. He turned to two new correspondents brought him by the Borgia book. One was James J. Walsh, a New York physician. The other was G. T. Maquay, William Waldorf Astor's secretary. Maquay had acted for Astor when Rolfe attempted to sell him the genealogy. The transaction aroused Maquay's interest so that he read Rolfe's *Chronicles of The House of Borgia* and wrote to comment on it to Rolfe. From that letter developed a considerable exchange of letters. On 16 July, Rolfe asked Maquay to find a patron for the projected work.[23] Walsh, Rolfe asked to be his patron.

In the course of a series of letters which appeared in *The Saturday Review* discussing Pope Alexander VI, Walsh had defended the Borgian pope and Rolfe's account of him. Rolfe was so pleased that he could not refrain from thanking Walsh in a letter dated 28 January 1903. Now, on 28 July, Rolfe asked Walsh for a 'lump sum' of perhaps £1,000 to give him confidence, sweet-reasonableness, strength to 'use' himself 'well and aptly'. With a 'lump sum' he could pay up his 'really paltry embarrassments' and then rest for a month at sea, rid his soul of 'horrible dreams' and get back to work without the worry of saving boot-leather on a long walk or of lacking a clean shirt and collar when he needed to see a publisher. Rolfe admitted that he had been unable to make anyone understand the urgency of a 'lump sum'. But he explained that he was not adept in the 'art and mystery of mendacity'. Besides, he could never remember that others were not as intelligent as he, and he feared that his 'cruel face' and 'haughty disdainful manner' aroused the 'most violent antipathy'. In return for a decent sum, Rolfe offered Walsh the same options Harry Bainbridge had had:

149

to buy the Borgiada and all rights to the information it contained, to buy it without the rights, or to become a partner and acquire a half-share in the fame and profit to be derived from a history of the Borgias which Rolfe would produce. He called the last a real opportunity for some young American millionaire who wanted to 'get high up in the tree of literature at one bound'. If none of this appealed to Walsh, Rolfe could offer him four complete books in exchange for enough cash to allow him to conquer his despair and to use himself. Rolfe insisted that he was certain and resolved to be certain that God had not created his 'very singular potential energetic and unique person-ality simply to be wasted'.[24]

The appeal to Walsh was not an appeal for charity. Rolfe had already refused the offer of a gift of money from Maquay, thanking him on 18 July for his kindness and saying that he could not 'take something for nothing'. He was determined to meet any circumstance too strong for him 'with clean hands'.[25] Rolfe, whose sense of business was not his strongest point, firmly believed that he had something to sell which was well worth buying and must sooner or later bring a good price. Therefore he wrote to Pinker in August to ask again for an advance. Since by now Pinker could surely 'fix a value' on Rolfe's work, the 'Reviews of Unwritten Books' had had favourable attention, and he had shown his ability to turn out literary work under un-happy conditions, Rolfe thought Pinker might make a 'substantial advance'. If not, Rolfe said, he must terminate their agreement. Although to so do would lose the benefit of Pinker's services and 'annul the success . . . won so far', Rolfe said that he saw no alternative, that he could not continue to work on the 'present lines'.[26] Pinker refused and Rolfe offered to call for his manuscripts. But his indigna-tion was half-hearted. A few days later he was advising Leonard Moore, Pinker's associate, how to approach Constable, how to 'pitch a yarn' about Rolfe as a writer bound to rise and with whom it might be well to be connected.[27]

His financial predicament and his prospects were unchanged, but Rolfe believed that if he held out until October the Royal Literary Fund would salvage him. On 3 July 1903, he had written to Roberts to ask whether he might renew his application to the Fund. According to Rolfe, Henry Newbolt had suggested this fresh application. That he did so is difficult to credit inasmuch as he had heard from Edmund Gosse and Julian Sturgis exactly why Rolfe had been denied funds in May. Yet, in writing to Newbolt in August, Rolfe referred to his plan to renew his application with an ease which took for granted Newbolt's knowledge of it. In fact, he had already filed an application. Disre-garding the professional coolness of Roberts's reply, dated 9 July 1903, Rolfe had asked for consideration at the next Committee meeting scheduled for 14 October.

His application could produce only pain and humiliation, although they came to Rolfe through a chain of events peripheral to this third appeal to the Royal Literary Fund. On 13 August, in taking in the letters from the postman, Rolfe found two from Henry Newbolt, one to himself and one marked private and confidential directed to Mrs. Griffiths. A few days earlier, Mrs. Griffiths's patience with Rolfe had worn itself out 'violently', and she had given him another ultimatum. He tried to annul it with talk of funds to come from *The Monthly Review* and Newbolt. Mrs. Griffiths then called on Newbolt to find out the truth about Rolfe's earnings and his prospects. Unable to talk with her at length, Newbolt wrote to tell her of his respect for Rolfe's ability but despite that he could not guarantee Rolfe steady employment. Although Newbolt urged her to be generous a little longer, his information goaded Mrs. Griffiths to a renewed threat and a new quarrel of gigantic proportions with Rolfe. That same day, she set down her side of the story in a long letter to Newbolt. Her only source of income was from boarders. She currently had one who paid her £1 1s. a week. From that she supported her son, a housekeeper, and Rolfe. By waiting three years for his success, she had lost £160, ruined her business, and, for her pains, got a bill of sale on her furniture. She wanted Rolfe's room to let to some advantage.[28]

Rolfe resented this traffic behind his back, and he hurried to say that he knew about it and to explain his position with Mrs. Griffiths in a letter written that same day. He answered Newbolt's charge of concealing details of his 'case' by charging Newbolt with 'imperfect' sympathy. As his letter went on, Rolfe's sense of abuse turned to self-pity. He said that he had no choice but to disappear since a grant from the Royal Literary Fund was improbable and in any event it must be inadequate and degrading. He asked Newbolt to write to various publishers if he could recommend Rolfe's work; but if the work was 'pretentious, unreal, superficial, valueless', as Rolfe feared, then, he urged, 'say so, and let me die'. But Newbolt's suggestion that Rolfe had not told the 'whole state' of his 'case' stuck in his 'gorge'. His tendency to demean himself disappeared and he then and there wrote a second letter. He reproved Newbolt for his letter to Mrs. Griffiths because, Rolfe said, it was belittling to him. He insisted that he was no 'common cadger', that he wanted no alms. He declared that Newbolt had no right to be told anything, a circumstance which was Newbolt's own doing. Newbolt had shown that he had no room in his life for Rolfe. He continued, 'I have so composed all my affairs that no one on the earth ever will be able correctly to read me, unless they shall have obtained the key from me . . . I keep the key. And I will keep it, even when I disappear . . . for the gods have not sent me a loyal heart to whom I can entrust it.'[29]

Newbolt's response informed Rolfe that the letter to Mrs. Griffiths and the reference to Rolfe's 'case' were attempts to investigate the accusations made against him by the trustees of the Royal Fund. For the first time Rolfe learned of these two accusations and of Newbolt's subsequent distrust. One was that Rolfe had already received more than one grant from the Fund, and the other, more serious one was that he had falsified his financial situation, that he had an adequate income from William Rolfe & Sons.

Rolfe had this information on 17 August, a Monday, and he at once sat down to write more letters. He returned the application form to the Royal Literary Fund, saying that despite circumstances of 'the most distracting description', he preferred to make no application to the Fund. He had obtained from Newbolt, Rolfe went on, 'particulars of two definite accusations' made by trustees of the Fund, accusations which amounted to 'a charge of fraudulent misrepresentation'. He insisted that he was the last man in the world to ask for help which he did not 'merit or need'. He asked Roberts to lay before the trustees his 'most strenuous protest' against the treatment he had received. He called himself the 'indignant victim' of a 'secret and baseless slur'.[30] As he had told Roberts he would do, Rolfe sent to Newbolt by the same post a 'directly substantial refutation' of the accusations, twelve pages written in 'burning torment'. He refuted both accusations firmly and truthfully. In the case of the supposititious income, Rolfe quoted pence and pound, showing that profits to date from William Rolfe & Sons under his management came to 17s. 5d., which went to his mother. He reproved Newbolt for writing to Mrs. Griffiths because, as a result of his letter, she had come to disbelieve Rolfe, thus adding 'a new terror' to his life. So far his letter had dignity and force. The last part asked for introductions to Dr. Moore of Oriel College, Oxford, through whom he hoped to approach the Toynbees with the Borgia genealogy; to Bernard Quaritch, the London bookseller, again for the sake of the Borgias; and to Edward Stanford, who could employ him as 'revisor and editor of the new edition of Murray's "Rome and the Campagna".' Although he expected to be 'adrift' at any moment, he meant to keep trying until that moment came.[31]

Rolfe sent a third letter to Dr. Walsh in New York. Rolfe had had no reply to his letter of 28 July in which various options were proposed for the purchase of the Borgia genealogy and the hypothetical sum of £1,000 was named. Frantic with pain and worry, Rolfe could not wait for an answer. He wrote that his affairs had come to a head, that his creditors were 'upon' him, that it was the dead season for publishing with little possibility in that direction until after Christmas. He went on to say that at any moment he might be thrown out into the street with nowhere to go and no one to help him: 'I must lean upon you. Save me from going mad, losing all chance of success with my work. I do not know where I shall be from hour to hour so I beg you to wire your help . . .'[32]

Walsh sent £10, one of those 'little bits' which Rolfe said only prolonged his agony. Yet that £10 served to fend off Mrs. Griffiths's repeated threats of expulsion. Rolfe appealed once more to Harry Bainbridge. 'Give me a chance to continue writing', Rolfe said, 'and I will be able to keep the whole lot of you, and my mother and sister as well, handsomely.' He implored Bainbridge to join forces with him; both must benefit if Rolfe had a place in which to work and peace of mind. He could not understand Bainbridge's failure to welcome the idea. Rolfe told Bainbridge, 'Things will continue to go damnably with me as long as I am prevented from going on working. I wonder that you have not realised that fact; and that you have not . . . accepted my offer to join forces.'[33]

Because he knew from experience who must finance such a collaboration, Bainbridge had avoided Rolfe for some time. He now relented and invited Rolfe to Shapwick. Rolfe replied on 12 September that he must delay long enough to read the proofs of his article 'Suggestion for a Criterion of the Credibility of Certain Historians' for *The Westminster Review*, and his opportunity was gone. When he was packed and ready to go on 21 September, a Monday, he found himself in tatters and with only 6*d.* in cash. Money which he expected from Bainbridge on the next day did not arrive. Neither did Bainbridge, whom Rolfe expected in response to a telegram. Instead he had a letter putting him off while Mrs. Griffiths scolded him and demanded that he leave without his possessions. This quarrel with his landlady was long lasting and harsh; one day she was 'abominably rude' and another, heaped 'horrible abuse' on him. But as Rolfe insisted he would even though he went 'raving mad in the process', he stayed at 69 Broadhurst Gardens, entreating Bainbridge all the while to send him £4 (of which 30*s.* was intended for Mrs. Griffiths), to take his possessions, to let him come to Shapwick, but above all to give him a chance to 'use' his 'undoubted abilities now running loose'.[34] His last appeal was dated 28 September 1903 and, like the others, it was fruitless.

In little more than a week, Rolfe had broken irrevocably with Newbolt. Rolfe waited uselessly for the letters of introduction he had requested until he was driven to say that sudden death would be merciful in comparison with his suspense and wasted efforts. By late September, he was directing letters not to Newbolt but to the Editor of *The Monthly Review* and soon, in the third person, he stated that Newbolt's conduct was 'not that of a man of honour', and he declared himself Newbolt's 'persequent enemy'.[35] That was on 6 October 1903. Although he continued to send rancorous notes to Newbolt, by 6 October, Rolfe had alienated himself from every editor who knew his work and from every literary associate except his agent.

[vi]

Shortly after 6 October, Rolfe's unnatural humility vanished, his relations with Mrs. Griffiths were on a sounder basis, and for the moment he was no longer dependent on anyone to give him 'personally a chance'. In fact, briefly, he hardly needed the help in getting 'little literary jobs' which Richard Whiteing, author of the novels *No. 5 John Street* and *The Yellow Van*, began to supply early that month. On Friday, 2 October, Whiteing had had Rolfe to dinner at the Whitefriars Club and on the Monday following wrote to ask Wilfred Meynell to read Rolfe's work and to do something for him. Whiteing, who knew nothing of prior transactions between Meynell and Rolfe, described Rolfe as 'a little weasel of a man almost tonsured with a close crop, and that indelible look of priest in every line of him which your seminaries seem to give whether they call or reject which even Renan bore to the last day of his life'. Whiteing said that Rolfe told a 'strange story of an attempt to live by learnedly popular books and much resultant commons. . . .' Whiteing had given his guest a lecture on 'not writing over people's heads' and Rolfe had listened 'with a smile that might have meant anything though it was meekness and acquiescence as far as it met' the eye.[1] Whiteing thought of taking lessons in Italian, and he put Rolfe in the way of work from time to time. Rolfe was much impressed with the Whitefriars' dinner, a weekly event at Anderton's Hotel on Fleet Street, and he decided to accept whatever help was to his liking. He had other expectations.

Within a few days after dining with Whiteing, Rolfe provided himself with a meagre independence by answering a newspaper advertisement for literary assistance. In mid-1903 the Rhodes Trustees had commissioned Colonel Owen Thomas to prepare a report on Rhodesian farming and advanced him a fee of £500. The subject was a timely one inasmuch as the Treaty of Vereeniging, which concluded the South African War, was little more than a year old and papers and periodicals filled their pages with plans relative to South Africa. Thomas's book was part of the British concern for colonialism in South Africa. Unable to put his material into publishable form, Thomas advertised for help. When Rolfe applied for the work, the 'obese magenta colonel of militia with a black-stubbed moustache and a Welsh-tongued proposition' engaged him. They entered into an agreement whereby Rolfe was to edit Thomas's book, later called *The Agricultural and Pastoral Prospects of South Africa*, for a fee of £25, an amount suggested by Rolfe. The sum was paid to him in instalments which commenced on 10 October 1903 and ended on 28 November 1903.

Rolfe, who immediately envisioned large undertakings, amplified his new assignment to Mrs. Griffiths and eventually supported his claims by paying her enough to restore her good humour. Indeed, when she had only a promise of payment, she was so mellowed by his expectations that she at last allowed Rolfe, who was still curious about it, to see the letter Henry Newbolt had written to her in August.

Of course, Rolfe found the letter offensive. He called Newbolt a 'blackguard' and announced that he was by no means 'done' with Newbolt. As soon as Colonel Thomas began his payments, Rolfe sent this letter to Newbolt:

> I know you will be sorry to hear that I have obtained a month's relief (from the difficulties in which you cast me) in the shape of a 'ghostship' to an agricultural expert, who provides the facts and fee for a booklet which I am writing for him to sign. I am thankful to say that I owe this job solely to my own exertions; and I put you in possession of the facts in order that you may have no excuse for further libellous statements concerning me.[2]

However consoling it was for Rolfe to attribute his misfortunes to someone else, he could do no more than threaten revenge. When Leonard Moore informed Rolfe, late in November, that *The Monthly Review* had rejected Rolfe's article called 'Esoteric Jewelry', he wrote to Moore, 'I hope it has been made plain to Mr. Newbolt that the article was not sent to him through me.' He forbade Moore to offer anything else to Newbolt or to his publisher Murray. 'I have not finished with Mr. Newbolt yet by any means,' Rolfe repeated to Moore and promised to do 'whatever else is necessary' when the occasion arose.[3] No such opportunity presented itself. Rolfe's capacity for revenge throughout his life, except for wounding words, was as impotent as his more noble delusions.

By 26 November, Rolfe's revision and editing of Thomas's *Agricultural Prospects* were complete.[4] Rolfe was pleased with the work he had done. He felt that his faith in himself was justified, that he had demonstrated another facet of his brilliance, and he had no hesitation in telling Moore that Pinker had failed to realise what an asset he had in Rolfe. He thought Pinker must be used to men who could do only one thing and thus could not conceive of a man such as Rolfe, who was able to 'do half-a-dozen things equally well'.[5]

Before Thomas made his last payment, Rolfe had another reprieve. In the first week in November he had acquired as much as £20 when he was reunited with John Gambril Nicholson, established since 1896 as a master at the Stationers' School. Instead of ignoring Rolfe or reminding him of unhappy times at Colwyn Bay in 1894 or their differences about the poem 'William of Norwich' in *Love in Earnest*, Nicholson welcomed visits from Rolfe and lent him money. Nicholson

155

eagerly reported on Rolfe and his doings to his antagonist of Christ-church days, Kains Jackson. After an account of two evening visits from Rolfe, referred to as Corvo, Nicholson spoke of him as looking 'well-preserved' because he used 'art in his make-up'. Nicholson had 'spotted' it on the second visit, and he decided that Corvo was no doubt 'equally meretricious in his manner; . . . a poseur'. With his schoolmaster's naïve faith in the power of fellowship and tolerance, Nicholson was confident that he had penetrated Rolfe's pose and that he could deliver Corvo from his mortal fear 'of all men, of all publicity, of all daylight upon him and his deeds'. Nicholson took pride in accepting Corvo without prejudice and giving him another chance to obliterate 'the last 20 years', an attitude 'the world' refused to take. He was determined to save Corvo from himself 'by purposely ignoring anything amiss in him', and he believed Rolfe responded gallantly. 'The man I knew and loved 20 years ago', Nicholson said, 'was bound to do so. . . . He is F. W. Rolfe; he assumes no other identity.'[6] Nicholson's anticipation of a 'miracle of healing' in Corvo-Rolfe was absurd. He was unaware that he needed healing except in the form of success and the cash it might bring. From Rolfe's point of view, even the visits to Nicholson were unsatisfactory. Rolfe disliked the unremitting presence of Frank Victor Rushmore, a boy of about fifteen whom Nicholson described as his 'dear young chum', so 'kind and indispensable'.[7] When Nicholson inscribed a copy of his book of poems A Chaplet of Southern-wood 'To F. W. R. from J. G. N. F. V. R. intervening', Rolfe returned it. He had crossed out his own name and written, 'Things being as they are, F. W. R. refuses consent to intervention'.[8] More than 'ten years' hell', attributable to others' blunders which no one tried to set right, could hardly be wiped out by a schoolmaster's complacency or senti-mentality. Rolfe was receptive only to the £20.

That £20, Rolfe was sure, was a mere stop-gap, because he expected £2,000 from the Borgiada. On about 18 November, he had exhibited it to Colonel Thomas; and Thomas, Rolfe insisted later, had promised to sell it for that amount.[9] While he waited for the sale to be effected, Rolfe was performing small tasks for Thomas such as writing letters or advising him about letters. For these he received small sums in cash.

These additional payments from Thomas plus Nicholson's contri-bution got Rolfe through the last weeks of 1903 and the first ones of 1904. According to Nicholson's New Year's letter to Kains Jackson, Rolfe was in an 'awful state'.[10] It was relieved only by Friday dinners with his mother and a short working visit with Hardy at Oxford, commencing about 10 January. Ten days later, Rolfe was back in Hampstead and back at his unflagging efforts to promote himself and his work. On 22 January, he sent a long letter to Arthur Henry Bullen asking for a commission to do 'an historical novel on the life of Pius II (Eneas Silvio de' Piccolhuomini).' Rolfe outlined a novel of ten parts treating the 'picturesque XV Century times' in 'vivid modern English'.

156

He proposed to illustrate it, as well, with 'exquisite outline drawings' of the frescoes at Siena, available for Bullen's inspection at the British Museum.[11] Bullen declined. At about the same time, Rolfe reported to Leonard Moore after a long talk with Colonel Thomas that a 'whole *ocean of literature*', both 'serial and book', was to follow the publication of *Agricultural and Pastoral Prospects*.[12] Rolfe assured Moore that when he had sold work currently in his hands, he would get more. The South African book was dangled before Moore and at the end of the month Rolfe showed him a 'private copy' of it. In a further attempt to call attention to his work, he sent to *Notes and Queries* for 13 February a short inquiry as to Henry Harland's exact reference on page 227 of *My Friend Prospero*: 'In the spirited phrase of Corvo, "here came my Lord the Sun".' Rolfe signed himself Nicholas Crabbe; as Frederick, Baron Corvo, he answered his own query in the 5 March issue of *Notes and Queries* with a reference to his Toto story which had appeared in *The Butterfly* in 1900, 'About What is Due to Repentance'.[13]

Unfortunately none of these produced cash so that while he waited for Thomas to sell the Borgiada, Rolfe was happy to accept Thomas's suggestion in February that he prepare for publication the typescript of *Agricultural and Pastoral Prospects* for a fee of £15. On 23 February, Rolfe received £10 of that amount, and the remaining £5 was paid him on 15 March. This arrangement with Thomas enabled Rolfe to go with Mrs. Griffiths when she moved in March from 69 Broadhurst Gardens, Hampstead, to 15 Cheniston Gardens, Kensington.

By the time of the move, Rolfe was inaccessible to nearly everyone he knew. On 19 March, in a letter to Kains Jackson, Nicholson remarked that he had not seen Rolfe for a month, that he refused both visits and letters. Nicholson went on, '*This* Corvo would be a failure anywhere. . . . But there *is* another being who is possible; but this . . . other self of his lives a crab life; and even when it emerges from its shell and its claws it is *that sensitive* that it suffers if the least thing touches it.'[14] Clothes in tatters and an 'awful state' hardly make for conviviality.

[vii]

Although the metaphor of the crab in Nicholson's letter implies his knowledge that Rolfe was at work on *Nicholas Crabbe*, Nicholson failed to take the fact into account. Rolfe's isolation suggested that he was eager to write without interruption. When he completed the book well before 1 July 1904, it was the second of three long pieces of fiction wholly his own and written wholly on his own initiative during the six terrible years which began when he came to London. These three books were not commissioned and none was a translation. In addition to *Nicholas Crabbe*, they include *Don Tarquinio* and *Hadrian the Seventh*. Rolfe's earliest reference to Hadrian occurred about 1895 at Holywell during a conversation between John Holden and Rolfe. When he was asked what he would do if he 'came into a million', his answer was immediate and serious. 'Become Pope,' he said. Judging by his prompt reply, Rolfe already had his dream of the papacy and his concept of the rights and duties of a pope. He vented them to Holden in a considerable harangue about bribery, the papacy, the curia, various colleges and functions, and the Jesuits. Holden asked what name he would take and alluded to an English pope. Rolfe 'almost shouted, "I shall be Adrian the Seventh!" ' As Adrian, he promised to make Holden Archbishop of Milan but vowed to withhold canonisation.[1] Rolfe first referred to the book in a letter directed to Kenneth Grahame and dated 21 December 1900. There Rolfe listed three historical novels among his several projects, 'Don Ghirlando's Diarium (A.D. 1528–30), Don Tarquinio's Holographs (A.D. 1492–1524), and Hadrian the Seventh (A.D. 1905).'[2]

The actual writing was already under way. Rolfe had started *Hadrian* in late summer, 1900, after he delivered the original version of *Chronicles of the House of Borgia* to Grant Richards and while he waited to hear from Richards or Frederic Chapman, acting for John Lane, about another commission which never came. He wrote in the attic room at 69 Broadhurst Gardens. There, under the slanting ceiling, in his armchair before the fireplace he sat with his writing-board on his knees and worked exactly as the early pages of *Hadrian the Seventh* say. Despite interruptions such as the unwelcome task of revising the Borgia book to Richards's specifications, problems with Lane about *In His Own Image* and the *Rubáiyát*, quarrels with Mrs. Griffiths, the attempted collaboration with Sholto Douglas, frantic efforts to sell the Borgiada, and the necessity for writing 'frightful rot' for monthlies and weeklies under a 'posse of pseudonyms', Rolfe finished a first draft before mid-March 1903. By that time he was revising and making a fair copy of *Hadrian the Seventh* in his elegant, affected script. The progress of his revision is easy to follow. Once he added a remark about Jesuits got from Walsh—that one-fourth 'is the Christians of the World'[3]—but that procedure was an exception. As a rule, Rolfe's letters derived from his book; that is, his letters to James Walsh written between 13 March 1903 (the date of his second letter to Walsh) and 29 June 1903 are filled with reflections of *Hadrian*. Sometimes these were phrases which he had used before and would use again with variations, such as his insistence that he found the faith comfortable and the faithful intolerable or the statement that it was not he who had lost the Athenians but the Athenians who had lost him. More often details in the book and the letters were identical; one example is a reference to Percy O'Sullivan, known years before at Oscott; another is to Rolfe's 'Divine

158

Vocation', and a third to blisters applied to the back of his ears.[4] Before the end of June, his task had grown irksome and the book, distasteful. He characterised it to Maquay as 'a really vulgar sentimental novel' written only for the money it might make. He found it very hard 'to be low' and harder still, when he was distracted in so many ways.[5] Also he recoiled from his own depiction of Catholics. 'I hate and abhor from the picture of modern Roman Catholicks whom I have drawn,' he told Walsh. But, as he had said before, he wrote entirely against his will, driven to it by Catholics, and he put down only what he knew.[6] As June began to fade, Rolfe yearned to be freed from his '10 foot attic', to be in the sun to work 'wholesomely' at Oxford.[7] Nevertheless, on 12 July 1903, Rolfe at last delivered Hadrian the Seventh to Pinker.[8]

For some reason known only to himself, Rolfe pretended disdain for Hadrian the Seventh almost to the day of its issue. On 25 June 1904, only two weeks before it appeared, he told Maquay that it was 'frantic vulgar sentimental balderdash, deliberately written to interest the "Library Public" and to make money'. Actually Rolfe meant very little of that. Certainly he wanted to make money, but even to Maquay he represented the book's hero as 'deliciously libellous' and the book as 'highly controversial, written from the inside with a scalpel'. Indeed, to Rolfe Hadrian the Seventh was more nearly a book which he spoke of elsewhere as 'lovely', a 'frightfully pretty witty subtle violet-and-white book, full of pathos and laughter and good sense and wild absurdity and real beauty'.[9]

Part of its satisfaction and beauty for Rolfe lay in the fact that it outdid life ten to one. For chaos and failure and cruel injustice, it substituted order and reason. He summarised Hadrian for Walsh as the 'history of one year's pontificate of an Englishman with the temperament of a cat and a predilection for American independence who finds himself lifted to Peter's Throne about A.D. 1910'.[10] Rolfe had had at hand a long time the materials for his account of George Arthur Rose who came to be the pope Hadrian. 'It should teach you a little more of ME,' he said to Walsh[11] accurately, since his idealisation of self is at the heart of the book and its action traces a year of Rolfe's life as he believed it could have been lived.

What acted as a catalyst for turning Rolfe's lonely, sordid, pathetic struggle into the wisdom and success in life of Hadrian VII and his joyous achievement of rest and love in death is a mystery. Perhaps it was the talk with Holden of the pope Adrian. At some time after his talk with Holden and even as he wrote to prescription for almost nothing and quarrelled with Mrs. Griffiths and Grant Richards and Slaughter and Lane and Trevor Haddon, Rolfe became a stubborn advocate of his own dream. For the remainder of his literary career, Rolfe's subject was the search for love, whether lost or achieved, as in every book one character recurred who was sometimes a hero and who always turned out to be Rolfe.

In the case of *Hadrian the Seventh*, Rolfe's vision solved two pressing dilemmas with one grand sweep. A good Victorian, he regretted the distance he felt between himself and the world, the fact that he was 'strange, uncommon . . . not a "man among men" like other people'.[12] He swore that he had a vocation and, as Hadrian the Seventh, he pictured himself as a man who got his just deserts in spite of animosity and intrigue. He set himself above reconciliation with the world as the centre of a powerful system whereby he could mete out rewards and punishments with rigorous justice. Hadrian's nobility was flawed by Rolfe's belief that when he suffered someone must pay, but this was counterbalanced by a determination to restore Catholicism to Christ. The pope's mission was apostolic, and, as Hadrian, Rolfe took literally and seriously the 'formula' of his enthronement which made him 'Ruler of the World, the Father of Princes and Kings, the earthly vicar of Jesus Christ and saviour.'[13]

To these offices Hadrian brought the effect of 'felinity upon caninity', by which he meant the effect of simplicity upon complexity.[14] For Rolfe, Christianity was not satisfied by form and ritual. The responsibility of each Christian extended to every part of life, and each soul was accountable to its creator. By incantation, he said, he communicated directly with the 'invisible Omniscient'.[15] The fact that he equated such an intense faith and its rewards with 'felinity' is in keeping with Rolfe's love of cats. Was Rolfe not known to talk in the light of the moon to ten or more staring cats at one time? Rolfe told Maquay that if he liked the 'Feline Man', he would like Hadrian.[16] Hadrian's comfort and confidant was Flavio, a yellow cat.

As the 'Feline Man', Hadrian began by removing himself from the red velvet and ormolu of his quarters and providing instead 'clean bare spaces and simplicity without frippery'.[17] He showed a predilection for inconsistency, the humane, and the magnanimous. He laughed at theologians' 'straw-splitting' as an example of the 'undevelopable fossil which goes by the name of consistency'.[18] He offered the Church to the poor, the depraved, the weak, those who could not conform. He denounced the 'farce of organised charity' with words, a gesture, or money wherever he saw individual need.[19] He was liberal with friends and dependents and generous with a few enemies. To Hardy of Jesus College, Oxford, and to his family under the name Strong, Hadrian showed real gratitude for friendship. To a young Italian who had served him, he gave the secret of Rolfe's colour photography as insurance against hard times. Men of the Church who had helped Rolfe—Monsignor John Dey and Father George Angus—became cardinals under Hadrian. For men whom Rolfe admired, Hadrian created an ideal position such as the directorship of a college of historical research for Dr. Richard Barnett, by whom was meant Richard Garnett.[20] Hadrian treated his enemies as Rolfe thought they deserved. For some he had only abhorrence. Father Beauclerk is

160

among these. He is first mentioned as a 'detestable and deceitful Blackcote' who robbed Hadrian of years of labour. Once he is referred to as a 'harebrained and degenerate priest'. Then he figures as the Black Pope, the General of the Jesuits, Father St. Albans, to whom Hadrian delivered an admonition to the Jesuits that they stop pretending to be 'Superior Persons', stop giving themselves airs, stop the use of hansom cabs and billiard tables, try to be honest, try to treat the poor fairly and to love all men. Finally he calls Beauclerk a 'detestable scoundrel' and relegates him first to a mad house and then to the colonies.[21] Hadrian's strongest animus, however, is reserved for Mrs. Crowe and Jerry Sant, who are in Rome at the expense of England's Liblab Party to blackmail the pope for the benefit of the Socialists, a part of the Liblab coalition. Sant, by whom Rolfe denotes the 'letter-thief' who failed to carry out Champion's directions in 1894[22] plus a seasoning of Keir Hardie, is the author of an attack which in reality was that of Aberdeen's *Daily Free Press* on Rolfe. Mrs. Crowe, by whom is meant Nancy Gleeson White, is named as a main source of the information for the attack. Hadrian exhibits a particular detestation for her. She is castigated as lecherous enough to 'make advances as obvious as abrupt and as shameless as a dog's,' an affront to Hadrian's 'feline temper'.[23] His loathing of Mrs. Crowe goes beyond the demands of the book. It is instinctive and pathological.

So intimate an exposure was not a part of Rolfe's plan for the novel. Neither was the implicit pederasty in Hadrian's admiration for the 'brown boy' who rowed the fisherman's boat at Lake Nemi, his delight in the virile limbs of his chamberlains, and his extravagant wonder at the sight of the small prince of Italy.[24] But at its most explicit, *Hadrian the Seventh* is not mere self-exploitation. Rolfe makes no saint of himself. Without piety, he was too deeply religious for that and, whether self-deceived or not, too conscious of his difference from his fellows, too aware of his eccentricities—there had always been a 'fundamental element of reason' about them, he said—and too bemused by them.[25] His emphasis on physical fitness, his inveterate smoking, his sensuous joy in cleanliness all belong to Hadrian. Rolfe's association of the clean with the angelic accounts for his fear of reptiles.[26] Hadrian's passion for cupboards, for boxes and neat shelves built into the apartments at the Vatican give Rolfe away as the inhabitant of cramped lodgings, a man who has never known enough space of his own. Rolfe's pride in his voice, his personal fastidiousness, his intellectual arrogance, even his small appetite, his admiration for semiprecious stones, and his handwriting are Hadrian's. So is his resentment at growing old; contact with ageing humanity, he said, made 'his juvenile soul shudder', but he had a profound love for 'lovely live things'.[27]

Perhaps Rolfe's—or Hadrian's—concept of simplicity played him false in his role as Father of Princes and Kings. The villains of *Hadrian*

161

the Seventh and the characters which activate the dénouement are Jerry Sant and Mrs. Crowe. As Socialists they are treacherous. Rolfe associated them and their party with the treatment which Champion, here named Dymoke, had received in the early nineties. Hadrian also argued against Socialism as a dangerous manifestation of democracy. He denied the 'dogma of Equality' as a 'diabolical delusion' and upheld the idea of diversity, the principle of Aristos 'the Best'.[28] He advocated what he termed a twentieth century version of autocracy, 'Aristos, the Strong Man', who emerges from conflict. This implies a more solid position than Rolfe took when he explained his reluctance to become a 'militant socialist' to Hubert Bland on the grounds that to do so would damage his means of livelihood, a statement made when Rolfe wanted help from the socialist Bland.[29] Through Hadrian, Rolfe supports dictatorship. He identified 'Aristos' with the most autocratic ruler of Western Europe, William II, Emperor of Germany, whose friendship for England was already in question, a friendship Hadrian strongly advocated. Thus Hadrian's stand is a forerunner of Rolfe's in his article 'Concerning England and Germany' written some time after 1905.[30] Hadrian's advocacy of Italy's king was another matter altogether, having to do with the vexed relations between state and papacy in Italy soon after Victor Emmanuel III succeeded to the throne. In William, grandson of the 'Divine Victoria', Hadrian saw England's firmest ally. William's autocracy had defeated Socialism in Germany. Yet, although Hadrian explained England's distrust of Germany as mistaken in his 'Epistle to the Princes' where he divided the world into five spheres, he kept separate Germany and England.[31]

It was all a dream. Rolfe's dearest illusions about himself and what he was fit for had no substance. Even as Hadrian he was fallible and a victim. The truth of Rolfe's vision lay in that realisation. When Sant, Socialist assassin, killed Hadrian, Rolfe once more faced his self.

Nothing interested Rolfe as much as his self, a fact which accounts for the autobiographical element in all Rolfe's fiction. He had to the highest degree the self-consciousness or in his case the self-interest which is the mark of the autobiographer. He might have said with Gerard Manley Hopkins, as by implication he did, 'I find myself both as man and as myself . . . more distinctive and higher pitched than anything else I see.' Rolfe was his own hero whether in past or present fact or in imaginative transformation. Toto told his tales to a well defined concept of Rolfe. He was a reliable by-stander in 'An Unforgettable Experience', that account of a woman declared dead who is brought back into life. An examination of himself in a similar situation brought him to the foreground in 'How I Was Buried Alive'.[32] But the autobiographical content is not merely a matter of how much or how little. Its preponderance in 'How I was Buried Alive', for example, or in *Stories Toto Told Me* was dictated by the nature and form of his fiction. Rolfe very likely never underwent Yeats's 'moment of

162

revelation', when he was 'self-possessed in self-surrender'. Rolfe, however, was deliberately bringing his imagination to play on external events, fitting them to a projection of self or the projection to events. One might be as important as the other and both, as a means to fiction, must outweigh self-knowledge or even Rolfe's psychic needs. As in crises of emotion, his letters to Father Beauclerk and Henry Newbolt moved from shattered ego and fact to healing and self-justification, so Rolfe's explicit account of his personal history served him as self-justification. Nevertheless he adapted it to fiction. Every secondary character in *Hadrian the Seventh* was taken directly from Rolfe's experience. Although not one is more than a mechanical man wound up to participate in Rolfe's game of Hadrian, all have autobiographical reality. It is in the focal point of the book, the character Hadrian, the only one with the dimension and variability of humanity, that the book dissolves (in a cinematic sense) into fiction and again into fact. However completely Hadrian is endowed with Rolfe's identity, it is Hadrian who blurs the boundaries between autobiography and fiction.

In other words, Rolfe was not writing autobiography, and neither its presence nor the extent of it is a basis for evaluating *Hadrian the Seventh* as a novel. Graham Greene had read Symons's *Quest for Corvo* so that he knew what he was talking about when he compared *Hadrian*, a 'novel of genius', with Francis Thompson's *The Hound of Heaven*. D. H. Lawrence wrote about the book in 1925, almost ten years before *The Quest* appeared so that he was speaking of *Hadrian* only as fiction when he praised it as a 'clear and definite book of our epoch, not to be swept aside. If it is the book of a demon as Corvo's contemporaries said,' Lawrence went on, 'it is the book of a man demon, not a mere *poseur*. And if some of it is caviare, at least it came out of the belly of a live fish.'[33]

The recurrence of autobiography in most of Rolfe's fiction, however, is an insistent biographical fact. What Rolfe knew of his own consciousness, what he made of it, how he transformed it and why demand attention. How he related it to his personal environment can not be ignored. It is important that, as he progressed in his self-explanation he also progressed in the emphasis on his subject, the painful search for love. Surely it is significant that Rolfe's autobiographical concern diminished or enlarged with his fortunes. The fiction in which autobiography predominates came out of grim misery, the agony of disappointment, failure, loneliness, and fear. It made bearable his self to himself and the terrible years commencing in 1893, almost unrelieved in squalor and pain, acquired a meagre pattern.

Nicholas Crabbe is a narrative of Rolfe's literary career from 1899, when he came to London from Holywell, until about the close of the year 1902. The 'history of his first literary period', Rolfe named it, and in the same breath he referred to *Hadrian the Seventh* as the history of his ecclesiastical and artistic career.[34] In *Hadrian*, or so he told Walsh, there was a 'distinct assertion of a secondary personality'. In *Nicholas Crabbe*, Rolfe dwelt on his primary personality, that is the character which he 'received through the stars' of his 'nativity from the Maker of the Stars'.[35]

Rolfe believed firmly in astrological influence. In the matter of 'prognostic astrology', he generally followed the Church. He could not reconcile with his conscience as a Christian the practise of such astrology habitually, although he admitted that he had exploited it several times for himself. But on the whole, Rolfe was averse to using astrology for prediction because he was not certain where white magic ended and black magic began. In that respect he looked askance at Aleister Crowley's methods as those of a charlatan and belittled his self-acclaimed powers. He told Ralph Shirley, editor of *The Psychic Review* and publisher, that Crowley's 'ecstasy' was only the ' "rapture" which St. Francis of Assisi & . . . Nicholas Crabbe attained without masquerades using solely the simple incantation Deus meus et Omnia.'[36] On the other hand, Rolfe was convinced that the stars controlled each man's nature, but its development rested on will power.[37]

Rolfe confirmed his reliance on astrology in the name Nicholas Crabbe. The first name was that of Rolfe's grandfather, who had moved the family business to 61 Cheapside in London. In 1804, Nicholas had written a tragedy and then 'stifled his literary muse'. The surname Crabbe was taken from Rolfe's astrological sign, the crab for those born under Cancer. This sign identifies Nicholas Crabbe with Rolfe inasmuch as he summarised Crabbe's nature in terms of his own horoscope. He wrote about himself:

> Inability to feel, except when I'm changing my shell: inoffensiveness till I'm attacked: and then the most violently amazing ability of nipping and pinching other people's rawest and most secret sores and Tenacity, the faculty for holding on even at the expense of my claws.[38]

Rolfe's description of Nicholas Crabbe reads in part:

> He never attacked for the mere sake of attacking: but people who poked at him, or trod on him, had reason for bewailing the cruel, violent unexpected inevitability of his crunching grip. He never let go; and he never ceased to persecute and harass.[39]

This astrological identity is confirmed by non-astrological likenesses between Crabbe and Rolfe, such as their addiction to meals at one or another Express Dairy, their joy in the sight of the 'proud serene carriage' of some boy, and their unalterable fear of women.[40]

Indeed, Nicholas Crabbe as a fictitious person or a thin disguise for himself—and often both—held Rolfe's interest for the rest of his life. *Nicholas Crabbe* was hardly complete when Rolfe referred to a character in another book on which he was at work, 'Rose's Records', as a 'Crab, frightfully ferocious when poked at: but on the other hand, the Moon made him very soft inside.[41]' Crabbe is the hero of *The Weird of the Wanderer* and *The Desire and Pursuit of the Whole*. Rolfe used a form of his name, Crabmaid, as a signature for at least one unpublished essay; the dedicatory prologue of *Don Tarquinio* is written as from Crabs Herborough; and he referred to Crabbe in letters as a friend, an acquaintance, and a semi-mythical personality in whom Rolfe could objectify himself.[42]

In *Nicholas Crabbe*, the metaphor of Crabbe first ratifies the autobiographical element. Then it dominates the book's most prominent imagery, which is largely derived from the crustacean. In addition to the hermit crab in his cave, Rolfe refers often to shells, palpi, feelers, claws, antennae, carapax. And last the metaphor of Crabbe enfolds the concept of the artist with his 'sensitive longing soul' and his determined faith in himself, ill at ease with the pretensions of literary London and at the mercy of his publishers who were aware of his gifts but unwilling to pay for them and of his own mistakes in judgement.

But Crabbe is not merely a crustacean stereotype. He is a 'most distinct identity'. Before coming to London, he had resolved that he would neither seek nor speak unnecessarily to anyone. He had determined to stifle his 'natural predilection for a gregarious existence' and to ally himself with no person or group. He rejected 'all kindness, all praise, as the offspring of pity or of envy or of contempt'.[43] The result was marked individuality and with that had come not only a 're-markable' imagination but also a 'fastidiousness' which was made up of equal amounts of boredom, aloofness, contempt and 'fine feeling'. Rolfe said of Crabbe:

He was . . . reserved and sensitive, sympathetic and tenacious, persistent and impatient, impressionable and emotional. He was beginning to understand the necessity of selfishness for the protection of his individuality: and on these lines, he was becoming self-possessed, self-reliant, strong, and potent.[44]

That Rolfe believed himself to be what he described in Crabbe is undeniable. But the characterisation of Nicholas Crabbe also serves to establish him as the protagonist of a book with the subtitle *The One and The Many*. Rolfe, as Hadrian, had agonised that God had made him strange, unusual, unknown to his fellow-men. Crabbe, too, in his earnestness about the solemnity of living must pit his individuality against the Many and ultimately, as in effect Hadrian had done, allow it to make him the victim of the Many.

In *Nicholas Crabbe*, possibly because autobiography and fiction, truth

165

and poetry (grim as it was), are in reasonable balance, the Many who are Crabbe's antagonists consist of more thoroughly explored characters than those of *Hadrian*. That is not true of every character. The publishers Slim Schelm, a 'beery insect' by whom is meant John Lane, and Doron Oldcastle, a 'scorbutic hobbledehoy' by whom is meant Grant Richards, are alive as far as they go. They are out and out scoundrels and their behaviour is predictable. So perhaps is that of their associate, the shrewd, hustling Abrahams (Isaac Isaacs, later Temple Scott), who changed his name to Church Welbeck as he went up in the publishing world and adapted himself to greater income, greater importance, and the most fashionable dress. Rolfe's anti-semitism prevented his developing the kindness suggested in this character, and he remained only an ostentatious clown whose promises were always broken. Similarly the painter based on Trevor Haddon and the literary agent Vere Perkins, based on Stanhope Sprigge, enacted only treacheries and stupidities. The portrait of Edward Savage as Neddy Carnage is caricature.

On the other hand Sidney Thorah, Rolfe's fictional representation of Henry Harland, is a character of real dimensions. Rolfe recorded Thorah's feverish restlessness, his factitious modernity, his affectation of decadence, and his plain vulgarity when he has had too much to drink. Thorah is a would-be aesthete who mouths the superiority of the artist and his vision while his 'literary equipment' consists of 'only one set of characters and only one plot'.[45] His unconsidered and self-serving advice to Crabbe is as calamitous as Schelm's and Oldcastle's villainy. At first Crabbe believed Thorah when he said that he would like to be the man if Crabbe ever wanted a man to talk to. But that delusion vanishes before Thorah's shrill clamour; and when Thorah refuses Crabbe's dedication of *Daynian Folk-Lore (In His Own Image)*, the friendship between the two men ends.

Nowhere in Rolfe's fiction is the discrepancy on a social level between the One and the Many more skilfully presented than in an episode composed and inserted in the book more than five years later. The episode recounts a party to which Crabbe went at Thorah's insistence. His hosts were the Arkush Annalys, by whom is meant Edith Nesbit, author of books for children, and her husband Hubert Bland. The setting, a garden in Kensington, 'where the flower-beds were outlined with fairylamps and everything was lovely and amusing', the champagne, his hostess in chiffon and diamonds, Thorah screaming 'pseudepigrams', are in sharp contrast with Crabbe's 'imperscrutable face and his grim air'. Although Crabbe had a delightful evening, he 'came away utterly failing to understand what it was all about, or what return was expected from him'. Above all, he was disappointed in his expectation that he would have 'an opening offered to him'[46] because he needed one.

After all, when he saw a need in others, Crabbe did what he could to supply it as with Robert Fulgentius Kemp. He is the only thoroughly imagined character in *Nicholas Crabbe*. Kemp had a real-life model in Sholto Douglas, but Douglas and Rolfe met only once or twice[47] so that no similarity between fact and fiction necessarily exists in the representation of Kemp's self-containment, his sensitivity, and his manliness. Crabbe first encountered Kemp as he swam in the Serpentine. Meeting him again by accident, Crabbe realised that Kemp, an Oxonian working as a telegraph boy and earning too little to survive, needed help. He offered the younger man living space in his flat with the understanding that he never disturb Crabbe and his work. After a time he learns that Kemp's sight is almost gone, that he cannot work, that he is hungry and wants only to die. Crabbe delicately restores Kemp's will to live and, with understanding and generosity, helps him to a feeling of independence; but in so doing Crabbe exhausts his funds and drifts into debt.

Meanwhile Kemp and Crabbe begin a literary collaboration, and in this *Nicholas Crabbe* returns once more to autobiography. The collaboration is identical with Douglas's and Rolfe's on 'Reviews of Unwritten Books' and 'Thirty Naughty Emperors'. In fact the very same titles are used as, for example that of the essay on Eliogabalus prepared for 'Thirty Naughty Emperors' called 'A Goat in Priest's Clothing'; it still exists, a manuscript of fifteen pages by Douglas, transcribed and corrected by Rolfe.[48] It was the study which he used as a 'specimen' of 'Thirty Naughty Emperors' when he first broached the subject to Pinker.[49]

The collaboration between Kemp and Crabbe is autobiographical in another, more tenuous and far more important way. As Sholto Douglas had briefly answered Rolfe's yearning for the 'Divine Friend', so Kemp in *Nicholas Crabbe* answers Crabbe's faith that friends, lovers, are 'but truly two halves of one whole.'[50] Unlike W. H. Auden, for instance, with his passion for diversity and his reliance for fulfilment on a loved one who is ' "other" than the lover', Crabbe (or Rolfe) wanted identicalness. He found it in Kemp. He rolled his cigarettes in a deft way which mirrored Crabbe's way, they both liked the same kind of cigarette paper. They shared an 'intense undying admiration' for 'sacred exuberant exquisite' Oxford.[51] Apparently their voices were similar, or so Rolfe described them. Of Kemp's voice he wrote that it was quiet, sensitive, and full of 'minor vibrations like a muted lute'; of Crabbe's, once that it was low and minor and once that it was a 'strong low voice like the pang of a lute-string (F# minor)'.[52] Kemp exhibited the best of his nature in return for Crabbe's kindness and understanding. Above all, their collaboration was an ideal one such as Rolfe wanted much of his life. He described it in *Nicholas Crabbe*:

> In course of the work, the workers themselves came closer together, closer in amazement at and admiration of each other's

extraordinary genius. Crabbe was astonished by the nimbleness, the profundity, the dazzling wit, the chaste taste of Kemp. Kemp shouted applause at Crabbe's mordant irony, his delicate certainty of touch, his patience and dexterity in producing beauty of form....

MS. after MS. was written and emended and revised and rewritten again and again, until the two keen minds were wholly satisfied. Arguments and quarrels took place, without a vestige of ill-nature; and no difference was passed over until it had been threshed out thoroughly and solved. Each was willing to give in. Each was open to conviction.[53]

Such perfection is a dream and, like the illusion from which *Hadrian* was created, it vanished. Kemp recovered his sight and was reunited with a friend of long standing, Theophanes Clayfoot (a fictitious name for Douglas's companion Arthur Graham). With Clayfoot there was no place for Crabbe and, when in great need he asked for help, Kemp terminated all pretence of friendship. Like Hadrian, Crabbe—against his practical reason, to be sure—had lived up to his faith in Christian charity; and for doing so, he, the One, was the victim of the Many. He was left 'alone and naked—all alone with the Alone'.

The theme of the One and the Many is boundless, admitting endless human complexity and endeavour. The innocent, the obsessed, the fool for his faith, those who will not or cannot compromise, the man of pure heart, may live high tragedy. Unfortunately, Nicholas Crabbe's heart was no purer than Rolfe's and however firmly the author underlined the hermetic existence, side by side, of Kemp and Crabbe and Kemp's delicacy—'fresh and stainless as a primrose', he wrote once[54] –the truth is all to plain. Rolfe understood the fact. As the narrator of *Nicholas Crabbe*, he explained that he made no excuse for Crabbe. Rolfe went on, 'I simply am telling you patently of the things which he did he ought not to have done, and of the things which he left undone which he ought to have done: and, that there should be no health in him is not singular.'[55] Rolfe was coping with the One and the Many in a way he had described in *Hadrian the Seventh*, masking himself in an image and looking at it and the feeling it aroused 'like a child at Punch and Judy'.[56] Although such an autobiographical element may abridge the theme, it still fits Rolfe's definition of fiction got from Charles Reade, 'a thing done being merely another word for Fact'.[57]

Precisely the periods of time which Rolfe devoted to *Nicholas Crabbe* and to *Don Tarquinio*, the third book completed during the years in London, are impossible to establish. Various letters contain references to books in progress after *Hadrian the Seventh* was finished, but they fail to specify which book. On 26 June 1903, he told Pinker that the typescript of 'An Ideal Content' would be available in a few days and added that another book was 'half done'.[58] Rolfe meant not a half-written book but the 'half done' typescript of *Hadrian the Seventh*, since he sent to his agent both an autograph copy and a typescript of *Hadrian* on 12 July. Four days later he complained of being at 'a loose end' until his new book appeared; so he can hardly have been seriously at work, in July, on another one. Only in mid-September was there talk of something else. In a letter dated 13 September 1903, he complained to Pinker of having a 'most awful time', of three 'precious weeks' wasted because he had no place in which to work and a 'new book boiling' in his brain.[59] That was *Nicholas Crabbe*.

The word 'new' is the key. *Don Tarquinio* was not new. It was first mentioned in the same letter as *Hadrian the Seventh*, one dated 21 December 1900 and directed to Kenneth Grahame.[60] According to Rolfe's prologue addressed to his brother Herbert, *Don Tarquinio* originated in a suggestion from Isaac Isaacs (Rolfe names him only as 'a certain idiot'). Isaac's suggestion came from his association with Grant Richards when Rolfe was commencing *Chronicles of the House of Borgia*, a book from which *Don Tarquinio* derived. Don Tarquinio's fortunes turn on a service rendered to Cesare Borgia. The romance tells how Don Tarquinio, under the Great Ban and with his family estates in Rome sequestered, restores his name and wins his lady (in service with Lucrezia Borgia) by running with a message in cypher lettered on his back from the Roman palace of Cardinal Ippolito d'Este to a village in the Alban mountains, Velletri, thereby enabling Cesare Borgia to escape from Charles VIII, who holds him hostage. Caesar, in turn, intervenes with the Pope so that the Great Ban is lifted from Don Tarquinio's family and the rest of his happiness falls into place. Rolfe's delight in Rome and all things Italian, his delight in the male human body and in the rich elegance of Renaissance princelings, and his familiarity with all these served him well in this production of an ingenious story overlaid with magnificence of setting, both totally and charmingly artificial.

Don Tarquinio, in some form, was one of the manuscripts Isaacs retained in New York without payment. But Rolfe had kept a copy of *Don Tarquinio*, according to his preface; and when he happened on the manuscript, he determined to make something of it. At first he thought of recasting it as a play and even went so far as to make a sketch for it in dialogue form. He abandoned that and then prepared two non-dramatic versions, one with Don Tarquinio as his own narrator and one with a 'modern rather slangy story-teller' speaking in his own words. He was still at work on one or the other in December 1904. In a letter dated 3 December 1904, he told Maquay about sequels to *Hadrian the Seventh* which he was writing and which he wanted to finish as soon as he could 'get this Cesare Borgia story off' his chest. He said that it was more than half revised. At Christmas of that year, 1904, he showed it to his brother Herbert. By 15 March 1905, Rolfe had submitted the 'slangy' version to Chatto & Windus, who rejected it but agreed to publish the 'antique version'.[61]

Don Tarquinio was published on 18 May 1905. From early December to 18 May may seem too short a period in which to complete and publish the book. Yet the production of *Hadrian the Seventh*, a much longer work, occupied little more time. On 1 October 1903, Chatto & Windus, who published *Hadrian the Seventh*, had not yet seen it. Calling it 'rather a strange book', George Webster of Methuen & Co. refused *Hadrian* on that date.[62] In fact, Rolfe was trying to ascertain from Pinker as late as 17 May 1904 whether the number of publishers who had 'declined' *Hadrian* was ten or twelve. But by 25 June 1904, Rolfe had read proof on 144 pages out of some '400 odd' and submitted his design for a cover. *Hadrian the Seventh* appeared on 14 July 1904. With *Don Tarquinio*, Rolfe saved endless delay by dealing directly with the publisher. He had quarrelled with Leonard Moore a year earlier and, although his last extant letter to Pinker is dated only three days before publication of *Don Tarquinio*, that is 15 May 1905, Rolfe had ceased sending him manuscripts almost two years earlier. He had gone directly to Chatto & Windus with his manuscript of *Don Tarquinio* 'beautifully written, on fine paper, and bound in white buckram' with one of his 'gorgeous black and white designs' drawn on the cover.[63]

Obviously, then, the precise dates for beginnings and endings are unavailable, but it is reasonable to state that the re-making of *Don Tarquinio* followed immediately after the completion of *Nicholas Crabbe* and that the work on *Nicholas Crabbe*, including the time in which it was being typed, dates from about 13 September 1903 until 29 June 1904. That date is definite. On 1 July, a Friday, Rolfe wrote to John Lane, 'I sent you on Wednesday a typescript of my new book entitled *Nicholas Crabbe*'.[64]

[viii]

Rolfe's motives in sending *Nicholas Crabbe* to John Lane are dubious. For Lane to publish a book containing the broad depiction of himself as Slim Schelm is unthinkable. Yet Rolfe fully expected Lane or someone to publish. Despite the unmistakable and libellous portraits of Richards, the Harlands, Ella d'Arcy, and others as well as Lane, Rolfe saw to it that *Nicholas Crabbe* made the rounds of the publishing offices. In 1907 he was still persevering with the book and, what is more, with John Lane. Rolfe asked Hubert Bland to intercede for him with Lane; and when Bland refused but offered to approach another publisher, Werner Laurie, Rolfe eagerly accepted and said, 'The publishers who refuse N.C. are fools. There is such a jolly lot to come about him.'[1]

Although he failed to sell the book to Lane in 1904 or 1907 or any other time, Rolfe had the satisfaction of putting both Lane and Henry Harland into a towering rage. As soon as he read it, Lane sent *Nicholas*

Crabbe to Harland. Aline Harland wrote for her husband on 5 July 1905 with his opinion that *Nicholas Crabbe* was criminal libel, that sending it to Lane constituted legal publication, and that Lane must keep the typescript while he had his solicitor force Rolfe to declare in writing the falsity of the libellous statements, promise never to repeat them, and agree to the destruction of all copies of the book. Lane then wrote an inflammatory letter to Rolfe; in it, the publisher threatened Rolfe with legal action. On 7 July, Rolfe answered as offensively as he could, declaring that *Nicholas Crabbe* was a romance and nothing more and that Lane and his 'friends (so-called)' had 'sniffed "lampoons & libels"' where none are'. Rolfe said, 'I was not aware that you had any friends; and I certainly do not know them. So I merely point out that, had my book been what you stupidly call it, it is hardly likely that I should have submitted it first to you.' He assured Lane that when the typescript was returned, he would examine it with care in order to find out what had put Lane 'into such a maniacal & rhapsodical fury'. He belittled Lane's threats as 'bounce' and 'bogeys', refused to accept responsibility for Lane's aggrieved misapprehensions and then urged him to read *Agricultural and Pastoral Prospects of South Africa* by Owen Thomas when Constable issued it.[2]

That last admonition matched another which Rolfe had sent a month earlier when, on 10 June 1904, he had advised Henry Newbolt to read the same book. 'It may teach Mr Newbolt a lesson,' he wrote.[3] The year 1904 should have been a banner year for Rolfe. It provided him with unusual opportunities for invective and splendid chances to demonstrate various sides of his genius. He had two books in print that year, *Hadrian the Seventh* signed with his name and *Agricultural and Pastoral Prospects*, both from prestigious publishers, not to mention another book completed, *Nicholas Crabbe*, one almost written, *Don Tarquinio*, and possibly four in progress. What is more, *Don Torquinio* suggested that he had unequivocally found his 'singular and proper handicraft', one which he described as 'rather solid and very brilliant and picturesque historical fiction based on unusually extensive researches in historical fact'.[4] To put a final fillip to all the rest, Rolfe received the offer of a bishopric.

In fact, 1904 was as bitter, as dreary, as disheartening as any year Rolfe had had since coming to London. It began, as most recent years had, with a stay of about ten days in Oxford with Dr. Hardy. Rolfe spoke of Hardy as a 'poor Oxford Don' who was going blind owing to glaucoma and 'likely to be in difficulties in the near future'. Rolfe complained of the work which he did in reading examination papers for Hardy, how it took his every minute, occupying him from 9·30 in the morning to 11.30 at night. Then 'limp as any rag', he could do nothing except 'fall on sleep'.[5] But Rolfe loved Oxford—only a fool would fail to be happy there 'when the weather is weather', he said— and Hardy, whose circumstances Rolfe so cheerfully denigrated, was his one friend, a man with whom he enjoyed talking and the only man, he told Maquay, with whom he was 'on speaking terms'.[6] Above all, Rolfe was well fed and he lived without cost at Oxford.

On 20 January 1904, Rolfe returned to Hampstead and to his precarious habits. On Friday evenings he went to his mother for dinner. On Sunday morning he was 'always at the Oratory not far from the Calvary' between eight and half past nine.[7] He got down once more to the composition of *Nicholas Crabbe*, still unfinished in January, and to his work with Colonel Owen Thomas, and he continued his endless attempts to prod Leonard Moore to greater efforts on behalf of his unpublished works.

In the spring when Rolfe changed his residence and went with Mrs. Griffiths to 15 Cheniston Gardens, Kensington, the pattern of his activities hardly changed. He was still getting straight in mid-April, and it was May before he had letter paper printed with his new address. Meanwhile, in April, *The Magazine of Commerce* published 'The Commercial Future of Rhodesia', signed by Owen Thomas but written almost wholly by Rolfe. He maintained that he wrote or helped write two other pieces for Thomas, but they remain untraced.[8] In April, too, the Rhodes Trustees arranged with Constable for publication of *Agricultural and Pastoral Prospects of South Africa*, a disposition which Rolfe thought advantageous. He boasted to Moore of his 'own roundabout (but quite inevitable) way' of getting what he wanted. The only problem was to wait for his share of what was to come.[9] By 5 May, Rolfe was once more at the recurrent effort to make something of the Borgia genealogy, now looking to Maquay for help with it. He set a value of £4,000 on it and referred Maquay to Hardy for 'bona fides'. He did not push Maquay, however, possibly because he had so many more matters to attend to that the Borgias had to remain 'in the corner' and possibly too, as he complained in a letter of 10 May, because he was exhausted from 'South African affairs'.[10] The amount of £12 was still due from that quarter, but four days before it was paid, that is on 24 June, Rolfe was so badly in need of cash that he tendered the proofs of *Hadrian the Seventh*, on which he was at work, as a 'warranty of good faith' and borrowed a 'few pounds' from Maquay. When he had tried to give such help earlier, Rolfe had refused it because he 'saw no future'. With *Hadrian* assured of publication, he asked Maquay to renew his offer. The next day Rolfe thanked Maquay for the loan and with typical inconsistency went on to say that he had made a private 'deed of gift' of all his interests in *Hadrian* to his mother.[11]

Whatever his intentions, Rolfe's gift of his rights in *Hadrian the Seventh* was an empty one. It appeared on 14 July 1904 and it went almost unnoticed. Rolfe was hard put to find reviews. By 25 October, he was calling the book 'a "novelist's success" but not a commercial one', and he admitted that it had not yet paid expenses. In mid-November, Chatto & Windus issued a flier in an attempt 'to prevent Hadrian from being lost'. But nothing helped. In March 1905, in a hostile letter to Father Beauclerk, Rolfe pretended to be surfeited with praise of *Hadrian* and by then it had attracted some individual attention; but as a commercial venture, it had escaped comment. On 9 December 1904, Rolfe told Maquay that its sale was poor and that Chatto had decided not to issue a 6d. edition.[12]

As his expectations from *Hadrian* proved false, so Rolfe's transactions in the South African affair ended in catastrophe. *Agricultural and Pastoral Prospects*, published by subvention to the amount of £240, appeared on 4 October 1904, but by that time Rolfe had come to regard his connection with South Africa as 'distinctly rum'. After 29 June, when Thomas made his last payment of £12, Rolfe found it impossible to squeeze another penny from Thomas. Rolfe tried. He knew that the Rhodes Trustees supported Thomas's project, and he thought he saw possibilities. He wrote letters alleging payment due for what Thomas regarded as mere friendly advice. He tried to hold Thomas to what Rolfe insisted was an agreement made in the previous November that the colonel would sell Rolfe's Borgiada for not less than £2,000.[13] When Rolfe's letters grew tiresome and abusive, Thomas responded, according to Rolfe, by menacing him. The crucial letter, dated 20 July 1904, was one in which Thomas 'associated himself with Father Oswald O.S.B. & Mr. George Angus, two Catholic clergymen (*latebrosa & lucifuga natio*),' who, Rolfe maintained, had been 'calumniating' him secretly for years. He retracted the charge against Angus, who had offered him shelter in the Oscott days, but he bluntly applied the term rascal to Father Oswald, whose secular name was Hunter-Blair and whom Rolfe had first met as he went north to Oban in 1886.[14] In any case, Thomas's 'threatening letter' once more brought Rolfe's litigiousness into play. In May of the previous year, Rolfe had asked Pinker to recommend a solicitor who was not necessarily a specialist in literary cases but a good 'Fighting-Man'. Pinker had named Barnard & Taylor of Lincoln's Inn Fields.[15] Now Rolfe took not only his grievances in respect to Thomas but also the Borgiada and his tale of one book in progress, four books ready for publication, and the recently published *Hadrian* to Churton Taylor. Somehow Rolfe managed to fire Taylor's imagination. He agreed to undertake the case against Thomas and to make Rolfe a small weekly allowance contingent on the case. Here was a good bargain, exactly what Rolfe wanted on a grander scale, and he agreed. Needless to say, his approval diminished as time went on. Rolfe's summary of the situation as he saw it in a few months and set it down in a letter to James Walsh reads:

Notwithstanding that I am a dreamer, I actually wrote *Agricultural & Pastoral Prospects in South Africa* (Constable) for an expert of the Chartered Company & Rhodes Trustees to sign. He kept me alive while I was doing it; but afterwards, openly gibing at my powerless poverty,

173

refused to make good the promises on which he had obtained my services. I found some lawyers who, on the security of all my own published & unpublished works, sent him a writ for £2,000 and allow me enough to starve on till the case comes into court.[16]

The writ by which Rolfe claimed £2,000 from Thomas was issued on 6 August 1904.

Some time in September, Mrs. Griffiths, his landlady, learned of the impending lawsuit and of Rolfe's allowance from Barnard & Taylor. It was not enough to meet his indebtedness to her and the lawsuit meant that another of Rolfe's expectations of money to be made, of good fortune almost within reach, had proved to be a fantasy. One by one, the props which kept up his credit with Mrs. Griffiths had collapsed: Richards, Lane, Newbolt, the Borgiada, and now Thomas; not one was left him by which to support his illusions or his credit. Mrs. Griffiths put him out. Once more—and for the last time—Rolfe was homeless in London.

Part IV

1904 – 1908

[i]

When Mrs. Griffiths evicted Rolfe, he went to his mother and sister. At the end of October, he wrote to Maquay about his situation, 'I had to leave Cheniston rather hurriedly in Sept; and to come ... where my Mother and Sister (for whom I am responsible) have started a small school. They were in need of me; and I had no other place to go.'[1] The Rolfe women had managed to open a kindergarten and little girls' school called St. Alphege, at Broadstairs. Broadstairs lies on the north coast of the Isle of Thanet, midway between the popular watering-places Margate and Ramsgate. Affording no variety shows, no band concerts, no promenades for holiday makers, Broadstairs is much quieter than its neighbours. Once it had been a favourite resort of Charles Dickens and George Eliot, but it is the very symbol of the provincial and somnolent against which Ronald Firbank warned his sister in 1912, when he urged her to remember that 'no trains worth catching pass by Broadstairs'.

For Rolfe, Broadstairs was exile. His only pleasure was bathing in the sea which, in mid-November, he said he had done every morning since his arrival. He performed necessary chores for his mother, moving quietly about the school in his freshly laundered but worn clothing. When St. Alphege began publication of a magazine, *The Fleurdelys*, Rolfe designed the front cover and prepared copy for the printer. But he felt 'fixed' at Broadstairs, wasting time and energy because he lacked means to 'move about' and use himself or to arrange publication of his various manuscripts. Without that and without a place in which to work, he saw no way to deliver himself from his enforced stay with his mother and sister.[2]

Yet Rolfe's work provided almost the only relief from the gloom and boredom of those months at Broadstairs. By 3 December 1904, he had sold two essays from the series 'Reviews of Unwritten Books'. *The Gentleman's Magazine* published 'Cicero's Oration for Joan of Arc' and 'Shakespeare's Tragedy of King Charles the First' and sent Rolfe a half-guinea in payment. He applied his half-guinea to sending off other articles to other and better paying editors.[3] And he kept at his writing. His methods, as described to Maquay were hardly orthodox. 'I'm getting wonderful assistance by night in dreams,' Rolfe said. He went on:

Where I can continue to fight off the exhaustion in the morning, I write down stuff which appeals very strongly to my sense of the

177

ridiculously ought-to-be as well as to my critical faculty. However, I can't tell how these works will pan out until I get them on paper and through their first revision.

Most of his books, he explained, were totally altered by revision except 'the brilliant flashes' which he recognised as not his own but the result of the occession.[4] Whether by dreams and occession or by putting pen to paper, Rolfe completed both versions of *Don Tarquinio* at Broadstairs.

In addition Rolfe was busy with two other pieces which had increased to four by March 1905. The first of these was called 'Rose's Records'. He was already at work on it in November and by 3 December 1904, it was sketched out and its 'skeleton . . . more than half-clothed'. In fact, he had shown a 'bit' of it to Chatto & Windus. Planned as a follow-up of *Hadrian the Seventh*, 'Rose's Records' consisted of a series of papers written by George Arthur Rose (who was elevated to the papacy as Hadrian) and handed to Rolfe 'in a pigskin portfolio' after the murder of Hadrian with a label 'in the well-known paparchal hand-writing "For Mr Rolfe to publish".'[5] The second piece, entitled 'Ivory Apes & Peacocks', was also designed as a series of imaginary letters. Directed to Rolfe after publication of *Hadrian*, they supposedly came from persons named in *Hadrian* such as Cardinals Semphill, Carvale, Talacryn, Van Kristen, Ranga, and Sir John Devine; from Nicholas Crabbe, one of the 'tired wan clean men with corns on their right middle fingers and jackets bulging along the lower edges'; from the two orphaned sons of Toto Maidalchini and Beata Beatrice of *In His Own Image*, two 'straight-limbed straight-eyed boys of 16'; and from 'the Northern Emperor Wilhelm and the Southern Emperor Vittoremanuele'; and possibly from 'the Ninefold King'. These letters discussed Hadrian's attitude toward three matters: 'the good things of the world, i.e. Ivory; Woman, a very elaborate disquisition as to why He could not understand or know anything at all about Her, i.e. *the Apes*; Man, i.e. Peacocks.' Rolfe was certain it would make 'very tasty reading'.[6] He had settled on the use of fictitious letters to avoid exposing his own feeling, especially bitterness. Rolfe was the whimsical editor of the letters, the 'Barnum of both shows'. He meant to disclose his characters' emotions while he as 'daw (corvus monedula) would peck at them'.[7] By 15 March of the next year, Rolfe had added two more titles to his list. Still at Broadstairs, he outlined them to his brother in a letter of that date. One of these two was 'The King of the Wood', which Rolfe called a 'romance of Diana's grove at Nemi . . . where the priest (Rex Nemorensis or Flamen Dianae) *had* to be a runaway slave to pick the Golden Bough (mistletoe) from the oak in the sacred grove and to slay his predecessor'. The second was 'Duchess Attendolo', which told of the 'amazing courtship of Duchess Sforza and her four legal marriages within one month to the Duke her

178

husband'.[8] Rolfe said he had already commenced these, and he may have; but two weeks later, that is on 27 March, he was revising the two books derived from *Hadrian*.[9]

Rolfe's dream of *Hadrian the Seventh* seemed momentarily to have come true in December 1904. He was offered not a papal crown but a bishop's mitre. The offer came from a 'Syro-Chaldaic prelate' named Vernon Herford. Herford began his ecclesiastical career in 1892 as a Unitarian minister; some four or five years later he founded a small, still active sect called The Evangelical Catholic Communion and constructed for his faithful a place of worship, The Church of Divine Love. For himself he claimed the title Bishop of Mercia and Middlesex. In 1902 on a missionary's journey to South India, he acquired another bishopric when Mar Basilius, a schismatic Roman Catholic priest of Goa, consecrated Herford and gave him the name Mar Jacobus and the status of British Administrator of the Syro-Chaldean Metropolitan See in India. In London once more in 1904, Herford read *Hadrian the Seventh* and 'precipitately' offered Rolfe a bishopric over '25,000 Xtians and 20 churches'. Rolfe might just as precipitately have accepted. His eagerness for recognition of his vocation needs no emphasis. Herford offered him a chance all at once for priesthood and episcopal position and power. But from the first Rolfe said that a man who offered him a bishopric must be 'a fraud and a schismatic' and that what was wanted was an apostate. Herford was less a fraud than a crackpot, but there was little likelihood of his being 'an ambassador from the divine ones inhabiting olympian mansions'.[10] Rolfe had to be sure. He explained his intentions to Maquay on 16 December:

> Vernon Herford, it appears, was introduced to Hadrian by Richard Whiteing of *The Yellow Van*, a fine talker whom I respect. If V.H. is a friend of his, I shall only tell him my opinion and for ever after hold my peace. If not, I'll ask Bernard & Taylor (who are conducting my case against the Chartered Co.'s expert) whether it is desirable to send V.H.'s papers to Labouchere. You understand that, being in shady circumstances myself, I'm not anxious to pop into publicity unnecessarily. Poverty is my unpardonable crime (and sempiternal coronal) although I do work like a free slave for the love of the thing and like a convict in the ergastulum for fear of the lash. But I am frightfully afraid of having my crime proclaimed and my toil annulled.[11]

Whiteing was no help; so Rolfe wrote directly to Herford, asking him whether he was 'in communion with the Roman See; and the cause and reason' of his application.[12] Herford cannot have affirmed communion with Rome, and Rolfe, whether for expediency or faith, refused Herford's offer, thus terminating this strange mockery of his most ardent desire.

These transactions, which began in early December and continued until late in the month, did nothing to enrich the Christmas season for Rolfe. Nor did his prospects. Except for his annual January stay at Oxford, he had nothing to anticipate and could only wait until his suit came to trial. Had it not been for Maquay, Rolfe's Christmas in 1904 must have been extremely shabby and bare. In the first days of December, Maquay wrote to say that he was busy with plans for leaving London, but before he went he wanted to send a turkey to Rolfe for Christmas. When he replied, Rolfe assured Maquay that such a gift would be most welcome and then asked him, as he packed, to look out for old clothes he would be willing to give to a Broadstairs resident about Maquay's size and 'quite a "decent sort" ' who was 'paralysed' for lack of a wardrobe. Rolfe wrote again in a week to remind Maquay of the clothing: 'dark jackets and waistcoats, mackintoshes, woollen undergarb', every kind of wearing apparel. So Maquay, who doubtless knew that the 'decent sort' was Rolfe, first sent a hamper with food and then a quantity of used clothing. And Rolfe, in Maquay's linen, his trousers and jacket, and his boots—three sizes too small but 'fitted to a grateful recipient'—sat down with his mother and sister and possibly his brother Herbert to take his Christmas dinner from Maquay's huge turkey, so delicious that Rolfe could easily say that he had never 'tasted a better bird'. In mid-November, he had lamented that he was 'frightfully in want of a sphere, since circumstances' prevented his shaping his own.[13] For a man on a meagre allowance, no home in which he rightfully belonged, and no visible future, Rolfe had done rather well that Christmas.

[ii]

The next five or six weeks held nothing as good or as satisfying as that Christmas dinner. In January, Rolfe went to Oxford for ten days or so to do his usual stint for Dr. Hardy. Because his allowance from Barnard & Taylor was too small to allow him lodgings in London but large enough to make a difference to his mother and sister and because he had no place else to go when he left Oxford, Rolfe returned to Broadstairs. Once more he took up his chores at St. Alphege, keeping the coal scuttles filled and the dust down on the stairs and in the school-room. He was still at work on some version of *Don Tarquinio* and intermittently concerned with his new books, 'Rose's Records' and 'Ivory, Apes, and Peacocks'. But the seaside in January is bleak and the sea, much too cold for bathing. If Rolfe had any consolation for his enforced stay at Broadstairs, he failed to voice it.

In February, however, Rolfe's position began to change. That month *Hadrian the Seventh* brought him two most gratifying letters, one because

180

it permitted him to affirm his rectitude in the face of Catholic machinations and the other because it was filled with extravagant praise of his work from an unexpected and serviceable source. The first of these letters came after almost two years of silence from Rolfe's enemy of the Holywell days, Father Beauclerk. He had found himself in *Hadrian* and, shortly before 19 February 1905, he wrote to remark on Rolfe's 'psychic bitterness' and to ask why he was treated as an enemy. Rolfe's reply, written on that date in his most elegant hand, was succinct and unrelenting. He declared that he treated Beauclerk as an enemy because his acts were 'absolutely inimical', a fact which Rolfe refused to explain again and again. He suggested that Beauclerk refresh his memory by referring to *Hadrian* and the two volumes of Toto's stories. Rolfe assured his correspondent that if he were moved to make 'tardy reparation for the nine years of horror' just past, Rolfe would not be 'unchristian or ungracious enough' to decline consideration of the priest's proposals. The letter emphatically held Beauclerk accountable for the bitterness which he detected in Rolfe. Beauclerk protested immediately in a long letter that he had at no time, consciously or unconsciously, wished Rolfe harm and the priest offered his friendship. Rolfe was adamant. He refused to allow Beauclerk to justify himself in any way. He had nothing to do, Rolfe said, with Beauclerk's wishes but only his acts, and those had so far been hostile. Rolfe recalled how the priest had offered promise after promise and then refused to honour even one, thereby making of Rolfe 'an articulate & monumental scandal'. He reminded the priest how he had abused his strength and his advantages to drive Rolfe into the workhouse. Friendship on his part, Rolfe said, was impossible: 'You, & others who have followed your example, have extirpated that tender plant, root & branch. It will not bloom again, until the soil is fertilised & new seeds are sown. You have an utterly sterile plot to work on.'[1] He was willing, however, to allow it to be cultivated, and to demonstrate his sincerity Rolfe offered to exhibit 'original research of unique & popular importance' to Beauclerk and two other Jesuits. Rolfe was offering to show them his Borgia genealogy, and he did so not to let them see the kind of thing Catholics had been 'trampling on' but only in order to please and amaze them. But Father Beauclerk was stubborn, too, and once more, in a letter dated 24 March 1905, he asserted his good will. He maintained that he was doing his best to make amends through daily prayer and insisted that Rolfe fabricated causes for his bitterness, that it was his 'genius & destiny to be continually at cross & crab-like purposes' with his surroundings. Rolfe denied the cogency of anything in Beauclerk's letter. He refuted each argument and then suspended the correspondence for the time being by telling Beauclerk that his 'heavy inaccessibility to ideas & the tedious orthodoxy' and his ridiculous estimate of himself as well as his impenitence had only deepened Rolfe's distress.[2]

The second and more promising letter came from Robert Hugh Benson. Born in 1871, he was the fourth and youngest son of Edward White Benson, Archbishop of Canterbury. In 1903, after eight years as a priest of the Church of England, Benson was received into Roman communion. Late in the same year, he went to Rome and to San Silvestro in Capite as a novitiate for priesthood, to which he was ordained in June 1904. Benson returned then to England to study theology, and to do so he had his bishop's permission to live in Llandaff House under the supervision of Monsignor Barnes, another convert who was chaplain to Catholic undergraduates at Cambridge. The flurry created by the conversion of a son of the Archbishop of Canterbury, especially in the *Church Times*, was long past so that Benson had had many months of peace and quiet in which to attend to theology, write his own books, and cultivate his personal predilections. Among them was *Hadrian the Seventh*. Having read it with mounting excitement, he looked for other books by its unknown author and found the two collections of Toto's tales. These became his bedside books. In February 1905, Benson wrote to declare his admiration of the books and his interest in their author. 'I hope', Benson said, 'you will allow a priest to tell you how grateful he is for *Hadrian the Seventh*. It is quite impossible to say how much pleasure it has given me in a hundred ways, nor how very deeply I have been touched by it. I have read it three times, and each time the impression has grown stronger of the deep loyal faith of it, its essential cleanness, and its brilliance.' Benson urged Rolfe to bring out another book as quickly as possible, but, as Maquay had already suggested, to put aside all bitterness.[3]

Rolfe had long been aware of the Bensons. As early as 1882, he had put into his scrapbook a rubbing of a brass in the cloister of Winchester College commemorating Martin White Benson, Hugh's eldest brother who had died the year before at the age of seventeen.[4] No one with the Catholic awareness which Rolfe had could have failed to know about Hugh Benson's conversion. But he was wary of Hugh, or so he told Herbert Rolfe. In a letter of 15 March 1905, Rolfe lumped Benson with the arch-enemy Father Beauclerk and said he had never met an honest Catholic. Rolfe told his brother that if any of 'these devils think that they quietly can confuse and delay and make of none effect, they'll find themselves mistaken. I am very sweet and suave with them, but quite inexorable, and I give them as much information as they deserve and plenty of food for thought'.[5]

Nevertheless, admiration such as Benson's was irresistible. Rolfe replied and one letter led to another so that well before Rolfe wrote that comment to his brother, he and Benson were in frequent correspondence. Benson had put *Hadrian* among the three books from which he wished never to be separated although he objected to the account of Socialists in it and thought of pasting together the pages on which it occurred. Rolfe gravely protested that paste could not

182

eliminate the Socialists but might well prove a breeding ground for microbes,[6] and Father Hugh left the leaves of *Hadrian* untouched. He was wholly ready to follow Rolfe's suggestion in almost every way. He was inclined to identify Rolfe with Hadrian, to see in Rolfe Hadrian's sanctity and wisdom. Because the priest was certain that Rolfe's influence must be a good one, he introduced by letter a sporadic friend whose pseudonym as a writer of fiction was E. V. de Fontmell and whose real name was Eustace Virgo. Rolfe described him as the kind of man who was always 'getting stranded (in silk underwear)'.[7] Often short of funds, Virgo was usually 'at war with all the world' so that his relations with Benson alternated between 'loyal manly friendship' and 'absolutely rabid quarrels'.[8] One bone of contention, according to Virgo, was his 'entirely sincere and somewhat austere paganism', and he firmly believed that Benson expected Rolfe to ameliorate it.[9] Virgo was mistaken. Benson expressed his delight that Rolfe was a 'proper pagan.' Surely, 'all sound Catholics must be that', Benson said.[10]

The letters exchanged between Benson and Rolfe grew increasingly intimate. *Hadrian the Seventh* led to literary questions and answers. Benson consulted Rolfe about a book to be called *Richard Raynal*. Rolfe sent unpublished manuscripts—'An Ideal Content', 'Reviews of Unwritten Books', *Songs of Meleager*, and a part of 'Rose's Records'[11]— to Benson, who read them and attempted to find a publisher for everything except 'Rose's Records'. On 5 March, Benson sent an invitation to visit him (and Virgo) and confided a tendency to quarrel with his best friends. The visit was impossible but Rolfe explained that the reason both he and Benson did not always get on with their friends was in their astrological signs, one a crab and the other a scorpion.[12] Rolfe cast Benson's horoscope; and Benson handed himself over to Rolfe with fervid self-anatomising. On 24 June, when he was hardly settled after a move from Llandaff House into the rectory behind Cambridge's Catholic Church of Our Lady and the English Martyrs, Benson described his new room and said Rolfe must see it. Five days later, Benson wrote of a time perhaps two years away when he hoped to leave Cambridge and retire to a 'small country Mission in a sweet and secret place, and be perfectly happy' for the rest of his life. He told Rolfe, 'Pray that this may be so, and then come and join me there; and we will live in two small cottages, and not speak to one another till 2·30 p.m. I am intolerable and intolerant until that hour.'[13] This scheme grew into a colony of cottages, each within an 'encircling wall. . . . No lion shall be there, nor any ravenous beast. But the redeemed shall walk there.'[14]

Rolfe was not far behind. When *Don Tarquinio* appeared on 18 May, he sent a copy to Benson at once. Despite his determination to be reticent and calculating with this priest, Rolfe compulsively laid bare himself and his life, both in and out of the confessional. He divulged the horror and shame of the Holywell workhouse, fearful that his stay there might be cause for a rupture of his developing relationship with Benson. Benson was promptly reassuring. 'May I say quite plainly', he wrote of the workhouse, 'that I cannot conceive of anyone with whom I wish to have anything to do . . . regarding it as any kind of a bar under any kind of circumstances? I do not exaggerate when I say I regard it as I regard a wound received in battle.'[15] Rolfe went on with his self-exposure. The allegations of the attack in Aberdeen were denied, Father Beauclerk was castigated, the case pending against Colonel Thomas was explained, and even Mrs. Gleeson White's unseemly behaviour, recapitulated. By October, when Benson was addressing him as 'My dear man' and incorporating him with Eustace Virgo into the character of Chris Dell in a novel called then 'The Waster' and later The Sentimentalists, Rolfe had accounted for his whole unfortunate but paltry life.[16]

Rolfe made some of these disclosures during an 'ascetic walking tour' on which he and Benson went together in August. It was Benson's proposal that they set out with one or two shirts, a tooth-brush, and a breviary, that they go only into villages where a 'mass house' was available, that they sleep in out-of-the-way inns and eat their meals where they found them. It was a brave undertaking since Benson and Rolfe had not met. Each was apprehensive about dis-appointing the other, and each vowed to dismiss his preconceptions,[17] and they agreed to go, starting from Cambridge.

Benson and Rolfe met for the first time at Cambridge in Benson's room with its brown floor, its hangings of green 'arras cloth' and its white walls against which Benson had set furnishings in use for many years—a mahogany writing-desk, an oak chest and a scarlet-hued leopard skin which had 'sentiments'. Between 1905 and 1908, a stream of young men including Ronald Firbank, Philip Kerr, Vyvyan Holland, and Shane Leslie, who were called Bensonians, came to that room for comfort or inspiration or both. Rolfe came there, too, on a Saturday in August 1905 and sat with Benson or looked out of the windows at the cathedral's stone devils and angels and listened to the peal of church bells and to the clatter of horses' hoofs as the trams were hauled up Hill's Road.[18]

What each man saw when he faced the other for the first time might well be significant. Did Hugh Benson answer to the portrait drawn by an admirer, the novelist Mrs. Lindsay, in The Guide Book and the Star? It runs in part:

He's medium height, and blond, with straight butter-coloured hair . . . which needs cutting. His face is rather full and more oval than square. . . . His nose makes his whole face youthful. It's short, aquiline, and has arched nostrils. His mouth is confusing—a fascinat-ing mouth. It's tender and dogged; sensitive and yet shapeless;

emotional but rigid. . . . It's the mouth of a man who could bite; but he'd bite with tears in his eyes. . . . He has a habit of thrusting out his chin, and he stammers a little: not apologetically or painfully, . . . but quite cheerfully. He doesn't mind at all.[19]

Or did Rolfe see at once the man whom he later caricatured as The Reverend Bobugo Bonsen, 'a stuttering little Chrysostom of a priest, with the Cambridge manners of Vaughan's Dove, the face of the Mad Hatter out of *Alice in Wonderland*, and the figure of an Etonian who insanely neglects to take any pains at all with his temple of the Holy Ghost, but wears paper collars and a black straw alpine hat'?[20] And Benson; what did he see? Did Rolfe seem to be what he wanted to be, a man 'so vivid, so serene, so supremely non-curant, so exclusively aloof, & distinct from every other living thing on this orb of earth'? Did he give the impression that he reflected the character given Nicholas Crabbe, 'noticeable simply & solely because he was so exquisitely simple & sole—so singularly & so pellucidly complete in himself, & apart'?[21] Or perhaps Benson saw instead the person whom Eustace Virgo described, 'a man of about the middle height with a pair of curious and uneasy black eyes, in one of which he attempted in vain to wear a monocle. His fingers were covered with huge rings of tarnished silver, engraved with cabalistic signs.'[22] Whatever Rolfe's view of his companion may have been, Benson's was the kinder one because he was infatuated with some non-existent Rolfe.

Little is known about Benson's and Rolfe's excursion. They discussed Rolfe's Borgiada, they read together Hubert Bland's *With the Eyes of a Man*, and their regard for each other grew so strong and their mutual amiability so great that the two ended their tour by going together to Tremans, Benson's mother's home situated on a country lane near Horsted-Keynes in Sussex. When they arrived they found there Arthur Benson, Hugh's oldest living brother who was the editor with Lord Esher of Queen Victoria's letters, a writer, and later Master of Magdalene College, Cambridge. He spoke of himself as 'rather vehement, sharp, contemptuous and a busy mocker'.[23] He was also a stimulating conversationalist and a genial despot given to intimate friendships with all manner of men and few women. Obviously Arthur Benson and Rolfe might have been companionable in a number of ways, but there is never room for more than one despot at a time. Arthur disliked Rolfe at once and proved unwilling to let Rolfe show himself to any advantage. As Mrs. Benson summed up the situation, Arthur was courteous to Rolfe, but 'a mind that works in such a very different manner is not favourable to unfettered talk'.[24] None of this altered Hugh Benson's enthusiasm for Rolfe or Rolfe's acceptance of the eagerly offered friendship. Either at this time or soon thereafter, so euphoric was he, Rolfe agreed to suppress 'Rose's Records' and 'Ivory, Apes and Peacocks' owing to Benson's reluctance for him to exhibit any sort of severity. At Benson's instigation, Rolfe made a bonfire of the drafts of both pieces.[25]

Well before Benson's and Rolfe's tour, the priest had sent Eustace Virgo to Rolfe. Virgo had found himself unable to continue at Cambridge for financial reasons; so Benson asked Rolfe to invite Virgo for a visit. Not only would this help his finances but association with Rolfe, Benson believed, must also improve Virgo's spiritual state. Rolfe replied that unfortunately he was about to go to Oxford, but that his rooms at Broadstairs during his absence were available to Virgo. So Virgo went off to Broadstairs, arriving two days before Rolfe's departure. Within those two days, Rolfe gave an exaggerated account of himself, pleased to have a new audience and content with the impression he thought he was making. In fact and rightly enough, Virgo believed almost nothing he heard. Try as he might, he disliked poor Rolfe immediately and instinctively. 'Eccentric' and 'egocentric' were two of the milder terms Virgo applied to his host, and he was more happy than not when Rolfe departed for Oxford, leaving Virgo in possession for at least six weeks.[26]

Precisely when Virgo's visit took place or exactly when Rolfe was at Oxford in 1905 after January and before December is impossible to determine. His movements throughout that year and much of the next are uncertain. He was at Broadstairs in February and March. He was there, too, immediately after *Don Tarquinio*'s publication on 18 May 1905. His mother and sister had moved their school to more desirable quarters, still in Broadstairs, but Rolfe continued in the earlier premises, 'camping out' in their empty house, where he may have remained until their lease terminated 'at Midsummer'.[27] The brief period in August—no more than ten days—which he spent with Hugh Benson can be accounted for. That he was at loose ends and frantic for some way to turn is plain from another attempt to exploit the Borgiada; this advertisement appeared in the personal column in *The Times* on 15 September 1905:

A PRIVATE INDIVIDUAL is desired to FINANCE a LITER-ARY UNDERTAKING. The advertiser has sole access to unique historical documents and information. Particulars and references at interview. Apply J.L. care of Messrs. Barnard & Taylor, 47, Lincoln's -inn-fields, London, W. C.

This notice, with slight modifications, was published again in mid-October.[28] There is no further documentary indication of Rolfe's whereabouts until early December, when he was at Oxford.

Rolfe's presence at Broadstairs in May and at Oxford in December is attested by letters to Barnard & Taylor, his solicitors, having to do mostly with his pending suit against Colonel Thomas. Rolfe took an active part in all the plans for it, giving advice and counsel at every turn. In May he had yet to learn the 'complete Scheme of the manner' in which they proposed to present his case, but he thought he ought to. 'I am fairly convinced', he wrote, 'of the possibility of presenting it in an unanswerable fashion'; and he was entirely convinced that with a knowledge of the legal form and an opportunity to weigh details, he could remove any doubts his attorneys might have. Thereafter Barnard & Taylor showed him every document and sent him copies of letters transmitted to Thomas's solicitors, because on 6 December, he approved Barnard & Taylor's steps toward compromising the case but declared that they had not been explicit enough. He recalled Thomas's threats of July 1904 involving Father Oswald and George Angus and declared plainly that before he would 'consent to entertain the bare idea of a compromise', he must have an 'unqualified withdrawal' of the charges made by Thomas.[29] Two days later, Rolfe knew that compromise was most unlikely and he proceeded to give his solicitors instructions as to how to act: serve Thomas at once with a 'Ne exeat regno' and 'instantly apply for discovery of the drafts & revised typescripts named in statement of claim'. Rolfe approved the Statement of Claim but found the Advice on Evidence inadequate and incomplete. Despite exhaustion, pain from a cyst on his chin, and overwork, he offered to sit down with his solicitor and a shorthand writer at any time between the eleventh and the sixteenth of the month or after Christmas in order to compile a 'complete synthesis of the case'.[30]

Even in the absence of documentary evidence, it is unquestionable that Rolfe was at Oxford frequently and for extended stays in 1905, commencing with the Michaelmas Term of that year and, except for short absences, remaining well into January 1907. In the latter part of 1905, Dr. Hardy was revising and enlarging his *Christianity and the Roman Government*, first published in 1894, by adding to it six essays which had already appeared elsewhere. The new volume was called *Studies in Roman History*. In this work, he was dependent to an unusual degree on Rolfe, a fact which Hardy acknowledged in his preface. There he declared that the book could not have been prepared without the assistance of Rolfe, that he had revised the essays and undertaken the entire correction of proofs.[31] Furthermore, because his sight was dimming and his health fragile, Hardy required constant help from Rolfe with students' papers.

Although the work for Hardy gave Rolfe some stability and enough income to contribute 5s. to the Fabian cause out of admiration for George Bernard Shaw, Rolfe's financial situation was as precarious as ever. Once more in the spring of 1906 he attempted to profit from the genealogy of the Borgias. This time he asked for a meeting with Hubert Bland, a journalist and essayist and ardent Fabian, because Bland's picture in *With the Eyes of a Man* made him look 'as man-of-the-worldly as possible' and the scheme for use of the Borgiada, involving 'two or four thousand pounds' was a 'big affair' for men of the world. Of

187

course Bland had neither four nor two thousand pounds available for Rolfe. Instead Bland invited Rolfe and with him Hugh Benson to Well Hall and involved Rolfe again in a social life as puzzling as that he had known with the Henry Harlands. The parties at Well Hall gave Rolfe a new scene to add to *Nicholas Crabbe* and characteristically Bland and E. Nesbit, his wife who wrote successful children's books, attempted to help Rolfe publish over a period of years.[32]

During this same period, meanwhile, the remainder of Rolfe's life was determined insofar as exterior events determine it. Before 10 May 1906 he had a proposal from Hugh Benson that he and Rolfe collaborate on a 'really startling novel' about Saint Thomas of Canterbury. It was to be told as a supposed translation from Old French by a fictitious monk called first Gervase and then Robert. It was the method of both *Don Tarquinio* and Benson's *Richard Raynal*. According to Rolfe, Benson decreed that he would provide and write the story because Rolfe could not 'invent'. Rolfe was to give the novel 'historic verisimilitude' and literary form because he could tell a story 'more fascinatingly than any man alive'.[33] What Benson actually said, according to a letter dated 11 February 1907, was, 'What you can do (Good Lord, how you can!) is to build up a situation when you've got it; but you can't move along. You are a vignette-, a portrait-, not a landscape-painter, a maker of chords, not of progressions'.[34] Both were to be named as authors, but because only a third of the work was assigned to Rolfe, he refused to take the half of the profits Benson offered and settled instead on a third. On 10 May 1906, Benson sent a summary of the book in three parts to Rolfe and asked for comments at once so that they might start. Benson said that his method was 'to work like lightning, and then take a rest. I can't plod *at all*'.[35]

The entire arrangement suited Rolfe. He had sought collaboration at Holywell with John Holden and in London with Sholto Douglas, both unknown; now here was Robert Hugh Benson, an impeccable Catholic, successful and important, offering it to him. This time Rolfe must play a minor part, but he happily set to work collecting material and drawing sketches. Furthermore, Rolfe and not Benson kept recurring to the book after the first proposal. Not until 6 August 1907 did Benson at last make a division of labour. Rolfe was to apply his talent in 'scalloping and embroidering' by writing the chapters made of 'exquisite lacework' and to supply facts for Benson's chapters; Rolfe must write parts of those. At the same time Benson sent a 'scheme of chapters' to Rolfe, who added little except questions and suggestions, and sent the material back to Benson. There the affair rested.

[iii]

By early August 1907, Rolfe had been deeply involved for more than a year with Harry Pirie-Gordon, a young man who, like Robert Hugh Benson, helped determine Rolfe's remaining years. Harry, the only son of moderately wealthy parents, Edward and Mrs. Pirie-Gordon, had come up from Harrow and matriculated at Magdalen College, Oxford, in January 1902. He read history, in which he received his degree in June 1905. In his last undergraduate year, he had submitted an essay on Innocent III, pope from 1198 to 1216, for the Arnold Prize without success. His enthusiasm for Innocent III and study of the papacy was undiminished, however. After a summer with friends, among them Harry Luke, on Iona, a tiny, bleak, windswept island west of the westernmost tip of Mull, which is off that part of the coast of Scotland where Oban lies, Harry Pirie-Gordon went to Rome. There he spent part of the autumn and winter at work in the Vatican Library. While in Rome, he was presented to 'two or three cardinals' and got to know several members of the Sacred College and the Papal Court by sight. He began also to take considerable interest in the currently strained relations between the Vatican and the Kingdom of Italy. When he returned to England and to his college at Oxford for a postgraduate year, he learned that the author of *Hadrian the Seventh* was acting as Hardy's secretary and living at Jesus College. Pirie-Gordon determined to meet him. And so, one midnight, 'gigantically attired in a coat-dress with high (but huge) vermilion heels', he sought out Rolfe to roar with 'amplitudinous' drawl and 'deep guffaw', his interest and admiration for *Hadrian*.[1] Rolfe was flattered by Harry's admiration and by his attempts to identify living persons from the fictitious names given them in the book. In any case, Harry Pirie-Gordon was a large, charming, generous young man who was careful to indulge his most eccentric whims. He had a particular interest in bizarre clothing and uniforms; he loved medals, insignia, embroidery. Even in private life his 'brobdignagian wardrobe' ran to scarlet waistcoats and evening dress of white bound with violet moiré. He had read widely; he knew a great deal about twelfth- and thirteenth-century Italy and he loved the gorgeous panoply of those and succeeding times. His and Rolfe's liking for each other was instantaneous. Rolfe soon declared about Harry that 'anything more invigorating, sustaining, than his indefatigability, his wit, his pathos, his quaint young outlook on life, is impossible to conceive'.[2]

Harry introduced his closest friend, Harry—later Sir Harry— Luke, to Rolfe and in no time the two young men told him about their

189

scheme for founding the semi-monastic, secular Order of Sanctissima Sophia solely for the purpose of enlarging the world's learning. They had already 'hammered out' most of their rules for the Order during the summer of 1905 while staying in the Bishop's house at Iona.[3] Rolfe was immediately fired by the idea. He responded seriously, setting himself up as a 'wise autocrat' to get the order well started and accepting the post of provost under Harry as 'Lieutenant of the Grandmagistracy'. And Pirie-Gordon, delighted with Rolfe's acceptance of the Order, ceded Rolfe authority to formalise it. He began at once to design 'sigils, blazons, banners, and . . . dresses'. He created at least two devices, one in black and white and a larger one in yellow and white, and a billing form printed in purple and white on white paper advising that cheques be made payable to Harry Pirie-Gordon.[4]

As the summer holiday, the Long Vacation, approached, Pirie-Gordon invited Rolfe to his home, Gwernvale at Crickhowell in Breconshire. Convinced that neither his means nor his tastes made him a suitable guest of 'so stupendous a personage', Rolfe held back. But when Mrs. Pirie-Gordon reinforced her son's invitation, Rolfe accepted and on 7 August 1906 began a short visit which was soon extended to 26 September 1906.

Gwernvale, in use today as an inn, is at the northern edge of Crickhowell, a market town five or six miles from Abergavenny. A spacious building shaped like an inverted L and faced with stucco over brick, Gwernvale sits well back from the main road on a steep rise broken by a flat lawn where Maypole dancing was traditionally an annual event in the Pirie-Gordons' time. Within, the bedrooms occupy the first floor. The stairs which lead to it from the ground floor begin in a wood-panelled hallway which is lined on all sides with small shields ornamented with coats-of-arms. The dining room, a fine library, and a yellow drawing-room were all on the ground floor. Visible from the windows of the drawing-room and the bedrooms above it are the fast-flowing Usk River at the bottom of a meadow which slopes away from the other side of the road and beyond that, as the ground rises again, the Crickhowell workhouse.

It haunted Rolfe. When he looked out, even on a dark day, there it was, and his letters of those years contain more than one reference to workhouses and their immanence in his life. Yet his stay at Gwernvale was sheer delight. Not only did he like the Pirie-Gordons and Charlotte Handly, Mrs. Pirie-Gordon's sister who lived with them, but they liked him in return. He exerted himself to be a satisfactory guest. His conversation and his idiosyncracies proved interesting. When the neighbours came to Gwernvale for dinner, as often happened, they were amused at the sight of Rolfe's spectacles, the lens set in his grandfather's silver frames 'with their wide flat sides and many joints'. And they were 'rather thrilled at meeting a man who dressed for dinner in a soft white shirt and a grey velvet dinner-jacket, who

190

wore silver rings of curious shape and explained that the spur-rowel set in the thickness of one of them was for use in case he might meet a Jesuit and have to gash him across the forehead so as to blind him temporarily with the blood running into his eyes while he, Rolfe, made his escape. He even let it be supposed that the ring had already been successfully used for that purpose.'[5] He got on well with the guinea-fowls, the hens, and the peacocks, the dogs Missy and Dingo, and the Gwernvale cat as well as eight or nine others from the neighbourhood. He and Harry often sunbathed in the walled orchard or they climbed Black Mountain behind the house, resting in the heather as they went. When Harry Luke came, he joined in their walks and in their nonsense as they lay in the heather. Once, according to Pirie-Gordon, the three played at 'composing savouries'. They were unanimous 'about putting a mushroom baked in milk upon a roundel of fried bread and surmounting it with a small square of cold grouse: Rolfe then suggested the addition of five drops of lemon-juice but gracefully accepted Sir Harry's amendment of "half a mulberry" on the ground that the lemon juice would be too sharp.'[6] Rolfe's solemn manner, so easily turned from silliness to seriousness, amused Pirie-Gordon. He and Rolfe worked well together on a revision of the rules for the Order of Sanctissima Sophia. On hot days, after they bathed in the Usk, the two lay naked on the shady bank of the river and worked at a final version of the rules which Harry eventually ran off on a Roneo machine in about six copies.

The remainder of Pirie-Gordon's and Rolfe's time, that summer, went into literary work. Often they took it with them into the walled orchard or to the heather which grew so profusely on the slope of Black Mountain. They worked first on preparing Harry's failed essay on Pope Innocent III for publication. Rolfe made several contributions to the book, all outside the text: Appendix II on Innocent's consistories; a design for the cover, handsomely produced in gold on scarlet; the Latin imprimatur in which he claimed (falsely, according to the evidence of both Pirie-Gordon's and Rolfe's statements) that he typed the book; and the dedication, carefully worked out in English and Latin to mean, in Rolfe's translation, 'The Son gives, sets apart, & dedicates these First fruits to his admirable ideal-companion & Father, & to his tireless, loving & worthy to be loved Mother.'[7] In respect to the text, Rolfe persuaded Harry to introduce several 'Graecocorvine' words into the essay, to transliterate KH instead of CH for the Greek, and to reduce the length of his sentences.[8] Some of Rolfe's preoccupations, such as his distaste for Socialism, are present in the book; but however great his influence in such details, the book belongs to Pirie-Gordon, not to Rolfe, as he later maintained.[9] Nevertheless, from this venture came Rolfe's designation of Pirie-Gordon as Caliban and himself as Prospero.[10]

Prospero and Caliban were the names under which the two books of a collaboration between Pirie-Gordon and Rolfe were published. Rolfe suggested the collaboration. Pirie-Gordon had on hand an unfinished story which he had written after reading H. Rider Haggard's *The World I Desire*. The story had to do with a modern man who relived his previous incarnations and thus came to identify himself with Odysseus. Rolfe converted Harry's romance to Nicholas Crabbe, and it was Crabbe who fell back into times past. Although Pirie-Gordon undertook to write the book in a division of their labours, Rolfe dictated the character of Crabbe, calling to Pirie-Gordon's attention 'The Armed Hands', a recent, unpublished short piece by Rolfe in which he wrote his most flattering depiction of Nicholas Crabbe.[11] This book became *The Weird of the Wanderer*.

The second product of the collaboration was *Hubert's Arthur*. It began in *Innocent the Great*, where Arthur of Brittany, his companion Fulke the Flame, John Softsword, and others who figure in *Hubert's Arthur* occur. After much exchange of ideas and musing on historical novels, Pirie-Gordon and Rolfe determined to write 'History As It Ought To Have Been And Very Well Might Have Been, But Wasn't'.[12] Thus they had no scruples about adjusting the facts of history to their own purposes or about constructing fictitious heraldic devices, a particular interest of Pirie-Gordon. They meant to write in the manner of William of Tyre and of *Itinerarium Regis Ricardi*. The mode of presentation was one Rolfe had already used in 'An Ideal Content' and *Don Tarquinio*, a supposed translation from an original document.[13] As *The Weird of the Wanderer* was Pirie-Gordon's charge, *Hubert's Arthur* was Rolfe's.

[iv]

None of these projects was complete when Rolfe returned to Oxford on 26 September, so that his letters to Pirie-Gordon were filled with accounts of what he was doing for *Innocent the Great* or *Hubert's Arthur* and suggestions as to what Harry ought to do for *The Weird* or articles he might write. Unfortunately, Rolfe's work for Hardy had to take precedence over these far more interesting activities. But the luxurious stay at Crickhowell had been unsettling, so that Rolfe's letters were also filled with vast discontent. During the summer holiday he had asked to be released from his duties in a letter to Hardy, who was in Jamaica, but the letter miscarried. Some time in early October, Rolfe recapitulated the letter in a conversation with Hardy. Pirie-Gordon had encouraged Rolfe to address Hardy, thinking he would at once be 'more agreeable financially'. Rolfe, in reporting the whole affair to Pirie-Gordon, quickly disabused him and went on to say that Hardy 'in his godlike way' was regretful, he hated the inconvenience of finding another secretary, but 'being godlike', he was far too proud to say so or to 'move a hair's breadth' to keep him. Instead, Hardy had advertised for a replacement.[1] None materialised, and Rolfe's complaints were increasingly frantic. He was certain that his whole future must suffer by staying at Oxford. He told Harry's mother that his four completed books, 'The Songs of Meleagros of Gadara, . . . the only complete collection in the world, Reviews of Unwritten Books, a series of 24 witty, learned but quite easily understood essays . . . a novel about Don Tarquinio's relations called Don Renato (or An Ideal Content) and a modern novel about friendship and literary life called Nicholas Crabbe (or The One and the Many)' must stay on his table until he had made a success with 'another book or books', when the publishers would then take anything he wrote. Yet he could not see the slightest possibility of being able to write another book. His present circumstances precluded it. He was fast being exhausted by the term's work and he was sure to be a wreck when the vacation began. Yet he was forced to stay where he was and do this work 'simply for bread and butter'.[2] All he wanted was 'Time and Opportunity', but to have these he must first have cash. Rolfe hoped to get around that ever pressing need by eliciting another invitation to Gwernvale.

Rolfe's lamentations, however, were not directed solely to the Pirie-Gordons. Because he fully expected his lack of funds to be remedied by his suit against Thomas, Rolfe also complained to his solicitors Barnard & Taylor. On 22 November, he objected strongly to the fact that his case had been postponed and would not be heard until 17 December. He repeated the grievance which he had explained to Mrs. Pirie-Gordon, that is, that because of lack of cash, his books were not making the rounds of the publishers and he was prevented from 'pursuing the uninterrupted pushing' of his work, the only means he knew to assure success. He promised to do all he could to 'fall in' with his solicitor's arrangements, but he warned them that at the moment it seemed impossible to hold out until 17 December. He found life hardly worth living under the present circumstances.[3]

To bear witness to his unhappy and worrisome state, Rolfe had developed another cyst on his chin and dark suspicions about Chatto & Windus's dealings with him and his two books published by them, Hadrian the Seventh and Don Tarquinio. He questioned Chatto & Windus's half-yearly account of sales and royalties and on 3 December, he asked his solicitors whether they had investigated. Having noticed that Chatto & Windus were advertising works under the 'signed "Imprimatur"' of Archbishop Vaughan, his former patron, Rolfe concluded that the Catholics were once more scheming against him and had influenced Chatto & Windus to mislead him and to do what they could to insure the failure of his two books. He hardly expected Barnard & Taylor to credit his statement, but he pressed them to ask the publishers for an explanation of their accounts and their neglect of

193

his books. Even when the solicitors assured him that the publishers' accounts were accurate, Rolfe still believed that Chatto had been 'got at'.[4] In the matter of the cyst, his physician Dr. Sankey had advised a more serious operation than in the previous year. Rolfe hoped to postpone it until after 17 December, and he made every effort to keep the cyst out of 'knife's range' by the use of an ointment, Antiphlogistine.[5]

As his problems enlarged, Rolfe's patience grew shorter. Although he thought himself very likely to be 'adrift' without the faintest notion as to where to go, he threatened on 5 December 1906 to resign that very week from his 'engagement' at Oxford. Of course he did no such thing. He stayed there to await the hearing of his court action against Colonel Thomas. He had made what he thought was every preparation for it. 'I shall not be content', he told Barnard & Taylor, 'with anything short of complete victory,' and for this he thought he ought to be prepared at 'all points'. The plan was first to discredit Colonel Thomas and then to prove his default on promises made to Rolfe, especially in his alleged guarantee of £2,000 from the sale of the Borgiada. As early as March 1906, Rolfe was transmitting to his solicitors information about Thomas got clandestinely from a staff-clerk in the War Office who in turn had it from a personal friend. Rolfe was still on Thomas's trail and offering 'clues' in late November. He suggested a Mrs. Newton-Jackson to testify as to his relations with Thomas, 'how the overtures came from HIS side', how Rolfe held aloof until the Colonel made good his promises. He thought Lord Rosebery, a Rhodes Trustee, might be called as a witness to Thomas's dishonesty. Rolfe had exchanged more than one letter with 'Ld R,' taking 'jolly good care' always to explain himself quite clearly. In mid-November, Rolfe was eager to testify and confident of making a successful appearance, unless he was 'taken unawares, fuddled, or bullied'; if that happened, he must have an opportunity in re-examination of explaining himself.[6] Two weeks later, however, he was protesting that he could hardly go into court, disfigured and in pain from the cyst. By mid-December, although he declared himself in 'quite a fighting mood', Rolfe reminded Barnard & Taylor that he was a 'physical wreck' and asked them to arrange all possible indulgence. He needed to be 'watched, directed, & helped as far as possible'.[7]

At the last minute, that is on Saturday, the hearing scheduled for Monday, December 17, was postponed once more. Nevertheless, although his face was bandaged and Barnard & Taylor had failed to supply his allowance, on 16 December Rolfe went to London where he stopped with Pirie-Gordon in Barkston Gardens until 21 December. During those few days he resorted to Turkish baths in an effort to soothe his nerves and his cyst. On 21 December, he accompanied his host to Gwernvale, Crickhowell, for the Christmas season, and he remained there until 15 January 1907.

194

On the following day, a Wednesday, Mr. Justice Walton heard Rolfe's suit against Colonel Thomas in the King's Bench Division. While the suit had been only an academic matter, an occasion for exchange of opinion with Barnard & Taylor, an opportunity to communicate both information and instructions and to dabble in legal terminology, Rolfe's irrepressible self-confidence made anything except a verdict in his favour unimaginable. His friends believed with him. When the hearing was set for 17 December, Hugh Benson had planned not only to attend but also to bring with him two young men, 'Phillip Kerr (s. of Admrl Ld Walter) and a Luminous Innocent named Burke', so that they might see and hear Rolfe's impregnable superiority confirmed by the court. Eventually, Benson came alone as did Harry Pirie-Gordon. As the time for the hearing approached Rolfe grew more and more nervous. The wait for the £2,000 in damages which he anticipated was hardly bearable. The case itself was simply one man's word against another's, and the verdict depended on credibility. Colonel Thomas had raised and commanded the Prince of Wales's Light Horse. His son Robin had commenced service at the age of thirteen as a bugler under his father, and together they went through eighty engagements. The boy had been awarded the King's Medal. Lord Kitchener had directed Thomas to start all the remount farms in South Africa and entrusted him with their maintenance. The Rhodes Trustees, of which Lord Rosebery, once Prime Minister, was a member, had assigned Thomas the project which had involved him with Rolfe. The discrepancy between Thomas and Rolfe in a conventional society need hardly be stressed. A more recent writer who had his own experience of the law courts, Ford Madox Ford, once observed that conventions and traditions (a large part of the law) work for the preservation of the average and conventional and for the extinction of proud, resolute, and unusual individuals. The application to Rolfe is easy. Besides, in this instance the question keeps recurring as to whether he had a legal or a moral or any kind of right to Thomas's £2,000. When Rolfe was put on the stand and Thomas's solicitors, Wontner & Sons of Ludgate Hill, forced him to testify to his way of life, the verdict was inevitable. Mr. Justice Walton found for the defendant, with costs.

[v]

Frederick Rolfe was routed. 'I feel', he wrote to Pirie-Gordon three days after the trial, 'exactly as though I had been beaten with beet-roots and Mangold-worzels all over, especially on my face, neck, and hands —quite sore and bruised by the court full of eyes which banged on me all Wednesday.' With rare humility, impressive and pathetic because it was rare, Rolfe continued:

It appears to me that I was a great fool. Not such a fool as my advisers: but a fool. Several things were omitted which ought to have been put in . . . The whole thing was hurried far too much. Really salient points were not even mentioned. However, I told B. & T. that I never COULD do things right the first time; and as they didn't give me a second shot, I've no more to say. I'm sure they did their best. And I'm not going to complain. This is only an explanation *for you* because I value you.[1]

He spoke of a letter of sympathy from Harry's mother and confessed that his own mother was 'heavy' on his chest. He even concerned himself about his Oxford creditors, asking Pirie-Gordon to advise him whether to say anything to them since they had said nothing to him. He had had so many ways to use that £2,000.

Rolfe could no longer endure his clerical duties at Oxford, too dull to absorb him. Once more he asked Hardy to release him if only for that term. Hardy's unfailing friendship since their first association at Grantham had often been Rolfe's only support both materially and psychologically in the direst circumstances. Now Rolfe had the compassion to wonder how Hardy would manage, but he asked no questions when Hardy made some kind of arrangements and on 4 February 1907, Rolfe was free to go. He moved himself and his possessions into Gwernvale on that date. Six days later he reported that the Egyptian book, by which he meant *The Weird of the Wanderer* was 'coming on magnificently and that he was both happy and inky'.

At the end of the year, when he feared he might lose the Pirie-Gordons' hospitality, Rolfe told Harry, 'You have all been more kind and infinitely more *understandingly* sympathetic than any other people I ever met; and I hate to think of parting.'[2] Indeed while he remained with the Pirie-Gordons at Crickhowell, he continued as inky and perhaps as happy as at any time in his life. He enjoyed the invitations to tea and dinner with the neighbours such as the Reeses, the Woodmans, the Sandemans, and after early September Richard and John Dawkins, until Richard went back to Athens and his position there as Director of the British School of Archaeology. Rolfe was eager to put the Order of Sanctissima Sophia into action by assigning each man his task. Neither Harry Luke nor Pirie-Gordon, co-founders of the Order, took it as seriously as Rolfe. He refused to design new arms until the Order was at work, and he protested again at the end of the month that what both Harrys wanted was 'not to be ruled or worked'. He threatened to resign his offices and let them 'eat thistles' at their ease. They would die of their 'own decay (festered first)', Rolfe predicted.[3] He kept after Harry Pirie-Gordon, too, in the matter of

Innocent the Great, urging him to get on with it and advising him about the terms of his contract with Longmans Green.[4]

Although Rolfe liked writing no better than ever—'I DETEST the job,' he said once in December[5]—he took satisfaction in his ability as a writer. Now at Crickhowell, he had time and opportunity and an absentee collaborator, who was at Oxford. He stayed close to some version of *The Weird of the Wanderer* until it was ready for Mrs. Pirie-Gordon to type. Before 10 June a typescript fully signed by both authors went to Macmillan. By late May he was deep in the composition of *Hubert's Arthur,* sending off questions and comments to Harry. In June, Rolfe complained of its being 'an awful piece of work', but he was convinced that it would be 'unlike any book ever written' and that it would pay.[6] His resurgent optimism seemed justified when, later that year but before 24 November, he reached an agreement with Francis Griffiths for the publication of *The Songs of Meleager* and *Don Renato, An Ideal Content.*

From February onward, Rolfe had made every effort to keep alive Benson's interest in their proposed collaboration on the book about Thomas à Beckett. When Benson first advocated it, he had stressed the benefits which must accrue to Rolfe: his public rehabilitation by the association of their names and the financial gains because Benson was a popular novelist whose books sold well.[7] As soon as Rolfe was settled at Crickhowell in February 1907, he had indicated his willingness to go ahead, but on 11 February, Benson said that St. Thomas was 'unthinkable' at the moment; he promised to consider it after Easter. After Easter, Benson said he would do the Beckett book if it were possible, but that he 'simply couldn't—one must follow one's currents'.[8] It was mid-July before Benson showed real interest; at that time he had a plan for exchange of 'vignettes, phrases, *technical* facts, customs'. On 6 August, he showed enthusiasm about the book for the first time. On that date he instructed Rolfe as to what he should do and sent to him a scheme of chapters. Meanwhile Rolfe had made his own scheme, which went to Benson.[9] For three days, commencing 26 August, Benson was a guest at Gwernvale. Rolfe had talked of him with so much admiration that Pirie-Gordon invited Benson. During that visit he and Rolfe renewed their agreement so that in early October Benson began to write the first chapter and Rolfe, the second. By 10 October, Rolfe had completed his chapter, sent it to Benson, and got it back again with suggestions as to how to shorten it and still keep it 'vivid and interesting'. More important, Benson said, Rolfe must 'please hurry up. Polish afterwards. Just let it run, now, full tilt; otherwise there will be no go in it.'[10] On the next day Benson wrote again to insist that Rolfe hurry. Within the month, Rolfe had another letter from Benson rebuking him for his failure to send his assigned share-to-date of the book. The letter went on, 'I shall soon be immersed in other things, unless something comes from you. You know I

197

can't write except at full pressure. I cannot dribble. Just off to town. Nearly mad!'[11]

When Benson returned from London, the collaboration was at an end. He informed Rolfe that in town his unnamed agent according to some accounts and his publisher according to others had decreed that the book about St. Thomas would sell better without Rolfe's name on the title-page. In fact both agent and publisher were involved. Before 5 September 1907, Benson's agent had referred to him an offer of an advance of £400 and 25 per cent royalties for an historical novel. Benson had tried to satisfy the offer with the book on Thomas à Beckett and had asked his agent to negotiate. The result was an agreement conditional on Benson's signing the book as sole author. His financial arrangement with Rolfe was to remain unchanged and Rolfe's share must increase with better sales. Benson asked Rolfe's consent. Rolfe refused despite Benson's promise of £100 on the day of publication and several hundreds of pounds from sales. Rolfe insisted that the original agreement with Benson meant independence and that the new proposal made him a 'sponger upon other people's charity'.[12] Benson then offered Rolfe a fulsome acknowledgement of his assistance. Rolfe still refused. Finally Benson proposed to turn everything prepared for the book over to Rolfe and to let him finish and publish it as his own. Although Rolfe accused Benson of having driven 'a coach and six through the spirit of the original understanding and over the dead body of its letter',[13] he at length assented to Benson's demands. As soon as he did, Benson shelved the book. 'I'm simply mad for want of time,' he wrote to Rolfe on 20 November 1907. 'That was why I was in such a hurry a month or two ago. I had time then. I haven't now; and God knows when I shall have it again.'[14]

Benson acted in this questionable transaction from want of money and resentment. His sonnet 'Hero Worship' contains these lines:

Almost a very god thou wert to me;
  Haloed with brilliant virtues: every grace
  Lived in thy look and shone about thy face:
I bowed beneath thee, loved, feared, worshipped thee.
Then in my folly and my jealousy
  I let my critic thoughts prevail apace,
  Which entered, swarming, tore thee from thy place,
And dashed thee down in wrath and enmity.[15]

If these verses were an apology for his treatment of Rolfe, the key word is jealousy. When Benson visited Gwernvale in August, he cannot have failed to see Rolfe's easy affection for the Pirie-Gordons and in turn his position with them. Indeed Benson was there owing to that circumstance. Furthermore the happy collaboration with Harry on both *The Weird* and *Hubert's Arthur* offered an example of harmony in work which Benson and Rolfe had not attained. Last of all, Rolfe had asked

Benson's advice before settling at Gwernvale in February because its location made difficult the performance of his religious obligations. In August, Benson found Rolfe turning to the elder Pirie-Gordon for counsel.[16] Benson at Gwernvale was the outsider, a position he did not accept easily. His brother Arthur's distaste for Rolfe, Rolfe's dubious status with Catholics, his shabby life, his homosexuality seemed to weigh more heavily than the priest's devotion.[17]

Furthermore Benson wanted money to satisfy his dream of a house of his own in the country and a colony of congenial friends around him. His first explanation of the request that Rolfe allow his name to be eliminated as a collaborator on the Thomas à Beckett book, directed to Edward Pirie-Gordon, emphasised the financial aspect, the fact that his publisher wanted a book from him alone for which he would receive a considerable sum. Later Benson implied other reasons for his failure to honour his agreement, but he still came back to the matter of money when he wrote about Rolfe to Pirie-Gordon on Christmas Day 1907:

> As to my suffering through him—I have always been perfectly aware that Catholics dislike and suspect him. . . . But if he is so anxious that I shouldn't suffer—why on earth did he insist upon his name appearing with mine, when, both on this account, and on the pecuniary side, I should 'suffer' far more than on the alternative I urged on him? That is the kind of thing that makes me wonder whether he does care one atom about my convenience and my reputation.[18]

Before he wrote either letter, Benson had acquired Hare Street House at Buntingford and for the rest of his life it filled much of his mundane thought.

The house and the money it necessitated further complicated the relations between Benson and Rolfe. That situation derived from Rolfe's extreme poverty. His allowance from Barnard & Taylor had stopped. It had been paid him on the contingency that the suit against Colonel Thomas would yield £2,000 from which the solicitors could recover the amount already paid to Rolfe. When the verdict went against him, they no longer saw any reason to pay his stipend. By June he was complaining to Pirie-Gordon of having only one and three-pence and being unable to take care of his weekly laundry bills unless he could borrow from Benson '(and break his heart)'. Rolfe added that he intended to break 'B.'s heart' in order to keep at his work.[19]

When the Pirie-Gordons and Harry Luke began to plan an extended tour of Greece and the Middle East, Rolfe conceived the idea of joining the two Harrys in March 1908 for visits to castles of the crusaders, mediaeval fortresses strung across Syria and Palestine. He wanted to act as photographer for the expedition. In November

199

1908, he asked Barnard & Taylor for a loan of £500 to enable him to go; profits derived from his photographs would repay the loan. Barnard & Taylor agreed to lend the money at 7 per cent for a period of three years, but they required a 'surety', a guarantor. Rolfe, indomitably sanguine, was certain that he would be able to repay the entire loan. As he told Mrs. Pirie-Gordon, if the photographs did not pay off, 'one has two books now in the press'—*Don Renato* and *Songs of Meleager*— 'and in 3 years' time one would certainly have the Thomas book and the *Weird* and *Hubert's Arthur* all out, to say nothing of other books'.[20] He approached Father George Angus, who had befriended him years before and continued to exchange letters with him. Angus refused, saying he never acted as surety for anyone. Rolfe thought of Richard Dawkins but wisely did not ask. By 2 December, he realised that he could find no surety. Edward Pirie-Gordon helped him to write a letter to that effect to Barnard & Taylor.[21]

Rolfe then asked for an advance of £100, basing his request on the continuing collaboration with Benson on Benson's terms to which Rolfe had agreed. He asked Benson to provide a statement to support his claim. Barnard & Taylor lent him £100 to be paid in two parts, but for extra security they took steps to insure Rolfe's life.[22]

Arrangements for this loan, completed in January 1908, were far more pressing than securing funds for travel. Harry Pirie-Gordon with his mother and Harry Luke left Gwernvale on 19 November 1907, proceeding to Rome, where Mrs. Pirie-Gordon remained with friends and the two young men went on to Athens. After various expeditions, the three met at Haifa on 24 February 1908. In either the last week of January or the first in February, Edward Pirie-Gordon left Crickhowell to join his wife and son. Gwernvale was closed until the family returned. Rolfe knew that would be the case when he first approached Barnard & Taylor for a loan in November. When he realised, in December, that he could not join the travellers owing to his inability to borrow the £500, he also realised that the closing of Gwernvale must once more leave him homeless and without means to go on with his writing.

Rolfe decided that there were two ways open to him. One was to get a small advance from Barnard & Taylor and take a room at Crickhowell's Crown Inn; from there he might have access to the Pirie-Gordon's library and thus he could finish *Hubert's Arthur*. The second was to 'live on Benson and do the *Thomas* book.' Rolfe turned first to the priest because he had said that 'when all else failed' he would gladly take Rolfe in, that he need never worry again about the workhouse or having to sleep outdoors. Benson's response to Rolfe's request, however, was the offer of the 'situation of caretaker in his lonely house 2 miles from Buntingford at 8s. a week'. There Rolfe was to 'look after the place, do the gardening, and fowls, and be a 2-mile walk and a train-journey from Mass for seven months'. He was to consider himself not a guest but a paid servant, bonded to repay his 'journey-money' out of his first earnings.[23]

Benson's offer reached Rolfe on 10 December. He was slow to reply and when he did he refused to live in Hare Street House, a priest's house, without the archbishop's approval. He called to mind his experience in the house of Father Gerry at Steichen and asked Benson to apply for Archbishop Bourne's permission. Benson made no such request. On 14 December, he wrote to Edward Pirie-Gordon explaining his position and his attitude toward Rolfe and stating that he must arrange for a caretaker for the house at Buntingford at once. On 20 December, Benson wrote to say that he had done so.[24]

Still other differences with Benson widened the breach between him and Rolfe. Benson, for some reason, attempted to prevent Rolfe's communication with Eustace Virgo. Rolfe in reply loudly praised Virgo and talked of joining him in Italy, where they might 'live in peace together'. When Edward Pirie-Gordon tried to lessen the animosity between the two men shortly before Christmas, Benson was feeling self-righteous and abused enough to say that he would make no overtures to Rolfe. Much to Rolfe's distress, Benson failed to give him a Christmas blessing.[25]

This whole sequence of events from Benson's defection in the matter of the collaboration to his withholding his Christmas benediction brought real pain to Rolfe. For a time he pretended unconcern; possibly he entertained the hope that the difference with Benson was temporary. When Rolfe told Harry Pirie-Gordon how Benson had 'shelved *Thomas*' and bought Hare Street House, Rolfe added, 'For the last fortnight, he has been exploding like a Baby over a new toy. When he cools down, he may return to decent behaviour. At present I am rather tired of him.'[26] He even made jokes by telling Dawkins that though he adored the Catholic clergy, he fell 'into rows with them as a black-beetle falls into a basin'.[27] But by early January his old suspicion of Catholics and the clergy had revived. After describing his quarrel with Benson in a letter of 9 January 1908, Rolfe spoke of the priest's silence at Christmas and admitted that he was 'flabbergasted, stranded and don't like it at all'. He asked, 'What does it all mean? I simply daren't allow myself to think.'[28] He was stronger in what he told Mrs. Pirie-Gordon, saying that he was unable to account for Benson's behaviour except 'by an hypothesis' which he was 'frantically refusing' to consider. He explained that Catholic clergymen had behaved in this same way to him before with the idea of breaking him, 'heart and soul and body'. Thus Benson's conduct left him 'inconceivably frightened' and aroused all his 'old distrust of the clergy ... rampant and paramount'. He was especially fearful as 'this occasion' was caused by someone whom he had regarded as a 'true friend' and to whom he had confided all his secrets.[29]

Rolfe's neurotic fear of the Catholic clergy, centred on Benson, was aggravated by worry as to how and when he was to live after the Pirie-Gordons closed Gwernvale. He spoke more than once of the workhouse and of disappearing 'in corduroy and a blue belcher and a pseudonym'. He was weary of interrupted work, of 'hope deferred', of his eternal 'dance on volcanoes' and fearful that he might not emerge from the impasse in which he found himself. He described his life of dependence as 'quite infernal'.[30] Because this 'bestial state of uncertainty about the future' prevented his writing, Rolfe designed several vignettes in black and white—forgeries of Greek vases he called them—to scatter throughout the pages of *Songs of Meleager* and then started work on a frontispiece for *The Weird of the Wanderer*, 'Hermes singing before the areopagos of the Immortals', intended to make publishers 'jump at' the book.[31] But no problem was solved, nothing was settled, and once more a cyst appeared on Rolfe's chin.

[vi]

The cyst and his meagre resources, which threatened to disappear altogether in April, shaped Rolfe's activities for at least the six months following the end of January 1908. When Gwernvale closed and he was forced to go elsewhere, his first destination was Bristol. There Rolfe underwent hydropathic treatments meant to cure his 'awful chin' under the supervision of Dr. William Joseph Spoor, who managed the Bristol Hydro-Therapeutic Establishment. After about two weeks and an operation of a little less than four minutes without anaesthesia, the doctor dismissed him with the advice that he have absolute rest and a sea voyage.

Rolfe did what he considered the next best thing. He went from Bristol into northeast Cornwall and there on 19 February 1908 he took lodgings at 23s. a week, all included, with Mrs. Wilcock, a widow, who was the tenant on Helscott Farm situated three miles from Bude on the main road to Boscastle and Tintagel. The farm's location was a desolate one, 'high on granite cliffs with monstrous green mounds quite bare of trees undulating away and away to the horizon'.[1] Mrs. Wilcock lived in a farmhouse without running water, indoor plumbing, or electricity; but the dwelling in addition to a dairy, a kitchen, and dining- and sitting-rooms, had eight bedrooms so that in spring and summer she usually had lodgers. In winter Rolfe had the place to himself except for the widow and her two young sons.

The primitive conditions in which he lived, the 'savage grub', his tiny room were no hardship to Rolfe, but he had a sad time at Helscott Farm. He was lonely and thoroughly bored. His intent was to finish

Hubert's Arthur, but he had no heart for it and only dawdled at that and at the proofs of *Songs of Meleager* and *Don Renato*, a task which he found most distasteful. Rolfe tried walking, but the roads were rough and barren; he wandered whole afternoons on the main road without seeing one person. A month after reaching Helscott Farm, he had spoken to no one outside the Wilcock family except a doctor. By that time the wound on his chin, which had seemed to be healing, had opened and begun to 'suppurate'. He required medical attention and two weeks later complained of the 'amount of muck (including *4 goes of morphia*)' which he had swallowed and been 'buttered with'.[2]

Rolfe had still more woes. His creditors were demanding payment, and Barnard & Taylor refused to send him the unpaid balance of the loan which they had agreed to advance; they had been unable to secure insurance on Rolfe's life against the loan. At the end of April, the solicitors at last sent him £10, but within a week he learned that he needed 'half an hour's carving and bone-scraping' at a cost of £50. Although the doctor eventually decided against the surgery, Rolfe's anxiety and his pain were intense so that he was on edge all day and unable to sleep at night. At this point he had a gift of money from Richard Dawkins.[3]

His determination to live until eighty to disprove the insurance company's dark predictions, the anticipation of returning to Gwernvale, and the gradual development by letters of an intimacy with Dawkins kept Rolfe going. The letters between the two men were by mutual consent 'sub sigillo' so that they could write freely to each other. They wrote of their likes and dislikes, their reading, a considerable taste for erotic literature, and of each other's charm. Rolfe gave full details of his illness. He made much of a young Jew, Mark Markoleone, he had had assigned to him at Dr. Spoor's 'Hydro' in Bristol. Rolfe told about secretly and spontaneously baptising the boy and spoke of taking him along on the journey to Italy which Dawkins was agitating. Rolfe blew hot and cold about the journey as he faced more immediate problems, but by the time he went back to Gwernvale, he was enthusiastic about their travel plans.

Rolfe's return to Crickhowell and Gwernvale was set for 17 June. When he learned the date from Harry, Rolfe was hesitant about going back because of his illness. 'If I broke out into sores there', Rolfe told Dawkins, 'I should go stark mad and bolt. . . . Disease to me is something disgraceful, especially when it's visible. And "making-up" as I do is such a bother.'[4] In mid-May, he learned that the opening of the Pirie-Gordon house was postponed owing to the fact that Mrs. Pirie-Gordon had suffered a broken leg on 27 April near Kalat-esh-Shakif and was still recovering at St. Luke's English Hospital in Haifa. Meanwhile Rolfe's health improved so that he had no disease to take with him to Gwernvale. He returned there shortly before 29 June and on that date, a Monday, he went in the dog cart with Harold Palmer, the

Pirie-Gordon's coachman, to meet Harry and his parents at the railway station in Abergavenny.

Rolfe's life at Gwernvale and in the British Isles was almost at an end. During much of the next month, he spent a part of each day developing the photographs which Harry Pirie-Gordon had made on his tour. On 21 July and again on 22 July, Rolfe went to Abergavenny in the dog cart. One week later, that is on Wednesday, 29 July, he acknowledged a letter from Dawkins 'with joy'. Dawkins and Rolfe were almost ready to leave for Venice and to facilitate their plans and their departure, Rolfe was preparing to move in with Dawkins. Two or three days later Rolfe took the things he seemed most likely to want to Pendarren, the beautiful home situated high over Llangenny which Dawkins had recently inherited from his uncle John Doyle.[5] Rolfe returned to Gwernvale only once more. On 4 August, a Tuesday, both he and Dawkins dined with the Pirie-Gordons. Harry was away and had been since 13 July. He did not return until 6 August so that he may never have seen Rolfe after 13 July. Soon after 6 August, a week or ten days at most, Rolfe left with Dawkins from Pendarren and then from Abergavenny for Venice.

Part V

1908 – 1913

[I]

To know Frederick Rolfe, Baron Corvo, in Venice is to know him at his most Corvine, most Rolfean. All that Rolfe was, all that he had become in his more than thirty-five years of failure, disappointment and contemptible dealings, hardened in Venice. At no other time did he have greater need of a sense of peerless difference for psychic survival. At no other time in his life was Rolfe more essentially himself. He declared that in coming to Venice he had come to a 'new half of his life' and 'everything in it was different from the first half'.[1] Seemingly contradictory, that statement is in fact an affirmation and an explanation. His hope for priesthood ended in Venice. By 1910, his vow of celibacy as proof of vocation had run its course after twenty years and on the one hand he announced that he was 'not at all moved' to avail himself of 'liberty,' while on the other, he stated that he had had 'inward warnings of the exhaustibility of human patience'.[2] In either case, the dearest aim of Rolfe's life had worn itself out. Rolfe had not lost his faith. To the contrary. At the tip of his tongue, he had saints on whom to call in need. The outward signs of religion, the triptych of the Virgin Mother of Nikopoieia, open on Saturdays, and the names by which Christ's mother was known in Venice— Saint Mary of the Lily, Saint Mary of Grace, Saint Mary of Consolation, Saint Mary the Beautiful, Saint Mary of Good Health, Saint Mary the Fragrant, Saint Mary of Miracles, Saint Mary of the Angels, Saint Mary the Processional, Glorious Saint Mary of the Friars, Saint Mary Mother of the Lord—were constant sources of comfort to him.[3] He prayed without ceasing and by his own formula, *Deus meus et Omnia*, erected himself to 'face to face' communion with his God. After 'silent eternities', he took leave and came 'softly down, corrected, cleaned, his problems solved, his soul inspired with necessary news and necessary strength and necessary knowledge for guidance on the way'.[4] But without hope for the priesthood, Rolfe had no occasion for restraint so that he no longer held in check his intellectual arrogance. It spilled over with more and more malignance on whoever disagreed with him or failed to value him as he did himself. That he was never to know an 'earthly home', never to satisfy his 'soft warm hungry heart', never even to use his unused 'human sympathy', was plain. Hardship and insecurity had dogged him all his life and their threat was ever present. That these things were true was largely

207

inexplicable and fortuitous. And so for five years, driven not by reason but by instinct and emotion, Rolfe exercised his individuality without constraint. He took delight in the sun gilding the angel on the bell-tower of Sanzorzi, the 'myriad different kinds of night' in Venice, the body of a naked boy emerging from the water, and the water itself. It was there he fled 'to cultivate the garden of his soul in the loneliness of sea and sky, amid the sweet salt air, where the winds were as a quire of singers'.[5] He was calm in his out-and-out sense of intellectual superiority and consequent disdain for the 'resident aliens', the English in Venice. His suffering there from hunger, and exposure brought him to the point of death; but by way of compensation Rolfe lived for five years in his own way with his own illusions.

Dawkins's and Rolfe's lodgings in Venice were on the fourth floor of the Hotel Belle Vue et de Russie, a modest hotel with good food and comfortable rooms. These occupied the upper four floors of a building located on the Piazzetta dei Leoncini, an arm of the Piazza San Marco. The ground floor is still occupied by Thomas Cooke and Sons. Adjacent is the clock tower which stands almost in front of the entrance to the Mercerie. The hotel no longer exists; its quarters now house a glass factory. But access to the upper floors of the building, marked by a stone in which is cut 'BELLEVUE', is still up the stairs at 268 Calle Larga San Marco and the view from the south windows is exactly the one Rolfe saw, the façade of Saint Mark's and the bronze horses in the near view expanding to the two columns, one topped with a lion and one with a crocodile, at the ducal palace on the Piazzetta, and across the Molo to the Bacino with its *gondolas sandolos, topos, barchetos* and all the water craft in a constant flow of traffic.

Rolfe enjoyed the hotel. He liked the food, he could practise his Italian on the servants, and above all he admired the view. As for Venice, it was a city to be savoured in every way. Whether with Dawkins or without him, Rolfe began to explore the monuments, the picture galleries, the palaces, and the churches. Even the poorest, most neglected of the many churches, each on its own square, had a window, an altar, a quiet corner which proved worth his notice. Merely to be on the waterways or the 'populous alleys' turning and twisting up and over the countless bridges and down to the water was sheer delight. Almost from the day of his arrival, he had available a hired sandolo pupparin, a light vessel smaller than a gondola, and two boys, Carlo Caenazzo and Gildo (Zildo, in the Venetian dialect) Vianello, to man it. Rolfe got on well with the gondoliers. As he said of himself, it was far easier to be friends with people of that kind than with 'howling swells like the Gordons'.[6] He joined in their work so that soon he was rowing as a Venetian does and feeling proud of the stamina which enabled him to take long turns with an oar. With the two gondoliers, Dawkins and Rolfe ventured farther and farther onto the lagoons, especially the north one, carrying with them the camera and its equipment and Rolfe's huge Waterman fountain pen and the manuscript of *Hubert's Arthur* at which he worked when he was not at the oars. They photographed what they chose (Dawkins was as expert a photographer as Rolfe) and wherever they found seclusion they made pictures of Carlo and Zildo, nude. Zildo in particular had 'commended himself' to Dawkins, who swore that the boy was the image of Agias of Delphi and yearned for a picture of him in the sun against a 'whited wall'. Rolfe described the pleasure of those 'lovely late-August days' when he wanted to do nothing except sit in the *barcheta* and be rowed about and write his book until he was ready to row or bathe or eat or take his 'forty winks, and so on, again and again'.[7] These pleasures answered his notion of an ideal holiday for which Rolfe had appealed to Dawkins shortly before the two left England, that is to live naturally, satisfying impulses and desires without constraint.[8]

Dawkins should have been forewarned. Rolfe's fancies, which he lived up to fully, caused incessant bickering between the two men. Rolfe expected his host to relish 'loafing elaborately' and to relish paying for it. They had no precise financial agreement, however, nor did Rolfe know what Dawkins was prepared to spend, although he had taken a 'correct and generous attitude' by saying that money was not to matter.[9] Rolfe had made no secret of his poverty and according to his understanding, he was to repay his share of expenses from the sale of photographs made on this journey, but meanwhile he was almost wholly dependent on Dawkins. Once in Venice, the gratitude which he had talked about during the bleak days on Helscott Farm vanished and he no longer felt his 'penniless condition acutely'. He simply turned to Dawkins for every expenditure, knowing that Dawkins had recently inherited a considerable sum from his uncle John Doyle. Rolfe had been Dawkins's guest at Pendarren, also inherited from Doyle. Pendarren with its kennels and piggery was a fine estate and the house alone, with its terrazzo floors, its large and sumptuous rooms, its fine library, cannot have failed to leave an impression of wealth. But Dawkins was a prudent man unused to lavish spending. His protests about any expense, Rolfe met with ridicule or hectoring and he concluded that Dawkins was 'absolutely incapable of performing a noble (i.e., a free) act.'[10] Although Rolfe had been told that he must pay back everything, he was annoyed that Dawkins demanded cheques periodically for money lent, doled out 2½d. at a time for tobacco after Rolfe had asked for it, and saw to it that Rolfe spent the £12 he had borrowed from Edward Pirie-Gordon before he left Gwernvale.[11]

Their relations were increasingly strained and in less than a month they quarrelled. According to Rolfe, their quarrel had to do with their attempts to reach by boat a spectacular white wall against which

Zildo might be photographed. They could see it as they rowed on the main canal which runs from Torcello to Treponti but could find no way to it. What they sought was the small island of Sant' Ariano. When they grew impatient with the canals which took them nowhere near and, leaving the boat channel, tried to row acorss the shallows, the *sandolo* and its crew and cargo were stuck on a mud-bank for eight hours. Dawkins turned into a 'gibbering moist maniac'. He and Rolfe exchanged heated words until they were 'faint' and then Rolfe's 'notorious patience gave way with a loud yell, and embellishments of lurid notes and queries.'[12]

The two 'made it up' when their *barcheta* finally floated free and they returned to the Belle Vue. Rolfe said later that at that point he was ready to terminate the friendship; but Dawkins 'begged' so piteously ('sobbed and postured and gesticulated . . . for some hours of the night,' Rolfe wrote), saying he was lonely and friendless, that Rolfe resolved to be a 'true and loyal friend' despite the effort it cost him. As proof, he asked Dawkins to start him in Venice as a gondolier. Instead, Dawkins gave him approximately £30, enough to complete the six weeks' holiday as planned and to return to England. He told Rolfe to expect nothing more. Two days later, entrusting the camera and some of his possessions to Rolfe's care, Dawkins left Venice for Rome on a sleeveless errand. To show that he felt no malice, Rolfe accompanied Dawkins with his baggage in a hired *poppe* to the railway station at Venice and watched the train pull out.[13]

[ii]

These last five years of Rolfe's life started well enough. He continued at the Belle Vue Hotel with his bill brought up to date, and he retained the *sandolo* and the two gondoliers, Carlo, whom he pitied for having but one testicle, and Zildo, whom he admired for his 'white-toothed, red-lipped, long greenish-blue-eyed smile'.[1] In no time at all, owing to his 'aquatic activities', he was elected *Socio Ordinari* in the Royal Bucintoro Rowing Club, which gave him 'mooring, slaves, and all things desirable'. When he stepped into his *sandolo* thereafter, it flew the red cross of Saint George of England and the 'red and gold Vesillo' of the Bucintoro. He spent most of his time in the *sandolo* exploring the canals and waterways and venturing farther and farther onto the lagoons. Rolfe described one such expedition initiated by his curiosity about the white wall and the distant island which had contributed to the quarrel with Dawkins. After buying charts of the waterways south and north of Venice, Rolfe set forth with his two gondoliers on a 'perfect summer day of rich September', when the sky was a 'monstrous dome of turquoise, the water like a live aquamarine, the lights like bluebells and forget-me-nots . . . the shadows like sapphires and lapis lazuli'. They rowed out of the 'little rio' by the Bucintoro onto the basin of San Marco and then through several small, dark, cool canals until they came onto the north lagoon; there they swept along with the 'warm sea-scented wind and the flowing tide' until they came into the main canal of Burano and moored at a little inn, Albergo di Roma. After lunch, in the 'gorgeous golden sunlight of afternoon', they rowed away from Burano coming in to a narrow waterway between 'sandbanks all ashine with sea-lavender and samphire' and then at last to their destination, the little island of Sant' Ariano. The night was passed at the Albergo di Roma and the next day, back they went through the sunshine and over the sparkling waters to Venice.[2]

Rolfe was still in Venice well after the period for which Dawkins had provided. He could not bring himself to leave. By staying, it seemed possible, without offence, to 'cheat autumn and winter'. This man who found old age incompatible with his youthful soul felt in Venice 'no more than twenty-five years old, in everything excepting value-less experience and valuable disillusion'. He had seized youth again in 'solitude with the sun and sea.'[3]

The £30 which Dawkins had left soon ran out and by 6 October, with his bill at the Belle Vue mounting steadily, Rolfe was forced to appeal for help. On that date, in his *sandolo* 'rushing Buranoward at moonrise', he wrote to Dawkins not to thank him for hospitality and money but to ask for another £10, preferably forwarded by wire. He made no reference to his hotel bill but spoke of the expenses of photographic supplies bought from Ugo Pajola's shop near Saint Mark's Square and of the pictures he had at last made before the white wall of Sant' Ariano. 'I am bleeding money like a pig', he wrote, 'to get a perfect mass of unique photographs.' According to this letter and at least one other, he expected Dawkins to be titillated by the prospect of the pictures of the nude boys and consequently ready to pay for them.[4] Dawkins's answer by telegram and then by letter was a refusal, leaving Rolfe in debt by the following Monday, 12 October, for another week at the Belle Vue and the photographic supplies. Two days later, he sent sixty-nine rough prints to Dawkins and the reproach that £10 received a week earlier would have paid his bills and got him back to Gwernvale but that now he needed considerably more.[5] Without a word to Rolfe, Dawkins transmitted £15 through his bank by way of Turin to the Banca Commerciale Italiana, which sent a uniformed messenger to deliver the £15 or L375 to Rolfe. He refused it, not knowing or pretending not to know whether it was meant for him and, if it was, who had sent it. This was Rolfe's way of insuring that all money be transmitted directly to him. Meanwhile, he wrote to tell Dawkins about the incident and to ask to be relieved of the burden of Dawkins's possessions and 'all those nude negatives.' Rolfe

211

cautioned Dawkins that whatever arrangements he made for their removal must be made only with Rolfe for the sake of his credit. By the end of the month, after considerable inconvenience to Dawkins and more than one letter, Rolfe had the £15 in hand. With it he paid his hotel bill, but he complained that the sum was insufficient to redeem his property from the Monte di Pietà, the pawn shop, and to get him back to England.

Rolfe's complaints and requests for money were not limited to Dawkins. About 26 October, Rolfe wrote to Barnard & Taylor, who sent him £25 in accordance with their agreement with him which had involved insurance on his life. Sometime also in late October, Rolfe had £12 10s. from Harry Pirie-Gordon meant as passage-money for a return to England. In answer to questions from the Pirie-Gordons about his future and his income, Rolfe had evolved a scheme for a photography business on a grand scale inasmuch as to succeed, 'one must begin as one means to continue'.[6] The scheme amounted to nothing without financing and his only chance to get that, as Pirie-Gordon made clear, was to return to England. It all seemed a great nuisance, but Rolfe agreed. He told Pirie-Gordon to expect him at Gwernvale in the week of 8 November.

Rolfe planned to finish *Hubert's Arthur* and work with Benson on the book about Thomas à Beckett. Benson, he said, was screaming for him to finish the book. And in fact Benson had written impatiently a month earlier to ask various questions about the book. He said that he must have answers at once or he must do some other book to satisfy his publishers.[7] At the same time, Rolfe needed information from Pirie-Gordon in order to get on with *Hubert's Arthur*. By going to England, Rolfe was sure he could complete both books and acquire enough cash to return to Venice in February and open his business.

When the week of 8 November came, Rolfe stayed where he was. He had written in good faith to Harry Pirie-Gordon, but Rolfe had no real desire for a photography shop or to work with Benson. As for *Hubert's Arthur*, he could complete it in Venice as well as or better than anywhere else. He had already told Dawkins that the last proofs of *Don Renato* demanded his attention. To Pirie-Gordon, Rolfe explained that he had purchased his rail ticket and travel insurance and made every preparation to leave Venice on Sunday, 8 November, when he was faced with 'other unexpected liabilities to the amount of £20 stg odd'.[8] So, by mid-November Rolfe found himself 'another week to the bad' and, with 'fresh bills', in need of £32 if he was to get away. He was also in a fretful mood. 'Destruction of a fine illusion'—that of friendship, perhaps, or the friendship of Dawkins—'and the worry of putting a good face on despair,' he confessed, 'annoy me dreadfully.'[9]

So far Rolfe had been surprisingly successful at concealing from his Venetian associates any worry or despair he may have felt, and his credit was unimpaired. If the Bucintoro, his club, or Evaristo Barbieri, his landlord, had any idea as to the precariousness of his financial position, they fully expected Rolfe to find a way to make good his obligations. Even by mid-December, when he had moved into a cheaper room and was ridding himself of his hotel bills by burning them, he was a welcome guest at the Belle Vue. His room, number 27, was cold and dark, but he was still enjoying such comforts as afternoon tea and wine with his after-dinner cheese.[10] Rolfe's status with the Venetians at the Bucintoro, he upheld with his skill as an oarsman in the Venetian manner and his endurance, remarkable in a man of his age. He came and went at the Bucintoro, using their boats and facilities at will.

Rolfe's writing, however, contributed most to his credibility. In August and the glorious months of early autumn, he took with him his pigskin portfolio stuffed with rough drafts and notes each time he boarded the *sandolo* and there, in a cane armchair with his writing board covered with paper on his knees and his huge Waterman fountain pen in his hand, Rolfe wrote. When the weather worsened, he worked in the *salone* of the Belle Vue, bringing his work and coffee into the hall at '19 3/4 o'clock' and working there steadily until the house closed at one o'clock in the morning. In this way, by the end of November, Rolfe had finished the composition of a piece which he described as the 'Excommunication of Harmsworth and the new Order for damning him', an order of chivalry. This piece, published under the title *The Bull Against the Enemy of the Anglican Race* well after Rolfe's death, was a diatribe against cheap journalism but especially the kind exemplified in Alfred Harmsworth's *Daily Mail*. So intense was Rolfe's scorn for that particular paper, he had invented the term 'Dilimilism' and equated it with 'pills, advertisement, penny-in-a-slot, and motor-cars'.[11] In his *Bull*, Rolfe as Hadrian the Seventh wrote a scathing attack on Harmsworth, Lord Northcliffe. He begins by acknowledging that Nicholas Crabbe, a 'student of human and divine affairs, a lover of his Motherland', has exposed the iniquity of a baron of the United Kingdom who owns and edits a journal and has denounced him as an 'hysteria monger and enemy of the Anglican Race'. As Hadrian, Rolfe goes on to castigate Harmsworth as an exponent of penny-journalism and ends by erecting a 'rampart for defence from and for offence against his infernal onslaught', a new Order of Chivalry under the protection of 'Saint Gabriel Archangel and News-Bringer'.[12] Although *The Bull* is a magnificent display of reasoned invective, Rolfe's work on it at the Belle Vue was in no way as impressive to onlookers as his preparation of the fair copy of *Hubert's Arthur* to go to Pirie-Gordon. In his elegant and careful script, page by page, he set down his story on bank-paper bound with white buckram into a tall slim volume.

While engaged in this work, Rolfe first attracted the attention of Canon Lonsdale Ragg, the Anglican Chaplain in Venice, and Laura, his wife. They had come to the Hotel Belle Vue with their one child and her English nurse to escape the winter cold of their apartment in the Contarini Palace and to enjoy a few months of comparative quiet and freedom from the responsibility of a household before they left Venice to go to a parish at Tickincote in England. Lonsdale Ragg remains a shadowy figure. An admirer described him as saintly, sensitive, and unworldly; he was also diplomatic and tactful.[13] He was unquestionably patient, as his dealings with Rolfe indicate. He was an educated man, who had achieved a First Class in 'Greats' and Theology at Oxford. In the preceding year, his *Dante's Italy* had been published. Ragg was a man of some presence who, because he was abroad, encountered a far more diverse and sophisticated society, especially among the English in Italy, than he would have in most English parishes. Later, in Rome, through the offices of Lord Berners, Ragg had the distinction of officiating at Ronald Firbank's first burial. In Venice, in 1908, Ragg was a regular guest at the *salons* which Horatio Brown held each Monday evening exclusively for men at Ca' Torresella. Frequently Ragg was at the receptions which Lady Layard held each Tuesday evening at Palazzo Capello. Mrs. Daniel Curtis, whose Palazzo Barbaro often housed Sargent and, several times, Henry James, made Ragg welcome. Helen, Countess of Radnor, trained his choir for a Christmas service in Venice. He took ices, syrups, coffee, wine with Venetians and other Italians, Germans, Greeks, French, all the charming and gifted and merely well-born who came to Venice in the early years of the century. Yet Ragg fails to emerge as either a Trollopian Hardy or a Grantly or as himself. Even Rolfe's depiction of him as Warden, the clergyman in *The Desire and Pursuit of the Whole*, gives Ragg no substantiality; the characterisation is a caricature of the hungry hypocrite. Only once, when Rolfe goads him to a denial of humane responsibility because of their different faiths, does Ragg appear to be a living, breathing man. Mrs. Ragg is another matter. She, too, appears in *Desire and Pursuit*, where she is shown to be a pretentious, intrusive affirmation of her husband. In fact, she was observant, severely honest, and sharp-tongued. Although what she wrote about the Anglo-Venetian society of which she was a part conforms with the reverential attitudes of the nineteenth and early twentieth centuries, still her acerbity and distaste for the obtuse are clear. Without doubt, she was more aggressive than her husband in practical matters. Although Canon Ragg eventually asked Rolfe to stop writing to him, Mrs. Ragg and not her husband took the first step in that direction by returning unopened Rolfe's letters to Canon Ragg. According to her own account, she had no trust in Rolfe from the beginning and more than once accused him of affectation and conceit. In no time she developed a passionate antipathy for this man who had 'neither patrician birth nor breeding nor the sentiments of one of "nature's gentlemen".' She described him as a 'cad with an intermittent streak

214

of genius'.[14] It was Mrs. Ragg, in her search for rooms at the Belle Vue, who noticed Rolfe's huge fountain pen and then looked at its owner in the only comfortable chair in the dark little *salone* of the hotel. That he was English and might be a nuisance caused her and her husband to hesitate momentarily about taking the Belle Vue's rooms, but they decided that since Rolfe was Roman Catholic and spoke Italian, he must have his own circle of friends and would not be their responsibility. They determined to disregard him except for civilities.

Who encouraged anything more between the Raggs and Rolfe is impossible to say. Mrs. Ragg accused Rolfe. From the first she suspected that he was eager to 'scrape acquaintance' and she told how he jumped from his table in the corner of the hotel dining-room to pass the Raggs a pitcher of water or a condiment, how he attempted conversation with their child's nurse when they met on the stairs, and how he borrowed light reading matter from her husband. Rolfe laid the blame with the Raggs. In a letter to Pirie-Gordon, he mentioned the fact that 'a pack of English' were running after him and that Ragg had made the 'most comical attempts to know' him.[15] Ragg and his wife interrupted Rolfe as he worked in the *salone*, forced cigarettes on him, and inquired with greedy tactlessness about his antecedents. But Rolfe resisted them and every other member of the English colony. 'What's the good of making new friends', he asked, 'when you may be denounced at the *questura* for debt any day?' When Lady Layard, whom he called the Queen of England in Venice, pressed him to come to a reception at Ca' Capello, he told her that something had gone wrong with his affairs in England, that he was at the edge of ruin and very likely to be without an income. These he called disabilities sufficient to 'disqualify' him from 'association with persons more securely situated'. He ended, 'I beg Your Ladyship to confine Her attention to those, and be pleased to leave me alone.'[16] At the same time and with the same 'flaming sincerity' he wrote to the Raggs. Dated 3 December 1908 and directed to Canon Ragg, the letter reads in part:

> And will you and Mrs. Ragg be so kind as not to take any further notice of me. I find myself in financial difficulties and on the very verge of trouble with creditors, a situation extremely undesirable in one's acquaintance. So I should take it as a favour if you will let me give you this warning to drop me quietly in time.[17]

What Rolfe told Lady Layard and Ragg was true. His financial status was deteriorating rapidly. On 23 November 1908, at about the time he first encountered Canon and Mrs. Ragg and less than a week after he had lamented his rashness and imprudence to Pirie-Gordon and acknowledged that his 'detention' in Venice affected his work and his future, Rolfe wrote to Barnard & Taylor, asking them to increase the insurance on his life and thereby make him a further loan or allowance large enough to enable him to have a 'clear year of solid work' in Venice.[18] By mid-November, the solicitors had supplied Rolfe with almost £500. Meanwhile, after having them a month, Rolfe had failed to return corrected proofs for *Don Renato*, to which Barnard & Taylor held the rights. They denied his request to increase the insurance on his life and brushed aside all talk of an allowance. Rolfe quickly told them that by stopping help to him now they risked the loss of all they had spent. When they misunderstood one of his letters to the extent of thinking he intended to get a job and concurred with the idea, Rolfe was puzzled and resentful. He declared that the only job he would do at all was writing books or running a photographic business in Venice and for one he needed £150 and for the other L15,000. He refused to attempt anything else. 'I have been battered out of the Church and battered out of Art,' he said. 'If I am to be battered out of Letters, too—Oh very well. I make no more attempts.'[19] If Rolfe had any cash by late November, it came from overdrafts.

His friend Pirie-Gordon was concerned enough to ask Barnard & Taylor to arrange for the British Consul to send Rolfe home. Pirie-Gordon offered £5 from Benson and £10 from himself toward expenses and wrote to tell Rolfe what he had done. Rolfe objected to any transaction with the consulate. His aim was to keep up the appearance of solvency with the English and with Barbieri and at the same time secure financial aid from England. Early in December he asked Dawkins not to interfere with the lies he was telling to keep afloat and he urged Pirie-Gordon to leave everything to Barnard & Taylor. They might be inclined to shirk their responsibility by turning everything over to Benson and Pirie-Gordon, knowing them to be rich; but in the long run the solicitors were sure to do what was right.[20]

By mid-December, Barbieri could no longer believe in Rolfe's façades nor could he ignore Rolfe's hotel bill. The hotel keeper consulted Canon Ragg and inquired about Rolfe and his prospects. Ragg spoke of Rolfe as a published author, tried to reassure Barbieri by saying that the book on which Rolfe was at work was sure to produce funds, and then agreed to pay for Rolfe's meals for the next three weeks, a period including the Christmas season. Barbieri decided to be patient a while longer, especially since the room Rolfe occupied was unheated and undesirable. He told Rolfe exactly what had happened so that the following morning Rolfe asked Ragg for an interview.

That night after dinner Rolfe delivered himself of a passionate account of the persecutions he had suffered including those inflicted by Dawkins and Benson. From that time, relations between the Raggs and Rolfe expanded. They often had their coffee together in the hotel lounge, and the two men had protracted conversations there or in the dining-room. Rolfe helped Ragg correct and revise his book *The*

Church of the Apostles. When the Canon and his wife dressed to go out to dinner or to the opera, Rolfe had compliments for Mrs. Ragg.

When the Raggs began to urge him to accept the invitations he received from the English in Venice, Rolfe resisted. He was happy to show Venice to visiting Englishmen such as Father Hugh Pope, who stayed briefly at the Belle Vue, *en route* from Rome to England. Rolfe spent two days in November talking books, the Church, and Venice with Pope and taking him as far as Torcello in one direction and, in another, the Armenian Benedictine monastery of San Lazzaro, an island lying off the Lido.[21] At this time, too, Rolfe offered his services to the English Hospital, located in an historical house in Rio della Croce on the Giudecca. The building, a delightful private home today, still retains its garden and its beauty. The hospital was the special charity of Lady Layard, who had founded it in 1903 and appointed her niece Olivia du Cane as its first directress. In Rolfe's time that position was filled by Edith A. Chaffey, a cheerful, capable, energetic woman who talked in breathless rushes. Rolfe's services consisted of rowing patients, mostly sailors, about in a Bucintoro *sandolo* every afternoon when the sun shone. He reported to Pirie-Gordon that the convalescents thought 'no end' of him as did the 'Matron, a Chaffey', and Lady Layard, who adored the hospital. Rolfe added, 'I choke 'em all off.'[22] As indeed he did. Courtesies to a visitor and help for the hospital were agreeable, but, as he had done with the Raggs, Rolfe 'abruptly, altruistically, and not ungenerously' begged to be left alone. He refused to 'mix with strange people' while his affairs were in their current state. He refused to make friends because he was 'in violent danger of wanting friends soon'.[23]

Eventually Rolfe capitulated. There was no gainsaying Miss Chaffey. She delighted in organising entertainments for her patients rather like children's parties, and she insisted on Rolfe's presence at these and at 'tea-fights'. The word of his attendance got around and seemed to weigh against talk of unsavoury relations with his gondoliers. He began to receive invitations not only from Lady Layard but also from the Frederick Edens, whose garden, naturally called 'The Garden of Eden', lay across the canal from the hospital, and from others, the Bonds and the Taplins. Ragg persuaded Rolfe to go to one of Horatio Brown's Monday nights. Brown, whom Rolfe later described as having a 'bluish smack-of-cheek-red face . . . a pursed mouth, a tight waistcoat splayed over a pudding . . . and longish knock-kneed shanks', lived with his elderly mother at Ca' Torresella. He is best known now for his association with John Addington Symonds, but during his lifetime Brown had a reputation for scholarly work on Venetian history and, in Venice, for his hospitality. The winter regulars at his Monday nights included William Hulton, Augustus Montalba, Prince Hohenlohe, whose Casetta Rossa was commandeered during the war for Gabriele D'Annunzio, the Reverend Charles Williamson, Humphreys Johnstone, and Ragg. Rolfe pretended disdain for the company and for their conversation and he thought Ragg's rendition of the lament from *Aïda*, hilarious. Even so, he went at least once with Canon and Mrs. Ragg to the Fenice for opera. Mrs. van Someren, the American wife of a Dutch doctor practising in Venice, first met Rolfe there in the box which the Raggs occupied, and he showed her a key contained in a massive silver ring on his finger, calling it the 'Master Key' to his possessions.[24]

That meeting occurred on the night of 28 December 1908; the Raggs were at the Fenice that night and, when they emerged, heard of the earthquake and tidal wave which had devastated Calabria and Sicily. Rolfe at once volunteered to collect clothing, blankets, and whatever was offered for the survivors in the South and for the empty-handed refugees who flooded into Venice. He spent days in his *sandolo* receiving contributions and taking them to the barracks of Santo Zaccaria for shipping to Messina and coastal points where they were needed.

All in all the period from mid-November to early February was unusually rewarding. He had much pleasure in the first mass of Christmas celebrated by the Patriarch in Saint Mark's and much pride as an Englishman in doing his work for the earthquake victims. He also enjoyed the opportunity of suggesting the 'beautiful and exquisite' Lieutenant Italo Felici for membership in the Order of Sanctissima Sophia. Rolfe's greatest satisfaction lay in completing *Hubert's Arthur*. He had first to secure Pirie-Gordon's contributions, a section having to do with the crusade in Jerusalem and another short 'bit' which was 'extremely good and fine and amazingly literary and picturesque',[25] and to incorporate them into the book. By 27 December, Rolfe could tell Pirie-Gordon to expect the book in two weeks— and 'such a BOOK as neither you nor any one . . . has ever dreamed of before this.'

Finishing *Hubert's Arthur* took a week or so longer than Rolfe had predicted, but at last it was ready, 'two tall narrow-paged beautifully written volumes bound in white buckram, containing the knowledge and the experiments of several lifetimes'.[26] Rolfe had Thomas Cook forward the two volumes to England. He had made a gift of *The Weird of the Wanderer* and *Hubert's Arthur* to Pirie-Gordon. Because Barnard & Taylor had declined to re-insure his life and provide him with a year's income, Rolfe was determined that they would profit from neither book. He wanted Pirie-Gordon to market both books as his own and pay Rolfe whatever seemed fair, first deducting a small sum owed to Edward Pirie-Gordon. At the same time, Rolfe hoped that he had made amends to the Pirie-Gordons. 'Oh it is abominable to be thought a beast,' Rolfe wrote. 'Of course it is unseemly for a 48er to perform the male equivalent of flinging his drawers over the

218

windmills. That ought to be done about 20. But that is all I have done after all'.[27]

In the last statement, Rolfe was inaccurate. By-passing Barnard & Taylor was close to felony. His share of income from the two books belonged to the solicitors in payment for money already spent. Rolfe's disgruntled attempt to ignore them could in no way improve his unhappy financial position. By the time he sent off *Hubert's Arthur*, he owed close to £100 in Venice, and most of it to Barbieri of the Belle Vue. Rolfe might well have decided to go back to England. Such a decision would not have paid his debts, but it would have ensured him shelter and food. The Pirie-Gordons were entirely willing to receive him at Gwernvale, and for a time Benson said that he was ready to have Rolfe as a guest.

But Rolfe could not be separated from Venice, a fact which grew increasingly clear to Harry Pirie-Gordon. Unsolicited, he packed up most of Rolfe's winter clothing and sent it to him, and at the end of December he tried once more to provide for his friend through Barnard & Taylor. Harry asked them to add enough to the £10 he could contribute, the £5 (£10, if possible) to come from Benson and whatever might be got from Dawkins so that Rolfe's continuing hotel bill in Venice to the amount of L45 per week for twelve weeks could be paid. Barnard & Taylor initiated a correspondence with Barbieri, who proved both reasonable and generous. He agreed to accept L50 a week not as full weekly payment but as a partial payment toward Rolfe's current expenses. Before 28 January, Barbieri received the first cheque under this arrangement, a cheque for L100 toward two weeks' expenses. Pleased with this accommodation, Barbieri showed the cheque to Rolfe.

Rolfe acted at once. He first sent a letter to Dawkins saying that his part of the donation would be returned. Next Rolfe wrote to tell Pirie-Gordon that under no circumstances could Benson and Dawkins be allowed to help. Rolfe then reported that Barbieri refused to accept the cheque toward current expenses, that he regarded it as a small payment on account for past indebtedness, and that unless 'arrears were cleared' by the last Saturday of the month, he was going to the police. Rolfe said it was all a misunderstanding owing to Barbieri's inability to read English and Barnard & Taylor's ability to make an 'amazing mess' without regard for their client, himself. Obviously Rolfe lied. He wanted every penny spent for him to go through his own hands. He believed that he had fabricated a position for himself with Barbieri which made his credit elastic. He had followed the same tactics with Mrs. Griffiths, his Hampstead landlady, and had railed at Newbolt for upsetting them. Rolfe had no intention now of letting his supposititious status with Barbieri disintegrate owing to the misguided efforts of such 'muckers' as his solicitors, incited by a tyrannous Hugh Benson, eager to haul him back to England and force him to write the book on Thomas à Beckett. Pirie-Gordon could do nothing except notify Barnard & Taylor. They promptly washed their hands of the matter, first repudiating their agreement with Barbieri. Naturally, he was angry and, after writing a letter to the solicitors which flatly denied the truth of Rolfe's statement, told Rolfe on 9 February, a Tuesday, that unless he paid a substantial part of his debt by the following Monday, the police would be called in.[28]

For a reason known only to himself, Barbieri relented and allowed Rolfe to stay at the Hotel Belle Vue, his bills mounting daily, until 14 April 1909. Late the night before, an incident occurred which precipitated Rolfe's eviction from the hotel. The incident was the culmination of a series of events which arose from Rolfe's constant talk about his assets and his laments at their mismanagement by his agents in England. By the one he meant not only Barnard & Taylor but also Pirie-Gordon, whom Rolfe suspected by April of dark conspiracies with Hugh Benson. By the other, Rolfe meant his books published and unpublished plus his Borgia genealogy and four incomplete books stored in England. Among the completed works, of course, were *The Weird of the Wanderer* and *Hubert's Arthur*. He had given them wholly to Pirie-Gordon; but now, while he acknowledged only partial ownership of *The Weird*, he began to claim *Hubert's Arthur* as his own and to castigate Harry Pirie-Gordon for failing to market either. To demonstrate the truth of everything he said, Rolfe offered the fact that *The Academy* had published a short piece of his, 'Deinon to Thely', on 9 January 1909, that he had learned by chance only in March of its appearance, and that his agents had not collected the unpaid fee in April.[29] Ragg, who had moved with his wife and child from the Belle Vue to Palazzo Barbaro as the guest of Mrs. Daniel Curtis, made a suggestion which he thought very likely to enable Rolfe to benefit from his assets; that is, that he let Ragg introduce him to a resident Englishman named Edward Hardcastle, who said he had once been associated with the banking firm of Rothschild. Rolfe hesitated, but the Raggs appealed to him in the name of friendship and he gave in.

When he went to call on Hardcastle at his hotel, the Grand, Rolfe says he found a man with the 'vacancies and dusty dryness of canute old age . . . rheumy-eyed with monocle and tinted nose'. According to Rolfe, Hardcastle spoke only after smacking his lips and then he talked only about himself. Discouraged, Rolfe reported to the Raggs, but when they insisted he prepared a full account of his affairs in which he acknowledged indebtedness of over £200, no cash, and a bill for £80 due on 12 April. On a second visit to Hardcastle, over tea served in his hotel bedroom, they at last got to Rolfe's affairs, and Hardcastle convinced Rolfe that his problems were minimal. He came away with the assurance from Hardcastle that Rolfe's affairs were his affairs and the draft of a letter for the London bookseller Bernard

Quaritch, who was sure to have in his pocket a financial partner for Rolfe.[30]

Any and everything seemed possible. Rolfe was so grateful to the Raggs that he speculated on a Steinway Grand awaiting them when they reached England as a suitable gift. He 'gave his news' to Barbieri and on the strength of it, he and Rolfe concluded an agreement whereby Rolfe signed a bill for £140 on which Barbieri's bank was willing to advance money at once. In return Rolfe could stay at the Belle Vue until the end of the year, another eight months, when payment would be due. It was so reasonable that Rolfe cheerfully signed the bill, received from Barbieri a written statement of terms, and 'settled calmly and peacefully down to plan his new campaign'. The next day, he must 'scratch together' a financial summary to submit when Quaritch produced the desired partner.

That was on 13 April. Shortly before midnight Rolfe was awakened 'from his first sleep' and told he had a visitor. He went below to find Hardcastle and Barbieri. Hardcastle had come, he said, to save Rolfe from trouble with his landlord. Rolfe thanked him and indicated the settlement with Barbieri concluded only that day. Hardcastle inquired as to the terms and Barbieri gave the visitor the two documents, the bill and the agreement, which he proceeded to read aloud in bad French and a 'growing odour of rum'. After a considerable disquisition, also in bad French and an aura of alcohol, Hardcastle tore the bill and the agreement into shreds and tossed them in the air. When Rolfe went back to bed, Hardcastle was still lecturing Barbieri on financial practices, smacking his lips, and exuding the smell of rum. The next morning at breakfast Barbieri confronted Rolfe with an ultimatum: he must pay his bill before noon or leave the Belle Vue before sunset. Rolfe had no choice. After lunch, taking with him a kit-bag which held some clothing and such things as razors and toothbrush, his Waterman pen, a portfolio of papers, and a burberry, Rolfe went to the Bucintoro Club.[31]

[iii]

April 1909—or what was left of it—was indeed a cruel month for Rolfe. The season at Venice was getting under way as usual. On the very day he was forced to leave his hotel, the German Emperor, whom Rolfe admired so extravagantly, came to Venice. In the midst of festivity and the first green of spring, Rolfe was spending his waking hours at the Bucintoro Club because he had no other place to go. When darkness fell, he sat wrapped in a cloak and pretending to meditate until midnight in his boat moored by the English Garden.

221

Then he lay down on the floor of the boat and slept fitfully, wakened sometimes by his fear of thieves and the water-police and sometimes by the slap of water as a fisherman's craft passed near him. If it rained, he walked the night through wrapped in the cloak. Keeping clean was a problem; he lacked tobacco, and he was hungry. He was resolved, however, not to make a spectacle of himself before either the Italians or the 'resident aliens'; he was unwilling to give them the satisfaction of knowing he suffered. Simultaneously, he wanted others to feel responsible for his misfortunes. Only a few days after he stopped sleeping in the boat, the *pupparin*, he warned Pirie-Gordon that he need expect no help in evading the consequences of his false friendship, that Rolfe was 'simply engaged in dying as slowly and as publicly and as annoyingly . . . as possible'.[1]

Rolfe was only a little better off when he moved into the Raggs' dismantled and unheated flat on the fifth floor of the Palazzo Contarini Corfu. On one of his aimless perambulations, he had encountered Ragg, who invited Rolfe to serve him and Mrs. Ragg by staying in their flat while their household goods were got ready for shipment to England, although in fact no such service was needed and Mrs. Ragg could see no reason for Rolfe's failure to go to Venice's 'Night Refuge', the Senzatetti. After inspecting the flat, Rolfe agreed to stay until the arrival of the Wilson Line's boat which was to load the Raggs' effects. Mrs. Ragg spoke of the flat as having polished floors, marble fireplaces, and a tiny frescoed oratory. She listed the furnishings still available in it when Rolfe moved in as a mattress and pillows, two old blankets, a stool, and a kitchen table. She said the flat had electricity so that Rolfe could cook, and her husband supplied the food. Although both she and Rolfe saw what they wanted to see, his description is more graphic. He revelled in the views from the flat, 'Canalazzo to beyond the Salute on the one hand, and (on the other) over the marvellous tiled roofs and chalice-like chimneys and verdant terraces and gardens and solemn byzantine bell-towers . . ., across the blue lagoon to the snow-clad battlements of the Alps seventy miles away.'[2] Inside he found a lavatory in the chapel, shavings, planks and crates littering the floor, broken crockery, a naked iron bedstead, a broken chair and table, a gas-ring for cooking, and a cupboard with assorted articles. These included 'five cigars, eight cigarettes, two half-penny rolls, an orange, an apple, a half-litre of stale red wine, a handful of sodden chocolate fondants, the end of a packet of tea, and a cardboard box of dried milk to be liquefied in boiling water'.[3] Most repugnant of all was the 'steadily undisturbed accumulation of filth' and at night the discomfort of the wire bed-springs and the 'scatter of sportive rats'. Because he had no electricity, no lamps, no candles, his nights began at sundown. He was always hungry. Thus Rolfe lived from about 22 April or 23 until 8 May.

From 14 April, when Barbieri evicted him, until the Raggs closed their flat, Rolfe grew more and more certain that everything and everybody had turned against him. For the sake of the sandwiches usually served with the whisky, Rolfe dressed himself in a lavender coloured flannel suit and a white guernsey and went, one Monday night, to Horatio Brown's. The company was distinguished; Brown's mother, a 'wonderful, tottering dame of ninety in black satin and lace and diamonds',[4] made an unusual appearance, and Prince Hohenlohe, Lord Rosebery, and his son Neil Primrose were present. There were jokes from one man-of-the-world to another about Rolfe's sleeping in the *pupparin* and much talk of gondoliers. But there were no sandwiches, and Rolfe came away as hungry as he had gone. On 13 May, Rolfe sent John Gambril Nicholson an account of the evening written 'on a scrap of dirty paper with no envelope'. He told how he had 'chatted for two hours . . . though he was starving', since there was 'no food going at that "at home".' If Rolfe hoped for help in response to his letter, in which he also complained of his 'life as a vagrant', he was disappointed. Nicholson felt nothing but scorn, as his remarks to Kains Jackson make plain: 'Now I could excuse Corvo for being such a liar (we all do a bit ourselves) but not for being such an ass. A pederast who couldn't touch Rosebery for a quid or two when starving is no use on this earth; he can't adapt himself to environment; and I can't lend a hand to Unfit Survivals.'[5] Before Rolfe sent off his laments to Nicholson, a letter came from Quaritch to say that he could not provide a financial partner. Rolfe posted the letter with a covering one to Hardcastle, asking for further directions. Hardcastle made no reply. Rolfe went often to the English hospital, partly to serve, partly to keep up appearances, and partly to supplement his meagre diet with the hospital's bread and butter at tea-time. When Miss Chaffey suddenly posted a notice which placed a 5d. charge on tea, Rolfe gave up a precious 6d., despite her protests and, thinking the notice was directed at him, went to the hospital no more. In mid-May when a visitor to Venice invited him to a tea-picnic at the hospital, Rolfe refused on the grounds that he was not wanted there unless he had something to give 'in the shape of service' and that the people at the hospital could only find it unpleasant to be civil to him.[6]

The 6d. which Rolfe left at the English Hospital was a part of a guinea sent him by Pirie-Gordon. With it was a letter importuning Rolfe to return to England, where he could live with Benson and write the book on St. Thomas.[7] To Rolfe that plea was the ultimate treachery. Robert Hugh Benson had preached the Lenten Sermons at San Silvestro, the English church in Rome, commencing on 28 February and ending on 28 March. On his return journey, Benson visited Venice as the guest of Arthur Spender, who lived at the Palazzo Condulmer on the Rio de Tolentino. Rolfe, with what he called his 'soft warm hungry heart', seriously believed that Benson was in Venice 'to look him up and make an honourable amend'. During

Benson's stay, Rolfe made himself available on the public thorough-fares and at the Bucintoro Club, hoping for a meeting; but none came. Benson's heart was tough. He listened to what Spender, who had met Rolfe at Horatio Brown's, had to say and during a gondola ride some time after 4 April he had a long talk with Ragg about Rolfe, but Benson made no move to see Rolfe. What the priest wanted was an apology—'anything in the nature of an apology', he told Pirie-Gordon.[8] He must have known Rolfe could not apologise. Instead, perhaps in June, Rolfe composed a letter to Benson which said in part:

> I was not surprised when you came to spy but did not dare to face me in Venice: nor even when you tried to defend yourself to a chance parson by pretending that you had been defending me at the Scots College of Rome. It is what I should have looked for in such a Self-Loving Coward as you have shewn yourself to be.[9]

More and more was Rolfe persuaded that every hand was against him, that he was every man's victim.

The events which followed the Raggs' closing their flat only served to add to Rolfe's conviction. When Mrs. Ragg told him that the boat which was to take the family's possessions ahead of them to England was in port, Rolfe asked to do something in return for the shelter given him and proceeded to use his huge fountain pen filled with red ink to write the labels for trunks and boxes. Such benevolence did not last long. As the hour for his departure came closer, Rolfe's rage and frustration overflowed into a letter to Harry Pirie-Gordon dated only Saturday, but which was 8 March 1909. Some of the letter reads:

> Last night was my last night in this empty house . . . I have not slept in a bed or changed my clothes for 15 nights, God knows where I shall sleep tonight. The weather is cold and wet. In this fort-night, I have had 5 lunches, 2 dinners, 3 breakfasts, and 8 afternoon-teas only. I have been 39 hours with nothing whatever to eat or drink.[10]

The rain was heavy when Rolfe turned over the keys of the flat, and he had nowhere to go. He had a meal at the nearby Trattoria agli Alboretti, to which Ragg had introduced him, and for the rest of the night he walked to and fro on the Fondamenta delle Zattere. Com-mencing with that night, Rolfe had two days and nights in the open without tobacco or more food or drink.[11]

On Monday, 10 May, Rolfe once more encountered Ragg, who offered to raise money to enable him to go back to England respec-tably and with his clothes washed. Rolfe refused Ragg's proposal and refused all help except on his own terms, a 'commercial' arrangement between himself and a financier who would take over his 'paltry debts' and undeniable assets and 'set him free' to continue his work.[21]

This discussion led to some talk on Ragg's part about the ethics of Rolfe's behaviour and on Rolfe's part about Hardcastle and Ragg's responsibility for the old man's inadequacies. Rolfe maintained that since Ragg had got him into his present difficulties through Hardcastle, it was Ragg's obligation to get him out. Not to do so was to desert him and, in a larger consideration, it was little short of criminal, according to Rolfe, to let a man of his 'calibre' be wasted.[13] Driven past endurance, Ragg screamed, 'Of course you know, I'm not really bound to help you, seeing that you're not a co-religionist!' Ragg added that Rolfe should seek help from his friends if he had any.[14]

At first Rolfe failed to understand the extent of Ragg's self-disclosure. At first Ragg's remark was far less important in fact than it would be in fiction. Later, in his presentation of Ragg as Warden in *Desire and Pursuit*, Rolfe highlighted Ragg's 'obsolescent sectarian bigotry'. It was a masterly comment on Warden's pretence at philanthropy and subsequent desertion of the man whom Ragg had taken up 'so very precipitately & insisted on befriending so very resolutely'.[15] But when Ragg was goaded to speak, Rolfe gave more importance to Ragg's remark that Rolfe should seek help from friends if he had any. On 11 May 1909 in a letter to Ragg which Rolfe wrote because he felt himself 'abused beyond the endurance of a block' and 'wounded deeply in mind as well as body', he acknowledged that Ragg's talk about not being a 'co-religionist' and about raising money to get him back to England stuck in his 'gorge'. Rolfe went on to say that it was the next sentence which had pained him more. 'I am quite well aware', Rolfe wrote, 'that I have no friends. Had I any friends, I should never have been allowed to endure what I have to endure.' Nevertheless, nothing—'no pressure, sentiment, or suffering'—Rolfe declared would cause him to 'smirch' himself with the 'deridable futility now masquerading as Charity'.[16]

Rolfe had hardly posted his letter when he had a note from Ragg urging him to be sensible and to go back to England, and again Ragg offered to provide money from his own pocket or that of Hardcastle to get Rolfe back first class with his clothes washed. Ragg's note was conciliatory, even touching on his own outburst. He asked Rolfe to pocket his pride and resentment, to do as he 'would be done by'.[17]

Rolfe refused to be placated. With Ragg's note before him, Rolfe wrote again, typically not once but twice. He denounced the criticism of the ethics of his conduct; he denied truthfully that he had encouraged the attention of the British in Venice; and he refused to be 'deflected' from his perfectly plain and simple and 'entirely reasonable position'. Rolfe went on:

I do hope . . . that any quasi-friendly feeling which you may have cherished for me will prevent you (any of you) from adding to the poignant outrages against my divinely-given 'senses'—outrages

225

complacently regarded as suitable to me every moment now—by worrying me further to consult the convenience of others rather than my own. *Here I am; but here I stay.*

The letter made much of Benson's treachery and Hardcastle's neglect. Rolfe asserted his lack of cash and of prospects and his expectation of facing his 'fate' alone even as he forgave those who had deserted him. He then said, 'I am thus deliberately defiant because I am desperate in the fullest intention of the term.'[18] By the next day, Rolfe had convinced himself of his rectitude. He had brooded enough on his misery to conclude that Ragg was responsible for it and that he had a 'severe account to settle' with Ragg. He must be made to know who was at fault. Ragg, his friends, and the Hospital had asked for and been given a 'fair chance of ministering to a good friend who is in trouble', but they had 'mucked it most magnificently and not by any means inconspicuously'. Rolfe said that he could understand Ragg's exasperation, but he had no intention of bearing more than his 'fair share of such an imbroglio'.[19] Thereafter Ragg rated high among Rolfe's enemies. These were all the people whose evaluation of Rolfe was not as high as his own and who had shown themselves unwilling to sacrifice their property and their influence for him. Help for Rolfe was in the interest of art, and those who refused it were part of a giant conspiracy. Later in the month, that is about 23 May 1909, Rolfe wrote the first of a number of jeering letters to Ragg. He set the tone of most of the letters in the first one by parodying Ragg's habit of using 'dear person' as a form of address; Rolfe began his letter 'Extremely Silly Person'.[20]

While Rolfe weltered in his despair and wrote the inimical letter to Ragg, Ragg had already made an attempt to help Rolfe by writing to Hugh Benson and inquiring about two matters. The first was Rolfe's claim to valuable assets under the mismanagement of his solicitors. The second had to do with his charge that Pirie-Gordon and Benson had entered into a conspiracy to withhold financial aid and Rolfe's papers and thus his means of livelihood so that he would be forced to return to England and write the book about Thomas à Beckett, not with Benson but for him. Benson's reply was neither patient nor realistic. Of course he denied the charge of conspiracy, but he had little to suggest beyond showing the solicitors Barnard & Taylor that people were interested in Rolfe and would be willing to administer any funds the solicitors might provide.[21] Ragg persevered. In a letter dated 22 May 1909, he asked Barnard & Taylor about Rolfe's prospects from future publications, for any sum of money which would justify Barbieri's readmitting Rolfe to the Belle Vue and about the status of his life insurance policy.[22] Nothing substantial came from this letter, either. That Rolfe even knew that they had been written is most unlikely.

In any case, Rolfe had other enemies with which to deal. There were Hugh Benson and of course Harry Pirie-Gordon. In a letter to Harry dated 18 May, Rolfe declared their enmity because no friend could behave as the three Pirie-Gordons had. The letter was filled with instructions as to what to do with the manuscripts of *Hubert's Arthur* and *The Weird of the Wanderer* and what not to do with the proofs for *Don Renato*, how to behave in the matter of 'Deinon to Thely', published in *The Academy*, and how to recover his letters from Hugh Benson. As to Pirie-Gordon's suggestion that he get a job, Rolfe refused outright. 'How can I get a job in tatters and slippers and no pocket-handkerchieves,' he asked and said that Pirie-Gordon should have got a job for him, such as reporting the Venice International Art Exhibition on approval.[23] On 28 May 1909, in a letter to 'My Dear Enemy,' Rolfe threatened to 'come straight back to Crickhowell Workhouse'—always visible across the Usk River from the front windows of the Pirie-Gordons' residence—and to die there or give Pirie-Gordon Senior the 'pleasure' of committing him to jail. Rolfe then declared that he had no roof over his head and no bed in which to sleep and that he had not eaten for twenty-four hours and had no possibility of eating for approximately another thirty-six.[24]

In fact Rolfe was living in reasonable comfort with adequate food. When he wrote that letter to Pirie-Gordon, Rolfe had been a resident of the Trattoria agli Alboretti, a modest establishment situated near the Academy, for almost three weeks. The Alboretti was the property of Angelo Scatturin, who operated a restaurant on the ground floor and maintained living quarters for his family and for three guests on the first floor. Two days and nights after leaving the Raggs' flat in the Palazzo Contarini Corfu, Rolfe had enough money from somewhere to go to the Alboretti for a meal of beefsteak with bread, cheese, and wine.[25] Because Ragg had paid Scatturin in advance for a meal for Rolfe, the innkeeper refused payment. Rolfe, however, insisted on paying his own bill and then engaged one of the guest rooms with pension at L5 a day. Rolfe said that he moved into the Alboretti on the strength of £2 2s. received from *The Academy* for his story 'Deinon to Thely'. He considered it a payment on account, calculating that at the rate of £5 5s. per thousand words, the rate he had stated when he submitted the manuscript, *The Academy* still owed him £16 5s. 6d. Nevertheless the £2 2s. converted to L52·80 and would 'see him through a clear week' at least.[26] That *The Academy* was the source of Rolfe's funds is most unlikely. On 14 May, four days after Rolfe had moved into the Alboretti, Pirie-Gordon wrote to say that he had asked *The Academy* for a cheque in order to forward it; and four days after that, in a letter to Pirie-Gordon, Rolfe said he still had not had the money.[27] Wherever he got his funds or whether he had funds or merely traded on Ragg's credit, Rolfe had certainly become a

227

resident of the Trattoria agli Alboretti some time on 10 May. Many of his possessions including papers were held at the Hotel Belle Vue, but what papers and clothes he had at the Bucintoro Club Rolfe moved to the Alboretti and settled in on that date.

As long as he stayed at the Alboretti and for some time after he left, Rolfe occupied himself with composing an answer to Edward Carpenter's *Towards Democracy*, a book of the 1880s which Rolfe had read in the past few years. In 1908, in a discussion of Walt Whitman's poetry, he had recommended *Towards Democracy*, which derives from Whitman, to Dawkins and spoke of writing a reply. 'Under certain circumstances, e.g. if I had a really fine steam-yacht and could go on long, long dreamy voyages,' he told Dawkins, 'I should most certainly write a book in the same manner, but far *finer* and call it *Toward Aristocracy*.'[28] Still lacking the steam-yacht but moved by Carpenter's 'perfectly sumptuous verses' and its 'damnissable' doctrine which set him 'rearing in revolt', Rolfe began a 'big book of verses as a counterblast' to *Towards Democracy*.[29]

The concept of aristocracy as excellence was an intrinsic part of Rolfe's fixed ideas. He provided the best summary of it, negatively stated, in a letter to Harry Pirie-Gordon written on 19 June 1907. Rolfe said:

It's a matter of principle with ME not to yield a single inch to dirty Demos, not to have any sort of truck with the beast excepting when I have him on a chain. And I affirm that concession is wicked and shameful, and all attempts to improve him by equality fatuous and futile. Drive your beast, lash him well, and make him go your way if you can: but don't attempt to run in harness with him, unless you want him to swallow you down his miry throat.[30]

Rolfe blundered when he did not understand the threat to liberty and human dignity implicit in authoritarian rule. His poverty had consigned him too often to a nameless place among the masses of people who allow the democratic process to function. From his experience, democracy offered neither service nor protection. He knew well the mediocrity it fosters, and he found such mediocrity totally antipathetic to his sense of self. His faith was in the distinction of individuality and excellence and its capacity, well used, to lead if not to the good and the beautiful at least away from the vicious. That attitude informed his *Bull Against the Enemy of the Anglican Race*, the attack on Lord Northcliffe's concept of the popular press. Indeed Rolfe's thanks to heaven that he was nothing if not reactionary[31] is apparent throughout his work. Nicholas Crabbe's surrender to the metaphysics of kingship in his description of the new-made King Edward and his share in the pageantry of the procession as it went by the Marble Arch towards the 'divine' Victoria's 'exsequies' reflected Rolfe's convictions.[32] His acknowledgement of the mystique of king-

228

ship is in *Hadrian the Seventh* and 'Deinon to Thely', the piece published that year, 1909. 'Concerning England and Germany', an unpublished plea for greater harmony between the two countries at a time when their relations were worsening, is an apology for autocracy. And now, in May 1909, according to Rolfe, he was engaged in expounding a 'new whole duty of man, from the gardener's boy and the scullery-maid, . . . up to the King and the Pope in their progress *Towards Aristocracy* on the road which leads to the Best'.[33]

[iv]

Rolfe surely gave little time to the composition of the 'magnificent hexameters, bright iambics, melodious hendecasyllables' of 'Toward Aristocracy' during his stay at the Alboretti. Throughout that time and immediately afterwards, he wrote innumerable letters meant to establish himself financially so that he could anticipate at least a year of comfort and quiet work in Venice. As each prospect disappointed him, he cast about frantically for another, meanwhile rebuking those who failed him, pitying some for imperfect vision, threatening others, or taking what he hoped was vengeance. As he had told Ragg, Rolfe was desperate in the fullest intention of the term.

By 18 May 1909, he had written twice to *The Academy* in an attempt to collect payment for 'Deinon to Thely', and on or about that date he wrote again, directing his letter to Lord Alfred Douglas, *The Academy's* editor. Rolfe informed Douglas that he was not to use the title Baron Corvo since the Baron 'had died of acute Barabbitis' after the publication of his Borgia book and that no one in England (meaning Pirie-Gordon) was authorised to collect his 'dues'. Rolfe wanted payment in English notes sent to Venice by return post. By 29 May 1909, he had acknowledged receipt of £2 2s. and on that date he thanked Douglas for copies of *The Academy*, just arrived, and once more asked for his entire fee which he set at £5 5s. per thousand for about 3,500 words. The only answer came not from Douglas but from Douglas's managing editor, T. H. Crosland. His 'hectic letter' said that he did not know Benson, that he had not asked for contributions from Rolfe through Benson, that the full fee was £2 2s. Again Rolfe wrote to Douglas, insisting that Benson, who knew Rolfe's prices, had submitted several of Rolfe's manuscripts at Douglas's request and asking for the return of all manuscripts, including that of 'The Bull of Hadrian VII Against the Enemy of the Anglican Race', sent to *The Academy* from Venice.[1]

Rolfe had better have saved his energy and his postage. Benson was as relentless as polished stone; he had already denied all account-ability in Rolfe's difficulties with *The Academy*. Crosland was clever and gifted but unreliable. Probably the only person in all England more quarrelsome than Rolfe was Lord Alfred Douglas. Twenty-five years later he spoke of 'Deinon to Thely' as 'most brilliant' and took full credit for its publication. To Rolfe, he made no answer. Instead Crosland wrote to repeat that he knew nothing of Benson and in any case the periodical had at no time solicited material from anyone and certainly it had not asked Benson to secure contributions from Rolfe. Crosland went on to say that he had chosen 'Deinon to Thely' for publication, that Douglas had seen neither Rolfe's letters nor his manuscripts, and the whereabouts of these was unknown.[2] Rolfe never saw them again.

In a somewhat bemused letter to Crosland, Rolfe seemed to accept the loss of both money and manuscripts philosophically. In fact, the collapse of his hopes for additional income from *The Academy* put him into a rage. He was convinced that the entire situation was Benson's doing, another example of 'customary unscrupulous Roman Catholic practices'. Rolfe believed that 'alluring' him to trust his 'serial mss' to *The Academy* and the resultant losses were planned in order to force him not only to help Benson write the book on St. Thomas but, worse, to make him write the greater part of it at the same fee. Early in June, Rolfe sent a letter to Benson, refusing 'definitely and finally' to do the book with him. The letter was hardly necessary. Despite a statement to Ragg that Rolfe was welcome to co-operate with him, Benson knew that he and Rolfe could not possibly work together. But Rolfe had to have his say. He wrote in part:

> I will not be the 'Ghost' of an author who uses his spiritual power to force me to do temporal work for him on the same terms which I was to have had as his equal & collaborator ... As you seem to have forgotten that 'when' my 'back is against the wall' I become 'magni-ficent' you may blame your monster as much as you please, but yourself chiefly as his creator.[3]

As soon as he had the final letter from Crosland and realised that no more than £2 2s. was forthcoming and that his manuscripts were lost, Rolfe composed a tirade against Hugh Benson to be sent as an 'open letter' to Eustace Virgo, Stuart Reid of Duckworth & Co., and *The Athenaeum*, among others. Rolfe started with his final refusal to write the book 'about Thomas of Canterbury'. He explained the circum-stances of collaboration, how Benson had forced him to withdraw from their original agreement and then described the means by which Benson had tried to 'bully' him into writing the book while depriving him of the 'very privilege which was the essence of the collaboration, *viz*., the public association' of their names as co-authors. Rolfe con-cluded by saying that he had treated Benson with forbearance in the hope that he would amend but that now, with patience exhausted, he had 'formally broken off' with Benson. 'I can do better for myself', Rolfe said, 'than in the toils of a perjured tyrant.'[4]

Rolfe's frustration and anger at Benson spilled over onto Pirie-Gordon as Benson's confederate. 'Your Benson,' Rolfe called him and said of him, 'He has ruined my soul and I am quite content to pit my body against him.' In the letter to Benson written in early June, Rolfe had warned him of 'fairly complete arrangements for explosions to occur' in England even when Rolfe was not there 'to light & tend the fuses'. He repeated the warning to Pirie-Gordon, that is that 'various calculated unpleasantnesses' might be expected at Crickhowell throughout the year.[5] Rolfe's threats were absurd. Plain nonsense was the more specific one of publishing either in Italy or in France a polyglot translation of an obscene book signed R.H.B. with the Pirie-Gordon arms on the cover. It was to be 'decently printed and bound in vellum with the ordinal badge and imprimatur' of the Order of Sanctissima Sophia, 'all in violet'. Benson was alarmed enough to write about it to Pirie-Gordon, but Rolfe's threats of vengeance amounted to no more than candles in the wind.

When Rolfe put one of his threats into effect he did at least as much harm to himself as to his intended victim. Almost from the time he sent *Hubert's Arthur* in manuscript as a gift to Pirie-Gordon, the authorship and ownership of that book and of *The Weird of the Wanderer* were vexatious. After Longmans rejected *Hubert's Arthur*, Pirie-Gordon asked Henry Marriage Wallis, who wrote popular novels under the name Ashton Hilliers, to read the manuscript and suggest changes to make it more saleable. Rolfe refused to consent to the alteration of a single word until several publishers including Smith Elder, Macmillan, Murray, and Duckworth had declined it. He upbraided Pirie-Gordon for his 'intermittent playing with the *magnum opus* of a starving man' and declared that it was 'awful' to see him treating 'such a pearl like an animal with a penchant for acorn'.[7] Then Rolfe demanded a formal agreement defining the literary rights in both books. When he had such a document from Pirie-Gordon whereby all rights in both books belonged to him and he could alter the name and contents of either book and publish either one anonymously or as by 'C.H.C. Pirie-Gordon and Another' in return for half of net proceeds from publication or sale, Rolfe refused to sign. He accused Pirie-Gordon of acting in anger and of making a 'hideous mess' of Rolfe's affairs and then 'chucking them sulkily back' at him. Rolfe wanted *The Weird* sent to E. Nesbit, Mrs. Hubert Bland, who he believed would arrange publication more quickly and more advantageously than Pirie-Gordon. He delayed in sending the book and when he at last wrote to Mrs. Bland asked not to send *The Weird of the Wanderer* but to store Rolfe's possessions with her instead of at Gwernvale. Rolfe went into another rage. He attacked not only Harry and Benson, but Mr.

231

and Mrs. Pirie-Gordon as well. In a letter dated 4 June 1909 he wrote to Pirie-Gordon with magnificent illogicality:

You have prevented me from seeing my Mother all this time; and now you are going to make me her murderer: for the scandal into which you force me will certainly kill her as well as me. This is what you and your people and Benson will have to bear the brunt of. . . . What I shall never understand is that a perjured blackguard and robber of the poor, like your Benson, who solemnly swore to me that I never under any circumstances should have to go to the workhouse again—and a discontented Christian like her [Mrs. Edward Pirie-Gordon] who affirmed again and again 'You must not leave Gwernvale except for betterment'—can, simply to assuage the self-love which my bitter words have pierced to the core, basely desert a fellow-creature for months together, interfere with his property without his consent and despite his agonized intreaties, ostracize him, destroy his credit, and reduce him to the state in which you see me—and then feel deeply pained because he is what you have made him. . . . Those two people, Benson and your Mother, feel deeply: and ought to have known better. At least, though natural resentment caused them to wish to persevere in driving me through agony to fury, their so-called Christianity should have suggested the opposite.[8]

Helpless in his fury, Rolfe went on to rage against Edward Pirie-Gordon and Harry, whom he charged with 'spewings' and 'vomitings' in his letters and with 'dirty pusillanimous poltroonery'. He informed Pirie-Gordon that unless he acted differently before the following Wednesday, a statement would go to the Publishers' Association and Rolfe would start for England on that day. He then composed a concise statement intended for the president of the Association. In it he summarised The Weird and Hubert's Arthur, called himself author of nine-tenths of both, and forbade the publication of either book while he was away from England.[9]

Persuaded that Pirie-Gordon was engaged in some kind of trickery with Don Renato for the benefit of Barnard & Taylor, Rolfe also wrote early in June to Francis Griffiths, who had engaged to publish that book and Songs of Meleager. In his letter, Rolfe denied Pirie-Gordon's authority to act for him and asked for news of the two books. When he had no response by 18 June, Rolfe withheld his consent for publication of either title until he had 'passed proof dies binding etc.'.[10] His career as a published writer was halted. Although it was a temporary cessation, it could not benefit him. But he was pleased because he was satisfied that he had struck at Pirie-Gordon and his solicitors, Barnard & Taylor.

Before mid-June Rolfe had learned that his hope for rescue from his financial troubles through Barnard & Taylor was as illusory as his prospect with *The Academy* had proved to be. When he wrote to Barnard & Taylor on 27 May to dissociate himself from Pirie-Gordon, he suggested with heavy sarcasm that they might find time to communicate with him, Fr. Rolfe, their client. He had not had word from them in six months. The next day he wrote again and this time he charged them with failure to exploit his Borgia genealogy or to help him to do so, with neglect in quickening his 'publishers' energies' or in hiring a literary agent to do it for them, and with indifference to his problems as demonstrated by the fact that they had not increased his life insurance before the lapse of six months made necessary his return to England for a new medical examination. Under the circumstances, he wanted to revise the 'nature of their connection' or transfer his obligations to more interested administrators and he asked Barnard & Taylor to name the amount needed to free him from obligations to them. When the solicitors finally broke their long silence on 7 June 1909, they freely admitted having done little to encourage sales of Rolfe's published books, or publication of those awaiting it. Rolfe then demanded their justification for allying themselves with Benson and Pirie-Gordon and dropping all communication with him. Rolfe declared that until he had it he was withholding consent for all publications, not to defraud his solicitors but to protect himself.

The real purpose of Rolfe's letter, however, was to offer Barnard & Taylor two options. One was to continue to act for him, bringing much more vigour to their job. In that case, Rolfe said that they must face the necessity of increasing their investment in him by £1,000 to a total of £1,500. He called it a 'very moderate sum in comparison with sums invested by other investors in other authors.' He named Arnold Hannay and Henry Harland but thought better of it and crossed out their names. Then Rolfe went on to explain how the £1,000 was to be sent: £300 paid to him by 1 July and two payments of £100 each on 1 October and 1 January. They were to retain the additional £500 for emergencies. The second option asked only that they confirm Pirie-Gordon's report that they intended to cut their losses on him. In that case they must send him the Borgia genealogy so that with it he might obtain credit to prolong his life while he looked for a new financial partner. Rolfe presented his situation as of the 'most precarious description.' He wrote:

I have no friends at all now. I owe about £150 here. My goods papers & clothes are sequestered. I *live* anyhow & have no means whatever wherewith to work or even to carry on correspondence. Consequently I have completed arrangements for relinquishing all hope of pursuing my career and for applying to the F.O. for means of repatriation so that I may go & end my days in Crickhowell Workhouse.[11]

If Rolfe thought he would melt the heart of Barnard & Taylor, he was mistaken. When they replied under the date 15 June, they denied all responsibility for him. Their unconcern threw him into a fury of letter writing and expostulation. On 18, 19 and 21 June, Rolfe pelted Barnard & Taylor with scathing epithets, the mildest of which were 'imbecilic' and 'stupid'.[12] In addition, he denounced them to the Law Society and entered into lengthy correspondence about them, but he had no alternative to accepting Barnard & Taylor's repudiation of him.[13]

Rolfe had already cast about for someone—anyone—to provide a way out of his difficulties by taking over from Barnard & Taylor what he called his assets. He had written long letters with a careful outline of his achievements and possibilities to anyone he thought might serve him. One letter went to a Captain D. in Venice. He even sent a prospectus to Dawkins, though he could hardly have expected much from that quarter.[14] Rolfe's most likely benefactor all along had seemed to be Barbieri, keeper of the Hotel Belle Vue. Barbieri had signed a bill for him once, and only Hardcastle's drunken antics had upset the arrangement. Five days after moving into the Alboretti, Rolfe began a campaign meant to recover what he had lost—and a little more—on that heartbreaking occasion. To Barbieri, he gave the assurance that he was done with such stupid people as Ragg and Hardcastle and their friends, that henceforth he would manage his own affairs, given 'means and opportunity'. These, he hoped Barbieri would provide. He asked Barbieri to receive him again at the Belle Vue and to renew the note at the bank for L2,000 so that Rolfe could have £525 in order to negotiate for the sale of his four unpublished works. He named them as *Nicholas Crabbe*, 'Review of Unwritten Books', *The Weird of the Wanderer*, and *Hubert's Arthur*. To persuade Barbieri of his sincerity, Rolfe said that he could return to England with his fare paid and his clothes washed, but he preferred to stay in Venice in order to pay his debts. Nevertheless, Barbieri was sceptical. He declared that he wanted deeds, not words, and he reminded Rolfe of several broken promises.

Rolfe insisted that he had made his promises in good faith because he had believed in Barnard & Taylor, Pirie-Gordon, Ragg, and Hardcastle. 'I am the victim of these people,' Rolfe said, '& it is due to them, not to me, that my promises are broken.' He went on, 'I am NOT a dishonourable person, and it utterly infuriates me to be made to appear like one by these false friends in whom I have been fool enough to trust.'[15] He offered Barbieri a lien on his manuscripts as soon as they came from England and supervision of all efforts made to market them. After a talk with the hotel keeper, Rolfe sent him a rough draft of the prospectus prepared for Dawkins and others. Rolfe was sure that the logic of his argument, the same argument made to Barnard & Taylor, must appeal to Barbieri. In essence it said that if Barbieri wanted what was owed him, he must lend Rolfe more, he must relieve Rolfe of the 'empty horror' of his days and the 'sore discomfort' of his nights and make it possible for him to work. Within the week, Rolfe was impatient for Barbieri's decision. 'The suspense is killing,' he said, 'and prevents me from finishing another book'.[16]

While he waited to hear from Barbieri, Rolfe tried another tack. No later than 22 May, he asked for help from Horatio Brown at the urging of John Gambril Nicholson, who said Rolfe ought to 'pocket his pride' and tell Brown about the 'awful trouble' in which he found himself. In a day or two, Rolfe replied to Brown's question as to how he could be of use. He laid his current position—'homeless, starving, penniless, sponging, & liable to be finally ruined'—at the door of Colonel Owen Thomas and the Rhodes Trust. Describing in singularly mild terms the failure of Barnard & Taylor to manage his affairs properly, Rolfe asked to be considered not as an object of charity but as a 'business proposition'. This obsessive hawking himself about as a good business proposition seems never to have impressed Rolfe as absurd. Horatio Brown attributed Rolfe's unhappy situation to 'too high an estimate of himself', but that statement oversimplifies his conviction of wisdom and sense of competency. Brown did not recognise these since he sent a bank note to Rolfe by return mail. Rolfe sent it back with this note, 'Thank you very much: but alms nauseate this stomach more than emptiness. Note returned.'[17] Charity was all Brown had to offer Rolfe. More than once he had shown an eagerness to talk with Brown, but only if Brown summoned him. Brown evaded a meeting.

All correspondence might have ended when Rolfe refused the bank note, but he kept it open. At the end of May, when he at last had a copy of *The Academy* containing his story 'Deinon to Thely', Rolfe sent it to Horatio Brown as a 'specimen of £18 7s. 6d.' On the strength of this publication, Rolfe asked Brown to take one of two steps, guarantee his landlord £200 sterling payable in a year or advance him a loan of £100 at once in return for a lien on 'the serial rights & copyrights' of his 'nineteen new Venetian Toto Stories'.[18] Rolfe had started these tales at the end of August 1908 when the glory of Venice was new and breathtaking. A miscellaneous notebook-diary contains a series of entries for that period when he could not resist setting down descriptions of what he saw. Under the date 26 August 1908 he wrote, 'Heaven was blazing quickly with saffron & purple & rose[.] The Lagoon was one wide monstrous gem a gleaming amethyst streaked with topaz & with gold arabesques[.] And the islands floated on it in umbrous shadows[.]' Three days later he tried again: 'Silhouetted against the glory miles away twinkled the little lights of the Lido. Behind in every shade & tone of grey through blue to heliotrope ascended the majestic moon in a rain of silver sheen.' In subsequent and undated entries on five leaves are notes for Toto stories. 'Why

235

Sammarco is never finished' is one; another is 'Story of the Valle dei Sette Morti'.[19] The latter had been told Rolfe by the gondolier with the 'slow, sweet, splendid smile', Ermengildo Vianello called Gildo or Zildo. He was the model for the Venetian Toto. In a letter written to Pirie-Gordon in December 1908, Rolfe had said that because he was 'in a violent and deliberate passion' he had torn up and drowned the Venetian Toto stories.[20] To Brown, Rolfe promised to put them into final shape and send them out for publication. Brown's refusal of both propositions is attested by a note which Rolfe wrote about 31 May: 'I am sorry. It was my last hope. *E nihilo nihil fit*, & I shall not attempt it.'[21]

Brown might very well have been Rolfe's last hope. Barbieri had already decided against Rolfe's proposals. On the same day as he wrote the note to Brown, Rolfe wrote also to Barbieri, protesting against his accusation of idleness and his shortsightedness in refusing every part of Rolfe's scheme, thereby making it impossible for his debt to be paid. He reproached Barbieri for 'sheer pigheadedness' and prejudice derived from Canon Ragg and others.[22]

The truth was, Barbieri was anxious enough about Rolfe to write to Pirie-Gordon and ask whether Rolfe's publishers would guarantee £200 to him, payable when Rolfe's books were published. With that security, Barbieri was prepared to furnish Rolfe with room and board at the Belle Vue so that he could 'recuperate and rest his brain and body' and thus be able to 'set to work with renewed vigour to his literary pursuits.'[23]

Rolfe meanwhile had other avenues to explore. He had asked Barbieri's permission to go to his locked basket, held at the hotel against his debt, and to take from it a workman's blue linen suit. It was the one he had worn so long in Holywell. Now he hoped it might help him to find work. He failed to get access to his basket, but Rolfe nevertheless applied simultaneously to five English residents of Venice who kept gondolas and to one German, Prince Hohenlohe, for a job as second gondolier. He offered himself as well as poultry manager to Frederick Eden, and to all six he offered a week's probation. Five expressions of disinterest promptly came back; one recipient, the Reverend Charles Williamson, ignored the application.[24]

At the same time, Rolfe appealed to the British Consul, Edward de Zucatto. In his attempts to find someone other than Barnard & Taylor to assume responsibility for his affairs, Rolfe had sent de Zucatto, as a matter of record, a prospectus such as had gone to Dawkins.[25] On 31 May, Rolfe asked the Consul to intervene on his behalf with Barbieri, to try to make him understand that help on Rolfe's terms was good business. He wanted the Consul to tell him, too, how to earn his living until someone could be found to underwrite him, and he wanted the Consul to act as his agent in finding a Venetian, any Venetian, who might do so. Rolfe also asked what arrangements could be made for returning him to England. He made clear that he would accept nothing in the way of charity but 'only such honourable "assistance and protection" ' as was required by his passport.[26] Rolfe's determination to stay in Venice at any cost was crumbling. Impotence, isolation of spirit, a sense of injustice done him were undermining his resolution. He had no 'tools of trade', he could get no work, he was hungry, his landlord at the Alboretti, Angelo Scatturin, was increasingly peremptory. Rolfe had only pride and hatred to sustain him. On 11 June 1909, he asked for repatriation.[27]

While he waited for authorisation to come from England, Rolfe kept alive as many of his old quarrels as possible and even started a new one. He complained to the vice-president of the Bucintoro Rowing Club about the insolent and neglectful servant Gigio, who had refused Rolfe the use of a canoe, allowed his club cap and jersey to be stolen from the drying line, ignored orders to put the *pupparin* 'Crab' into good condition, and corrupted Fausto, once a good servant but now imitative of Gigio. In a letter to Pirie-Gordon, Rolfe threatened to starve quietly, prolonging the process by conservation of his energies. He posted his statement 'Concerning Benson'. He flailed Barnard & Taylor and revoked his agreement with the publisher Francis Griffiths. He was outraged when he learned that Barbieri had written about him to Pirie-Gordon. He demanded—and got—from Ragg a retraction of an alleged statement that Rolfe was unwilling to return to England because he was wanted by the police there.[28] By mid-June his relations with Scatturin were openly hostile. For almost two weeks, Rolfe had been reduced to subsisting on two rolls a day, or so he told Doctor Van Someren, because his indebtedness to Scatturin prohibited him from having meals at the Alboretti and he had no funds to buy more than rolls. On 21 June, a Monday, the landlord had given him a week to pay or to expect the police and by Thursday Rolfe had decided to give himself up to the Questura two days hence unless the Consul advised otherwise.[29]

Rolfe was on good terms with almost no one except the Consul, de Zuccato, and Doctor Ernest Van Someren, whom Rolfe had met first with the Raggs at the opera in January. Early in June, he called on Van Someren and described his plight and a few days later wrote to thank the doctor for sympathy and to pour out his complaints about his inability to get a job and his antipathy for Ragg. Shortly afterward, and before 18 June, Rolfe returned 5 francs (the equivalent of 4s, or $1) sent him as a gift by Van Someren. With the money went the explanation, 'I have the best of all guidance. It says NO to anything of this kind.'[30] As a man who had shown himself a true friend, Van Someren was carefully excluded from a list made for the Consul, a list of the English living in Venice against whom Rolfe had grievances. De Zuccato had become the repository of Rolfe's records in case of inquiries and of his confidences and complaints. Rolfe anticipated de

Zuccato's help with the police if relations with Scatturin of the Alboretti came to that.

Yet, Rolfe had no hesitation in withdrawing his application for repatriation and turning down the railway ticket offered him at the end of June. In the first place he could not accept it while his 'bona fides' were questioned in Venice, a reference to Ragg's supposed accusation that Rolfe was wanted by the English police. In any case, a ticket without other 'assistance and protection' was neither what his passport guaranteed nor what he needed to recover his property and his work. He thought it preferable to go without food for two days and nights in Venice, where 'at least he might be still, than to starve for the same period of time in the stress & turmoil of a railway journey', which last ordeal, Rolfe said, was 'calculated to render' him incapable of 'compassing' his purpose in going to England, that is, the adjustment of 'complicated financial difficulties'.[31] Rolfe was so indignant at officialdom's interpretation of the 'assistance & protection' called for in his passport that he composed a letter about it, still unpublished, to the London *Times*.[32]

The fact is, however, that deliverance from his immediate troubles had presented itself to Rolfe. By 25 June, he found himself with both a friend and funds. The funds, amounting to L500, doubtless came from Lord Rosebery. At the end of May, when he was casting about desperately for a means to stay in Venice and preferably re-establish himself at the Belle Vue, Rolfe had first written to Rosebery. The letter was ostensibly to thank him for his inquiries, as reported by Horatio Brown, about sleeping in the *pupparin* 'Crab'. Although he asked for nothing, Rolfe confessed his poverty and attributed it to his ruin at the hands of Colonel Owen Thomas and the Rhodes Trustees, of which Rosebery was one. Less than a month later, Rolfe wrote this effusive letter, undated, to someone whom he addressed only as 'My dear Lord:'

> It is impossible for Me to make You know what relief & joy you have given today. I fear most horribly to bore one who knows me so little: but I really and truly am amusing & a life long fighter against becoming a sponger. I am a giver, rarely a getter, a tremendous worker when I can only get freedom to work & an exquisitely elaborate loafer by sheer grace. Such an one never has friends. He can not keep them. And he never can be at his best alone. Always remember that I am at your service. If I could make you half as happy as you have made me today, I should do well. A Thousand sincere thanks.[33]

If the L500 was from Rosebery, Rolfe was making a fine distinction between alms, which he rejected, and what he thought owing to him. Whatever made the gift acceptable, it enabled Rolfe to join forces with his new friend George Demain Cooke.

[v]

George Demain Cooke is one more person whose name might have died with him had he not been associated with Rolfe. Rolfe described him as a 'stumpy little clean-faced ruddy one, with a calm voice, and the benevolently pug-doggy manner of stubby curates'.[1] Cooke was or pretended to be an artist. The only estimate of his abilities comes from Rolfe, who saw with a vision wholly unlike Cooke's. Cooke was caught by the new ideas of contemporary painting on show at the Ca' Pesaro, where only the year before the first exhibition of the Opera Bevilacqua La Masa had been held. To Rolfe such painting mistook 'the large for the great, the weird for the wonderful . . . the How for the What, . . . technique for type'.[2] Cooke had come to Venice from somewhere in Egypt. How he had got to Egypt or from where is unknown. When he left Venice, he went to Milan, and after that he disappears with his wife, his child and his debts.

Rolfe encountered Cooke first at the Bucintoro Club when Venetians called on Rolfe to speak to him in English 'for gentility's sake'. That occurred in the first days of June, and for at least two weeks thereafter he tried to avoid Cooke. Then, on 18 June, he wrote to tell Cooke why. The letter begins:

> The reason why I avoid you is that I don't know how much you are in with the English here. And the reason why I hold off you on that account is that I am not going to have my life complicated any longer by persons for whom I entertain a feeling of fastidious disdain, in that they have most magnificently mucked the very best chances of their lives of behaving with the daring Christianity which fable ascribes to Englishmen.[3]

Rolfe went on with an account of his situation and of how he was brought to it. For good measure he sent an almost identical letter to a Mr. Taplin, an Englishman living with his wife in Venice. Taplin took the letter as Rolfe said he meant it, an explanation to acquit him of intentional discourtesy, and no more is heard of Taplin. Cooke, however, 'persisted in amiability' and by the end of the month showed himself eager for Rolfe to join him, his wife, and his small daughter in a flat in the Calle dell' Angelo. For lodging in an attic at the top of the house, Rolfe contracted to pay L25 a month and for his meals, L1·50 a day. He agreed to act as Cooke's gondolier, rowing him to sites appropriate for painting. The two men formed a partnership on the 'principle of "halves" ' in case there were any earnings. In conformity with this stipulation, Rolfe proceeded to pay Cooke L250, obviously half of his recently acquired funds, though later Rolfe maintained that he was paying for his room and board in advance. But he did not stop there. He redeemed a brooch belonging to Mrs. Cooke from the Monte di Pietà for L6 and he spent L20·50 on the Cooke child.[4] Cooke was delighted with such lavishness. Although he was only less hard up than Rolfe, Cooke declared that his quarterly remittance, due late in July, would set things right. He went with Rolfe to settle his affairs at the Alboretti, where after some bargaining, Scatturin accepted L100 from Rolfe and Cooke's guarantee for L93·50, still unpaid. Rolfe moved at once to the attic room in the Calle dell' Angelo. That was on 25 June. A week later he reported the fact in glowing terms, finding it 'most gratifying' that Cooke, a 'brother Catholic', had come forward spontaneously to relieve his immediate problems.[5] Rolfe failed to say that it was his money which had occasioned Cooke's spontaneity.

Rolfe's enthusiasm for Cooke was misplaced. Rolfe took him onto the multifarious waterways of Venice when the weather permitted, and one versified while the other sketched. Cooke achieved nothing except a few 'daubs' and much tippling. If Rolfe was at work on 'Toward Aristocracy' as he says, he accomplished little. Once he promoted a scheme with Cooke for obtaining the Venetian agency for a marine engine. He investigated American, British, and French engines, but as most of his schemes did, this one came to nothing.[6] Once Cooke, in Rolfe's name but without his knowledge, borrowed L22·50 from Dr. Van Someren, used half of it for current expenses and from the other half gave Rolfe L2 as his 'share of the plunder'. Rolfe objected less to the abuse of Dr. Van Someren's confidence than to the size of his share; it was a transgression against the partnership. When nothing in the way of cash was available someone borrowed from Mrs. Cooke's relations or something was pawned. Even Rolfe's cross which hung on a chain around his neck went to the Monte di Pietà to help the household.[7] The best that can be said for the month following 25 June is that Mrs. Cooke's food was good, Rolfe was working outside as he wanted, and he had a bed and in his pocket a diminishing supply of cash into which Cooke dipped now and then by borrowing a franc or so until his allowance was paid. The two men were tragi-comic clowns with Rolfe the gull waiting for salvation through Cooke's remittance.

When it at length arrived, a sum of no more than L850, Rolfe found himself only one of many creditors, some from Naples and some from Venice, all with prior claims. They all wanted their share, and there was not enough to go around. Rolfe got L10. The Venetian landlord was so truculent that Cooke with the help of Rolfe and the *pupparin* hastily moved his family from the flat in the Alley of the Angels to a 'crimson plush bed-room in a common noisy lodging-house' (with kitchen privileges) kept by a Signor E. Rossi in Via Garibaldi. No provision was made there for Rolfe. Because the rent for the flat was paid until the end of July, Cooke directed that Rolfe stay in his garret and take his meals with the Cookes in their new quarters. Rolfe spent the day after the move in the boat with Cooke, watching him doze or listening to him whine about his wife. Rolfe was kept waiting in wind and rain for his dinner until 9·30 that night and then offered a 'plate of coagulate risotto undergoing the attention of a cloud of blue-bottles and mosquitoes' in a filthy kitchen; in one corner was set the toilet common to all lodgers in the rooming house. Rolfe reported that he plastered a double-handful of the rice over Cooke's face, broke the plate over his head, and left. Rolfe had had enough of this man whom he called a most 'PORTENTOUS FOOL' and who resembled nothing so much as a puff-ball.[8]

Only a month after he had joined the Cookes in their flat, Rolfe was once more in a desperate situation. He had the right to exactly one week in the garret in the Calle dell' Angelo and no more than a few *centesimi* in his pocket. Because Cooke owed him L215·50, a sum reached after careful calculation involving Rolfe's laundry at L6, the L10 received from Cooke on 19 July, the L22·50 'cadged' from Van Someren, Rolfe's nutriment, his hire as gondolier, L14 lent to Cooke, and other transactions, Rolfe was in the unaccustomed position of creditor instead of debtor; but he stood no chance of collecting, as he soon learned. On 26 July, a Monday and the day following the break with Cooke, Rolfe first wrote to ask for payment before 4·0 p.m. on Tuesday. 'After your treatment of me,' he told Cooke, 'that is as long as I intend to starve for your convenience.'[9] Thereafter, always setting a new deadline for payment, Rolfe wrote letter after letter to Cooke. He appealed to Cooke's English agent Alfred Cox and Son; to his Italian agent Aldo Jesurum; to Mrs. Cooke's relations, Signors Tomich and Mitti-Zanetti; to the Consul; to every one he could think of; and when Cooke moved to Milan, Rolfe threatened to warn the Consul there of Cooke's misdeeds and his moral state unless Cooke paid his debt. Rolfe had no more success than his own creditors had with Rolfe. By 25 July, then, he had lost or squandered his L500, so joyfully received a month earlier. He had not been paid for his work as Cooke's gondolier. When his right to the attic room terminated at the end of the week, he would have no roof under which to shelter.

[vi]

Rolfe found an answer to his needs in Dr. Ernest Van Someren. He knew that at the end of June, Van Someren had had words with Lady Layard about Cooke's 'voluntary attempt' to solve Rolfe's difficulties. Rolfe had congratulated the doctor for his 'pluck' in taking up a cause 'before that questionably mannered person' who had it 'in her power' to damage the doctor.'[1] At the end of July when Rolfe could see no way out of his plight, he remembered Van Someren's courage and sympathy; and so he threw himself on the doctor's mercy. Out of sheer kindness Van Someren offered Rolfe a room, his meals and, in exchange for pocket money to the amount of L10 a week, some menial household tasks in the Van Someren residence, the Palazzo Mocenigo-Corner. Today the Palazzo Mocenigo-Corner houses the National Customs Office. It is a severe, classical building of the mid-sixteenth century fronting on the Rio di San Polo. Its rooms are spacious and darkly elegant, its staircase, wide. The room allotted to Rolfe was a small one on the first floor landing, looking onto a garden. Its only heat in winter was a paraffin stove, but he first took up residence there in a time of pleasant weather, 30 or 31 July.

Rolfe was a guest in the Van Somerens' home and, except for the few chores, he was treated as one. He had his meals with the family, that is the doctor and his wife and at least two children. In the event of guests Rolfe took his food on a tray in his room by choice. In either case he ate what the Van Somerens ate. It was doubtless an austere diet, since both Doctor and Mrs. Van Someren were food faddists. Mrs. Van Someren was the daughter of Horace Fletcher, after whom the practice of eating only when hungry and of masticating what was eaten with great thoroughness was called 'Fletcherism'. Fletcher, an American of considerable wealth, had worked with Van Someren in the scientific study of nutrition. Thus the Van Someren table was plentiful but severely limited in every other way by the doctor's theories on health and nutrition. Nevertheless, Rolfe had enough to eat, an infrequent circumstance in his immediate past, and in Ivy—Mrs. Van Someren—an intelligent listener when he held forth in his precise speech on various subjects but especially on Catholic ritual and betrayals by false friends. Once or twice, when Mrs. Van Someren mentioned the Benson family or she was critical of Rolfe, he left the room in a rage. But often, in his well-cut and well-washed clothes, Rolfe stayed after dinner, while the doctor made the rounds of his patients, to hear Mrs. Van Someren play the piano.[2] That he did not play for her in turn is most unlikely. Rolfe's chores were performed in the fore part of the morning. Eventually, he spoke of himself bitterly as an 'unsalaried facchino, a lighter of fires, a carrier of water, a maker of cream, a hewer & porter of firewood' and complained at the waste of his time.[3] He soon grew irritable, too, at daily exposure to the Christian charity which had prompted the doctor to take him in. 'It's not joyful', he lamented, 'living with a pious crank, eating crank food sauced with the most unctious of rancid piety.'[4] He came to feel constricted by the requirements of routine and respectability and began to yearn for a freer existence than was possible with the Van Somerens. At first, however, Rolfe was glad to have his daily bread assured although it was cut from a health-loaf,

242

and he accepted his household tasks as necessary and attended to them regularly. They left him with most of each day to do as he liked.

From the moment he fell on hard times in Venice, Rolfe declared that his friends' treachery had deprived him of ten years' work and of his literary career. He told Barnard & Taylor that his writing had stopped in May, that having no means to work, he must relinquish his literary career. Accusations directed at both Benson and Pirie-Gordon were that they wanted to rob him of his career. He told Horatio Brown that 'false friends' had put him into an 'impotent position' where he could neither benefit from his past productions nor compose new ones. When Barbieri called him idle, Rolfe insisted that if that was true it was the fault of those who kept him from working.[5]

Of course these charges, that he was prevented from writing and that his literary achievements had been annulled, were without foundation. Rolfe and no one else had shaken Barnard & Taylor's confidence by demanding too much and by failing to return the proofs of *Don Renato* in a reasonable time. In anger and the spirit of revenge, he had prohibited publication of his unpublished books. Furthermore, he had never stopped writing. No matter how difficult his existence, how ravaged by cold and hunger and the conviction of misuse, Rolfe had managed to write. He finished *Hubert's Arthur* even while Barbieri was alternately calculating returns from it and threatening him with eviction. He had commenced 'Toward Aristocracy' at the Alboretti and despite hunger and the threat of the Questura, which Scatturin held over his head, he had gone on with it and continued to do so while he served Cooke as gondolier. By the time he moved to the Palazzo Mocenigo-Corner, Rolfe had composed a number of short pieces about Venice and started the novel *The Desire and Pursuit of the Whole*. He had enough unpublished material and enough of that uncommitted by 18 June to write to Leonard Moore for the first time in five years with a view to re-establishing himself with a literary agent. In that connection, on 26 June, Rolfe listed the details of his literary career. In addition to his six books already published, he referred to four books ready for publication, by which he meant *Nicholas Crabbe*, 'Reviews of Unwritten Books', *The Weird of the Wanderer*, and *Hubert's Arthur*; four books half-done by which he meant 'The King of the Woods', 'The Burrowers', 'Towards Aristocracy', and *The Desire and Pursuit of the Whole*; and a 'lot of odds and ends'.[6]

In that last group, Rolfe included at least two of the three pieces which years later were published as *Three Tales of Venice*[7] and which, in 1913, appeared in the June, July, and September issues of *Blackwood's Magazine*. The three are 'An Ossuary of the North Lagoon', 'Venetian Courtesy', and 'On Cascading Into the Canal'. The third tale, composed later than the other two, was written at some time between 26 June 1909, the date of Rolfe's letter to Moore, and 27 September, when

Rolfe sent 'An Ossuary of the North Lagoon', 'An Open Confession', and 'Daughter of a Doge' with 'On Cascading Into the Canal' to a literary agent in London.[8] Which of the other two, 'An Ossuary of the North Lagoon' or 'Venetian Courtesy' is earlier in composition is open to question. Rolfe had made a fair copy of 'Venetian Courtesy' by mid-July; some time between 15 July and 17, he recorded in his letter book that he had sent it to Mrs. Bland. About two weeks later he was anticipating the return of the manuscript of 'An Ossuary' from England, where it had been refused publication by the *Westminster Gazette*.[9]

The three tales are autobiographical. Each is a metaphor for Rolfe's idealisation of himself. Their narrator, who participated fully in the events he recounts, is called Nicholas Crabbe and he is what Rolfe thought he showed himself to be in Venice, a remarkable boatman and swimmer (he no doubt was), an incontrovertible but kindly master among servants, a man instinctively superior and acknowledged as such because he was exemplary of the finest English character. It was a great deal more than the kind with which he credited George Demain Cooke when Rolfe spoke of Cooke's 'sangfroid, or obtuseness, or insensibility' as the 'most densely stolid British thing' he had encountered.[10] Rolfe admired *sang froid*, but his idea of excellence in British character also involved acceptance of one's own merit, sensitivity to its recognition by others, clean living, worldliness, and much more. These were what he wanted the 'resident aliens' to observe in him, to envy and succumb to. He told Ivy Van Someren that he 'almost fainted with joy at the wild idea', mistakenly got from something she said, that one of the English residents in Venice was 'plucking up courage . . . to make peace with him'.[11] It is regrettable that Rolfe could not evaluate them as Lady Gregory, more than once a guest in Venice of Lady Layard, evaluated them, 'normal and simple well-bred people' whom one needed from time to time 'as a rest to one's mind'.[12] But Rolfe's pride and his sense of unrecognised worth stood in his way. He resented their safe lives and he very much wanted their approval. Yet, although the 'Resident Aliens' had warm clothes for winter and boots which let in no water, they were well fed and, on the whole, they responded genially to each other, not one of them could have walked the Zattere all night as Rolfe did after leaving Ragg's flat, cold and wet and homeless, and have seen the 'daffodil-coloured dots of the lamps outlining the long island of Zuecca, shining through an old silver-coloured mesh of falling rain'.[13]

That is not the only notable description in the three Venetian tales. They abound with passages reflecting not only Rolfe's delight in Venice but his skill with language as well. His interest in words had long been apparent in his frequent and extravagant coinage, so extensive in *Don Renato* that he had compiled a glossary for the book.[14] As his letters show, he liked his own phrase-making. Over and over he used such statements as 'I find the Faith comfortable and the Faithful intolerable'. Another favourite had to do with his dread of meeting 'that awful expression of face "Now, I do hope, to God, that you're not going to ask me to do anything for you".'[15] In these three tales, however, Rolfe's language is imagous of his rich visual perceptions or precisely suited to vignettes of personal relationships. He displays a swaggering, amused, lusty Nicholas Crabbe—himself— with Dawkins, English sea captains, gondoliers, innkeepers, petty officials, the Guardia Notturna, and a compendium of Venetians. All together, these are three masterly tales in a consideration of Rolfe as a writer, demonstrating his ability as a chronicler rather than a discoverer or interpreter of experience.

[vii]

The Desire and Pursuit of the Whole began as much the same thing, a chronicle. It is a chronicle of Venetian life as Rolfe lived it in the person of Nicholas Crabbe from 28 December 1908, the time of the Messina earthquake, to the break with George Demain Cooke. It tells with scathing satire how supposed friends in England and foolish scoundrels in Venice, both English and Italian, brought Crabbe to the brink of ruin and how he kept alive. To that, Rolfe added material which made of the book a tender account of homosexual love, disguised as Nicholas Crabbe's love for Zilda, a girl who dressed and lived as the boy Zildo.

The agreement with Dr. Van Someren enabled Rolfe to devote most of each day, as long as he stayed at Palazzo Mocenigo-Corner, to the composition of *Desire and Pursuit*. Although he had said, even toward the end of their partnership, that he felt 'fairly serene' with Cooke and he obviously did some writing in his garret in the Alley of the Angels, the arrangement with Van Someren promised more opportunity to work than Rolfe had had since leaving Gwernvale. He was determined to make the most of it. Immediately after his introduction into the doctor's household, he warned Cooke against breaking in on him with 'fatuous jabber'. A week later, Rolfe told the Consul that as Van Someren had 'kindly' given him the chance to begin his new novel of Venice, he was trying to shut himself up entirely to work at it without interruption.[1]

Rolfe had in fact started *Desire and Pursuit* earlier than his letter to de Zuccato indicates. Whether 'radiantly unworded' or actually on paper, the book existed in some form at least by mid-July, when Rolfe declared contemptuously that his interest in Canon Ragg and the 'whole crowd of dreadful people' who composed the English colony was 'fiercely but absolutely academic' and that he intended to study them microscopically. He told Ragg, 'I am . . . laying traps to catch your pettiness, your pusillanimity, your vanity, your absolutely narrow outlook, your bourgeois cruelty to inferiors & unfortunates, your notorious tuft-hunting & abject worship of Mammon, your appalling caricature of Christianity.'[2] Rolfe was anatomising his associates—and these included Barbieri and, briefly, Scatturin—in order to continue the 'frightfully interesting and highly discreditable' odyssey of Nicholas Crabbe. Rolfe is the narrator and, as Crabbe, Rolfe is also his own hero. He is a 'shy proud man who has been idiotically abused, vilely wronged, & is resentful & touchy but not unreasonable.'[3] He is plagued by his past in the persons especially of Benson and Pirie-Gordon and their supposed collusion with Barnard & Taylor and beset in Venice by Ragg, Lady Layard, Horatio Brown, Miss Chaffey of the Hospital, George Demain Cooke, the two inn-keepers Barbieri and Scatturin. That part of *Desire and Pursuit* is as near the truth as Rolfe's bitter resentment and egocentricity let him understand it. His attitude is adumbrated in a letter written about 19 September in which he asked Horatio Brown for his influence and recommendations in finding a job. He told Brown, 'I am so sick of people of my own class that I will jump at a chance of entering the class of menials. I PREFER to have to clean boots & barks, to wear a blouse or a uniform, & to touch my hat to my masters.'[4] Although Rolfe had no love for such work and he was careful of his position with Van Someren's servants, nevertheless he believed what he wrote to Brown. The attitude of the letter to Brown is essential to *Desire and Pursuit*. Rolfe's experience as Nicholas Crabbe with 'festering congeries of human beings, all with loves of their own, all with hates of their own, all with unintellectual indifference to and ignorance of him, his absence of love, his ravening appetite for it, his constant presence of odium'[5] is the first layer of composition.

The second layer tells of the fulfilment of love between the girl-boy, Zilda-Zildo called Zildo, and Nicholas Crabbe. Crabbe, cruising in his topo after the earthquake which struck the south of Italy on 28 December 1908 lands at a small island and finds among the dead scattered everywhere one living but unconscious girl under the wreckage of a smashed house. She is seventeen, 'straight-limbed, and strong, almost as sexless as a boy, white as milk and honey with thick short light-brown hair'. Crabbe appraises her from head to toe and concludes that she is a 'grand broad-chested thin-flanked waistless boy by intention but a girl by defect'.[6] He takes her to his boat and revives her. When Crabbe wants her to go back to the island to recover her dowry, a leather purse containing more than a hundred gold pieces hidden in the hollow of an olive tree, she refuses. She is Ermenegilda Falier, recently a worker on her uncle's island-farm, but she had been born a Venetian, the last descendant of an ancient family established by a twelfth-century Doge of Venice. Ermenegilda is the orphaned daughter of Bastian Falier who had reared her as a gondolier, a boy.

This episode in *Desire and Pursuit,* so fundamental that out of it comes the book's dénouement, existed separately in a truncated, crude version as 'Daughter of a Doge' at least as late as 14 October 1909. On that date Rolfe instructed a London literary agent to send his manuscripts, including those of the Venetian tales, to Mrs. Bland. Among them was 'Daughter of a Doge'.[7] Since he had sent the several short pieces to the agent in good faith and hoped to secure £180 from their sale, Rolfe must have comprehended the suitability for *Desire and Pursuit* of Zilda-Zildo and her relationship with Nicholas Crabbe after mid-October. Whether then or at another time, he adapted 'Daughter of a Doge' to the novel, reworking the short piece, expanding it and making it more immediate by the characters' enactment of events instead of presenting them in a summary as he had done in the earlier version. This expanded version Rolfe integrated with the misdeeds of his treacherous friends and thus made of them *The Desire and Pursuit of the Whole.*

The integration commences when Ermenegilda, or Zilda, not only refuses to go back to the island but also protests that she wants to serve Crabbe and vows that she will never leave him. He then faces the question as to what to do with her. His answer is reached after long thought and comparison with Shakespeare's and Maurice Hewlett's girls disguised as boys. Crabbe at last concludes that Zilda has 'phenomenally perfect boyishness,' that she is, by habit and by inclination, 'simply a splendid strapping boy—except for the single fact that she was not a boy but a girl'. Yet, her hair is cut short, her 'pectoral muscles' are flat and vigorous, her waist is that of a boy who has rowed standing in the Venetian manner, and she is as firm and 'supple as the narcissus of Pompeii'.[8] She ought to be a boy, and she shall be one and serve him as she wishes. And so Zilda becomes Zildo, and his future and Crabbe's are joined.

Homosexuality, and more particularly pederasty, as a subject for literature was much in Rolfe's thoughts throughout the composition of *Desire and Pursuit.* In either the spring or early summer of that year, 1909, he had sent to John Gambril Nicholson and his boy-lover Frank Victor Rushmore a 'specimen' of some 10,000 words, an experiment in formulating homosexual activities as though they were his own. It was a test of vividness and plain-speaking meant to reach the senses without the vulgarity of current pornography. He chose Nicholson and Rushmore, Rolfe told them, because they would be able to give 'some unique criticisms in the shape of *their* personal experiences, which . . . must be singularly pretty—Victor now being of an age & education to provide an intelligent analysis of his side of the question'. The test was a success in that at first Nicholson emitted 'hysterical ecstasies of joy' and returned a commonplace account of his own experiences without the slightest delicacy which belongs to 'what is & can be the most idyllic thing in this world'. Then Nicholson reversed himself. He said he had never felt so 'wicked' and he determined to wipe from his mind what Rolfe had written and to give up Victor's embraces. Both Victor and Nicholson implored Rolfe to write no more.

Rolfe was incensed. He reminded Nicholson of his 'piteous asseveration' that when he was a boy, Rolfe had done him the unkindness and injustice of rejecting Nicholson's advances. But when Rolfe tried to make amends by putting aside the restraint which was his constant rule and coming out with the discussion of a matter interesting to all —Victor, Nicholson, and Rolfe—and one about which Rolfe reminded Nicholson, 'You have the practical experience which I have not', then both Victor and Nicholson asked him to discontinue the subject. Eventually, after a talk with Edward Carpenter, the author of *Towards Democracy*, Nicholson burned Rolfe's manuscript.[9]

While he was contending with Victor and Nicholson over their demands that he stop such writing and their inability to distinguish between a confession of real actions and literary sketches, Rolfe was expecting a visitor to Venice, Charles Masson Fox. Nicholson announced Fox's immanent arrival in Venice and asked Rolfe to afford what courtesies he could to Fox. Nicholson explained that Fox would call on Horatio Brown and expressed the hope that the association with Brown would not prevent a meeting with Rolfe. Nicholson also warned Rolfe against any attempt to 'exploit' Fox 'for gain'. Rolfe promptly pointed out to Nicholson his presumptuousness for his warning and assured him that if Fox came with an introduction and treated him at least as an equal, he would do what his circumstances permitted; or, if Fox wanted to hire him as a *barcariol*, Rolfe declared that he would keep his place and do his job thoroughly. He added, 'Having no friends, I should welcome the opportunity of making one.'[10] He repeated to Brown the offer of hospitality to the limit of his circumstances and stated without reservation that he had no designs on Fox. Rolfe meant what he said, but after their meeting Fox opened the way for Rolfe to attempt to extract money from him by the most insidious means and at the same time to test his literary powers on a subject of compelling interest. When Fox reached Venice, he had with him an American unidentified beyond his surname Cockerton. They failed to get in touch with Rolfe at once so that their association was short, but insofar as time permitted Rolfe made known to the visitors the waterways of Venice and the boys who haunted them: Carlo, Gildo, Fausto, Piero, Giuseppe, and others. That the three men were all of the 'same tastes & habits & dispositions' in respect to these and other boys was soon apparent, but no intimacies developed. Leaving L120 with Rolfe, Cockerton and Fox soon went to Florence with the

248

intention of returning to Venice, a plan which they abandoned and instead went to England.

In September, while Cockerton and Fox were still in Italy, Rolfe sent to Fox the first of a series of letters which may well be the most painful and the most erotic homosexual letters in English. Certainly they are more pitiable and far more perverse, owing to Rolfe's intentions in writing them, than, for example, V. Sackville-West's autobiographical statement in *Portrait of a Marriage*. Their readers have found in them what they looked for. On the one hand is the opinion that the letters expose Rolfe as a corruptor of the innocence of youth, an insatiable and unrepentant sodomite. On the other hand is the contention that these are begging letters and as such accounts not of real adventures but of imagined ones put together from vast reading in the literature of homosexuality and skilful invention so as to give pleasure to Masson Fox by making him 'see & feel'. Such an apology finds ample support in what Rolfe said about his work to Fox, 'Writing's a poor sort of job: but I want to get mine as perfect as I can. And it's only perfect when I succeed in exciting my reader, carrying him out of himself & his world, into my world & the things which I am describing.'[11] Further-more, Rolfe's vow of twenty years' chastity taken in 1890 and his statement, made to Nicholson, that he was innocent of pederastic experience are adduced as evidence.

That these are begging letters and that their success, in Rolfe's eyes, was dependent on his ability to transport Fox to Venice in fancy and in fact are undeniable. He told Fox that he wanted his writing to recreate what he described in his reader's imagination.[12] Rolfe began with an effort to arouse Fox with descriptions and promises of boys unlimited; he might then commission Rolfe to secure a flat and hold the boys in readiness for a visit from Fox. Twice, once in November and once in December, Rolfe spoke of taking two boys, Carlo and Peter, to Falmouth, where Fox conducted timber and shipping businesses and for several years acted as Russian and Swedish Vice-Consul. Rolfe thought it an opportunity to return courtesies extended him when Fox had been in Venice in a manner sure to 'enchant' Fox.[13] But Rolfe liked better his suggestion that he hire a small place of his own in Venice, where he could entertain the boys—not only Carlo and Peter but others as well—and have them available for Fox's arrival. Rolfe promoted this enterprise in his first surviving letter to Fox and thereafter repeated it at intervals. After about two weeks, he wrote that if Fox could get him out of his financial 'pickle' and on his feet again, he in turn would engage a flat and boys at any time and for as long as Fox wanted. In December he once more offered to arrange a place to be ready for Fox's holiday next autumn and to have a new set of boys available since Carlo, Zildo, and the rest would by then be much too big for Fox's taste. In February 1910, Rolfe was still urging Fox to join him in a flat at the top of a palazzo on the canal running around the square of San Giacomo del l'Orio, a flat with sunny rooms directly over the square and the church 'more than 1,000 years old & wonderfully quaint' with a view over Venice to the Alps on one side and the Lido on the other.[14] By February, however, less than five months after the first letter was written—and the letters continued until late July 1910—Rolfe's efforts at seducing Fox to a Venetian holiday were half-hearted and although he referred more than once to the boys, so radiant in the summer of 1909, his letters turn into those of an ageing man and increasingly they are out and out pleas for financial help. They are filled with accounts of Benson's treachery and Barnard & Taylor's mismanagement of his affairs until they differ hardly at all from any number of Rolfe's letters to other correspondents from whom he hoped for help in one way or another.

Yet the Venice Letters cannot be dismissed as an ingenious mode of begging. Whether the events recounted are true or not, the fact that Rolfe wrote them to solicit money and in so doing got interested in their literary merits and their effect on Fox does not eliminate the 'ramping sexuality' of perhaps half of them. What they are and what they expose about Rolfe goes far beyond their initial purpose. Rarely is it possible, outside fiction and the annals of crime, to observe so deliberate an attempt to excite lust for financial gain. That the promise to supply boys of fourteen or fifteen not yet active sexually was a necessary part of his attempt seems not to have disturbed Rolfe in the least. If he had not already corrupted the young, as charged, he was entirely willing to do so. Repeatedly he asked Fox to send a promised photograph of 'two entwined'; it would be an excellent means of educating some of the boys in Venice, especially the untried ones who 'naturally would be the most satisfactory'.[15] Perhaps Rolfe believed what he told Fox, that is that a 'passionate boy' must have an outlet and that his 'nature' prefers another male. Rolfe insisted further that the boy who enjoys the love of a male keeps his 'youthful freshness & vigour infinitely longer' than the boy who turns to girls for sexual activity. Thus, while Rolfe urged that the 'present set' be used and cultivated at once or they would 'flower at Easter, fruit at midsummer, & be pollen by autumn',[16] he was prepared to initiate younger boys for Fox's pleasure.

There was, of course, another more tender and generous side to Rolfe's relations with these boys. He bought Peter, his brother Giuseppe, and Carlo white linen suits and jerseys with red sashes with money supplied by Fox. When he could, Rolfe treated the boys to the 'cinematograph' and sometimes went with them. When Fausto was discharged from his job at the Bucintoro, he and Zozzi the Greek sought out Rolfe to ask for his intervention. Because he had not paid his dues and dared not show his face at the Club, Rolfe could do nothing except give each boy a 'small tip' and a cigarette and call his impotence to help others 'damnable'. He felt even more helpless when

Peter Venerando, too, lost his job as *barcaiuolo* on a bark carrying fire-wood for Gildo's father and as a result was 'wan with want of food, hunched up & shivering with cold', miserable.[17] He was sick at having nothing to share with Peter. Indeed, Rolfe was at ease with these boys and he felt for them a real sympathy.

Rolfe also wanted to be like them in some ways inasmuch as he prided himself on his ability to row, standing, as they did and to be at home in the water as they were. That fact is a symptom of Rolfe's particular, egocentric sexuality. Rarely has any man left so clear an account of his own sexual nature and his passionate hunger for its fulfilment. However rampant their sexuality, these are letters not of fulfilment but of obsession and frustration. In Rolfe's seventeen surviving letters to Fox, there is only one record of fulfilment.[18] That occurs in a letter started on 20 January 1910 and continued in two parts, one dated 25 January and one, 27 January. In the last part Rolfe tells how he took Peter to Burano the day before, thanks to a gift of money from Fox. Peter and Rolfe met by agreement, Wednesday, 26 January, on the Fondamente Nuove, and Rolfe explained to the boy what money was available and offered him money to meet real needs or a day's pleasure. Peter chose the second with 'My pleasure is to be with my Paron.' Rolfe's account continues, 'Fancy a great big boy of seventeen being as sweet as that. And he took my bag—I had a satchel full of papers for the sake of looking business-like—and declared himself at my disposition.' Such eager submission was a stimulus to Rolfe's desire and thus important to his enjoyment. Despite 'fiendish' weather, snowy and cold, they took the steamer to Burano, where they lunched at an inn on beef and wine and cheese. Meanwhile Rolfe had had a 'scaldino of charcoal placed in a bedroom' in preparation for a siesta. Rolfe goes on:

> Then Piero & I went upstairs. I never saw anyone slip out of his clothes as he did—like a white flash—he must have unlaced his boots and undone all his buttons on the way up. Then he turned to help me. He was scarlet all over, blushing with delight, his eyes glittered and his fingers twitched over my clothes with eagerness. As for his rod—lawks! As I came out of my guernsey he flung himself back on the bed, across the bed as he knows I like it, throat up, ankles crossed, thighs together & body expectant.

Rolfe then tells how they 'raged together' until the 'end came simul-taneously', how they 'laughed and kissed, rolled over & cleaned up & got into bed to sleep embraced'. Rolfe was awakened by a gentle voice, 'Sior, Sior, with permission!' And Peter's 'rod was rigid & ready.' Peter 'laboured with the sumptuous abandon of the true artist' and Rolfe in turn became excited; they wrestled 'close-locked' until they 'finished the matter', when Peter exclaimed, '*Oh! che bel divertimento!*'

251

As a rule, however, Rolfe was without money and lacking a place in which to entertain a boy who might offer himself freely. His occasions of frustration were numerous. Unable to go to Florence, where Fox's companion Cockerton had found an especially desirable male, or to enjoy his 'numerous opportunites' in Venice, Rolfe harped on a past conversation with Fox, how he and Cockerton preferred 'the small, the 14' while Rolfe's preference was for 'the 16, 17, 18, & large'. He told Fox:

> A soft little body is all very well to lie in one's arms all night: but it cannot give me furious joys. I want one long enough to be face to face with me while I thrust through its thighs, & strong enough to give me as much joy as I take. (Oh when? Oh when?)[19]

Rolfe's agonies of yearning, almost always without a specific object were an expression of appetite, of unadulterated sexuality. His walks took him into the Ghetto to look at Jews because in his opinion a 'satisfactory Jew', owing to his 'spunk', was 'worth a dozen gentiles'. Or he went to the harbour-end of Zattere to watch 'lusty youths' load the ships. Although he contemplated the professional 'practitioner' Amadeo Amadei in all his beauty—'muscular sweet flesh', his skin of 'rosy satin firmness and softness', his black eyes and strong white teeth and his red mouth 'like blood'—Rolfe's chief interest was what Amadeo would be like 'in use'. Rolfe declared about the young man, 'I'm certain that a Saturday to Monday at Padua would simply be one long violent bout of naked wrestling & furious embracing so strengthening & invigorating to mind & body that I should be set up for a month.'[20] He had modelled his Venetian Toto after Gildo and had photographed him clothed or naked and admired his skin, his eyes, and his body, 'long & muscular' but 'plump enough to damn a saint and as hot as fire'. Still, Rolfe stayed away from Gildo, held off by his 'sulky dignity'. Then when Rolfe bought the suits and sashes for the boys but failed to include Gildo, he was 'desolated in spirit'. Using Peter as an intermediary, Gildo asked Rolfe's forgiveness for his earlier behaviour. He said that he had 'practised regularly' with Peter since March and wanted 'another chance of displaying his skill and accomplishments'.[21] Despite his knowledge that Peter and Gildo were lovers, Rolfe was at once enchanted and tormented. He wrote to Fox:

> I think that Gildo's complete change of front, his fervent anxiety to go, & do where Peter went and did, his simply complete ascent [from sulky dignity] . . . to sparklingly brazen incontinence was the most comical & also the most genuine & lovable feature of the whole affair. And I'm sure you can imagine far better than I can tell you the tantalising tortures which I suffer in consequence. To have offered the very thing I have been yearning & still burn for, offered unreservedly & not be able even to touch it.[22]

252

Rolfe had not managed to satisfy his desire when Gildo celebrated the New Year, 1910, by slipping away from Peter and going with Carlo to the Fondamenta Osmarin, where each boy enjoyed 'five girls one after another stark naked and in broad daylight from 2 to 4 p.m.'[23]

Well before that escapade took place, Rolfe had enshrined his version of Gildo as Zilda in 'Daughter of a Doge' and adapted the short piece to *The Desire and Pursuit of the Whole*. The relationships between the factual Ermenegildo Vianello and the fictitious Zildo-Zilda are their lineage and their appearance. Both, according to Rolfe, were exquisite in their 'perfect boyishness', sweet of flesh and smile with 'ingenuous lagoon-coloured eyes'. To Zilda, Rolfe gave the family name of her supposititious ancestor, the fourteenth-century doge Marino Faliero or Marin Falier as Venetians call him. Falier had conspired to wrest the power of state from the Council of Ten for the benefit of the doge, and for his pains, he was beheaded. Young Vianello, while not a descendant of a doge like Zilda, was the son of an ancient family once prominent in Venetian affairs but by 1908–9 simply hard-working, self-respecting tradesmen. Vianello senior was alive as Zilda's father was not. Indeed after the earthquake of December 1908, Zilda was entirely alone, a fictional circumstance which made possible an absolute union between her and Nicholas Crabbe in his 'desire and pursuit of the whole called love'. This situation is emphasised by the fact that Zilda, born on 1 January, is the astrological complement to Crabbe's—or Rolfe's—birth in Cancer. The chief difference between the real and the fictional, however, is in characterisation. Gildo Vianello was volatile, capricious, undisciplined, eager for sensation. Zilda was infinitely pure and above all docile. When Crabbe determined to keep Zilda as Zildo aboard his topo, he instructed her as his servant that her special duty was to save him from trouble, to stand between him and the rest of the world, to know what he wanted without being told, to have it ready at the moment he called, and to obey his will 'in all things without question'. Zilda acquiesced in all these requirements. Throughout the book, her every effort as Zildo is to anticipate Crabbe's needs, to watch over him, to serve and preserve him. Zildo and Crabbe together are indeed two halves of one whole ultimately 'crowned and rewarded by Love'.[24]

These divergences from reality in Rolfe's characterisation of Zildo-Zilda and the tale of her association with Nicholas Crabbe are important biographically, perhaps more important than the record of his supposed abuse from Pirie-Gordon, Benson and other assumed friends. Zilda's purity and her gentle and invariable yielding to Crabbe as her master, her willingness to sacrifice herself for him, even to deny an independent self of any kind, unmask the demands of his ego. Rolfe knew they were excessive, that he was very far from being perfect in his loneliness, but he was not content with anything short of 'The Unique and the signory of it'.[25] Only on his own terms could he exist in close communion with his fellow creatures, and no creature outside fiction was capable of such selflessness. As for the homosexuality implicit in the hero-heroine, it is too apparent to need enlarging. Zilda in her derivation from Ermenegildo Vianello discloses Rolfe's sexual needs and the fantasies they provoked. That he used the 'literary eccentricity' of the 'girl in boy's guise'[26] demonstrates, on the other hand, the hopes he had for *The Desire and Pursuit of the Whole.* No one else, neither Barnard & Taylor nor Pirie-Gordon, had any rights in it, and he was convinced he could sell it to advantage. 'I am doing a modern love story of Venice,' he said, 'which will have to be read at least by everyone who comes here.'[27] Thus he took no risk of offending publishers or public. Rolfe meant *Desire and Pursuit* to be his salvation.

[viii]

Ivy Van Someren said that while Rolfe lived at Palazzo Mocenigo-Corner, he rarely left the house and he had no visitors. She said that he kept to his room on the landing, at work most of every day on his writing.[1] On the whole, that was true. Rolfe felt himself 'tied' to the house partly because of his wardrobe. He called it appalling and in autumn 1909 he worried how he was to get through the winter, 'keeping warm & presenting a decent appearance'.[2] Under his jackets he habitually wore white guernseys; but they were so difficult to keep clean that he asked Masson Fox to send him dark blue jerseys with high collars and perpendicular lines in the knitting. After they arrived, Rolfe still felt unable to show himself 'decently in public', and he was reluctant to leave the house. In any case, where had he to go? He was no longer welcome at Brown's Monday evenings, he felt himself an interloper at the hospital, and indeed he no longer associated with the English residents in Venice.

On All Saints Day he went across the lagoon on a 'bridge of boats' to the cemetery at Sammichele, where 'all Venice' was with 'candles & flowers & lamps', decorating the graves of the dead. Since no one remembered the English dead, Rolfe proudly took flowers to their graves set apart in a section for Protestant burials. He then informed Miss Chaffey of the English Hospital with special mention of the burial urn of a ship's engineer who had recently died at the hospital. Afterward, Rolfe sauntered along, 'grim, sad, lonely', until he saw Peter, Carlo, Gildo and five more boys on their 'wicked knees' around the grave of a comrade. 'Abashed' by his poverty, Rolfe was prepared to go on alone, but one of the boys saw him and called out, and they were 'all over' him with 'cheerful friendly salutations'.[3] Such an excursion was unusual. When Rolfe had money he left the Palazzo Mocenigo-Corner only to buy tobacco, to get his boots repaired, to join the gondoliers at the cinema. At very rare intervals he went to the Bonvecchiati, a restaurant, to supplement the Van Somerens' diet (once he described a lunch as consisting of stewed celery, dry toast, and water) with steak and red wine. Sometimes he went for a smoke and a long walk.[4] But these were exceptions to his usual practice.

Certainly, after September, Rolfe was denied his favourite pastime, voyaging on the canals and the lagoon. At the end of that month, after a day with the sea and sky for his 'sole companions', he had damaged the *pupparin* as he fought wind and tide in a passage from Malamocco back to Venice. Driven ashore at Poveglia, a fort, he was forced to go on and was then taken in charge by the *carabinieri* on suspicion of spying. Rolfe turned this episode into a great adventure; he used it for a short piece called 'Arrested As A Spy' and made it the occasion for a lecture on the 'Cosmic Comic View-Point' to Benson and Pirie-Gordon. Rolfe pointed out to both men that 'Mirth alone' keeps men sane and that 'Life is Mind out for a Lark'.[5] Rolfe had a great deal more to say to Benson, careful to inform him of the wrecked *pupparin* since his 'small spy Spender' could know nothing of it or of Rolfe's reflections. These began, 'How much more I enjoy myself than you!' He suggested that Benson discard his 'shield of impenetrable pomposity' that he 'stop sulking & come out on the blue blue blue turquoise sapphire & (sometimes) indigo lagoon'. Rolfe went on:

> You build as for eternity—as though Death did not lie in wait for you—a house is suspended in air of which, for every brick you lay on, another silently drops out into space. And your career of a popular preacher—are you much more successful than the celluloid dog who chases an asbestos cat through hell? But I—I have reached the Realm of White Light through the Ravine of Ultra Violet despair and I chuck my insults at devouring time & impale the inevitable on a smile.[6]

These are fine words. They represented Rolfe's exhilaration after an intoxicating opportunity to be a living and breathing Nicholas Crabbe of *Three Tales of Venice*.[7] But damage to the boat was a serious matter; it leaked 'like a sieve' and needed to go to the '*squero*' for repairs. Until it did, it was useless. Owing to his failure to pay his subscription to the Bucintoro, he was unable to use another boat belonging to the club and so he had no means of 'getting about'.[8]

As the year advanced, Rolfe's lack of heavy clothing made his going out less frequent and his discomfort greater. Fortunately he had dry boots, thanks to a cheque received at the end of October from a Mrs. Eram of Portland Place, London. She had spent the spring and early summer in Venice and in some way made Rolfe's acquaintance. After her departure, that is on 22 July 1909, Rolfe wrote to her, ostensibly to apologise for his failure to provide photographs of her flat, as he had promised, or to tell her goodbye. His explanation amounted to a long account of his abuse from the Raggs, Lady Layard, and Horatio Brown and their unwillingness to amend. Mrs. Eram replied with an offer of £5, which Rolfe accepted, assuring her that £4 would go to Van Someren and the remaining £1 allow him to buy stamps and to have his boots mended.[9] In November, however, he said that he still wore summer clothes unchanged since April. He was forced to 'stick' on the landing of the Palazzo Mocenigo-Corner and there, too, he was painfully uncomfortable. With a minimum of exaggeration, he told Masson Fox in November about the 'absolutely devilish' two weeks just past:

> No tobacco. Alps covered with snow, 'bora' blowing up Adriatic one way & wind from Alps bringing simply perishing cold. And here I live & work & sleep on an *open landing* of this palace on the side which never sees the sun with *stone* floors walls ceiling & stairs, no privacy (it's the servants' stair) & *no heating arrangements whatever.* And I have but one thin blanket. *My dear, I'm simply dying of cold & hunger.* . . . I want proper clothes, warmth, light, & beef & wine.[10]

And so eventually Rolfe took to his bed for lack of heat. From his bed, with his one blanket and his clothes piled on that for warmth, Rolfe went on with his affairs. He worked at his new book, attempted to sell the books and stories already written, made various attempts to profit from his assets, and kept alive his enmities.

At times, these last three activities were indistinguishable as indeed they had been for several months. In mid-June, still at the Trattoria agli' Alboretti, Rolfe had determined to rely again on a literary agent to market his work. When he learned that Leonard Moore, his old friend once associated with J. B. Pinker, had joined the publishing firm of Cassell & Co. and was therefore unavailable as an agent, Rolfe wrote to Charles Francis Cazenove. By 23 September Cazenove and Rolfe had reached an agreement and a few days later Rolfe was promising Cazenove 'perfect confidence' and 'ideal loyalty' if he would work on lines Rolfe approved. He confessed that he badly wanted money, but he wanted it on his own conditions. These he stated succinctly: 'I will not consent in any circumstances whatever to be numbered with the ruck or to take any but a first & unique position.'[11] If Cazenove understood and chose to 'MAKE' him, Rolfe was prepared to double the usual commission. He instructed the agent to shelve *Nicholas Crabbe* until a demand for it was created by the sale of shorter pieces. Rolfe sent four manuscripts of about 3,000 words each to Cazenove, telling him to ask Mrs. Bland for more.[12]

Within the next week, Rolfe sent two more pieces to Cazenove, one an attack on Robert Hugh Benson called 'De Presbytero' and the other an attack on *The Academy* called 'De Academia'. Cazenove was told to dispose of these as he saw fit. An accompanying letter asked him to publish a notice that Rolfe had withdrawn from collaboration with Benson in the novel about Saint Thomas. As for *The Academy*, Rolfe wanted the return of his unpublished manuscripts, having concluded that to try for anything more was useless. To be plunged on such short notice into the very heart of Rolfe's rancour was more than Cazenove had bargained for. He took fright and by 14 October had cancelled the agreement with his new client.[13]

Although he was sorely disappointed, Rolfe made no protest in reply. He merely asked that his literary manuscripts and the copies of the letters to and from him be sent to Mrs. Bland. But to Fox, Rolfe complained bitterly. Already *'bunged up'* by exhaustion, he called Cazenove's repudiation 'another smack in the face'. Furthermore, it left him with '£180 sterling's worth of Venetian essays & stories' lying 'fallow' on his hands.[14]

Rolfe's principal aim was to find someone to invest in him and take over his assets from Barnard & Taylor and in return supply him with a sum of money commensurate with his evaluation of his manuscripts and thus relieve him of all obligations. When that was done, that is when the 'drag' was 'off the wheel', then the machine—himself—would 'move merrily'. He was sure Fox was making an effort to put him in touch with a likely prospect. Rolfe also asked Mrs. Eram to find 'some MAN of business', preferably a lawyer or financier with whom he could discuss a definite scheme for putting his affairs on a sound basis. He explained to Mrs. Eram that he needed a 'man of large ideas'.[15] A copy of a 'prepared & definite scheme' had gone to Cazenove, too, enclosed in the letter of instructions which Rolfe sent late in September. He had wanted Cazenove to make the necessary arrangements, thus providing more leeway in transactions with his literary properties and more opportunities for Rolfe to supply more 'stuff' for the agent to sell. Rolfe had tried to reassure Cazenove, however, by telling him that E. M. Knapp, recently of the Capital & Counties Bank in Covent Garden but currently at 27 Tavistock Road, Croyden, was moving in that direction.

In July, Rolfe had noted in his letter book, 'Wrote Knapp xxii asking where & could he take agency business.'[16] An affirmative reply had come back at once, and on 29 July Rolfe had written again to ask that Knapp swear his 'most solemn oath' to be 'leal, keen, & secret'; in turn, Rolfe promised to pay fifteen per cent of earnings. He gave a series of careful directions and, as he did so, characterised his three enemies, Robert Hugh Benson, Harry Pirie-Gordon, and Barnard & Taylor. With this letter, Rolfe enclosed a copy of his 'scheme', which he told Knapp to 'read, mark, learn, inwardly digest, copy, & return' and then do everything possible to put it into effect. With his incurable and unrealistic optimism, Rolfe later told Knapp, 'Succeed in helping me to succeed and you can give up banking.'[17] Rolfe looked for immediate results, but Knapp uncovered no potential partner for Rolfe until December.

Meanwhile there were other prospective partners. To Knapp, Rolfe suggested various solicitors and one bank manager, G. Searle of the National Provincial Bank of Finchley Road, where Rolfe had an overdraught of £30. And at the beginning of November, Rolfe somehow located a firm of solicitors in London with the reputation of undertaking unusual business. Whoever they were, they assured him that there would be no difficulty in finding a partner to manage his assets.[18]

Rolfe soon learned that a greater difficulty lay with Barnard & Taylor and Pirie-Gordon. On 7 November, Rolfe wrote to both, describing his opportunity. Although he had 'denounced' Pirie-Gordon to his neighbours and to his friend Henry Marriage Wallis and for good measure denounced Hugh Benson to the Archbishop of Westminster for his supposed collusion with Pirie-Gordon, from Pirie-Gordon Rolfe now demanded that the manuscripts of *The Weird of the Wanderer, Hubert's Arthur*, 'The King of the Wood', 'The Burrowers', and an *unnamed MS. about the Boy Popes Benedict and John* be sent to him prepaid.[19] From Barnard & Taylor, Rolfe demanded that they co-operate with any investigation the solicitor with whom he was 'in treaty' might wish to make and he reminded them that it was their stupidity which had incurred his current obligations for him. He asked that Barnard & Taylor exhibit copies of his six unpublished books, the Borgian genealogy, guarantees of Griffiths's acceptance of *Don Renato* and *Songs of Meleager*, and such manuscripts of unpublished works as he could induce Pirie-Gordon to entrust to them.[20] Neither Pirie-Gordon nor Barnard & Taylor replied. On 19 November, as he had already done in June, Rolfe reported Barnard & Taylor to the Law Society, declaring that the solicitors continued to withhold his accounts and his property and refused to make possible the transfer of his obligations and assets to another firm. He asked the society to 'intervene to end this prolonged scandal'.[21] Having had no acknowledgement from the Archbishop of Westminster relative to the denunciation of Benson for his supposed alienation of Harry Pirie-Gordon, Rolfe wrote again, also on 19 November, to ask the Archbishop for a reply. On the same day, he sent copies of his denunciation to Dr. Reid of Duckworth, T. H. Crosland of *The Academy*, and Benson's brother Arthur.[22] The next day, Rolfe reported his action in connection with Barnard & Taylor to Pirie-Gordon and demanded again that he restore Rolfe's possessions undamaged and free of expense. Rolfe asked, 'How long will your conscience let you torment and rob the man who opened a literary career to you?'[23] Still Rolfe received no satisfaction, and the only retaliation he could contrive was to prohibit the use of the designs he had made for the Order of Sanctissima Sophia.

Rolfe's faith that a partner would benefit from association with him

258

and that one must appear sooner or later never wavered. When Knapp at last produced a firm of solicitors, Hicks, Arnold and Mosely, interested in acting with and for Rolfe, he wrote once more on 8 December to both Barnard & Taylor and Pirie-Gordon.[24] Rolfe also sent a letter through Knapp to the interested solicitors, an account of his assets which included a number of short stories in the hands of Mrs. Bland and a tired recapitulation of the misdeeds of Barnard & Taylor and Pirie-Gordon.[25] Although they failed to respond to Rolfe, Knapp continued negotiations with Hicks, Arnold and Mosely until some time in January 1910, when he advised Rolfe that they had decided against an agreement. On 1 February 1910, Rolfe confessed that he was disappointed but 'not a bit disturbed or deviated', and he suggested various expedients to Knapp, including an advertisement in *The Times* or a financial journal. He declared himself willing to pay sixty per cent to a partner and urged Knapp to persevere.[26]

This time Rolfe made no attempt at reprisal against Barnard & Taylor or Harry Pirie-Gordon. He had already complained to Harry's father, Edward Pirie-Gordon. On 12 December 1909, before the 'Christmas season of peace & good will' began, Rolfe wrote to the elder Pirie-Gordon to ask whether he thought 'the rough & furious words & acts' which 'this awful year' had forced from Rolfe warranted Harry's actions, whether Edward thought Rolfe had been 'justly treated', whether it was 'defensible' to punish him in revenge. He assured Pirie-Gordon that the letter was written without thought of reconciliation (though he would accept it if it were offered) but only to settle his own 'personal point of view on this most horrible subject' before Christmas 'for reasons' which Pirie-Gordon could not mistake.[27]

Rolfe's assumption of injured merit at this pre-Christmas season was not for everyone. Miss Chaffey of the English Hospital had expressed gratitude to Rolfe, among others, in an informal report on the hospital's previous year. The report gave Rolfe his chance to manifest his disdain for the whole pack of 'resident aliens.' So, only a week before his letter went to Edward Pirie-Gordon, Rolfe sent out simultaneously identical letters to the five members of the English Hospital's board: Edith A. Chaffey, Lady Layard, Frederick Eden, Horatio Brown, and Augustus Montalba. The letter, written in the third person and dated 4 December 1909, protested against the 'unwarrantable use' of Rolfe's name in the 'eight-months-late Report' of the hospital. He pointed out that an author's name is his 'trademark' and that permission to use his was 'neither asked nor conceded'. Rolfe went on:

The similar liberty which Canon Ragg took, by including Mr. Rolfe's name (in defiance of explicit prohibition) in 'The Church of the Apostles' has already been severely reprobated to the publishers & emendation obtained. Without permitting himself to comment,

259

here, on the taste exhibited in these outrages, Mr. Rolfe does firmly maintain his right to choose his company; & he does not choose to appear in association with persons of the character of Canon Ragg, or with institutions of the character of Lady Layard's Hospital whose Committee he refused to join last April. He imagines, therefore, that the committee will see the propriety of withdrawing the present *Report*. . . .[28]

Rolfe was convinced that the members of the committee, but particularly Lady Layard and Miss Chaffey, were his mortal enemies ready at the least provocation to bring him to his knees, even if it meant damaging someone else. In October when he had assured Mrs. Eram of his intent to give £4 to Dr. Van Someren, Rolfe had quoted the doctor as saying of himself that he was 'living on God'. Rolfe then explained that without question the doctor was being made to suffer for supporting Rolfe, that Van Someren had been hunted out of the hospital, that he was 'avoided by English patients recommended elsewhere, & with a newly imported rival on the spot, he has little or nothing (really nothing) coming in'.[29]

Possibly that situation accounts for the fact that two weeks later, on 7 November 1909, Rolfe had assigned to Van Someren a 'lien to the amount of One Hundred Guineas sterling (£105 stg)' on *The Desire and Pursuit of the Whole* 'in payment for medical attendance & hospitality' which had enabled him to write it. This action implies a sincerely grateful Rolfe, but there always lurks the suspicion that the assignment was made as much to prevent the book's going to Barnard & Taylor as to insure revenue to the doctor. In any case, Rolfe continued to treat the book as his own unencumbered property. Some time before the month ended, Rolfe told Masson Fox that he was free to assign *Desire and Pursuit*, which he said was 'three parts finished'.[30] The next month, December, he offered Fox a 'first lien' on the new book for £200 and £2 a week for six weeks.[31] By late February, he was threatening Barnard & Taylor that if they failed to come to a satisfactory arrangement for a 'Competent Manager' of his affairs, he would 'give a sole charge' on *Desire and Pursuit* to someone else and publish it in America under a pseudonym. At the same time, he offered Barbieri, the Hotel Belle Vue's proprietor, a change from a second charge of £90 on *Desire and Pursuit* to a 'sole charge of £330 stg' if £300 were made available in a week.[32] This assignment and reassignment of books was another pattern in Rolfe's behaviour. He had first given *Hubert's Arthur* to Pirie-Gordon and then peddled it about as his own property. Similarly, Rolfe offered *Desire and Pursuit* wherever he thought he might make a deal even though he had already made one.

Whether or not his assignment to Dr. Van Someren was an empty gesture and one which Rolfe concealed or misused as he chose, still when those whom he thought to be Dr. Van Someren's enemies as well as his own gave him an opening, Rolfe was quick to demonstrate that 'no one on earth' could 'quarrel so unexpectedly & so ferociously' as he.[33] To fling Ragg in the faces of his foes gave an added savour to this quarrel, another opportunity to experience what Rolfe called the 'furious joy of loving enemies as enemies'.[34] To catch Ragg out as a hypocrite, to demand and get an apology for Mrs. Ragg's application to him of unwarranted terms such as 'extortionist', even to proclaim that Ragg was as much in debt as he to their landlord Barbieri and as short of cash, were real satisfactions.[35] But now Rolfe could remind Ragg's friends of his supposed misdeeds and, by lumping them with him, imply that they were all of a kind, all careful to ignore his needs but willing to prey on his reputation.

At the same time he could strike a solid blow in his on-going feud with the Raggs. On 3 July, Rolfe had learned from Mrs. Ragg that she had intercepted his letters and cards to her husband. In one such communication to Ragg, Rolfe had prohibited the use of his name in the acknowledgements in Ragg's book *The Church of the Apostles*. Since Rolfe had assisted with the proofs during the period of his friendship with the Raggs when they were all residents at the Belle Vue and since Ragg had not seen the prohibition, his author's preface credited Rolfe with 'a very careful and painstaking revision of the proofs'.[36] Rolfe saw it when Rivingtons sent him a copy of the book before publication on 27 July. With the statement before him, Rolfe attacked on three fronts with four letters, all written on 31 July 1909. One went to Benson and another to Edward Pirie-Gordon. Both advised the recipients to read Ragg's preface and 'be ashamed of having so readily snatched at an opportunity of suspecting evil'. The third was addressed to Ragg. It said, 'How dare you mention my name in your book (just received) after I explicitly prohibited you from doing so . . .? I am communicating with Messrs. Rivingtons giving my reasons for not wishing to appear in such company as yours.' The fourth was directed to Rivingtons. It told how Ragg had denied his responsibilities because he and Rolfe were not co-religionists and promptly turned him into the street. Rolfe concluded with the request that the publishers exclude his name 'from further editions of Canon Ragg's book'.[37] Rivingtons acknowledged his letter on 6 August, and there the matter rested until Rolfe saw the hospital report.

Rolfe then began to run his quarry to ground. Five days after his first letter to Edith Chaffey ('La Chaffey', Rolfe called her), Lady Layard, and the members of the hospital board, Rolfe wrote a second time to Miss Chaffey and refused to accept her personal apology for good intentions gone wrong. He insisted on an official reply, and on 19 December he wrote still a third time, reminding her how 'the Hospital had stuck up a notice in his face "Afternoon Tea 5d.".' On that same date, he demanded responses from Lady Layard and the committee to his protest of 4 December. When he had answers from each one separately, only Brown's satisfied him and to all but Brown, he returned disdainful acknowledgements. Rolfe had kindlier feelings, anyway, for Brown than for the other members of the committee. The death of Brown's mother in November had evoked a note of sympathy from Rolfe. The fact that Brown disclaimed all participation in Miss Chaffey's report was what Rolfe wanted, since it confirmed his charge of mismanagement of the hospital and left in doubt the existence of the committee.[38]

Meanwhile Rolfe turned his attention back to Rivingtons and Ragg's book. On Christmas Day he told the publishers that his patience with the Raggs was the cause of serious inconvenience, that 'new and intolerable liberties taken with him' obliged him to demand that they remove his name immediately from Ragg's preface. He asked that a new leaf be substituted in unsold copies of the current issue of the book and that his letter of 31 July 1909 be published in the *Church Times* and the *Guardian*.

Very likely this request to Rivingtons was one of the few pleasures Rolfe had on Christmas Day. A few days earlier, he had sent greetings to Benson, all three Pirie-Gordons, Ragg, Father Hugh Pope, and Hunter Blair. To the last two, Rolfe's message had been 'Quamquam es incredibilis'. To Ragg had gone a reminder of his words about a co-religionist and these lines translated from Michelangelo:

> He who lends wings of hope, while secretly
> He spreads a traitorous snare by the wayside,
> Had dulled the flame of love, & mortified
> Friendship, where friendship burns most fervently.

With these Rolfe had sent a re-ordered version of Matthew XXV, 41–43, which he began, 'I was anhungered, & ye gave me no meat: I was thirsty & ye gave me no drink.' The verses from Matthew went also to Benson and the Pirie-Gordons. To Harry had been added, 'A friend should bear his friends' infirmities: but Brutus makes mine greater than they are.'[39] In return Rolfe had greetings only from the gondoliers, a message from Nicholson about affliction being for one's good, and a postal order from Masson Fox. Rolfe began his Christmas worship with the 'Mass of the Eve of Saint Marks, and the Mass of Midnight at San Francesco Della Vigna, and the Mass of Dawn at the Frari'. He was 'frantically lonely', feeling more 'hideously forsaken and alone' than at any other time in his life. He told Masson Fox that 'neither beef nor turkey nor plum-pudding nor mince pies . . . passed' his lips and he adored them all. He was 'infinitely obliged' to Fox for the postal order because it enabled him to 'tip the 3 remaining servants'; otherwise they would have treated him as one of themselves and 'their insolent familiarity would have been intolerable'. The Van Somerens spent Christmas Day, from early morning to early evening, away from home with friends. Rolfe rushed from church to church, ending at the parochial mass of Santa Maria Odorifera in an attempt to collect 'such consolations as were accessible'. His mid-day meal was boiled rice and his dinner a 'scratch meal', the Van Someren family by then 'being fat with gorging at mid-day'. Rolfe was offended by the lack of 'Christian rejoicing at the table'. He found particularly distasteful the doctor, who 'grabbed and champed everything, smearing his face with food and whining platitudes'. As he left the table he remembered to deliver greetings from Ragg to Rolfe. Rolfe then rushed upstairs, his 'patience snapped off short', and wrote to Rivingtons.[40] It was indeed, as Rolfe said, an 'unchristian Christmas'.

When he had no satisfaction from his letter to Rivingtons, Rolfe wrote again on 6 January 1910 and yet again on 25 January. Three days later, he informed Miss Chaffey that Rivingtons had reprinted the entire preface (in fact, they had cancelled pages ix and x of the preface) in accordance with his request, and he cited it as 'an example of prompt & business-like politeness' which he 'cheerfully submitted for the emulation of Lady Layard's Hospital Committee (if there is such an entity) in regard to its recent report'.[41] In February, Rolfe was still demanding that Rivingtons make public his explanatory letter of the previous July, a libellous attack on Ragg.[42]

Underestimating life's magnificent irony, Rolfe told Dawkins early in 1910, 'You shall all get back the suffering & torment which you give.' Believing as he obviously did in retribution, Rolfe overlooked his own just deserts. That very letter of warning to Dawkins justified an accounting. It is, as usual, an outcry against the circumstances to which he has been brought by Dawkins's 'league with Benson & H. P-G. (O Precious Trinity, Miser & Priest & Peacock)' and a recital of his preparation of 'reckonings for all' who had injured him. But the letter is also a personal attack on Dawkins under the pretext of pity for his need to go in 'constant & consuming terror (a) of Toadies (b) Blackmailers'. The first threat to Dawkins's peace in Rolfe's view came from the £95,000 received from John Doyle's estate, a sum which included the sale-price of Pendarren for £15,000. Because of this wealth, he expected and suspected toadying. The second, Rolfe attributed to Dawkin's homosexuality, which Rolfe said he had been slow to comprehend. 'When you stood on my threshold the second night at Bellevue,' Rolfe wrote, 'I assure you that I hadn't the faintest idea, then, or till long after, not even when you displayed a package of French books. Here I blame no one but my own density. In matters of this kind, my practice is to dot each i & cross each t, & leave nothing to the imagination.'[43] And all the while Rolfe was on his way to his own accounting.

Despite the incredible number of letters he wrote and the elaborate schemes which lay behind them and the discomfort he endured in body and spirit, working sometimes little more than an hour or two a day and that under his clothes piled on his blanket for warmth,

263

Rolfe completed the first draft of *The Desire and Pursuit of the Whole* early in 1910. As late as September 1909, determined to 'write like blazes', he hoped to be done with the book by Christmas. Throughout the autumn months, he reported several times that he was writing as much, as hard, and as best he could under difficult circumstances. Soon after 8 November, Rolfe reported to Fox that his novel was three-fourths finished but that to complete it he still had a long difficult job to do, 'requiring knowledge, perseverance, concentration, & *incessant toil at full speed*'. He was sure that he had the necessary qualities, the will, the desire; but he was working at half his capacity because he was 'perished with cold & hunger'.[44] At the end of November, Rolfe lamented being a month behind in his work because of the 'beastly' occupation which helped pay his way with the Van Somerens, the 'chopping & carrying of logs'. Although he was suffering from a cold and suffering even more from Dr. Van Someren's method of treating it—eight days on barley water and thereafter only coffee and bread twice a day—he was sure the new book would be ready by February. Early in December he shut himself up to 'worry through' an 'exciting part' of the book. But at Christmas and well into the New Year Rolfe complained loudly of the chores he had to do for the doctor. Van Someren had reduced the number of his servants so that by mid-December Rolfe's duties were enlarged and his book was at a standstill. On 28 December, he assured Fox that the amount of wood the furnace consumed was unbelievable, that on that day, he had 'sawed & chopped & piled up logs about the size of a haystack', while his book was 'screaming for him to finish it'.[45] At the end of January, Rolfe was still resentful of the quantity of firewood which he must provide. 'It's a waste of time', he said, 'to chop the Dr's logs *when I ought to be writing*.'[46] Yet on 1 February 1910, Rolfe could tell Knapp that the new book was finished and he was revising it for 'faircopying'.[47]

[ix]

The completion of *The Desire and Pursuit of the Whole* led to the termination of Rolfe's residence with the Van Somerens at Palazzo Mocenigo-Corner and a harsh, hazardous period of more than two years. Although the first chapter of the book, differing from the published version only in minor details, was written and corrected on the pages which follow a letter dated 15 April [1910] in Rolfe's letter book and although in early June 1910, Rolfe said he had written his novel five times since July of the previous year, some form of *Desire and Pursuit* was fit for reading in the first days of March 1910.[1] When he and Ivy Van Someren lingered at dinner over their coffee after the doctor went to make his rounds, Rolfe talked enough about the progress of his new book to excite her interest and curiosity. She asked him several times to let her read it, and each time he told her to await publication. Suddenly, no later than 4 March, Rolfe offered his manuscript to her on one condition, that she reveal none of its contents to her husband. Mrs. Van Someren got through the first part with pleasure, but when she came to Rolfe's introduction of the Albergo Bellavista, by which he meant the Belle Vue, and his exposition of 'modern Venice', Mrs. Van Someren was affronted by his attack on the hospital and her friends. She refused to read more and told Rolfe so. He asked her to try another chapter, but this only enlarged her sense of outrage at the depiction of the people she easily recognised. She withdrew her promise to Rolfe, and when Dr. Van Someren returned, she described to him what she had read.[2]

Dr. Van Someren confronted Rolfe that very night. According to Ivy Van Someren, her husband told Rolfe that he must abandon the book completely or leave the house. Rolfe's account of what happened, repeated more than once and alluded to in writing to Van Someren, was more exact. It tells how the doctor was overcome by his 'religious mania' which 'burst out in a fresh and more fantastic direction than ever'. He produced the letter in which Rolfe had conveyed to him a first lien on *Desire and Pursuit* and 'passionately' destroyed it, declaring that 'Christ had recently been forbidding him not to muzzle the ox that treadeth out the corn'.[3] And so, maintaining that after the lien on his book was so summarily rejected he could no longer stay in the home of the Van Somerens because he was put into the 'beastly & intolerable position of a recipient of Christian Charity'[4] and this he refused to be, Rolfe left the Palazzo Mocenigo-Corner without breakfast on the morning of 5 March 1910.

Rolfe promptly sent an offer of a 'first charge' on *Desire and Pursuit* to Barbieri, who was on a visit to Milan, in exchange for shelter at the Hotel Belle Vue. Then he asked de Zuccato, the consul, to send a telegram to Masson Fox. It read, 'Homeless penniless wire money British Consul' and was signed by Rolfe. He called the next day, a Sunday, to collect Fox's remittance and the following day explained to Fox that he had quarrelled with the 'pious doctor' and had left his house on Saturday. Rolfe went on to say that he had not eaten since Friday and that he had passed the last two nights walking the Lido shore beyond the Excelsior Hotel. Although the cold was 'piercing' and the two nights spent outdoors had made him 'as stiff as a post', he reported himself as 'satisfactory and his 'spirits & determination undimmed'.[5]

That Rolfe survived the next several days is a miracle, especially since he was hoarding what funds Fox had sent him. To stay alive at night, he had to keep moving. Days were almost as bad. His membership at the Bucintoro had lapsed months ago and he was reluctant to show his face there. Yet there was no other place to shelter. If he ate, it was thanks either to the money from Fox or to someone else's generosity, possibly that of the gondolier Peter Venerando, although he still had no work. Even so, Rolfe subsisted for several days on a penny's worth of bread.

But by 15 March 1910, Rolfe had a settled place to sleep. On that date at the latest, he once more became a resident of the Hotel Belle Vue. Barbieri had taken the Clock Tower, which stands in the Piazza at the entrance to the Mercerie and adjacent to the Belle Vue, and was having it converted for an annex to the hotel. There, in the Tower, he found an empty attic which he allowed Rolfe to occupy in return not for a 'first charge' on *Desire and Pursuit* but for a small payment made from Fox's remittance. Rolfe had a fine view from the front windows— 'quite the loveliest view in the world', he said—but his comforts were minimal. He told Fox that 'carpenters & painters & stone masons & plumbers & water-closet makers' walked over him day and night. 'I was never so dirty in my life,' he added, '& having no boat & no privacy whatever, I can't even go to bathe.'[6] Still, on Friday or Satur-day, 18 or 19 March, Rolfe sent a boy from the hotel to the Palazzo Mocenigo-Corner to fetch his possessions, and he settled down to his hazardous existence.[7]

Once he had his papers and other goods in hand, Rolfe quickly got back to his preoccupations, to which, of course, he added his deter-mination to clarify his enmity to Dr. Van Someren. Rolfe soon seized on the discrepancy between the doctor's willingness to keep cash paid him previously toward Rolfe's expenses (such as the £4 got from Mrs. Eram's gift of £5) and his unwillingness to hold a lien on *Desire and Pursuit* because it 'violated Biblical principles'. In Rolfe's opinion Van Someren's behaviour had nothing to do with Christian ethics; rather it was the most blatant hypocrisy, putting the doctor in the same category as the Raggs, designated by Rolfe as the 'egregious Ragg & Raggage'. After all, the man who paid the money was the man who wrote the book. He began to badger Van Someren with demands for an explanation. When it was not forthcoming, Rolfe reported the doctor's failure to explain to his father-in-law Horace Fletcher, to the consul, to anyone who came to mind. And to Lady Layard at the end of March Rolfe wrote that he had 'ceased to inhabit Dr. Van Someren's staircase' and he implored her to permit 'that unfortunate man to earn a livelihood for his wife & family so that the "awful privations" of the past winter, uncomplained of but (of course) cheerfully ostended with Christian resignation, may no longer afflict the helplessly innocent' on his account.[8] Rolfe had long since revised his earlier estimate of the doctor 'as being as good as gold' and, in a note dated 17 March 1910, Rolfe told the doctor that his 'dishonesty of mind' was almost as boring as his hypocrisy was disgusting. 'I never want to see your food-splashed face again,' Rolfe wrote; 'you have had your chance, & you have mucked it most magnificently.'[9] He taunted the doctor by asking permission to dedicate *Desire and Pursuit* to him in gratitude for the opportunity to write the greater part of it, 'to spit out' his gag and 'become articulate'. Rolfe said that he wanted to repay Van Someren by giving him numerous chances for 'self-glorificatory whinings & complacently platitudinous self-depreciation'.[10] At last, on a card dated 9 April and addressed to 'Dear Ananias-Judas,' Rolfe told Van Someren that if his reasons for accepting the cash would not 'bear committal to writing—well & good. No man need depose to his own detriment—unless some . . . humbug has given him the pleasure of a conviction of sin'.[11]

With Mrs. Van Someren, Rolfe was more lenient, sending her an olive twig from Saint Mark's on Palm Sunday and making no attempt to belittle or chastise her but rather an effort to justify himself to her. He sent copies of letters he had received and he had written which showed how his attitudes toward Lady Layard, Miss Chaffey, and others connected with the hospital had developed. Rolfe was still reproaching Edith Chaffey for the unforgivable complacency of including his name in her report. In this connection, Rolfe tried to force young David Garnett, whom he had first encountered at the hospital, into his quarrel with Miss Chaffey and the members of the hospital board, with a view to discrediting them in England.[12]

Most of Rolfe's energies, however, went to his literary affairs. By 16 March 1910, a Wednesday, he had dispatched half of *Desire and Pursuit* to the American publishers Frederick A. Stokes Company, and he was carefully preparing the other half to follow on the next Monday.[13] Rolfe was determined to sell the book to advantage without allowing Barnard & Taylor or any one else to intervene. When Knapp indicated a friend's interest in serialising the book Rolfe began making a second copy almost before the first was finished, and by Easter Day, 27 March, he had four chapters ready to post and had started to copy the remaining twenty. With typical assurance, he prematurely reported both these ventures as firm offers to Fox on 31 March.[14] It was a day of heavy snow in Venice, and he wrote to Fox of '*instant need*' as he reported his 'prospects better'. He looked forward confidently to 'fees from two sources' for *Desire and Pursuit*, he had started a new book (*Amico di Sandro*), and he had an offer from William Rider & Son Limited, to publish *The Weird of the Wanderer*. That was one of the books Rolfe had denounced to the Publisher's Association. Nevertheless, a report to Fox of the offer might extract a money order from him or induce him to be more aggressive in finding a financial agent to deal with Barnard & Taylor.

Barnard & Taylor were a lacerating sore in Rolfe's breast. For months on end they had simply ignored Rolfe and when they finally wrote to him it was to say that they disliked the 'tone' of his letters. On 19 March, Rolfe had informed them of the offer for publication of

The Weird without disclosing the publisher's name; he added that he saw no reason to lift his prohibition on the book and thus the offer must be refused. He pointed out that Pirie-Gordon had stolen the book from him, and until Pirie-Gordon and Barnard & Taylor acknowledged their wrong-doing and proposed a fair share of income for him from his work, Rolfe meant to refuse all offers for all unpublished work from which Barnard & Taylor could benefit. On the same date, 19 March 1910, he sent a quotation from *The Tempest* to Pirie-Gordon; it consisted of Caliban's words, 'Remember to possess his books, for without them he's but a sot as I am.'[15] Meanwhile, prompted by Rolfe's low spirits and his determination to refuse Rider's offer, Knapp had conferred with Barnard & Taylor and reported a summary of their 'pleas' to Rolfe. These amounted largely to a charge that Rolfe had destroyed their security. Rolfe indignantly repudiated the accusation. 'What silly people B & T are!' he wrote. 'I haven't "destroyed" any of their security. I've just taken it back into my own hands, till they keep to their part of the bargain.' One by one he listed his grievances against the solicitors: they had broken their agreement; they had failed to provide him with sufficient income; for six years they had refused him his publishers' accounts; they retained the Borgia genealogy. Worst of all was the fact that they had taken 'that pageanting peacock H. Pirie-Gordon as their client knowing that he had robbed' Rolfe of '2 of their books' and all his 'life work & goods'. They had put him to the 'gravest suffering' and they declined to write to him. Rolfe said that he was entirely ready to sign an agreement for book publication of *The Weird of the Wanderer* and a new offer for serialisation, that week, if Barnard & Taylor would 'behave properly & make their Caliban of a client H P-G disgorge'. Otherwise he refused.[16] On 5 April, Rolfe repeated to Fox a determination to resist Barnard & Taylor's failure to 'come to terms' and insisted that he was 'going on' as long as he could 'wag a little finger'. Rolfe admitted, however, that in general 'things' were '*quite unaltered*', and that although he was eating as little as possible and as a result was 'delightfully thin & weak', food was a real problem. Thanks to money from Fox, Rolfe had a good supply of tobacco and he was anticipating a substantial meal with Peter and a bath. After such fortification, he could face his daily ration of a penny loaf until there was a change for the better.

Within ten days Rolfe was less sanguine and rightly so. Although Barbieri was willing to provide him 'a little good living & convenience' for doing his work if Rolfe could provide a guarantor and he had expectations from *Desire and Pursuit* augmented by the scheme of Ongania, the Venetian bookseller, to publish an Italian translation, Rolfe was helpless until Barnard & Taylor were 'cleared away'. Furthermore he had a 'horrid cough' which he feared might become 'phthisical' if he could get no exercise.

In fact, Rolfe was beginning a severe illness. Owing to exposure when he had walked the shores of the Lido throughout the cold, early spring nights, neglect deriving from the conviction that while he was actually forty-nine his body was as strong as at twenty-five, and insufficient food, he had contracted pneumonia. For a week, he alternated between periods of delirium and hazy weakness, when by stubborn determination he put together bundles of papers and photographs to be mailed to 'various enemies' before he died. On 22 April, when he could no longer force himself out of bed, the consul was notified. He cabled Whitehall, asking them to inform Fox that Rolfe was dangerously ill and penniless at the Hotel Belle Vue. The consul had Rolfe's brother Herbert notified as well, but he was in no way helpful. The next day, 23 April 1910, the consul delivered Rolfe, against his wishes, to the English Hospital, where he was taken in as a pauper. After a brief stay in the ward provided for British sailors, Lady Layard arranged for his removal to a private room.[17] There he lay so ill that he was given the Last Sacrament.

From the hospital, Rolfe sent a letter to Ivy Van Someren. He wrote it to 'ease his mind' of two things. The first had to do with Wilfred Blaydes, an English doctor who had recently commenced the practice of medicine in Venice. Rolfe wrote that Blaydes regularly paid porters of hotels summoning him twenty per cent of his fees. Thus Rolfe accounted for the decline in Van Someren's practice of the past few months and relieved himself and his enemies, especially Lady Layard, of responsibility for it. The second was more complex and more pitiable. His letter said:

I don't know how many minutes not delirious I can count up. But I can see that an enormously stupid thing has been done, in causing me to write a book. Then in forming a judgement & sentencing the criminal on *far less than half evidence.* Then the complication of the Consul compelling me to let those who wounded me feed me— processes like going through a cream separator emerging in vistas of turquetwill lampshades—cannot prevent what's done nor would it be honourable to either of us ii. But I don't know anything. No one speaks to me & things are carefully kept from me & I think & think & think till I *know* that I am thinking askew.[18]

Rolfe was right when he spoke so often of the soft inner body beneath the shell of Nicholas Crabbe. Certainly he thought himself 'idiotically abused, vilely wronged', as he had told Cazenove months before and he clung to that conviction even in sight of death. That he had to answer with *Desire and Pursuit* was owing to the intractability of his enemies, but it had to be done regrettable as it might be. He censured Mrs. Van Someren, too, for judging the malice of his book after reading less than half of it. Yet Rolfe acknowledged that she in objecting to the book, as he in writing it, had behaved as she must and nothing could be undone without loss of honour. He was hurt by her verdict on him, but he was more deeply hurt by those who failed to value him, the 'resident aliens', Miss Chaffey, Lady Layard, Ragg, Horatio Brown. And now he must undergo the humiliation of accepting help from them. Pleading mutual lack of understanding, Rolfe had offered the Raggs an 'olive branch' only to have it ignored. To Ivy Van Someren, he came as close as he was able to an acknowledgement that life is a twisted, bitter business and his part in it, perverse. For once he was humbled and his pride was spent.

Yet when Rolfe left the hospital on 11 May, nothing was very much changed. He sent a letter by way of the consul to thank Lady Layard for kindnesses at the hospital. She immediately suggested that anything else he had to say to her come the same way, and Rolfe agreed to accept the ostracism to which she had 'condemned him'. He was too weak to walk '20 paces' and under his ribs was a 'fluttering thing' which annoyed him immensely. But the next day he turned as much vigour as he possessed to his enemies. He wrote to Ragg, Dawkins, and Pirie-Gordon to inform them of his illness and to tell each that he was responsible.[19] Rolfe also renewed his entreaties to Fox, writing to 'implore substantial & immediate help' while he tried to 'pick up dropped threads'. His courage, Rolfe said, was untouched. He repeated this in a letter written six days later, that is on 18 May, to Dr. James Walsh in New York. Walsh had commissioned Rolfe to do research on thirteenth-century Venetian glass for inclusion as an appendix in a new edition of Walsh's book *The Thirteenth: Greatest of Centuries*. Rolfe put together a hasty bibliography and a few comments derived from Horatio Brown's translation of Molmeth's *Venice* and offered to write a treatise on glass and provide photographs if Walsh wanted them.[20]

Told to make a 'slow & gentle convalescence', Rolfe had instead done as much as he was able in return for a cheque from Walsh. What other energy he could summon, Rolfe turned to his literary affairs. He put off a decision on Rider's offer to publish *The Weird* until he could see absolutely no way to secure his rights in it as opposed to Barnard & Taylor's and to profit from his work. At last on 21 July 1910, he asked Rider for the return of his manuscript.[21] In early June, Rolfe began sending manuscripts and typescripts to Walsh, whom he expected to negotiate for their American sale through an agent. These were sent with Walsh's permission. Rolfe had inquired about an American agent in February, and Walsh had recommended Paul Revere Reynolds. In May, Rolfe asked to send his work for transmission to the agent with the suggestion from Walsh that Rolfe be 'run . . . for all he's worth'. He had assured Dr. Walsh that notwithstanding his present physical weakness he was 'keener & more resolute' than ever. 'I feel', Rolfe wrote, 'that my life has been handed back to me to have another try in.'[22] So, although he told Fox in a letter of 6 June 1910 that copies of *Desire and Pursuit*, *Nicholas Crabbe*, and *The One and the*

Many were idle in Venice because there was no 'tin to send them to publishers', on that same day Rolfe posted two manuscript volumes of *Desire and Pursuit* to Walsh. On 8 and 9 June, two typed volumes of *Nicholas Crabbe* (containing new material, the account of a party at the Blands' home in Eltham, Well Hall) went to New York, and between 10 June and 20 June, Rolfe sent eight 'Reviews of Unwritten Books', two short stories, and two Venetian essays to Walsh.[23]

Rolfe's letters and books were all posted from the Hotel Belle Vue. When Rolfe left the hospital, he was escorted by the consul, who took him to the hotel. There Barbieri had reluctantly taken him in and given him a 'den' on the ground floor. According to Rolfe, this was done in return for a 'first charge' on *Desire and Pursuit*. Later, Rolfe said that Barbieri had extracted 'an Assignation of ALL' his rights in the book during the period of delirium which preceded the entry to the hospital. But in a letter to Fox written little more than two weeks before he entered the hospital Rolfe had told how Barbieri had refused such a lien and said, "And what can a proprietor of an hotel do with a book[?] That's for the author."[24] Since the consul had insisted on Rolfe's return to the Belle Vue and Rolfe had nothing else to offer, Barbieri had accepted the lien in May.

In exchange, Rolfe got less than he thought his due. He 'grubbed' with the hotel staff, and his room at the back of the house looked into the Calle del Pelegrin, which leads from the Piazza San Marco to Calle Larga. He was close enough to the ground to touch the hats of the 'whores & drunks' who roared there all night long. In the day-time, the room got so little sunshine that he could work only with a light burning. Worst of all, the alley was invaded by rats who made a 'playground' of his room. There was little escape from his sunless quarters unless he went to walk at four in the morning. His clothes were so hideously shabby and his boots so worn that he could not bear to show himself by day in the streets, crowded since mid-May with people living on 'their fortunes, especially Russians and Americans', or with ordinary holiday-takers, and all with money to spend. In any case, Rolfe hardly felt well enough to leave his room. Even by early July, his recovery was so meagre that his hands shook constantly, his body 'tingled' inside, he had 'fits of giddiness', he could not lie on his left side for fear of stopping his heart, and he coughed incessantly with 'a chest filling up again'.[25] As the summer progressed, so did the number of mosquitoes; having no mosquito net, he was badly 'eaten and consequently . . . more or less feverish'. Barbieri began to be 'very shirty' so that by August, Rolfe began to foresee his eviction from the Belle Vue once more.

Such action might be to Barbieri's advantage; Rolfe had learned that by Italian law the only way Barbieri could benefit from the charge on *Desire and Pursuit* was through Rolfe's death. He believed even more strongly that Barnard & Taylor wanted him dead in order to

271

'scoop up' £450, the value of his life insurance policy. Since his effects —clothes, books, manuscripts—were already in Pirie-Gordon's hands, Pirie-Gordon, too, would benefit by Rolfe's death. To hinder further efforts on the part of the solicitors and Harry Pirie-Gordon to bring him to his grave, Rolfe again denounced Barnard & Taylor to the Publishers' Association as 'thieves' of his work and denounced both 'with full particulars to the Foreign Office' and once more 'appealed for "every assistance & protection" ' as required by his passport, as he interpreted it.[26] Indeed, his total circumstances were such that he danced 'on a slack wire all the time' and being 'so tottery' he found it, as he said with uncharacteristic mildness, 'rather difficult'.[27]

Yet Rolfe held fiercely to his belief in his manuscripts and typescripts sent to Walsh in New York. Deluded by his 'unspeakable sufferings' and his faith that at last he must succeed, he reported their arrival in New York weeks before he heard from Walsh. In a letter to Fox dated 1 August 1910, Rolfe wrote that 'The Desire & two others' (meaning *Nicholas Crabbe* and 'The One And The Many', naming them as two books) 'with eighteen long magazine articles' (a careless mistake for eight) had reached America and were 'being negociated as quickly as possible'. As he had said in another connection and as all too often was the case with Rolfe, his 'wish was father to the thought'. Thus, when de Zuccato, the Consul, offered him a 'passage to Dover or Newhaven 3rd class & without baggage', Rolfe refused it. It was his 'fatuous faith' that he had only to wait until he heard from Walsh to set himself right. While he waited, Rolfe kept count of the rats which he trapped and drowned in his 'slop-pail': thirty-six by 11 July, fifty-four by 1 August, and sixty-one before the end of August.[28]

By 28 August, Rolfe learned that his reliance on Dr. Walsh was misplaced. In fact, Rolfe's whole expectation of American publication was disappointed. When Walsh acknowledged receipt of the manuscripts sent him, he mentioned only *Desire and Pursuit* because that book was at the centre of his attention, but his letter left Rolfe with the fear that everything else—*Nicholas Crabbe*, the eight 'Reviews of Unwritten Books', short stories, essays—had been lost. In sending his work to Walsh, Rolfe had somehow confused the name of the agent whom Walsh had recommended. Instead of Paul Revere Reynolds, Rolfe wrote Paul Revell so that Walsh had wasted time trying to locate such a person and then was hesitant about approaching Reynolds without further instructions from Rolfe. Shortly after receiving the manuscripts and typescripts, Walsh had left New York for some time and now, as he wrote to Rolfe, Walsh was planning another journey of about three weeks' duration. Thus, nothing had been done to place Rolfe's work. But the real obstacle to immediate negotiation was *The Desire and Pursuit of the Whole*. Walsh had read it in order to talk cogently about it to an agent. While he admired the love story with its 'absolutely essential quality of a happy ending', the book had left him with a

272

'case of conscience'. It contained too many personalities too easily recognisable under their fictitious names. More important, Walsh hesitated because of the part Rolfe had given Robert Hugh Benson as Bobugo Bonsen. 'After all,' Walsh wrote, 'Father Benson is a correspondent of mine almost as you are and besides we have met and have had three precious hours of converse on all sorts of subjects in The Borderland Between Spirit and Matter.'[29] His delay, Walsh explained, was not out of neglect but out of the hope that Rolfe might alter his 'state of mind toward some of his former friends'. Rolfe's reply, dated 28 August 1910, was despairing. In addition to the fear that his work was lost, he regretted his intrusion on Walsh's life. And now he must implore Walsh not to give the work of his indescribable pain to his enemies. Rolfe wrote:

If your conscience will not let you help me to live, or to defend me, at least don't do anything else. Your letter has knocked me flat & gasping. If it had contained one word of encouragement it would have extended my credit, on which alone I have kept alive so long.[30]

Since Rolfe expected Barbieri to evict him at any moment, the matter of extending his credit was a serious one. He had kept a roof over his head on no more than promises and seeming optimism in Christchurch and London, and he had nothing more to offer for the 'filthy hole' in which he lived at the Belle Vue. But for once help came unsought from an unexpected quarter. The Reverend Justus Stephen Serjeant, en route from Rome to his rectory at Warboys, Huntingdonshire, spent a part of August at the Belle Vue Hotel. There he managed to strike up an acquaintance with Rolfe. It could not have been easy inasmuch as Rolfe was shabby enough to be ashamed of his appearance, made still less attractive by the transparent look which comes from acute illness. He was suspicious of all 'erastians', who might well turn out to be more Raggs. On the other hand, Rolfe was very likely grateful for any civility, owing to the fact that Barbieri and Matilde Delli, his secretary, did not even bother to say good-morning, and the hotel servants, whom Rolfe could not tip, 'snubbed and insulted' him. Furthermore, that Serjeant was a Rosicrucian helped break the ice, and he had much talk with Rolfe about astrological influences and mystical and occult signs. In time Rolfe decided that the visitor was 'extremely affable and a most exemplary thinker'.[31]

That opinion was due, no doubt, to what Serjeant thought about Rolfe's affairs. Rolfe confided details of his literary achievements— books published, books at the publisher, books ready to be published, and books not yet written, such as *Amico di Sandro*—and the treacheries which limited him. Exactly how much he told Serjeant is problematical. Rolfe maintained in a letter written to Pirie-Gordon on 6 September that Serjeant had heard nothing of 'infelicitous affairs'. But since Rolfe demonstrated to Serjeant's satisfaction that he was a

273

good financial risk waiting for a perceptive investor and that their signs were compatible and Serjeant was awaiting the settlement of certain legal matters when he would receive an inheritance, the two men decided to become partners. Serjeant was to negotiate with Barnard & Taylor as soon as possible after returning to England. A written but somewhat informal agreement provided that when Serjeant's legacy was paid him, he in turn would finance Rolfe so that he could devote himself to writing. The earnings on what he produced and sold would go to Serjeant.[32] When he left Venice in September, Rolfe wrote a letter introducing Serjeant to Harry Pirie-Gordon (the letter was never used) and, since there was nothing else he could do, Rolfe settled down to wait. He had his credit, his great expectations, which he carefully explained to Barbieri in order to keep his distasteful quarters at the Belle Vue and his meals, grudgingly given. But his illness, as he had come to realise, had done him more harm than he had first thought, and Serjeant's promises were for the indefinite future. As Rolfe said, he had had an 'unspeakably awful time these 21 months', and it showed no sign of lifting.[33]

[x]

Except for two letters, one to Dawkins and one to Ragg, no record of Rolfe exists for the months of 1910 which followed Serjeant's departure from Venice. Neither letter does more than confirm Rolfe's acrimony. The letter to Dawkins, dated 6 September 1910, reiterates Rolfe's 'blazing rage' with all his erstwhile friends who are comfortable and well-fed and who have deserted him and left him to 'horrible offensive torments'. He acknowledges his hostility to those who have robbed him of his work, his means of living, and his 'tools of trade', but he offers no olive-branches lest he be labelled a 'sucker-up, a toad-eater, the potential sponger' Dawkins thinks him to be. Rolfe ended his letter, 'It's no good writing any more. I shall never make you understand. You had a chance of making an equal and a friend. And you threw it away. We were both losers. But I'm the one who suffers. "*L'amor xe fato par chi lo so far.*" '[1] Rolfe wrote to Ragg more than a month later, that is on 14 October 1910. This letter is less bitter, but it is far more malicious than the one to Dawkins. Rolfe told Ragg that the letter was written in order to have the original in his diary rather than for Ragg's 'moral improvement', though he added, 'I am by no means happy about you as you are'. He went on to say that he was led to 'speak awfully' to Ragg because Ragg had informed the 'erastian resident aliens' that, according to Benson, Rolfe could always have a home with him and the 'aliens' had therefore concluded that Rolfe was making an 'altogether unnecessary martyr's suicide' of himself in Venice. After enumerating his not unwarranted complaints against Benson and the details of the life he must endure with Benson, Rolfe asked if it were any wonder that he avoided putting himself to 'hard labour in solitary confinement' when he could 'die quite comfortably of a second pneumonia on the open shore between Excelsior and Malamocco' at any time he pleased. He asked Ragg to retract the statement if it was his.[2] After these outbursts Rolfe was silent.

Indeed there is almost nothing else to be said about these months except that Rolfe suffered at least one severe bronchial attack and that his position with Barbieri deteriorated alarmingly. It was not helped by the collapse of his hopes for help from Walsh or by Rolfe's loud complaints about his inability to retrieve the manuscripts and typescripts which Walsh had sent back to him postpaid from New York. The customs fee imposed at Venice was more than Rolfe could pay.[3]

Rolfe surfaced again on 27 January 1911 because on that date Barbieri expelled Rolfe from the Hotel Belle Bue 'at a minute's notice . . . confiscating everything' and refusing him even ' *un foglio di carta*', a sheet of paper, as protection from the awful cold.[4] On the next day, Rolfe sent a postcard to Dawkins. It ran, 'Half-recovered from 2nd bronchitis this winter have been turned adrift again and am walking nights on the Lido. There is a thick white frost. Congratulations.'[5]

Rolfe's situation was desperate. Persuaded that Barbieri's aim was to kill him so as to benefit from *Desire and Pursuit*, Rolfe denounced the hotel-keeper to the Praetor and denounced his novel to the Publishers' Association. Consolatory as these actions may have been, they supplied nothing for Rolfe's maintenance. He had left the hotel with only the clothes he could put on in layers and a diary-letterbook on which to 'brood'. He was homeless; he was also in poor health. He was penniless, and no income can be assigned to him with certainty until about mid-March.

Shortly before 16 March 1911, Rolfe received £10 from the Consul. That sum was a gift from Alexandra, Queen Mother of England. Matilde Delli, Barbieri's secretary, moved by Rolfe's pitiable circumstances, had written to solicit help for him by reminding Alexandra of a patient whom she had greeted at the English Hospital during her visit to Venice the year before, and the Queen had responded with £10. It was turned over to de Zuccato, who presented it to Rolfe.[6]

Able once more to buy paper and stamps, Rolfe promptly wrote to Dawkins and to Walsh. On 16 March 1911, he informed Walsh that he had forfeited confidence and admiration because he was unworthy of them. Rolfe thereupon delivered himself of his resentment at Walsh's comfortable existence and at his treatment of Rolfe's manuscripts and he contemptuously repudiated Walsh's sympathy and inquiries as to how he might help as the 'feeblest hypocrisy'. Finally Rolfe described a recent letter from Walsh as 'most disgusting & disgraceful & most typically catholic'. The letter to Dawkins, dated 19 March 1911, was a repetition, almost word for word of a letter sent in September 1910, to which he had had no reply. To that Rolfe added an account of his current misfortunes, the fact that, in his third bronchitis of the winter, he was wondering how long he must wait for 'another and an efficacious pneumonia'. He expected no help; he wrote to prevent Dawkins's ignorance of the 'horrors' undergone and to have a record in his letter book.[7]

Rolfe sent only one more communication to Walsh, a rebuke for his 'ensconcement in sulky silence'. To Dawkins, in 1911, Rolfe sent one more short letter and two postcards. The second card, dated 29 September [1911] contains information as to how Rolfe survived. It said in part, 'To prevent undue complacency or blissful ignorance, you are warned that I am again existing in a boat on the lagoon.'[8] The boat was a *topo*, which Rolfe described as a strong bark with painted sail and rudder suitable for up to four passengers or for any work, with oars in the city or sails on the open lagoon'[9] How he secured the *topo*, how he kept it in operation and himself able to operate it are mysteries. In an unnamed and unpublished article on the character of Venetians, written in 1912, Rolfe spoke of covering the boat with a large water-proof tarpaulin.[10] It was under such cover and on the open deck of the *topo* that Rolfe lived for about six months commencing in September 1911.

It was a grim existence. Venice had long since ceased to be 'all opalescent sunbeams' for Rolfe. He no longer went on the lagoon, taking with him bread, cheese, and onion, and a flask of water for a day of 'dawdling about, sucking up wile & tenacity & endurance of evil' from his 'exquisite surroundings'.[11] Where he had once relished the 'lovely perfect solitude of wide horizons', in 1911 he was intolerably lonely, and, having no shelter except on the boat, he was forced to endure penetrating cold and violent storms of rain and wind.

Yet, in the eleven months which began with May 1911, Rolfe rewrote *Hubert's Arthur* and *The Weird of the Wanderer*. By May he already had a copy of *The Weird* sent him when he refused Rider's offer of publication in July 1910. In April 1911, a manuscript of *Hubert's Arthur* had gone to his mother, still living at Broadstairs, Isle of Thanet, when the Pirie-Gordons sent to her everything he had left at Gwernvale. She in turn sent a draft of *Hubert's Arthur* to her son. It was on this as well as on *The Weird* that he spent his long lonely hours in the boat, writing and rewriting, until at last in December 1911, *The Weird of the Wanderer* was revised for the sixth time and deposited for safekeeping in the Banca Veneta. *Hubert's Arthur*, its matter more subtle and less recently considered and thus less familiar, required far more work. Rolfe said that the final copy was his ninth.[12]

Before he had finished that ninth copy, Rolfe was forced to abandon

276

his life on the water. His account of hideous days and nights aboard the *topo* is contained in an undated letter to Serjeant. It said:

I am in an awful state; & I firmly believe that I'm finished if I don't get relief & a vacation instanter.

The last fortnight has been a chapter of misfortunes. I've been literally fighting for life through a series of storms. Do you realise what that means in a little boat, leaky & so coated with weed & barnacles by a summer's use, that it is almost too heavy to move with the oar, & behaves like an inebriate in winds or weather. I assure you it's no joke. And storms get up on this lagoon in ten minutes, leaving no time to make a port. I'm frequently struggling for 50–60 hours on end. Results, I've lost about 300 pages of my new ms. of 'Hubert's Arthur'. Part were oiled by a lamp blown over them: winds & waves carried away the rest. At every possible moment I am rewriting them: but horrible to say, grey mists float about my eye-corners just through sheer exhaustion. The last few days I have been anchored near an empty island, Sacca Fisola, not too far away from civilisation to be out of reach of fresh water, but lonely enough for dying alone in the boat if need be. Well, to show you how worn out I am, I frankly say that I have funked it. This is my dilemma. I'll be quite plain about it. If I stay out on the lagoon the boat will sink. I shall swim perhaps for a few hours, & then I shall be eaten alive by crabs. At low water every mudbank swarms with them. If I stay anchored near an island, I must keep continually awake: for, the moment I cease moving, I am invaded by swarms of swimming rats, who in the winter are so voracious that they attack even man who is motionless. I have tried it. And have been bitten. Oh my dear man you can't think how awful fearless ferocious they are. I rigged up two bits of chain, lying loose on my prow & poop with a string by which I could shake them when attacked. For two nights the dodge acted. The swarms came (up the anchor rope) & nuzzled me: I shook the chains: the beasts plopped overboard. Then they got used to the noise & sneered. Then they bit the strings. Then they bit my toes & woke me shrieking & shaking with fear.[13]

Terrified by the rats and crabs, tortured by loneliness and the certainty one day that he was losing his sight and the next that he suffered from cancer or angina or madness, able to manoeuvre his boat only with the greatest difficulty, Rolfe put ashore.

The *topo*, Rolfe turned over to a '*squero*' for repairs, which were calculated to take about two weeks. For himself, Rolfe somehow gained the confidence of Antonio Arban, manager of the Albergo Cavalletto at 1108 San Marco. Rolfe's casual reference to the hotel invites speculation that it was already known both to him and to Serjeant. Whether it was or not, Rolfe moved into the Cavalletto. He told Serjeant, 'I'm running a tick at the Cavalletto, simply that I may eat and sleep and write hard at restoring the 300 odd pages of *Hubert's Arthur*.'[14]

Again Rolfe fades from view. Only two statements about his activities ashore before April 1912 can be made with certainty. One is that at Christmas 1911, he sent venomous letters made up of a series of collects of his own composition to Pirie-Gordon and to Ragg.[15] The other is that he sent *The Weird of the Wanderer* in its sixth form to William Rider & Son Ltd. that same month, December 1911.[16]

[xi]

Before 2 April 1912, Rolfe had received his first remittance amounting to £50 from the Reverend Justus Stephen Serjeant. The legal proceedings which had delayed his legacy had been settled and, true to his word, he had taken up his agreement with Rolfe. Rolfe has left no record of his thoughts and emotions at the arrival of this money, the first of any amount to come his way in so long a time. Whether he was relieved or elated or merely complacent that at last he had received his just dues are matters only for conjecture. The earliest indication that the money had come is in a note, probably of 2 April 1911, to Dawkins informing him of the recovery of a changing-box. On receipt of the £50, Rolfe's first action having to do with anything other than his personal and immediate necessities, such as the purchase of boots and tobacco, had been to discharge enough of his indebtedness at the Belle Vue so as to recover his property as well as the changing-box which belonged to Dawkins. Rolfe entrusted it to Cook's for forwarding.[1]

Rolfe then gave his whole-hearted attention to himself. If he was not already there, he established his residence at the Albergo Cavalletto. It is a pleasant, well-run, small hotel which began operations centuries ago and is still in existence today. Antonio Arban, the Cavalletto's manager, was sympathetic and helpful; so Rolfe settled into this 'fourteenth-century pub'. He brought his possessions from the Belle Vue and arranged his room for the greatest convenience in their use. The room, a square, medium-sized one, was at the top of the stairs on the first floor. Rolfe had bookcases built on all four walls except where a washstand and a wardrobe stood and retained as furniture little more than a narrow bed on wheels. Usually he read and wrote, lying on the bed, his head propped on pillows, and when he required a book, he pulled his bed to the book by means of a stick with a curved handle which he hooked into a strut of the bookshelves. When not in bed, Rolfe dressed himself in a red blanket converted into a garment resembling a caftan and worked in the one

278

chair. Outside his room, he took to wearing a dark blue double-breasted suit similar to a naval officer's uniform and a peaked cap. His hair, grey and thinning, recovered its youthful auburn colour, thanks to a formula for mixing henna and *eau de cologne* got from Ivy Van Someren when he was her guest at Palazzo Mocenigo-Corner.[2]

But the glory of Rolfe's affluence was his gondola. In addition to the gondola, he had two other vessels. The larger was shipshape and conventional. For the smaller, Rolfe learned to use 'the earths employed by the fishermen for sail painting' before he had two sets of sails made to his specifications, one 'diapered with crabs and ravens' and the other painted with 'an elaborate design of heraldry at the prow, & a great Saint George (a Perseus-Poseidon-Hermes kind of nudity) at the poop'. He was especially pleased with that second set, so 'like antique velvet brocade' in appearance and so extremely conspicuous. The 'resident aliens' could hardly fail to be aware that their treatment of him, now that he had at last achieved his proper sphere, had been a miserable mistake. Although Americans stopped their gondolas in amazement to exclaim about 'the cunning' of the sails, his 'panther-skinned gondola' contributed still more to his 'picturesque life on the lagoons'.[3] John Cowper Powys, on holiday in Venice with his brother Llewelyn and the Louis Wilkinsons, tells how 'somewhere down by the Rialto, in a very narrow canal', they encountered as they were propelled through the water, 'a floating equipage that resembled the barge of Cleopatra, or perhaps . . . that ship, so often delineated in Greek vase painting, that carried the great god Dionysus on his triumphant voyage'. Powys went on to say that the bark, a gondola, 'was actually covered with the most wonderful skins of leopards and lynxes and it was handled by a Being who might very well have passed for the Faun of Praxiteles. In the stern, lying on a leopard's skin, was a personage who . . . was one of the most whimsical writers and one of the most beguiling men of the great world'.[4]

Powys referred, of course, to Rolfe. The Powys brothers and their companions had made Rolfe's acquaintance through their cousin Ralph Shirley. Although the relationship had not progressed very far owing to John's and Llewelyn's preoccupation with a young woman so complete that they were disinclined to make the social gestures needed to get on with Rolfe, he had written with great propriety to Shirley to say that he was very much 'struck' with the Powys brothers, that he had 'lunched them' and placed his gondola at their disposal and that he regretted their not letting him do more.[5]

Even as he wrote to Shirley about his cousins, Rolfe was correcting proofs of *The Weird of the Wanderer* for William Rider & Son Ltd., of which Ralph Shirley was managing director. In December 1911, when Rolfe had sent *The Weird* as revised during his stormy residence on the *topo* to Shirley, publication had been a sure thing. Shirley had repeatedly offered to publish an earlier version in 1910. Thus, on 3

279

April 1912, Rolfe had signed a contract with Rider and now, in June 1912, Rolfe discussed with Shirley the title of the book (one which he disliked), printers' changes in his manuscript, and the possibility of an American edition. The question of *Hubert's Arthur* also came in for considerable comment. Shirley had rejected it, and Rolfe wanted it sent from Rider's office to Smith Elder.

All this was a part of the substantial literary activity which Rolfe had commenced almost as soon as he had Serjeant's first remittance. As he told Shirley, Rolfe had 'quite a lot of saleable stuff', he would 'have occasion' for considerable money in the next year or two, and so he had to 'push' his interests. He would have preferred to deal with one publisher and he would have been content for Rider to publish two of his books 'with a certain amount of fuss', but while he was prepared to consider Rider first, Rolfe felt obliged to do the best he could.[6]

Rolfe's best consisted of literary efforts in two directions. One was writing. The book called *Amico di Sandro*, started in 1910, had advanced slowly. Because it was a fictionalised account of Botticelli told by his friend Sandro, a Florentine baker's boy, Rolfe decided to sharpen his knowledge of Florence. In mid-June, Rolfe went to Florence for a week or ten days to absorb the elegancies of that city. Mrs. Morgan Akin Jones, an American, met him in a dining car as they both travelled by train from Florence to Venice on 26 June 1912 and was impressed at once by the 'cultivated English voice' of which he was so vain. She spoke later of his charm, the Montenegrin cigarettes made to his order, his gondola with its tenor-voiced gondolier, both put at her disposal in Venice, and his delight in Venice and her legends.[7] Possibly Rolfe gave too much time to demonstrating his own and Venice's charm inasmuch as *Amico di Sandro* remains still a fragment with little of his awareness of Florence in it.[8]

Yet Rolfe started another novel, this one having for its hero Septimus Scaptia, a fifth-century bishop. The novel begins:

'I think that you are the most beautiful creature ever made by God': said the bishop, looking Silvius Prosdecimus straight in the eyes. 'And now I suppose that you are sick & never want to speak to me again': he added.

'No: why should I?' smiled the lad gravely.

'There is no reason why: it is merely the stupid habit of young males of your age when someone tells them a similar truth': bishop Septimus Scaptia declared.[9]

Silvius Prosdecimus is one of five boys, 'his brother Maurus, & his cousins, Honoratus & Domenicus Caloprinus, & their school-friend Arrianus Maturius', who have rowed out from their home in Altinum onto the lagoon between that city and Tauricellium to find an 'unfrequented & deep canal for swimming'. Rolfe described them: 'They were something more generous than the ragamuffin water-sprites who splash & yell near islands. They were evidently knightly at least, & pleasing to see, & though big and strong & capable, most singularly child-like and unformed.' They derived, of course, from Gildo, Piero, Carlo, and Rolfe's other associates among the Venetian gondoliers. Similarly the bishop is identifiable with Rolfe and his deathless view of himself as suitable for priesthood. In this new novel the bishop is aware that the boys discuss him and, eager to inform them that he is 'harmless & not negligible even by them, he laid aside his parchments & slipped out of his dalmatic & performed a neat header from his bark's poop'. . . . The book continues:

His bark was an ordinary open fisher bark with two sails, commodious enough & not too bulky to be rowed standing with the usual single poop-oar. This exercise pleased him. It was healthy & kept him young. He slept like a child at night beneath the wonderful dome of heliotrope, or of oriental amethyst, sown with enormous processions of constellations which covers the vast lagoon. Just before dawn, he rowed into the canal which bathes the parapet of his new cathedral precinct; &, indued with pontifical paludaments he celebrated the mysteries of the Unconquered Sun. Afterward, he sat high, enthroned above all in the centre of the apse, hierarchically weighted with tissue of gold with adornments of jaspers & carbuncles & sunstones, crowned with his mitre, holding his crook all crusted with gems, his eyes closed like the eyes of an ivory god rapt in ecstatic meditation while at his feet masses were sung by his canons. He had much food for meditation.

Although Rolfe made elaborate notes for the novel, filling pages with names, dialogue, sketches, and the outline of a Mithraic 'Company of Seven', he wrote little more than an explanation for the grounds of the bishop's meditations, a matter of 1,500 words at most.[10]

At intervals, however, Rolfe wrote or rewrote essays and short pieces on the Venetians. A second version of the tale published as 'Venetian Courtesy' was carefully set down and signed as by 'Frederick of Venice'.[11] He worked intermittently, too, on a long essay about Venetians. Inasmuch as he refers in it to his twenty-eight years as a Catholic and his five and a half years in Venice, this essay cannot have been started before mid-1913. Left untitled and unfinished, it may well have been the last piece of writing Rolfe attempted. It has the assurance of an experienced essayist and the imaginative and fresh individuality which marked Rolfe's best work. Either he was prevented from finishing it or he let it lapse from indifference or discouragement.

Certainly Rolfe was not heartened by the other kind of literary effort which he made in his own and Serjeant's behalf, that is to market his work. While he asked Shirley at William Rider & Son Ltd. to forward *Hubert's Arthur* to Smith Elder and wrote to that firm to announce its immanent arrival, Rolfe was coaxing Shirley to reconsider. At the same time, he was engrossed with details of the publication of *The Weird of the Wanderer*. On 28 June, two days after his return from Florence, Rolfe had notified Shirley of his intention to dedicate *The Weird* to his 'Florentine friend Domenica Comparetti', whom Rolfe described as a 'DCL of Oxford & a Senator of the Kingdom' as well as a 'fellow of all the chief European societies & academies'. Rolfe assured Shirley that Comparetti would do much for the book. As Comparetti had suggested, Rolfe had got French and Italian translations under way so that Shirley might start negotiations at once with French and Italian publishers. Nelson of Paris and Treves or Hoepli of Milan seemed likely prospects. In fact, Rolfe was working with Matilde Delli, Barbieri's secretary, at the Hotel Belle Vue, on a translation which in time he recognised as 'exquisitely D'Annunzian' and congratulated himself on how 'nicely' he had written.[12] Although he fretted over translations and proofs and revises of *The Weird*, the necessity for circulating *Hubert's Arthur* until it found a publisher was urgent. From Smith Elder, it went to Constable and from Constable to someone else and so on. Similarly Rolfe was posting *Desire and Pursuit* from place to place. On 7 May 1912, he submitted it to Smith Elder with a letter to remind them that for twelve years he had been trying to write up to their standards.[13] When Smith Elder rejected the book, he asked them to send it to Macmillan, and on it went to Unwin and then to Blackwood.[14]

Despite his letters and constantly moving parcels of manuscripts, Rolfe was able to place only what he called his 'Venetian book'. It consisted of 'Venetian Courtesy', which he had sent to Mrs. Bland in July 1909, and the two tales 'On Cascading Into the Canal' and 'An Ossuary of the North Lagoon', which he had tried to market in September through the agent Cazenove only to have them summarily thrust back at him by way of Mrs. Bland.[15] In June 1913, Rolfe reported to Leonard Moore that Blackwood was 'doing' the three pieces 'serially in Maga and afterward as a book'.[16]

Rolfe had renewed his correspondence with Moore some time in April, after about a year's fruitless efforts to sell his own work. By June he was again in the relationship of author-agent with Moore and trying to prod him to unusual efforts to sell *Nicholas Crabbe* with the promise of more manuscripts if that went well. And by July, he was asking Moore to do something—anything—to force Francis Griffiths to fulfil his agreements to publish *Don Renato* and *The Songs of Meleager*, agreements which Rolfe himself had repudiated by denouncing both books to the Publishers' Association. He instructed Blackwood, who had had their turn at *The Desire and Pursuit of the Whole*, to forward the book to Moore and early in October, Rolfe assured Moore that it was 'far and away the most urgent and profitable thing' he was ever likely to handle, 'all the other things being merely side-dishes'.[17]

When Rolfe wrote to Moore in April 1913, his affairs were rapidly deteriorating. The prosperous months beginning in late March or the early days of April 1912, when Serjeant's first remittance reached him, had been delightful to say the least. His room and meals at the Cavalletto were secure, and he ate well. He had money to replenish his wardrobe and supply himself with unbroken boots. His hostility and bitterness toward Dawkins, Pirie-Gordon, the Raggs, even Benson, seemed to have dissipated. He had worn out his attempts at vengeance on Benson; his letters to the Raggs had stopped. His last communications with Pirie-Gordon and Dawkins consisted of the venomous letter to Pirie-Gordon at Christmas 1911 and postcards to Dawkins sent on 31 May 1912. Serjeant had ended Rolfe's dealings with Barnard & Taylor by negotiating for their rights in his work. Now, he could listen with unmixed pleasure to a commemorative performance of Verdi's *Aïda* in Verona or view the Biennial Art Exhibition at Venice. He had his portrait painted, going in his best suit to sit for Covelli, whom Rolfe chose for his academic purity. Above all, he could make of himself as much of a 'wet-bob' as he liked. No longer was a boat a place of refuge, a place to hide. Throughout the spring and summer of 1912 and 1913, Rolfe made cruise after cruise, leaving Venice for days on end to explore the Vale of the Seven Dead Men, to sail past the Island of Tresse or of Sacca Sessola, and to go each time farther and farther, pushing toward Litorano Veneta or trying to reach Grado or Aquileja. Each cruise was lovelier, more glorious than the last and certainly more rewarding in its illusion of youth recaptured than the drudgery of setting down words which no one had the wit to read,[18]

Furthermore Rolfe had a companion (in addition to his sea-going dog) for his later adventures, Thomas Pennefather Wade-Browne. Early in 1913, Wade-Browne precipitately left a position as superintendent of a tea plantation in the highlands of Ceylon and came with no apparent purpose to Venice. There he settled into the Cavalletto Hotel. Norman Douglas, who knew Wade-Browne in Paris in 1918 and after, described him as a man with a 'crapulous turn of mind' and as 'obscene to the marrow'. His antics when Paris was bombarded, according to Douglas, displayed 'an outright love affair with death'.[19] Arban, who managed the Cavalleto, remembered Wade-Browne in a different way. Arban recalled him as an inconspicuous, reticent, rather forlorn man who walked awkwardly and noisily owing to the fact that he wore a surgical boot on one foot. In any case, Arban made Wade-Browne and Rolfe known to each other. Rolfe was delighted. He had an Englishman to whom he could show Venice and show himself as a knowledgeable Venetian. Rolfe took Wade-Browne on most of his cruises in 1913.

Nevertheless Rolfe's financial situation was quickly going from bad to worse. From early April to early December he had had almost £1,000 from Serjeant, who had had nothing in return. The legacy from which he had drawn the remittances was well-nigh exhausted, and he had marriage in mind. In early December, on the advice. of John Withers, his solicitor, Serjeant asked Rolfe to sign an indenture agreement. The document was executed on 11 December 1912.[20] Thereafter both the number and the amount of payments decreased until soon they stopped altogether.

That Serjeant would recover anything was most unlikely. Rolfe had made real efforts to place his manuscripts and he had failed. Certainly *The Weird of the Wanderer*, published on 16 November 1912, was not a successful book. William Rider & Son's December account, which Rolfe received in early March, had shown only eighty-two copies sold. On 12 March 1913, Rolfe wrote to the publishing firm to ask for a date on which his representative in England might inspect their books on his behalf. He declared that the sale of eighty-two copies was inadequate in view of Shirley's estimates and promises which included not only an advance of £40 but also extensive advertising, numerous reviews, and a plan to sell to certain booksellers at 'favourable terms' in return for buying the book in quantity. Now, when he questioned Shirley, Rolfe got only evasion and 'shifty treatment'. He had not been paid the £40, he had not been consulted as to the Press List, and he had had no opportunity to use both his purse and his influence in the matter of advertising. He advised Rider on the value of advertising and pointed out that after Shirley had sent his cousins, the Powys brothers, to inspect Rolfe's 'picturesque life on the lagoons in a Panther-skinned gondola or Venetian barks with painted sails', something might have been made of that. Rolfe wanted, too, an explanation of Shirley's statements that his two readers and Rolfe had been misleading when they represented *The Weird* as 'of a popular character' and that Shirley had not read the book until after the agreement for publication was signed in April 1912. The letter was mild for Rolfe, but it focussed on Shirley's statement that he had 'set his heart' on making *The Weird* a success. Rolfe apologised for the length of his letter by saying that it was inspired by a 'humanitarian motive . . . solicitude for the prevention of disasters' to their 'Mr. Shirley's heart.'[21] In the same post, he wrote to Shirley, expressing serious concern about his heart and giving that as a reason for the letter to William Rider & Son. 'Don't you worry,' Rolfe told Shirley. 'Go away & take a Rest-Cure. *Lascia fare a me.*'[22]

Rolfe enjoyed writing these letters, but neither one produced cash, and cash was what he needed. As he had done so often in the past when his need was extreme, Rolfe turned again to the scheme for elaborating his genealogy of the Borgias into a commissioned history of that noble family, based on their archives. Securing a few pounds from somewhere, Rolfe went off to Milan to promote the idea with Francesco Borgia and his son Cesare, who, Rolfe had said in 1908, were eager to serve him. Their attitude had changed. They gave him no

284

commission and, when he had spent every penny he had, he was forced to return dispiritedly to Venice.[23] In February 1913, he had commenced sitting to Covelli for his portrait; at that time paying for it was uncertain, but, counting on his reputation for 'lavish living to get him through', Rolfe allowed Covelli to complete the portrait.[24] Indeed by mid-March and possibly earlier, Rolfe was living almost entirely on the credit accruing from his reputation for extravagance.

But he had run his account at the Cavalletto too long. According to Arban, Rolfe owed so much as March 1913 drew to a close that eviction seemed inevitable. Yet, Arban had a genuine liking for Rolfe and was reluctant to turn him out. Instead, Arban found a flat for him which his dwindling resources and his credit might manage. The flat was on the top floor and at the front, overlooking the Grand Canal, of the Palazzo Marcello. The palace was acquired by the Marcello in the fifteenth century, rebuilt in the eighteenth, turned into flats early in the twentieth, and in 1970 was undergoing restoration. Standing squarely on the Canal a short distance from Campo San Marcuola, it is entered through a courtyard from the Rio della Maddalena. In the latter part of March, Arban arranged for Rolfe to move with all his possessions to the Palazzo Marcello.[25]

[xii]

At first the change of residence stimulated Rolfe. He wrote enthusiastically to Leonard Moore about his new home and its convenience, situated as it was on the Grand Canal so that he could moor a boat at the front door and go easily to the Cavalletto for his meals as Arban's guest. He gave much time and thought to decorating his new quarters, settling on the use of scarlet silk damask for his bedroom. His old enemy, Mrs. Ragg, told how he chanced to meet Nina, her former servant, and asked her to do some sewing for him. He took Nina to his flat, showed her his bedroom hung with the scarlet cloth and the curtains and bed-spread to match. He then asked her to make cushion covers of what he had left of the same material. When the covers were done, Nina asked a neighbour to deliver them to Rolfe. He failed to pay her then or later.[1]

By that time, probably May, Rolfe could pay no one. Every effort had failed. He had nothing and no prospects. Living on credit. Arban's generosity, and what little Wade-Browne could contribute, Rolfe spent most of the summer of 1913 on the water, his goings and comings dictated by weather and the need for supplies. Once ashore, at the end of each cruise, he tried his best to sell what he had written, largely through Leonard Moore. Although he retained the fresh vigour of his style, as in the unnamed essay on the Venetians, Rolfe's efforts at new composition were sporadic and half-hearted.[2] Years later, his brother Herbert spoke of the preoccupations, the obsessiveness which beset Rolfe. Herbert said:

> My brother was undoubtedly possessed—as some geniuses are— by an overmastering force, not malign in itself, though perhaps exceptionally susceptible to malign influence, which compelled him to wear his life out in efforts towards self-expression, the expression of an exceptional & gifted personality. I regard him as having been driven—far out of the beaten tracks of humdrum work which more ordinary mortals have to tread, in order merely to exist.[3]

But Rolfe was no longer driven. Well before the autumn rains began to fall on the lagoon in 1913, Rolfe had been purged of his obsession by repeated failure; exhausted and weakened by illness, he was an empty man. He was lost, despondent.

Aware of his hopelessness, Arban was worried about Rolfe and at some time after May he induced Rolfe to offer Wade-Browne the use of a room in the flat at the Palazzo Marcello and he urged Wade-Browne to join Rolfe. Thus Arban solved the problem of Wade-Browne's poverty and arranged for someone to keep an eye on Rolfe. The two men could care for each other whether ashore or at sea.

Rolfe made his last cruise of the 1913 season at the end of September. His vessel was wrecked and on the last day of the month he was towed back to Venice for repairs. On 3 October he anticipated putting to sea again in a week,[4] but the necessary repairs were extensive and the '*squero*', unsure of payment, worked slowly if at all. Rolfe was still ashore at the end of the month. On the last Saturday in October, 25 October, he went as usual with Wade Browne to the Cavalletto for dinner. They returned together to the Palazzo Marcello shortly after nine and sat in the *salone* of their flat talking together for more than an hour. Then each went to his bedroom.

Wade-Browne never saw Rolfe alive again. When he failed to emerge from his bedroom by mid-afternoon the next day, Wade-Browne investigated. He found Rolfe dead. He was lying fully dressed on his bed, where he had fallen at the onset of pain from a final heart seizure or what a formal inquest declared to be 'heart paralysis'.[5]

Rolfe's death was reported in England by a Reuter's dispatch published in *The Times*. Herbert Rolfe immediately set out by train for Venice, where, with the help of the English Consulate and especially Gerald Campbell, its Vice-Consul, Herbert attended to his brother's affairs. Rolfe's will named his brother Alfred, the schoolmaster in Australia, as his heir; but on the advice of Campbell, Herbert Rolfe claimed none of Rolfe's effects for the family, fearful that if he did he would be surrounded by a swarm of creditors. Herbert arranged for his brother's burial, which took place on Thursday, 30 October. Because the Municipality refused to sell him a grave in perpetuity, Herbert was obliged to buy one for a period of only ten years. At the end of that period, he entered into extensive negotiations with municipal officials and eventually bought a permanent 'resting place', to which Frederick William Rolfe's remains were moved with a religious ceremony on 12 January 1924.[6]

Having succeeded in nothing earthly which he attempted, having been denied everything the Church had to offer—except faith—Frederick William Rolfe at last came to rest. It is to be hoped that, like his own Hadrian, Rolfe was one of 'the dead' who 'found out the secret of Love, and are perfectly satisfied'. Rolfe maintained, always, as did Blake, that 'the soul of sweet delight can never be defiled'.

Notes

PROLOGUE

1. Frederick Rolfe, 'Armed Hands' (Martyr Worthy).
2. Ella d'Arcy, 'Yellow Book Celebrities' (Martyr Worthy).
3. Frederick Rolfe, 'An Ossuary of the North Lagoon', *Blackwood's Magazine*, June 1913, p. 815.
4. Cf. R. J. H. Jenkins, 'Richard Macgillivray Dawkins', *Proceedings of the British Academy*, 1955, p. 387.
5. Frederick Rolfe to R. M. Dawkins, Poundstock, Bude, 12 May 1908, in Frederick Rolfe, *Letters to R. M. Dawkins*, ed. Cecil Woolf, London, 1962, p. 116.
6. Cf. Cecil Woolf, 'Introduction' in Rolfe, *Letters to Dawkins*, p. 17 *n.* 2; A. J. A. Symons, *The Quest for Corvo*, London, 1934, p. 207.
7. Rolfe to Dawkins in *Letters to Dawkins*, p. 128; cf. Jenkins, 'Dawkins', pp. 382, 381, 384.
8. Rolfe to Dawkins, Crickhowell, 9 January 1908; Poundstock, Bude, 20 February, 16 April, 12 May 1908; Crickhowell, 29 [July] 1908 in *Letters to Dawkins*, pp. 77, 82, 102–3, 116, 127 *et passim*.
9. Frederick Rolfe, *Nicholas Crabbe*, New York, 1958, p. 101.
10. John Cowper Powys, *Autobiography*, London, 1934, p. 408.
11. Frederick Rolfe to C. Masson Fox, [Venice, 1909] (Texas).
12. Cf. Frederick Rolfe, *The Desire and Pursuit of the Whole*, London, 1934, p. 131.

PART I

[i]

1. Cf. 'A Brief Genealogy of the Firm of Messrs. William Rolfe & Sons'; Frederick Rolfe, *Don Renato An Ideal Content*, ed. Cecil Woolf, London, 1963, p. 15.
2. Cf. Frederick Rolfe, *Hadrian the Seventh*, London, 1904, p. 43.
3. A. T. Bartholomew, Autograph observations on visit, 28 December 1926, to Herbert Rolfe, dated 1 January 1927 in Bartholomew scrapbook (Texas).
4. Ellen E. Rolfe to the Editor of *The Spectator*, London, 27 December 1924; Ellen E. Rolfe to A. T. Bartholomew, Trevelyan, Hayward's Heath, Sussex, 22 April 1926 in Bartholomew (Texas).
5. (Martyr Worthy).
6. Rolfe, Untitled, incomplete holograph article on the Venetians dated as post-1906, because it is written on paper watermarked 1906 and placed in 1913 because it refers to 'five years' study of the Venetians' and to twenty-eight years as a Catholic (Martyr Worthy).
7. Frederick Rolfe to Leonard Moore, Hampstead, 9 October 1903, in Frederick Rolfe, *Letters to Leonard Moore*, ed. Cecil Woolf and Rabbi Bertram Korn, London, 1960, p. 37.
8. Frederick Rolfe to G. T. Maquay, London, 25 June 1904 (Berg); cf. Frederick Rolfe to Henry Newbolt, Hampstead, 12 August 1903 (Texas).
9. Rolfe, *Hadrian*, pp. 28, 371.
10. Frederick Rolfe to W. P. James, Oxford, 30 October 1906 in Frederick Rolfe, *Letters to C. H. C. Pirie-Gordon*, ed. Cecil Woolf, London, 1959, p. 38.

11. Frederick Rolfe, *Hubert's Arthur*, London [1935], pp. 105–6; cf. A. J. A. Symons, 'Introduction', in *Hubert's Arthur*, p. 3.
12. 'Testimonials in Favour of Mr. Frederick Rolfe' (Texas); Certificate signed by T. M. Jacombs, 1868 (Martyr Worthy).
13. Bartholomew, Observations (Texas); Rolfe, *Hadrian*, p. 17.
14. Frederick Rolfe to James Walsh, London, 4 June 1903 in Frederick Rolfe, *Letters to James Walsh*, ed. Donald Weeks, London, 1972, p. 15.

[ii]

1. Bartholomew, Observations (Texas).
2. Cf. three programmes of the Stationers' Company's School Swimming Club, 1879 (Bodleian).
3. Cf. Rolfe to Walsh, London, 4 June 1903 in *Letters to Walsh*, p. 15. Stanton came to St. Albans after 13 June 1875, but he probably did not hear confession until after 8 August 1875. See also, the memorial card for the Reardons in Rolfe's scrapbook (Bodleian).
4. 'Testimonials' (Texas); cf. Rolfe, *Hadrian*, p. 11.
5. Cf. a photo at the Bodleian; Rolfe to Walsh, London, 29 June 1903 in *Letters to Walsh*, p. 19; Rolfe, *Hadrian*, p. 44.
6. Rolfe to Walsh, London, 4 June 1903 in *Letters to Walsh*, p. 15; cf. Rolfe, *Hadrian*, p. 28.
7. (Bodleian).
8. Rolfe has placed an R by his contributions to *The Wintonian* for 4 February 1882 (Bodleian).

[iii]

1. P. 15.
2. Rolfe to Walsh, London, 4 June 1903 in *Letters to Walsh*, p. 15.
3. (Martyr Worthy); cf. *Desiderata*, 24 June 1955, p. 12.
4. John Holden, ALS to A. J. A. Symons, Antwerp, [July 1933] (Martyr Worthy).
6. Cf. G. G. Coulton, *Romanism and Truth*, 2 vols., London, 1934, II, 274.
6. Coulton, II, 274–7.
7. Cf. Cecil Woolf and Brocard Sewell, 'The Clerk Without a Benefice', in *Corvo, 1860–1960*, eds. Cecil Woolf and Brocard Sewell, Aylesford, 1961, p. 6; Rolfe, *Hadrian*, pp. 159–60.
8. Cf. Rolfe's Scrapbook for memorabilia of Grantham Grammar School (Bodleian).

[iv]

1. Rolfe, *Hadrian*, p. 381.
2. Father Edwards, S.J., F.S.A. to Donald Weeks, London, 3 December 1969.
3. Cf. Donald Weeks, *Corvo*, London, 1971, pp. 18–19; Woolf and Sewell, 'Clerk without a Benefice', p. 28; Vincent O'Sullivan, 'The Gall of Human Kindness', in *Dublin Magazine*, January–March 1935, p. 16.
4. Cf. The Right Reverend Sir David Hunter Blair, 'More Light on Baron Corvo', *The London Mercury*, May 1934, p. 625.
5. Hunter Blair, pp. 625–6.
6. Rolfe, *Hadrian*, p. 382.
7. Weeks, p. 23.
8. 25 December 1886, p. 1026.
9. Weeks, p. 36.
10. O'Sullivan, p. 19.

[v]

1. John J. Coyne, *St. Mary's College Oscott 1794–1969*, Farnworth, Lancs., [1969], p. 15.
2. Coyne, p. 20.
3. Symons, *Quest*, p. 64.
4. Rolfe to Walsh, Hampstead, 13 March 1903 in *Letters to Walsh*, p. 11.
5. Symons, *Quest*, p. 64; cf. Rolfe, *Nicholas Crabbe*, p. 30.
6. O'Sullivan, p. 25.
7. O'Sullivan, p. 22.
8. Cf. *The Universal Review*, 15 December 1888, pp. 585–91; *The Month*, May 1888, pp. [1]–3.
9. Woolf and Sewell, 'Clerk Without a Benefice', p. 21.
10. Cf. Weeks, p. 28.
11. Rolfe, *Hubert's Arthur*, p. 175.
12. Rolfe, *Don Renato*, p. 119.
13. Symons, *Quest*, p. 57. Cf. p. 60; Woolf and Sewell, 'Clerk Without a Benefice', p. 21.
14. Rolfe, *Hadrian*, p. 47.
15. Rolfe, *Hadrian*, p. 27.
16. Woolf and Sewell, 'Clerk Without a Benefice', p. 21; Weeks, p. 31.
17. Rolfe, *Hadrian*, pp. 27–8.

[vi]

1. John Gambril Nicholson to Charles Phillip Castle Kains Jackson, Rydal Mount, Colwyn Bay, 8 April 1892 (Berg).
2. Cf. Rolfe, *Hadrian*, p. 392.
3. Cf. Weeks, p. 38; Timothy d'Arch Smith, *Love in Earnest*, London, 1970, p. 66.
4. Cf. Weeks, pp. 38–9; below, pp. 29, 33.
5. (Edinburgh).
6. (Bodleian).
7. Cf. Frederick Rolfe, 'A Suppressed Letter', in *The Tablet*, 31 August 1889, p. 337; Frederick Rolfe, 'Christian Archaeology in Rome', *The Tablet*, 21 September 1889, pp. 457–8; Cecil Woolf, *A Bibliography of Frederick Rolfe*, London, 1972, p. 142.
8. Cf. John Gambril Nicholson, *The Romance of a Choir-Boy*, London, 1916, p. 20.
9. (Bodleian).
10. (Bodleian). This text, taken from the manuscript, differs from the printed text in punctuation, one or two words, and the use of the ampersand. Cf. *The Art Review*, April 1890, p. 128.
11. *Whitehall Review*, 11 May 1889.
12. Cf. The Very Reverend Alexander Canon MacWilliam, 'Fr. Rolfe and the Scots College, Rome', *Innes Review*, Autumn 1970, p. 135 and *n* 20.
13. (Bodleian.)
14. E. B. S[teynel], 'Afternoons in Studios: Henry Scott Tuke at Falmouth', *The Studio*, 1895, pp. 90–6.
15. Cf. d'Arch Smith, pp. 60, 61–2.
16. *Memoirs of a Misspent Youth, 1872–1896*, New York, 1933, p. 26.
17. (Martyr Worthy).
18. Unpublished (Donald Weeks).

[vii]

1. Cf. Rolfe, *Hadrian*, p. 382.
2. Cf. MacWilliam, p. 135, where Campbell's final report for college records is quoted; above, p. 26.
3. (Bodleian).
4. *Atalanta*, January 1890, p. [221].

5. Cf. Frederick Rolfe to the Editor of *Blackwood's Magazine*, Rome, 4 February 1890, with two enclosures, 'From the Whitehall Review' and 'Ottava rima: The Three Ages of Love' (Edinburgh). The poem also exists in at least one other manuscript, a part of the Walpole Collection (Bodleian).
6. See below, p. 46.
7. For a different opinion, see Weeks, p. 46.
8. Frederick Rolfe to [the Editor of *Blackwood's*], Casi di S. E. La Duchessa Carolin[e] Sforza, Genzano di Roma, 10 June 1890; cf. Rolfe to the Editor of *Blackwood's*, Scots College, Rome [1890] (Edinburgh).
9. Cf. Symons, *Quest*, p. 70.
10. Cf. Weeks, p. 50; Rolfe, *Hadrian*, p. 284; Charles Kains Jackson, 'Points for Bartholomew', dated March 1926 (Texas).
11. Cf. Symons, *Quest*, p. 70.
12. Symons, *Quest*, p. 71.
13. Symons, *Quest*, p. 75.
14. MacWilliam, pp. 130-1.
15. Cf. Weeks, p. 45.
16. MacWilliam, p. 133.
17. Cf. MacWilliam, p. 133 and *n* 18; Plate V (facing p. 132); Weeks, p. 48.
18. Frederick Rolfe, *Hubert's Arthur by Prospero and Caliban*, London, 1935, p. 84.
19. Cf. Woolf and Sewell, 'Clerk Without a Benefice', p. 22; Symons, *Quest*, pp. 70-73, 76; MacWilliam, p. 136.
20. Woolf and Sewell, 'Clerk Without a Benefice', p. 25.
21. Cf. Woolf and Sewell, 'Clerk Without a Benefice', p. 23; Weeks, pp. 43-4, 51, 53-4.
22. Cf. MacWilliam, p. 135; Weeks, p. 49.
23. Frederick Rolfe to Marquess Ruvigny, Christchurch, [7 January 1892] (Martyr Worthy); cf. Rolfe, *Hadrian*, pp. 29, 382.
24. Frederick Rolfe, *The Desire and Pursuit of the Whole*, London, 1934, p. 33.
25. Rolfe, *Nicholas Crabbe*, p. 114.
26. In *Letters to Walsh*, pp. 15-16.
27. MacWilliam, p. 136; Rolfe, *Hadrian*, pp. 291-2
28. Rolfe to Walsh, Hampstead, 13 May 1903 in *Letters to Walsh*, pp. 10-11.
29. Symons, *Quest*, p. 76.
30. Cf. above, p. 30; Coulton, p. 89, *n* 7.
31. Symons, *Quest*, p. 71.
32. Rolfe to Walsh, Hampstead, 13 March 1903 in *Letters to Walsh*, p. 10; Woolf and Sewell, 'Clerk Without a Benefice', p. 40.
33. Rolfe, *Hadrian*, p. 29; cf. above, p. 16.
34. Harry Luke, *Cities and Men*, 3 vols., London, 1953, I, 116; Frederick Rolfe, *The Weird of the Wanderer . . . By Prospero and Caliban*, London, 1912, p. 20.
35. Frederick Rolfe, 'About Doing Little Lavishly', in *In His Own Image*, London, 1901, p. 145. Cf. Rolfe, *Desire and Pursuit*, p. 33; Rolfe, *Hadrian*, p. 29.
36. Frederick Rolfe, 'About our Lady of Dreams', in *In His Own Image*, pp. 273-4.

[viii]

1. Frederick Rolfe, 'How I was Buried Alive', in *World Wide Magazine*, November 1898, p. [139].
2. Cf. MacWilliam, p. 129 and *n* 13; Symons, *Quest*, p. 57.
3. Symons, *Quest*, p. 73.
4. Cf. Weeks, p. 55; Frederick Rolfe to Henry Newbolt, London, 26 September 1903 (Texas).
5. MacWilliam, p. 134.
6. MacWilliam, p. 130. Cf. Weeks, pp. 53, 43-4.
7. Rolfe, *Desire and Pursuit*, p. 33. Cf. above, p. 22; Symons, *Quest*, p. 66.

8. Duchess Caroline Sforza-Cesarini to C. C. Gardner, Rome, 2 February [1892] (Bodleian).
9. Rolfe, 'How I Was Buried Alive', p. [139].
10. Rolfe, 'About Doing Little Lavishly', in *In His Own Image*, p. 161.
11. Rolfe, *Don Renato*, p. 28.
12. Rolfe, 'About These Tales, The Key and Purgatory', in *In His Own Image*, p. 207.
13. Rolfe, 'How I Was Buried Alive', p. [139].
14. Rolfe, 'About Doing Little Lavishly', in *In His Own Image*, p. 146.
15. Rolfe, 'About Doing Little Lavishly', in *In His Own Image*, p. 146.
16. Rolfe, 'About These Tales, The Key and Purgatory', in *In His Own Image*, p. 207.
17. Rolfe, 'How I Was Buried Alive', p. [139]. By Lago San Giorgio, Rolfe meant Lake Nemi.
18. Frederick Rolfe, *Don Tarquinio A Kataleptic Phantasmatic Romance*, London, 1905.
19. Cf. Baron Corvo, 'Stories Toto Told Me. I—About San Pietro and San Paolo', and 'Stories Toto Told Me. II—About the Lillies of San Luigi', in *The Yellow Book*, October 1895, pp. 209–24.
20. Rolfe, 'How I was Buried Alive', p. 144.
21. Kains Jackson, 'Points for Bartholomew' (Texas); cf. Rolfe, *Nicholas Crabbe*, pp. 13–14.
22. Rolfe, 'About Doing Little Lavishly', in *In His Own Image*, p. 146.
23. Duchess Caroline Sforza-Cesarini to C. C. Gardner, Rome, 2 February 1892 (Bodleian).

PART II

[i]

1. 'Baron Corvo More "Wide World" Adventures of a Nobleman from Aberdeen', *The Daily Free Press* [Aberdeen], 8 November 1898; Rolfe, 'How I Was Buried Alive', p. 146. Cf. above, p. 42.
2. Nancy Gleeson White to Charles Kains Jackson, [Christchurch, 1891] (Berg).
3. Cf. Weeks, p. 60.
4. Cf. Rolfe, *Hadrian*, p. 393; Weeks, p. 74.
5. Cf. Leonard Moore, 'Epilogue', in Frederick Rolfe, *Letters to Leonard Moore*, eds. Cecil Woolf and Rabbi Bertram W. Korn, London, 1960, p. 73; Weeks, p. 74.
6. Pp. 391–2, 393.
7. Nancy Gleeson White to A. J. A. Symons, London, 3 October 1933 (Weeks).
8. Cf. Nancy Gleeson White to Charles Kains Jackson, Christchurch, n.d. (Berg).
9. Pp. 139–46; cf. above, p. 31.
10. Cf. MS. in the Walpole Collection (Bodleian).
11. (Bodleian).
12. (Bodleian).
13. (Bodleian).
14. *The Pall Mall Magazine*, May 1906, pp. 575–76.
15. Frederick Rolfe to Charles Kains Jackson, Christchurch, 8 December 1891 (Martyr Worthy); Weeks, p. 64.
16. (Berg).
17. Weeks, p. 70.
18. Cf. Nancy Gleeson White to Kains Jackson, [Christchurch], n.d. (Berg).
19. Cf. *The Studio*, 15 July and 15 June 1893.
20. Kains Jackson, 'Points for Bartholomew' (Texas).
21. Weeks, p. 69.
22. Weeks, p. 70.
23. The painting is the property of Donald Weeks.
24. Weeks, p. 65.
25. Rolfe to Kains Jackson, Christchurch, 25 June 1891 (Weeks) and 8 December 1891 (Berg).

26. Nancy Bell (N. D'Anvers), *The Tourist's Art Guide to Europe*, London, 1893. Cf. Nancy Gleeson White to Kains Jackson, Christchurch, n.d. and Saturday Morning (Berg).
27. Rolfe, *Hadrian*, p. 394; cf. Rolfe to Walsh, Hampstead, 13 March 1903 in *Letters to Walsh*, p. 11.
28. According to Mrs. Gleeson White, her husband had left Christchurch as early as mid-September 1890. Cf. Nancy Gleeson White to Kains Jackson, Christchurch, Monday, 31 August [1891] (Berg).
29. Cf. Maria Tuke Sainsbury, *Henry Scott Tuke*, London, 1933, pp. 90–1.
30. Rolfe to Kains Jackson, Christchurch, 8 December 1891 (Berg).
31. Nancy Gleeson White to Symons, 3 October 1933 (Weeks).
32. Cf. Duchess Caroline Sforza-Cesarini to C. C. Gardner, Rome, 2 February [1892] (Bodleian); a letter from Nancy Gleeson White printed in 'Baron Corvo . . . A Nobleman from Aberdeen', *The Daily Free Press* (Aberdeen), 8 November 1898.
33. Cf. Weeks, pp. 74–5.
34. Duchess Caroline Sforza-Cesarini to C. C. Gardner, Rome, 2 February [1898] (Bodleian).
35. Cf. Weeks, pp. 63, 72 *et passim*; above, p. 42.
36. Rolfe, *Hadrian*, p. 52.
37. Frederick Baron Corvo, *Letters to Grant Richards* [Hurst, Reading, Berkshire], 1952, p. 1.
38. Nancy Gleeson White to Kains Jackson, Christchurch, 31 August [1891] (Berg).
39. Cf. Weeks, p. 73; Nancy Gleeson White to Kains Jackson, Christchurch, n.d. (Berg).
40. Nancy Gleeson White to Symons, London, 3 October 1933 (Weeks).
41. Cf. Nancy Gleeson White to Kains Jackson, Christchurch, n.d. (Saturday Morning) and n.d. (Thursday Morning) (Berg).
42. Cf. Weeks, pp. 72–3.
43. (Berg).
44. Rolfe, *Hadrian*, p. 393.
45. (Martyr Worthy).
46. Cf. Nancy Gleeson White to Kains Jackson, Christchurch, n.d. (Thursday Morning) (Berg).
47. Daly was not the licensee of the Red Lion Public House; Thomas Preece may have been.
48. Nancy Gleeson White to Kains Jackson, Christchurch, n.d. (Berg).
49. Nancy Gleeson White to Kains Jackson, Christchurch, n.d. (Berg).
50. Nancy Gleeson White to Kains Jackson, Christchurch, n.d. (Thursday Morning) (Berg).
51. Nancy Gleeson White to Kains Jackson, Christchurch, n.d. (Saturday Morning) Berg).
52. Cf. Duchess Caroline Sforza-Cesarini to C. C. Gardner, Rome, 2 February [1892] (Bodleian).
53. Nancy Gleeson White to Kains Jackson, Christchurch, n.d. (Saturday Morning) (Berg).
54. Nancy Gleeson White to Kains Jackson, Christchurch, n.d. (Berg). Cf. Frederick Rolfe to John Lane, Holywell, 29 November 1897 in Frederick William Rolfe Baron Corvo, *Without Prejudice One Hundred Letters to John Lane*, ed. Cecil Woolf, London, 1963, p. 28.

[ii]

1. Cf. Rolfe, *Hadrian*, p. 30.
2. Rolfe, *Hadrian*, pp. 29–30.
3. Rolfe, *Hadrian*, pp. 395, 394.

4. John Gambril Nicholson to Charles Kains Jackson, Rydal Mount, Colwyn Bay, 8 April 1892 (Martyr Worthy); cf. John Gambril Nicholson to J. W. Gleeson White, Brighton, 16 April 1892 (Berg).
5. Cf. Nicholson to Kains Jackson, Brighton, 16 April 1892 (Berg); Rydal Mount, Colwyn Bay, 8 April 1892 (Martyr Worthy); Nicholson to Gleeson White, Brighton, 16 April 1892 (Berg).
6. London, 1872.
7. Cf. Frederick Rolfe to W. T. Stead, London, 28 and 25 April 1892 in ' "Baron Corvo" and Mr. W. T. Stead', *The Daily Free Pesss* (Aberdeen), 26 November 1898, p. 4, cols. 6–7.
8. Cf. Weeks, p. 95; below, pp. 64–5.
9. O'Sullivan, p. 16; Moore, 'Epilogue' in *Letters to Moore*, p. 72.
10. Cf. Rolfe, *Hadrian*, p. 385.

(iii)

1. Cf. Weeks, pp. 88–9; 'Baron Corvo. More "Wide World" Adventures. A Nobleman from Aberdeen.' *The Daily Free Press* (Aberdeen), 8 November 1898, p. 5, cols. 1–3; R. F. Bandeen to Donald Weeks, Steichen, Aberdeenshire, 8 June 1968.
2. Hunter-Blair, p. 626.
3. Personal interview with Mrs. Irene Roth. When Malcolm Hay learned from Mrs. Roth that David Roth, her brother-in-law., collected Rolfe's MSS, books, and memorabilia, he promptly ordered the tree cut down and the carving removed; he sent it to Mr. Roth. It is now part of the Martyr Worthy Collection.
4. Cf. Weeks, pp. 90–1.
5. 'Baron Corvo', in *The Daily Free Press* (Aberdeen), 8 November 1898, p. 5; cf. Rolfe, *Hadrian*, p. 382.
6. Cf. Rolfe, 'An Unforgettable Experience', p. 324.
7. Frederick Rolfe to Mrs. Edward Pirie-Gordon, Crickhowell, 4 January 1908 in *Letters to Pirie-Gordon*, p. 76.

[iv]

1. Cf. 'Baron Corvo', in *The Daily Free Press* (Aberdeen), 8 November 1898, p. 5; Rolfe, *Hadrian*, p. 385.
2. 'Baron Corvo', in *The Daily Free Press* (Aberdeen), 8 November 1898, p. 5. Cf. Weeks, p. 91.
3. 'Baron Corvo. His Further Adventures in Aberdeen. The Baron and Mr. H. H. Champion', in *The Daily Free Press* (Aberdeen), 12 November, p. 5, cols. 1–3.
4. Cf. 'The Nude in Photography: With Some Studies Taken in the Open Air', *The Studio*, June 1893, pp. 104–8.
5. Cf. 'The Camera and Art', *The Studio*, July 1893, pp. 157–8.
6. 'Baron Corvo,' in *The Daily Free Press* (Aberdeen), 12 November 1898, p. 5.
7. Cf. 'Baron Corvo', in *The Daily Free Press* (Aberdeen), 12 November 1898, p. 5.
8. Rolfe, *Don Renato*, p. 322; cf. 'Baron Corvo', in *The Daily Free Press* (Aberdeen), 12 November 1898, p. 5.
9. Weeks, p. 99. Cf. 'Baron Corvo,' in *The Daily Free Press* (Aberdeen), 12 November 1898, p. 5; Viola Meynell, *Francis Thompson and Wilfrid Meynell*, New York, 1953, p. 133.
10. Cf. Weeks, pp. 97–8. Viola Meynell states in *Francis Thompson and Wilfrid Meynell*, p. 134, 'Meynell introduced Rolfe to the owner of the *Aberdeen Free Press*, and he was offered a post as "reader", which however was not to his mind.' In 1892, *The Daily Free Press* of Aberdeen was the property of Henry and William Alexander.

11. Weeks, p. 99; cf. Rolfe, *Hadrian*, pp. 390–1.
12. 'Baron Corvo', *The Daily Free Press* (Aberdeen), 12 November 1898, p. 5.
13. Cf. Weeks, pp. 101, 94.
14. 12 November 1898, p. 5.
15. Cf. 'Baron Corvo', *The Daily Free Press* (Aberdeen), 12 November 1898, p. 5.
16. Rolfe, *Hadrian*, p. 80; cf. Weeks, pp. 103, 159.
17. Cf. Henry M. Pelling, 'H. H. Champion, Pioneer of Labour Representation', *Cambridge Journal,* January 1953, pp. 222–38; Henry M. Pelling, *The Origins of the Labour Party 1880–1900*, Oxford, 1965, pp. 105–6, 113 *et passim*; Henry M. Pelling, 'Corvo and Labour Politics', *Times Literary Supplement*, 6 February 1969, p. 137.
18. Cf. 'Baron Corvo', *The Daily Free Press* (Aberdeen), 8 November 1898, p. 5.
19. Cf. Pelling, 'Champion', *Cambridge Journal*, January 1953, pp. 222–3.
20. Cf. Frederick Rolfe to the Fabian Society, Oxford, 15 February 1906 in Doris Langley Moore, *E. Nesbit A Biography*, Philadelphia, 1966, p. 183; Pelling, 'Corvo and Labour Politics', *TLS*, 6 February 1969, p. 137; George Bernard Shaw, 'Fabian Notes. The Election', *Clarion*, 2 February 1906, p. 5.
21. Frederick Rolfe to Hubert Bland, Crickhowell, 25 March 1907 (Benkovitz). Cf. below, p. 187.
22. Rolfe, *Nicholas Crabbe*, p. 109.
23. *Towards Democracy* was published in 1883. Cf. below, p. 228.
24. Frederick Rolfe to R. London, 24 March 1894 (Weeks).
25. 9 December 1893, p. [1].
26. Cf. Cecil Woolf, *A Bibliography of Frederick Rolfe Baron Corvo*, London, 1972, p. 145 *n* 1.
27. Cf. Rolfe to R, London, 24 March 1894 (Weeks).

[v]

1. (Weeks). R made marginal comments rebutting some of Rolfe's statements on Rolfe's letter and sent it to Champion. It was found among his papers; cf. Pelling, 'Corvo and Labour Politics', *TLS*, 6 February 1969, p. 137.
2. Rolfe, *Hadrian*, p. 386.
3. Rolfe, *Hadrian*, p. 30.
4. Cf. Symons, *Quest*, p. 60.
5. Cf. Rolfe, *Hadrian*, p. 30.
6. Rolfe, *Don Renato*, p. 197.
7. Rolfe, *Hadrian*, pp. 386–7, 30.
8. John Blount, 'Temptation', *The Holywell Record*, June 1897, p. 18. For an account of John Blount, see below, p. 80.
9. Rolfe, *Hadrian*, p. 391.
10. Rolfe, *Hadrian*, p. 388.
11. Cf. above, pp. 57–8.
12. Rolfe, *Hadrian*, p. 388.

[vi]

1. Frederick Rolfe, 'About the Cheek of Fra Sebastiano', in *In His Own Image*, pp. 15, 16.
2. Cf. Frederick Rolfe to Father Charles Sidney de Vere Beauclerk, Holywell, 2 December 1898 (Martyr Worthy).
3. Cf. Weeks, p. 124.
4. Rolfe, 'About the Cheek of Fra Sebastiano', in *In His Own Image*, p. 17.
5. For contrary accounts, cf. Symons, *Quest*, pp. 80–1; Weeks, p. 124.
6. Rolfe, *Nicholas Crabbe*, p. 109.

7. Mrs. Victoria Morris to Father Charles Sidney de Vere Beauclerk, St. Clare's Cottage, Pantasaph, 10 September 1895 (Martyr Worthy). Cf. [Frederick Rolfe], 'The Saint, The Priest, The Nowt, The Devil', *The Holywell Record*, 31 August 1897, p. 17, where Rolfe describes the Nowt (himself) as having had 'no luggage, no change of clothes, and no effects' when he arrived at Sewer's End, by which Rolfe is usually assumed to have meant Holywell. It is more likely that by Sewers End, he referred to the two Welsh villages Holywell and Pantasaph and applied the name to the *milieu* in general.

8. According to Weeks (p. 126), Rolfe moved from Pantasaph to Holywell about 14 April 1895, Easter Sunday. In an unpublished piece called 'Excommunicated' (Martyr Worthy), Rolfe describes himself as a resident of Holywell since July 1895. In a letter to Mrs. Morris dated 5 September 1895 (Martyr Worthy), he complains that a toothbrush and some soap were taken from his room 'last Wednesday week', a statement which implies that he was still at Pantasaph or had not yet removed so intimate a part of his few effects as his toothbrush in August 1895. A letter which Rolfe wrote to his landlady at Holywell, Mrs. Agnes Richardson, on 19 May 1897 (Martyr Worthy) speaks of being turned out 'last Tuesday week' after being a 'paying lodger for 21 months'. Again, that statement places the commencement of his residence at Holywell in the early days of August 1895.

9. Mrs. Morris to Father Beauclerk, St. Clare's Cottage, Pantasaph, 10 September 1895 (Martyr Worthy).

10. Frederick Rolfe to Mrs. Victoria Morris, Holywell, 5 September 1895 (Martyr Worthy).

11. [Rolfe], *The Weird of the Wanderer*, London, 1912, p. 57.

12. Rolfe to Mrs. Morris, Holywell, 5 September 1895 (Martyr Worthy).

13. Mrs. Morris to Father Beauclerk, Pantasaph, 10 September 1895 (Martyr Worthy).

14. 'Baron Corvo', *Daily Free Press* (Aberdeen), 12 November 1898, p. 5.

15. Frederick Rolfe, 'Excommunicated A Human Document' (Martyr Worthy).

16. Rolfe to Father Beauclerk, Holywell, n.p., 27 March 1905 (Martyr Worthy).

17. Cf. Frederick Rolfe, *The Attack on St. Winefride's Well Or Holywell Gone Mad*, Holywell, 1898, p. 2.

18. Rolfe, *Hubert's Arthur*, p. 15.

[vii]

1. Rolfe, 'The Saint, The Priest, The Nowt, The Devil', *The Holywell Record*, 31 August 1897, p. 18.

2. Rolfe to Mrs. Morris, Holywell, 5 September 1895 (Martyr Worthy).

3. Mrs. Morris to Father Beauclerk, Pantasaph, 10 September 1895 (Martyr Worthy).

4. Pp. 209–21.

5. 'The Princess's Shirts', *The Pall Mall Magazine*, May 1906, pp. 575–6.

6. Cf. Rolfe to R, London, 24 March 1894 (Weeks).

7. Frederick Rolfe to Frederic Chapman, Holywell, 27 August 1898 in *Without Prejudice*, p. 43.

8. London, 1898.

9. 'About What is Due to Repentance', pp. 276–75.

10. Cf. above, pp. 73–4.

11. Cf. above, pp. 40–2.

12. Rolfe, 'About the Fantastical Fra Guilhelmo . . .', 'Why the Rose is Red', 'About Our Lady of Dreams', 'About Beata Beatrice and the Mamma of Sampietro', in *In His Own Image*, pp. 3, 69, 276, 381–2.

13. Rolfe to Lane, Holywell, 16 March 1898 in *Without Prejudice*, p. 32.

14. John Holden to A. J. A. Symons, Antwerp, 14 July 1933 (Martyr Worthy).
15. Rolfe to Chapman, Holywell, 27 August 1898 in *Without Prejudice*, p. 43.
16. Holden to Symons, Antwerp, [July 1933] (Martyr Worthy).
17. Symons, *Quest*, p. 86.
18. Cf. Symons, *Quest*, pp. 86–7.
19. Holden to Symons, Antwerp, 27 July 1933 (Martyr Worthy).
20. Frederick Rolfe to Mrs. Tennant, Holywell, 13 and 27 July 1896 (Martyr Worthy).
21. Rolfe to Mrs. Tennant, Holywell, 10 July 1897; Mrs. Tennant to Rolfe, Holywell, 11 July 1897 (Martyr Worthy).
22. New York, pp. 61–[9].
23. Holden to Symons, Antwerp, [July 1933] (Martyr Worthy).
24. Holden to Symons, Antwerp, [July 1933] (Martyr Worthy).
25. Cf. Rolfe to Father Beauclerk, Holywell, 15 March 1896 (Martyr Worthy).
26. Rolfe to Father Beauclerk, Holywell, 15 March 1896 (Martyr Worthy).
27. Rolfe to Beauclerk, Holywell, 20 March [1896] (Martyr Worthy).
28. (Martyr Worthy).
29. Holden to Symons, Antwerp, [July 1933] (Martyr Worthy).
30. (Martyr Worthy).
31. 'The Saint, The Priest, The Nowt, The Devil', *The Holywell Record*, 31 August 1897, p. 17.
32. Symons, *Quest*, p. 82.
33. Holden to Symons, Antwerp, [July 1933] (Martyr Worthy).
34. Symons, *Quest*, p. 82.
35. Holden to Symons, Antwerp, 27 July [1933] (Martyr Worthy).
36. Holden to Symons, Antwerp, July 1933 (Martyr Worthy). Cf. Symons, *Quest*, pp. 84, 86.
37. Holden to Symons, Antwerp, 14 and 21 July 1933 (Martyr Worthy); Symons, *Quest*, p. 90.
38. Holden to Symons, Antwerp, [July 1933] (Martyr Worthy).
39. Rolfe, *Hadrian*, p. 51; cf. above, p. 8.
40. 'Stories Toto Told Me. III—A Caprice of the Cherubim'; 'Stories Toto Told Me. IV—About Beata Beatrice and the Mamma of San Pietro', *The Yellow Book*, April 1896, pp. 86–101.
41. Rolfe to Lane, [Holywell], 21 June and 10 July 1896 in *Without Prejudice*, p. 23.
42. Cf. *The Holywell Record*, July 1896, p. 24 *et passim*.
43. Symons, *Quest*, p. 93.
44. Frederick Rolfe to Father Joseph Flynn, Holywell, 9 April 1897; cf. Frederick Rolfe to N. J. Hanmer, Holywell, 29 July 1897 (Martyr Worthy).
45. Frank W. Hocheimer to Father Charles Sidney de Vere Beauclerk, Holywell, 13 June 1897 (Martyr Worthy).
46. Frank W. Hocheimer to The Reverend Father General, Holywell, 12 August 1897 (Martyr Worthy).
47. Rolfe to Mrs. Richardson, Holywell, 19 May 1897 (Martyr Worthy).
48. *The Holywell Record*, March 1897, pp. 8–14; April 1897, pp. 6–13; cf. May 1897, pp. 6–11; 22 June 1897, pp. 9–12; 31 July 1897, pp. 5–8; 31 August 1897, pp. 8–11; October 1897, pp. 9–11.
49. *The Holywell Record*, March 1897, pp. 20–2.
50. *The Holywell Record*, March 1897, pp. 18–20; April 1897, pp. 15–19; November 1896, pp. 15, 1–7.
51. (Martyr Worthy).
52. Rolfe to Mrs. Richardson, Holywell, 16 May 1897 (Martyr Worthy).
53. Rolfe to Father Beauclerk, Holywell, 4 June 1897. Cf. Rolfe to Hanmer, Holywell, 29 July 1897; Rolfe to Father Beauclerk, Holywell, 10 June, 10 July 1897 *et passim*; Hocheimer to Father Beauclerk, Holywell, 16 August 1897 *et passim* (Martyr Worthy).

298

54. Cf. Rolfe to Mrs. Richardson, Holywell, 26 May 1897; Augustine Watts to Father Charles Sidney de Vere Beauclerk, Liverpool, 29 May 1897; Rolfe, 'Excommunicated' (Martyr Worthy).
55. Cf. Rolfe to Mrs. Richardson, Holywell, 19 May 1897; Holden to Symons, Antwerp, 14 July 1933; Mrs. Agnes Richardson to Father Charles Sidney de Vere Beauclerk, Holywell, 13 July 1897 (Martyr Worthy).
56. Rolfe to Mrs. Richardson, Holywell, 19 May 1897 (Martyr Worthy).
57. Cf. Symons, Quest, p. 93; above, p. 86.
58. Cf. Holden to Symons, Antwerp, July 1933; Rolfe to Mrs. Richardson, Holywell, 26 May 1897; Rolfe to Father Beauclerk, Holywell, 12 June 1897 (Martyr Worthy).
59. Cf. Rolfe to Beauclerk, Holywell, 4 June and 10 July 1897 (Martyr Worthy).
60. Rolfe to Mrs. Richardson, Holywell, 19 May 1897, cf. Rolfe to Mrs. Richardson, Holywell, 16 May 1897 (Martyr Worthy).
61. Cf. Rolfe to Mrs. Richardson, Holywell, 26 May 1897; Frank W. Hocheimer to F. Llewellyn Jones, Holywell, 19 July 1897; Rolfe to Father Beauclerk, Holywell, 24 August 1897 (Martyr Worthy); above, pp. 80–1.
62. Cf. Frederick Rolfe to Thomas Corrigan, Holywell, 18, 21 and 27 June 1897, 1 and 3 July 1897; Frank Hocheimer to Mrs. Thomas Corrigan, Holywell, 10 June 1897 (Martyr Worthy).
63. Cf. Frank W. Hocheimer to C. W. Bell, Holywell, 5 July 1897; Frederick Rolfe to C. W. Bell, Holywell, 5 May 1898 (Martyr Worthy).
64. Hocheimer to Father Beauclerk, Holywell, 13 June 1897 (Martyr Worthy).
65. (Martyr Worthy).
66. Cf. Rolfe to Father Flynn, Holywell, 21 June 1897 (Martyr Worthy); Rolfe to Lane, Holywell, 25 November 1897 in Without Prejudice, p. 27.
67. Rolfe, 'Excommunicated' (Martyr Worthy).
68. (Martyr Worthy).
69. Rolfe to Mrs. Richardson, Holywell, 16 May 1897 (Martyr Worthy).
70. Rolfe to Lane, [Holywell], 25 June 1897 in Without Prejudice, p. 25.
71. Cf. Rolfe, 'Excommunicated' (Martyr Worthy); [Frederick Rolfe], 'Answers to Correspondents', The Holywell Record, October 1897, p. 25.

[viii]

1. Rolfe to Mrs. Richardson, Holywell, 26 May 1897; Rolfe to Father Beauclerk, Holywell, 7 October 1898 (Martyr Worthy).
2. In Without Prejudice, p. 29.
3. Rolfe, 'Excommunicated' (Martyr Worthy).
4. 12 August 1897 (Martyr Worthy); cf. above, p. 87.
5. Rolfe, 'Excommunicated' (Martyr Worthy).
6. Rolfe, 'Excommunicated' (Martyr Worthy).
7. In Without Prejudice, pp. 27–9.
8. 'Baron Corvo', Daily Free Press (Aberdeen), 12 November 1898, p. 5.
9. Hocheimer to Father Beauclerk, Holywell, 4 December 1897 (Martyr Worthy).
10. Cf. Rolfe to Father Beauclerk, Hampstead, 19 April 1903, and n.p., 27 March 1905 (Martyr Worthy).
11. Rolfe to Father Beauclerk, Holywell, 3 January 1898 (Martyr Worthy).
12. Rolfe to Father Beauclerk, Holywell, 3 January 1898 (Martyr Worthy).
13. Cf. Rolfe to Father Beauclerk, [Holywell], n.d. and Holywell, 31 March 1893 (Martyr Worthy).
14. Cf. Rolfe to Hanmer, Holywell, 29 July 1897 (Martyr Worthy).
15. Cf. Rolfe to Lane, Holywell, 4 June 1898 in Without Prejudice, p. 38; cf. Rolfe, 'Excommunicated' (Martyr Worthy).
16. (Martyr Worthy); cf. Rolfe, 'Excommunicated' (Martyr Worthy). When The Holywell Record ceased publication is uncertain; Hocheimer's letter implies its

existence in June 1898. The British Museum's file of the paper ends with the issue of October 1897 (it lacks September), and no other file of the paper is known.

17. Rolfe to Father Beauclerk, Holywell, 19 June 1898; Rolfe to Father Beauclerk, Holywell, 25 July 1898 (Martyr Worthy).

[ix]

1. Cf. Rolfe to Father Beauclerk, Holywell, 17 May 1898 (Martyr Worthy); Rolfe to Chapman, Holywell, 18 and 29 May 1898 and 16 July 1898 in *Without Prejudice*, pp. 36–7, 41; Rolfe to Lane, Holywell, 13 February 1898 in *Without Prejudice*, p. 31.
2. In *Without Prejudice*, p. 39.
3. Rolfe to Father Beauclerk, Holywell, 10 December 1898 (Martyr Worthy).
4. Rolfe to Father Beauclerk, Holywell, 2 and 10 December 1898 (Martyr Worthy).
5. Cf. Frederick Rolfe to Edward Slaughter, Holywell, [1 September 1897] in *Without Prejudice*, p. 28; Rolfe to Lane, Holywell, 9 February [1898] in *Without Prejudice*, p. 31. The colophon for *Stories Toto Told Me*, London, 1898, runs in part: 'Thus endeth the sixth of the nine and forty Stories Toto Told Me . . .'
6. Rolfe to Chapman, Holywell, 16 July 1898 in *Without Prejudice*, p. 41.
7. Cf. Rolfe to Lane, Holywell, 24 June 1898; Rolfe to Chapman, Holywell, 16 July 1898 in *Without Prejudice*, pp. 39, 41.
8. Cf. Rolfe to Slaughter, Holywell, [1 September 1897] in *Without Prejudice*, p. 29.
9. Frederick Rolfe to G. T. Maquay, Hampstead, 27 May 1903 (Berg).
10. April, pp. 15–19; May, pp. 12–14; June 22, pp. 15–17.
11. Cf. Symons, *Quest*, pp. 91–2.
12. In *Without Prejudice*, p. 38.
13. In *Without Prejudice*, p. 45.
14. 'Baron Corvo', *The Daily Free Press* (Aberdeen), 8 November 1898, p. 5. Cf. Louis de Rougement, 'The Adventures of', *The Wide World Magazine*, August 1898, pp. [451]–75. The serial continued.
15. Cf. 'Baron Corvo . . .', *To-Day*, 26 November 1898.
16. Cf. Rolfe to Father Beauclerk, Holywell, 10 December 1898 (Martyr Worthy).
17. Rolfe to Father Beauclerk, Holywell, 10 December 1898 (Martyr Worthy).
18. Rolfe, *Hadrian*, p. 305. Cf. Weeks, pp. 161–9; d'Arch-Smith, p. 71.
19. P. 305. Cf. Weeks, p. 163.
20. In *Without Prejudice*, p. 28.
21. Rolfe to Father Beauclerk, Holywell, 10 December 1890 (Martyr Worthy).
22. Rolfe to Father Beauclerk, Holywell, 2 December 1898: Cf. Rolfe to Father Beauclerk, Holywell, 25 July, 6 and 17 August, 9 and 24 September, 7 October and 4 November 1898 (Martyr Worthy).
23. Rolfe to Father Beauclerk, Holywell, 10 December 1898 (Martyr Worthy).
24. Cf. Rolfe to Father Beauclerk, n.p., 1 March 1905 (Martyr Worthy); 'Baron Corvo', *The Catholic Times and Catholic Opinion*, 16 December 1898, p. 9, col. 7.
25. Rolfe to Father Beauclerk, Holywell, 17 December 1898 (Martyr Worthy); Rolfe to Grant Richards, Hampstead, 6 March 1901 in Symons, *Quest*, p. 120.
26. Cf. Rolfe to Father Beauclerk, Holywell, 16 December 1898 (Martyr Worthy).
27. Cf. Weeks, pp. 146–8; Rolfe to Father Beauclerk, 19 April 1903 (Martyr Worthy); above, p. 90.
28. Frederick Rolfe to W. E. Scott-Hall, Holywell, 23 December 1898 (Texas).
29. Holden to Symons, Antwerp, [July 1933] (Martyr Worthy).
30. Rolfe to Father Beauclerk, Holywell, 19 April 1903 (Martyr Worthy).
31. Rolfe, *Nicholas Crabbe*, p. 30.

[x]

1. Cf. Rolfe, *Nicholas Crabbe*, p. 31.
2. Rolfe, *Hadrian*, p. 22.
3. Rolfe to Father Beauclerk, n.p., 27 March 1905 (Martyr Worthy). Cf. Rolfe to Walsh, Hampstead, 29 June 1903 in *Letters to Walsh*, p. 19.
4. Rolfe to Father Beauclerk, n.p., 1 March 1905 (Matryr Worthy).
5. Rolfe to Father Beauclerk, n.p., 19 February 1905 (Martyr Worthy).
6. Frederick Rolfe to Charlotte Handley, Poundstock, Bude, 20 March 1908 in *Frederick Rolfe, Letters to C. H. C. Pirie-Gordon*, ed. Cecil Woolf, London, 1959, p. 85; cf. Rolfe, *Hadrian*, p. 12.
7. Rolfe, *Nicholas Crabbe*, p. 52.

PART III

[i]

1. Rolfe, *Nicholas Crabbe*, p. 4; cf. Rolfe, *Hadrian*, pp. 1, 8–10.
2. Rolfe, *Hadrian*, p. 8.
3. Cf. H. C. Bainbridge, *Twice Seven*, London, 1933, pp. 76, 78; Rolfe to H. C. Bainbridge, [London], n.d.; 19 September 1899; Feast of Saint Partridge 1899 (Martyr Worthy); below, p. 112.
4. Cf. *Without Prejudice*, p. 110 *nn*. 60–1.
5. Rolfe to Grant Richards, London, April 1899 (Martyr Worthy).
6. Cf. Ella d'Arcy, 'Yellow Book Celebrities', unpublished MS., 6 pp. (Martyr Worthy); Rolfe, *Nicholas Crabbe*, p. 31.
7. Cf. Woolf, 'Epilogue', in *Without Prejudice*, p. 91.
8. Rolfe, *Nicholas Crabbe*, p. 16.
9. Rolfe, *Nicholas Crabbe*, p. 16. Cf. Rolfe to Richards, AN, [London], 13 March 1899 (Martyr Worthy).
10. P. 23. Cf. Rolfe to Lane, Holywell, 11 October, 9 February, 13 and 18 May, 24 June 1898 in *Without Prejudice*, pp. 44, 31, 36–7, 39.
11. Rolfe, *Nicholas Crabbe*, p. 23.
12. Rolfe, *Nicholas Crabbe*, pp. 25–6; Lane to Bartholomew, Cambridge, n.d. (Texas).
13. Rolfe, *Nicholas Crabbe*, p. 27.
14. Rolfe, *Nicholas Crabbe*, pp. 58, 34, 35.
15. Alfred Douglas to A. J. A. Symons, Hove, 11 February 1934 (Texas).
16. Rolfe, *Nicholas Crabbe*, pp. 37–8.
17. Rolfe to Richards, [London], 6 April 1899 in *Letters to Richards*, p. 1.
18. Cf. Rolfe to Lane, [London], 5 March 1899 in *Without Prejudice*, p. 46.
19. 2 April 1900, p. 5. Cf. Cecil Woolf, *A Bibliography of Frederick Rolfe Baron Corvo*, London, 1972, C77.1; Frederick Rolfe to Maurice Hewlett, London, 17 March 1902 (Royal Literary Fund); Rolfe to Lane, London, 19 June 1899 in *Without Prejudice*, p. 47; Rolfe, *Nicholas Crabbe*, p. 56.
20. Rolfe to Richards, [London], 7 April 1899 in *Letters to Richards*, p. 2.
21. Rolfe to Lane, [London], 19 June 1899 in *Without Prejudice*, p. 47.
22. Cf. Rolfe to Richards, London, April 1899 (Martyr Worthy).
23. Rolfe to Bainbridge, [London], 19 September 1899; n.d.; Feast of Saint Partridge [1899] (Martyr Worthy); cf. Bainbridge, *Twice Seven*, pp. 79–80.

[ii]

1. Rolfe to Richards, [London], 9 December 1899 in *Letters to Richards*, p. 3. Cf. Rolfe to Walsh, Hampstead, 13 March 1900 in *Letters to Walsh*, p. 11.
2. Cf. Rolfe to Richards, London, 20 November 1899, 16 May 1900 in *Letters to Richards*, pp. 2, 9.

301

3. Rolfe to Richards, London, 16 May 1900 in *Letters to Richards*, p. 9.
4. Cf. Rolfe to Richards, London, n.d., 27 February 1900 in *Letters to Richards*, pp. 2, 3.
5. Rolfe, *Hubert's Arthur*, p. 19.
6. Rolfe to Richards, London, 16 May 1900 in *Letters to Richards*, pp. 9–10.
7. Rolfe to Richards, Oxford, 25 July 1900 in *Letters to Richards*, p. 12.
8. d'Arcy, 'Yellow Book Celebrities' (Martyr Worthy).
9. Frederick Rolfe to Henry Newbolt, London, 25 September 1903 (Texas); cf. Rolfe, *Nicholas Crabbe*, p. 63, where Rolfe uses phrases identical with those in his letter to Newbolt.
10. Rolfe, *Nicholas Crabbe*, p. 212; cf. pp. 57, 60–2.
11. Cf. Rolfe, *Hadrian*, pp. 43, 151, 397.
12. Rolfe to Lane, [Hampstead], 15 January 1900 in *Without Prejudice*, p. 49.
13. Rolfe to Lane [Hampstead], 12 February 1900 (Texas).
14. Woolf, 'Introduction', in *Without Prejudice*, p. 17.
15. Cf. Rolfe to Richards, [Hampstead], 24 and 26 September, 19 October, 12 November 1900 *et passim* in *Letters to Richards*, pp. 17–19, 22–5.
16. In Symons, *Quest*, pp. 155–6.
17. *The Rubáiyát of 'Umar Khaiyam* translated from the French of J. B. Nicolas by Frederick Baron Corvo, London, 1924, pp. 2–3. Cf. Frederick Rolfe, alternate versions of stanzas 1–7 of *Rubáiyát of 'Umar Khaiyam*, holograph manuscript (Martyr Worthy).
18. Cf. Rolfe to Chapman, [Hampstead], 22 and 23 May 1900, in *Without Prejudice*, p. 50.
19. Frederick Rolfe to Temple Scott, [London], 4 May 1900, quoted in 'The Notes', in *Without Prejudice*, p. 108 *n.* 5.
20. Rolfe to Richards, Hampstead, 16 May 1900 in *Letters to Richards*, p. 10.
21. Rolfe to Chapman, Oxford, 12 July 1900 in *Without Prejudice*, p. 52.
22. Rolfe to Richards, Oxford, 19 July 1900 in *Letters to Richards*, p. 13.
23. Rolfe to Chapman, Oxford, 12 July 1900 in *Without Prejudice*, p. 52.
24. Cf. Rolfe to Richards, [Hampstead], 16 May 1900 in *Letters to Richards*, p. 10.
25. Rolfe to Richards, [Hampstead], 26 July 1900 in *Letters to Richards*, p. 15; cf. Rolfe to Chapman, [Hampstead], 23 May 1900 in *Without Prejudice*, p. 50.
26. Frederick Rolfe to Kenneth Grahame, [Hampstead], 21 December 1900; cf. Rolfe to Grahame, [Hampstead], 16 and 23 August, 15 September 1900 in *Baron Corvo to Kenneth Grahame*, [Hurst], 1962, pp. [7–8, 3–6].

[iii]

1. Rolfe to Walsh, Hampstead, 28 July in *Letters to Walsh*, p. 26.
2. Rolfe to Richards, [Hampstead], 24 September 1900 in *Letters to Richards*, p. 18.
3. Rolfe to Richards, [Hampstead], 26 September 1900 in *Letters to Richards*, pp. 19–20.
4. Rolfe to Richards, [Hampstead], 23 April 1901; cf. Rolfe to Richards, [Hampstead], 12 November, 19 and 27 October 1900; 30 March, 11 April 1901 in *Letters to Richards*, pp. 22, 24, 25, 33, 34, 38.
5. Rolfe to Richards, [Hampstead], 4 December 1900 in *Letters to Richards*, pp. 27–8.
6. Cf. Hunter Blair, 'More Light on Baron Corvo', *The London Mercury*, May 1934, pp. 626–7.
7. Cf. above, p. 118.
8. Rolfe to Richards, [Hampstead], 23 [two postcards] and 26 October 1901 in *Letters to Richards*, pp. 40–1.
9. In *Letters to Richards*, p. 46.
10. Rolfe, *Nicholas Crabbe*, p. 143. Cf. Rolfe to Richards, Oxford, 18 July 1900; [Hampstead], 13 August, 10 October, 4 December 1900 in *Letters to Richards*, pp. 14, 15, 20, 27.

11. Rolfe to Bainbridge, [Hampstead], 11 November 1901 (Martyr Worthy).
12. In *Letters to Richards*, pp. 29–31.
13. Rolfe to Lane, [Hampstead], 1 November 1900. Cf. Rolfe to Lane, [Hampstead], 15 January, 27 February, 12 July, 25 October, and 21 December 1900 in *Without Prejudice*, pp. 54, 49, 51–3; Rolfe to Walsh, London, 6 July 1903 in *Letters to Walsh*, p. 20.
14. Cf. Rolfe, *Nicholas Crabbe*, pp. 119–21; Frederick Rolfe to Arthur Stedman, Oxford, 4 June 1901 (Columbia University Libraries).
15. In Symons, *Quest*, p. 158.
16. Rolfe, *Desire and Pursuit*, p. 13; Rolfe, *Hadrian*, p. 11; cf. pp. 15, 12.
17. I Samuel, xvi, 12; cf. Holden to Symons, Antwerp, [July 1933].
18. Rolfe, *Desire and Pursuit*, p. 9; Rolfe, *Nicholas Crabbe*, p. 18.
19. Frederick Rolfe to Masson-Fox, Venice, 11 December 1909 (Texas).
20. Rolfe, *Nicholas Crabbe*, p. 163.
21. Rolfe, *Nicholas Crabbe*, p. 163; cf. Symons, *Quest*, p. 138.
22. In Symons, *Quest*, p. 139; Rolfe, *Nicholas Crabbe*, p. 164.
23. Symons, *Quest*, pp. 140–1; Rolfe, *Nicholas Crabbe*, pp. 164–5.
24. Cf. Symons, *Quest*, p. 141; Rolfe, *Nicholas Crabbe*, p. 165; Rolfe, *Desire and Pursuit*, p. 14.
25. Symons, *Quest*, p. 142.
26. Rolfe, *Don Renato*, p. 15.
27. Rolfe, *Nicholas Crabbe*, p. 60.
28. Rolfe, *Don Renato*, p. 24.
29. Symons, *Quest*, p. 142.
30. Cf. Holden to Symons, [Antwerp], July 1933 (Martyr Worthy); Woolf, *Bibliography*, p. 155; Rolfe, *Nicholas Crabbe*, p. 158.
31. Cf. Rolfe to Lane, Hampstead, 10 April 1902 in *Without Prejudice*, p. 62; Rolfe to Richards, Hampstead, 10 January 1902 in *Letters to Richards*, p. 43.
32. Symons, *Quest*, p. 143. Cf. pp. 139–42; Rolfe, *Nicholas Crabbe*, pp. 166–93.
33. Rolfe, *Nicholas Crabbe*, p. 193.
34. Cf. Rolfe to Lane, Hampstead, 8 and 16 February 1903 in *Without Prejudice*, pp. 79, 81.
35. Sholto Douglas to Frederick Rolfe, Southsea, Hants, 10 March 1902 in 'A Selection of Sholto Douglas's Letters to Fr. Rolfe', *Nicholas Crabbe . . . by Fr. Rolfe*, London, p. 253.
36. (Bodleian).
37. In 'A Selection . . .', *Nicholas Crabbe*, p. 257.
38. Symons, *Quest*, p. 146. Cf. Cecil Woolf, 'A Selection of Sholto Douglas's Letters to Fr. Rolfe', in *Nicholas Crabbe* by Fr. Rolfe, London, 1960, p. 252; Douglas to Rolfe, Southsea, 21 March [1902] in 'A Selection . . .', *Nicholas Crabbe*, p. 255.
39. Douglas to Rolfe, Southsea, [May 1902] in 'A Selection . . .', *Nicholas Crabbe*, p. 259. Cf. Rolfe to Lane, Hampstead, 17 April 1902 in *Without Prejudice*, p. 64.
40. Douglas to Rolfe, Southsea, 12 May [1902] in 'A Selection . . .', *Nicholas Crabbe*, p. 259.
41. Rolfe to Lane, Hampstead, 20 May 1902 in *Without Prejudice*, p. 66. Cf. Douglas to Rolfe, Southsea, 19 and 21 May 1902, 9 June [1902] in 'A Selection . . .', *Nicholas Crabbe*, pp. 262, 263, 266.
42. Rolfe, *Nicholas Crabbe*, p. 225. The Bodleian has seven 'Reviews' in Douglas's hand; nine were published of which the MS for one, 'Plato's "Dialogue on the Music of Wagner",' is included in the count of those at the Bodleian.
43. Rolfe, *Nicholas Crabbe*, pp. 218–19.
44. Douglas to Rolfe, Southsea, 5 June 1902 in 'A Selection . . .', *Nicholas Crabbe*, p. 265.
45. Rolfe, *Hadrian*, p. 106.
46. Douglas to Rolfe, Southsea, 5 June [1902] in 'A Selection . . .', *Nicholas Crabbe*, pp. 265–66; cf. Rolfe, *Hadrian*, p. 165.

47. Douglas to Rolfe, n.p., n.d.; Southsea, [August], 27 July, 22 and 24 June [1902] in 'A Selection . . .', *Nicholas Crabbe*, pp. 267, 269. 270, 271–2,
48. Cf. below, p. 145; Rolfe to Pinker, Hampstead, 17 and 20 January, 18 February 1903 (Texas); Rolfe, *Nicholas Crabbe*, p. [246].
49. Rolfe to Walsh, Hampstead, 7 July 1903 in *Letters to Walsh*, p. 20.

[iv]

1. Rolfe to Pinker, Hampstead, 18 February 1903 (Texas).
2. Rolfe, *Nicholas Crabbe*, pp. 124–5.
3. Rolfe, *Nicholas Crabbe*, p. 127.
4. Symons, *Quest*, p. 157.
5. Cf. Rolfe, *Nicholas Crabbe*, pp. 144–50.
6. Cf. Rolfe, *Nicholas Crabbe*, pp. 153–5.
7. Rolfe, *Don Renato*, pp. 20–1. Cf. above, pp. 125–6.
8. Rolfe, *Don Renato*, p. 25; cf. pp. 21, 13–14.
9. Rolfe to Lane, Hampstead, 9 April 1902 in *Without Prejudice*, pp. 61–2; Rolfe, *Nicholas Crabbe*, p. 212.
10. Rolfe to Lane, Hampstead, 9 April 1902 in *Without Prejudice*, pp. 61–2; Rolfe to Lane, Hampstead, 31 January 1902 (Harvard).
11. In *Without Prejudice*, p. 64.
12. Rolfe to Lane, Hampstead, 28 May 1902 in *Without Prejudice*, p. 66.
13. Cf. Rolfe, *Nicholas Crabbe*, pp. 211, 215; below, p. 138.
14. Rolfe to Lane, Hampstead, 28 May 1902 in *Without Prejudice*, p. 67; cf. Rolfe, *Nicholas Crabbe*, p. 216.
15. Rolfe to Lane, Hampstead, 2 December 1902; cf. Rolfe to Lane, Hampstead, 28 November 1902 in *Without Prejudice*, pp. 70, 68–9.
16. Cf. Rolfe to Lane, Oxford, 20 December 1902; Hampstead, 23 and 27 December 1902 in *Without Prejudice*, pp. 72–3.
17. Rolfe to Lane, Hampstead, 23 January, 1 and 8 February 1902 in *Without Prejudice*, pp. 76–7, 78, 80.
18. Cf. Frederick Rolfe, Application to Royal Literary Fund, 23 March 1902 (Royal Fund).
19. Rolfe, Application to Royal Literary Fund, 23 March 1902; Frederick Rolfe to Maurice Hewlett, Hampstead, 17 March 1902 (Royal Fund).
20. Cf. Rolfe, Application to Royal Literary Fund, 23 March 1902 (Royal Fund); above, p. 127.
21. Rolfe to Bainbridge, [Hampstead], 28 December 1901 (Martyr Worthy).
22. Rolfe to Bainbridge, [Hampstead], 26 December 1901 (Martyr Worthy).
23. Frederick Rolfe, unsigned holograph, 2 pp. (Martyr Worthy).
24. Cf. Frederick Rolfe to Henry Newbolt, London, 26 September 1903 (Texas).
25. Cf. 'Chronicles of the Borgias', *The Athenaeum*, 25 January 1902, pp. 115–16; 'The Parentage of Caesar Borgia', *Notes and Queries*, 1 March and 19 April 1902, pp. 176, 312; 'The Borgias', New York *Times, Saturday Review of Books and Art*, 5 April 1902, p. 235; 'A Letter to The Editor', *The Critic* (New York), April 1902, pp. 301–2; Rolfe, *Nicholas Crabbe*, p. 211.
26. Cf. Rolfe to Hewlett, Hampstead, 17 March 1902; Maurice Hewlett to A. Lawrence Roberts, London, 18 March 1902; E. G. Hardy to Royal Literary Fund, Oxford, 21 March 1902; Frederick Rolfe to A. Lawrence Roberts, 2 and 11 April 1902; Rolfe, Application to Royal Literary Fund, 23 March 1902 (Royal Fund).
27. Cf. Rolfe to Hewlett, Hampstead, 17 March 1902 (Royal Fund); Douglas to Rolfe, Southsea, 21 and 31 May, 17 and 27 July 1920 in 'A Selection . . .', *Nicholas Crabbe*, pp. 265, 264, 269, 271.
28. Cf. 'Tennyson in Mist' and 'A Knave of Hearts', *The Outlook*, 18 October 1902, pp. 321–3; 'December 1', *The Outlook*, 29 November 1902, p. 497.

304

29. Rolfe to Pinker, Hampstead, 2, 3 and 11 December 1902; cf. Rolfe to Pinker, Hampstead, 9 December 1902 (Texas).
30. Rolfe to Bainbridge, Hampstead, 11 December 1902 (Martyr Worthy).
31. Cf. Rolfe to Pinker, Hampstead, 23 December 1902; copy of telegram, Rolfe to Pinker, West Hampstead, 24 December 1902 (Texas). The manuscript of 'Live Pork and a Peall' is unknown.
32. Rolfe to Bainbridge, Hampstead, 27 December 1902, 4 September 1903 (Martyr Worthy).
33. Rolfe to Pinker, Hampstead, 9 January 1903; cf. Rolfe to Pinker, Hampstead, 23 December 1902, 8 January 1903 and copy of a telegram, Rolfe to Pinker, West Hampstead, 9 January 1903 (Texas).
34. Cf. Rolfe to Pinker, Hampstead, 24 and 28 January 1903 (Texas); Rolfe to Walsh, Hampstead, 28 January 1903 in *Letters to Walsh*, p. 10.
35. Rolfe to Pinker, Hampstead, 28 January 1902 (Texas).
36. Cf. Rolfe to Pinker, Hampstead, 13 February 1903 (Texas); Frederick Rolfe to W. W. Astor, Hampstead, 30 January 1903 (Berg); Rolfe to Pinker, Hampstead, 11 and 13 February 1903 (Texas). There are two letters dated 13 February 1903.
37. Frederick Rolfe to G. T. Maquay, Hampstead, 27 May and 16 July 1903 (Berg).
38. Cf. Rolfe to Pinker, Hampstead, 8 and 5 January 1903 (Texas).
39. Rolfe to Pinker, Hampstead, 19 January 1903 (Texas).
40. Cf. 'A Scented Garden' and 'Flipperty-Gibberty France', *The Outlook*, 21 February 1903, pp. 71-3.
41. Cf. Rolfe to Pinker, Hampstead, 11 February 1903 (Texas).
42. Rolfe to Pinker, Hampstead, 29 April 1903; cf. Rolfe to Pinker, Hampstead, 5 March 1903 (Texas).
43. Cf. Rolfe to Pinker, Hampstead 20, 22, and 23 April 1903 (Texas).
44. Rolfe to Pinker, Hampstead, 1 July 1903 (Texas).
45. Cf. Frederick Rolfe to A. H. Bullen, Hampstead, 22 July 1903; Rolfe to Pinker, Hampstead, 1 July and [July] 1903 (Texas).
46. Frederick Rolfe to Leonard Moore, Hampstead, 28 October 1903 in Fr. Rolfe, Baron Corvo, *Letters to Leonard Moore*, eds. Cecil Woolf and Rabbi Bertram Korn, London, 1960, p. 41.
47. Rolfe to Moore, Hampstead, 9 October and 5 December 1903 in *Letters to Moore*, pp. 36, 44-5.
48. Leonard Moore, 'Epilogue', in *Letters to Leonard Moore*, eds. Cecil Woolf and Rabbi Bertram Korn, London, 1960, p. 74; cf. p. 73.
49. Rolfe to Bainbridge, Hampstead, 13 February 1903 (Martyr Worthy).
50. Cf. Rolfe to Walsh, Hampstead, 13 March 1903 in *Letters to Walsh*, p. 12.
51. Cf. Rolfe to Pinker, Hampstead, 18 February, 23 April, and 26 June 1903 (Texas).
52. Cf. Rolfe to Pinker, Hampstead, 26 February 1903 (Texas).
53. Rolfe to Lane, Hampstead, 20 February 1903 in *Without Prejudice*, p. 82.
54. (Martyr Worthy).
55. Cf. Rolfe to Bainbridge, Hampstead, 22 September 1903 (Martyr Worthy); Weeks, p. 236; Mrs. Catherine M. Griffiths to Henry Newbolt, South Hampstead, 13 August 1903 (Texas).
56. Rolfe to Newbolt, Hampstead, 13 August 1903 (Texas).
57. Cf. Rolfe to Newbolt, Hampstead, 9 and 13 August 1903 (Texas).

[v]

1. Cf. Rolfe to Richards, Hampstead, 4 March 1902 in *Letters to Richards*, p. 46; Rolfe to Lane, Hampstead, 20 May 1903 in *Without Prejudice*, p. 65.
2. Cf. Rolfe to Walsh, Hampstead, 13 March and 28 July 1903 in *Letters to Walsh*, pp. 12 and 26.
3. Cf. Rolfe to Newbolt, London, 27 August 1903 (Texas); Rolfe, *Hadrian*, p. 43.

4. Cf. Rolfe to Bainbridge, Hampstead, 3 March 1903; 5, 8, 21 November 1902; 5 June, 29 August, 13 October 1903 *et passim* (Martyr Worthy).
5. Rolfe, *Hadrian*, p. 16.
6. Rolfe to Roberts, Hampstead, 23 March 1903 (Royal Fund).
7. Cf. A. Llewelyn Roberts to Frederick Rolfe, London, 24 March 1903 (Royal Fund).
8. (Martyr Worthy).
9. Cf. Henry Newbolt to the Committee of the Royal Literary Fund, London, May 1903; E. G. Hardy to the Committee, Oxford, 3 May 1903; Frederick Rolfe, Application to the Royal Literary Fund, 6 May 1903 (Royal Fund).
10. (Royal Fund). Both letters are undated. The comparison of the 'intellectual public' with the 'plucky boy', quoted above, is identical with a statement in a letter from Rolfe to Newbolt dated 5 May 1903.
11. Richard Garnett to the Committee of the Royal Literary Fund Hampstead, 20 April 1903 (Royal Fund).
12. (Royal Fund).
13. Cf. Edmund Gosse to Henry Newbolt, London, 12 May 1903 (Texas).
14. Cf. Julian Sturgis to Henry Newbolt, Compton, Guildford, Surrey, 14 May 1903 (Texas).
15. Rolfe to Newbolt, Hampstead, 14 May 1903 (Texas); Rolfe to Roberts, Hampstead, 17 May 1903 (Royal Fund); Rolfe to Maquis, Hampstead, 30 May 1903 (Berg).
16. Two anonymous reviews identified as Rolfe's appeared in *The Outlook* in 1903 after May, 'Microcosmic Macedonia' on 5 September and 'Galilaee, Vicisti', on 24 October; cf. Woolf, *Bibliography*, C96 and C97. Rolfe had first intended 'Notes on the Conclave' to appear anonymously, but it was published in *The Monthly Review* with his name. Cf. below, p. 149.
17. Rolfe to Walsh, Hampstead, 4 June 1903 in *Letters to Walsh*, p. 16; cf. Rolfe to Maquay, Hampstead, 27 May 1903 (Berg).
18. Rolfe to Walsh, Hampstead, 24 June 1903 in *Letters to Walsh*, p. [19].
19. Cf. Rolfe to Roberts, Hampstead, 3 June 1903 (Royal Fund); Rolfe to Walsh, Hampstead, 6 June 1903 in *Letters to Walsh*, p. 21; Woolf, *Bibliography*, p. 158 *n.* 2.
20. Rolfe to Walsh, Hampstead, 6 July 1903 in *Letters to Walsh*, p. 21.
21. Rolfe to Pinker, Hampstead, 8 July, 9 August, 25 July, 4 and 10 August, 5 March 1903 (Texas); Rolfe to Newbolt, Hampstead, 10 June, 3 August 1903 (Texas); *The Monthly Review*, August 1903, pp. 74–88; *The Westminster Review*, October 1903, pp. 402–14.
22. Rolfe to Pinker, Hampstead, 4 August 1903, cf. Rolfe to Pinker, 9 August 1903 (Texas).
23. Cf. Rolfe to G. T. Maquay, Hampstead, 16 July and 27 May 1903 (Berg).
24. In *Letters to Walsh*, pp. 23–6.
25. Rolfe to Maquay, Hampstead, 20 and 18 July 1903 (Berg).
26. Rolfe to Pinker, Hampstead, [August] 1903 (Texas). This letter is dated 12 February 1903, an obvious error made clear by internal evidence. A subsequent letter on the same subject is dated 13 August 1903.
27. Cf. Rolfe to Moore, Hampstead, 16 August 1903 in *Letters to Moore*, pp. 28–9; Rolfe to Pinker, Hampstead, 13 August 1903 (Texas).
28. Cf. Mrs. Catherine M. Griffiths to Newbolt, South Hampstead, 13 August 1903 (Texas).
29. Rolfe to Newbolt, Hampstead, 13 August 1903 (Texas).
30. (Royal Fund). Rolfe wrote another letter, dated 24 September 1903, intended for Edmund Gosse, J. M. Barrie, Julian Sturgis and Maurice Hewlett. In it he refuted one by one the charges conveyed by Newbolt. Whether he sent it or not is unknown; it exists in a holograph marked 'Copy' and is a part of the Rolfe–Newbolt material at the University of Texas.
31. (Texas).

32. In *Letters to Walsh*, p. [27].
33. Rolfe to Bainbridge, Hampstead, 4 September 1903 (Martyr Worthy).
34. Rolfe to Bainbridge, Hampstead, 18 September 1903; cf. Rolfe to Bainbridge, Hampstead, 22 and 28 September 1903 and a telegram, Rolfe to Bainbridge, 21 September 1903 (Martyr Worthy).
35. Rolfe to Newbolt, London, 6 October 1903; cf. Rolfe to Newbolt, London, 24 and 29 August; 17, 25 and 26 September, 6 October 1903 (Texas).

[vi]

1. Viola Meynell, *Francis Thompson and Wilfred Meynell*, New York, 1953, p. 134.
2. (Texas); cf. Rolfe to Moore, Hampstead, 9 October 1903 in *Letters to Moore*, p. 36.
3. Rolfe to Moore, Hampstead, 26 November 1903 in *Letters to Moore*, pp. 42–3.
4. Cf. Weeks, p. 241, where it is stated that Rolfe's work on Thomas's book lasted eight months. Later Rolfe said that he devoted 1,050 hours to the book. (Cf. Rolfe's Statement of Claim, Public Record Office, Reference J.54.1331). In February 1904, Rolfe was engaged to do 'press work', that is to make further revisions in preparation for publication, for a fee of £15(cf. below, p. 157)paid in two instalments, £10 on 23 February 1904 and £5 on 15 March 1904. (Cf. Defence in Rolfe and Thomas, Public Record Office, Reference J.54.1331-2351). Rolfe also functioned as a letter writer and general literary flunkey for Thomas, receiving small sums from the end of November as small jobs were completed and final payment of £12 on 29 June 1904. Thus he worked with Thomas from early October 1903 until 29 June 1904, a period slightly longer than eight months. But Rolfe's first and chief assignment from Thomas was complete by the end of November 1903. Cf. his letter to Moore dated 5 December 1903 (in *Letters to Moore*, p. 45) where he says, '. . . the thing is finished and is going through the last stages of typewriting and binding. It ought to have been delivered to the Directors and the Rhodes Trustees last week. It is certain to be delivered in the coming week.' *Agricultural and Pastoral Prospects of South Africa* was delivered to Constable before 22 April 1904 (cf. Rolfe to Moore, London, 22 April 1904 in *Letters to Moore*, p. 53) and was published in the following October.
5. Rolfe to Moore, Hampstead, 26 November 1903 in *Letters to Moore*, p. 43.
6. Nicholson to Kains Jackson, London, 20 November 1903 in d'Arch Smith, *Love in Earnest*, p. 126.
7. Nicholson to Kains Jackson, London, 19 March 1904 (Bodleian).
8. d'Arch Smith, *Love in Earnest*, pp. 126–7.
9. Cf. Rolfe's Statement of Claim, Public Record Office, Reference J.54.1331.
10. Nicholson to Kains Jackson, Chalklands, Tattingstone, Suffolk, [1 January] 1904 (Bodleian).
11. Rolfe to Bullen, Hampstead, 22 January 1904 (Texas).
12. Rolfe to Moore, Hampstead, [c. 22 January 1904] in *Letters to Moore*, p. 52.
13. Cf. *Notes and Queries*, 13 February 1904, p. 26; 5 March 1904, p. 193.
14. Nicholson to Kains Jackson, [London], 19 March 1904 [the letter is incomplete]; cf. Nicholson to Kains Jackson, Chalklands, Tattingstone, Suffolk, [1 January] 1904 (Bodleian).

[vii]

1. Cf. John Holden to A. J. A. Symons, Antwerp, [July 1933] (Martyr Worthy).
2. In *Letters to Grahame*, p. [5]. For a contrary opinion cf. Donald Weeks, 'Notes' in *Frederick Rolfe, Letters to James Walsh*, London, 1972, pp. 49–50 *n.* 10.
3. Rolfe, *Hadrian*, p. 277; cf. Rolfe to Walsh. Hampstead, 4 June and 28 July 1903 in *Letters to Walsh*, pp. 16, 23.
4. Cf. Weeks, pp. 226–9.
5. Rolfe to Maquay, Hampstead, 27 May 1903 (Berg).
6. Rolfe to Walsh, Hampstead, 28 July 1903 in *Letters to Walsh*, p. 23.

7. Rolfe to Walsh, Hampstead, 29 June 1903 in *Letters to Walsh*, p. 19.
8. Cf. Rolfe to Moore, Hampstead, 4 October 1903 in *Letters to Moore*, p. 34.
9. Rolfe, *Nicholas Crabbe*, p. 151.
10. Rolfe to Walsh, Hampstead, 29 July 1903 in *Letters to Walsh*, p. 26.
11. Rolfe to Walsh, Broadstairs, Isle of Thanet, 3 November 1904 in *Letters to Walsh*, p. 28.
12. Rolfe, *Hadrian*, p. 15.
13. Rolfe, *Hadrian*, p. 103.
14. Rolfe, *Hadrian*, p. 176.
15. Rolfe, *Hadrian*, p. 81; cf. p. 146.
16. Cf. Rolfe to Maquay, Hampstead, 16 July 1903 (Berg); [C. H. C. Pirie-Gordon], 'Epilogue' in Fr. Rolfe, *Letters to C. H. C. Pirie-Gordon*, London, 1959, p. 145.
17. Rolfe, *Hadrian*, p. 108.
18. Rolfe, *Hadrian*, p. 210.
19. Rolfe, *Hadrian*, pp. 176, 106, 121.
20. Cf. Rolfe, *Hadrian*, pp. 152–3, 401–2, 332.
21. Cf. Rolfe, *Hadrian*, pp. 15, 30, 277, 324.
22. Cf. above, pp. 70–1.
23. Rolfe, *Hadrian*, p. 199.
24. Cf. Rolfe, *Hadrian*, pp. 217–18.
25. Cf. Rolfe, *Hadrian*, pp. 15, 144.
26. Cf. Rolfe, *Hadrian*, p. 210.
27. Rolfe, *Hadrian*, pp. 86, 114.
28. Rolfe, *Hadrian*, p. 181.
29. Cf. Rolfe, *Hadrian*, pp. 279, 255; above, p. 68; below, p. 170.
30. (Martyr Worthy).
31. Cf. Rolfe, *Hadrian*, pp. 365–6.
32. Cf. above, pp. 97–8.
33. D. H. Lawrence, 'Baron Corvo', *Adelphi*, December 1925, pp. 502–6; Graham Greene, 'Frederick Rolfe: Edwardian Inferno' in *Collected Essays*, London, 1970, p. 133.
34. Cf. Cecil Woolf, 'Introduction', in *Nicholas Crabbe* by Fr. Rolfe, New York, 1958, p. 1.
35. Rolfe to Walsh, Hampstead, 4 June 1903 in *Letters to Walsh*, p. 17; cf. Rolfe to Walsh, Broadstairs, 3 November 1904; Hampstead, 29 June 1903 in *Letters to Walsh*, pp. 28, 20.
36. Frederick Rolfe to Ralph Shirley, Venice, 7 June [1912] (Bodleian); cf. Rolfe to Walsh, Hampstead, 4 June 1903 in *Letters to Walsh*, p. 17.
37. Cf. Rolfe to Moore, Hampstead, 9 October 1903 in *Letters to Moore*, p. 37.
38. Rolfe to Moore, Hampstead, 20 October 1903 in *Letters to Moore*, pp. 37–8. Cf. Rolfe to Newbolt, Hampstead, 17 August 1903 (Texas).
39. Rolfe, *Nicholas Crabbe*, p. 28.
40. Cf. Rolfe to Moore, Hampstead, 9 October 1903 in *Letters to Moore*, p. 36; Rolfe, *Nicholas Crabbe*, pp. 111, 158, 43.
41. Rolfe to Maquay, Broadstairs, 9 December 1904 (Berg).
42. Cf. 'A Goat in Priest's Clothing', signed Crabmaid (Bodleian).
43. Rolfe, *Nicholas Crabbe*, p. 43; cf. pp. 31, 20, 28.
44. Rolfe, *Nicholas Crabbe*, pp. 28–9.
45. Rolfe, *Nicholas Crabbe*, p. 58.
46. Rolfe, *Nicholas Crabbe*, p. 62; cf. p. 60.
47. Cf. above, pp. 129–31.
48. (Bodleian); cf. Rolfe, *Nicholas Crabbe*, p. 196.
49. Cf. Rolfe to Pinker, Hampstead, 29 April 1903 (Texas).
50. Rolfe, *Desire and Pursuit*, p. 49.
51. Rolfe, *Nicholas Crabbe*, p. 52.
52. Rolfe, *Nicholas Crabbe*, p. 96; cf. pp. 52, 31.

53. Pp. 218–19.
54. Rolfe, *Nicholas Crabbe*, p. 5.
55. Rolfe, *Nicholas Crabbe*, p. 239
56. Rolfe, *Hadrian*, p. 17.
57. Rolfe to Beauclerk, n.p., 27 March 1905 (Martyr Worthy); cf. above, p. 103.
58. (Texas).
59. (Texas); cf. Rolfe to Maquay, Hampstead, 16 July 1903 (Berg).
60. In *Baron Corvo to Kenneth Grahame*, p. [5]; cf. above, p. 118.
61. Cf. Rolfe, *Don Tarquinio*, pp. xi–xii; Frederick Rolfe to Herbert Rolfe, Broadstairs, Isle of Thanet, 15 March 1905 in Symons, *Quest*, pp. 170–1.
62. (Texas).
63. Rolfe to Herbert Rolfe, Broadstairs, 15 March 1905 in Symons, *Quest*, p. 171. The manuscript is apparently lost.
64. In *Without Prejudice*, p. 86.

[viii]

1. Rolfe to Bland, Crickhowell, 25 March 1907 (Benkovitz).
2. Rolfe to Lane, Kensington, 7 July 1904 in *Without Prejudice*, pp. 86–7; cf. Aline Harland to John Lane, Hampton Court, 5 July 1904 in Cecil Woolf, 'Epilogue', *Without Prejudice*, p. 90.
3. (Texas).
4. Rolfe, *Nicholas Crabbe*, p. 60.
5. Rolfe to Frederic Chapman, Oxford, 12 July 1900 in *Without Prejudice*, p. 52; cf. Rolfe to Walsh, Hampstead, 28 July 1903 in *Letters to Walsh*, p. 26.
6. Rolfe to Maquay, Broadstairs, 9 December 1904 (Berg).
7. Rolfe to Maquay, Hampstead, 22 July 1903 (Berg).
8. Pp. 296–9; cf. Woolf, *Bibliography*, p. 162 *n*. 1.
9. Rolfe to Moore, Kensington, 22 April 1904 in *Letters to Moore*, p. 53; cf. Rolfe to Maquay, Kensington, 24 June 1904 (Berg).
10. Rolfe to Maquay, Kensington, 6 and 10 May, 24 June 1904 (Berg).
11. Cf. Rolfe to Maquay, Kensington, 25 June 1904 (Berg).
12. Cf. Rolfe to Maquay, Broadstairs, 25 October, 17 November, 9 December 1904 (Berg); Rolfe to Walsh, Broadstairs, 3 November 1904 in *Letters to Walsh*, p. 28.
13. Cf. Rolfe's Statement of Claim, Public Record Office, Reference J.54.1331; above, p. 156; Rolfe to Maquay, Kensington, 24 June 1904 (Berg).
14. Cf. Frederick Rolfe to Barnard & Taylor, [Oxford], 6 December 1905, 51 November 1906 (Bodleian); above, pp. 18-19.
15. Rolfe to Pinker, Hampstead, 6 May 1903 (Texas). That Pinker advised Rolfe to take this particular complaint to Barnard & Taylor cannot be supported by extant letters. So far as can be ascertained, no letter from Rolfe to Pinker written in 1905 is extant. For a contrary opinion see Cecil Woolf, 'Introduction', in Fr. Rolfe, Baron Corvo, *Letters to C. H. C. Pirie-Gordon*, London, 1959, p. 16.
16. Rolfe to Walsh, Broadstairs, 3 November 1904 in *Letters to Walsh*, p. 28.

PART IV

[i]

1. Rolfe to Maquay, Broadstairs, 25 October 1904 (Berg).
2. Rolfe to Maquay, Broadstairs, 3 November 1904; cf. Rolfe to Maquay, Broadstairs, 17 November 1904 (Berg); Rolfe to Walsh, Broadstairs, 3 November 1904 in *Letters to Walsh*, p. 28.
3. Cf. Rolfe to Maquay, Broadstairs, 3 December 1904 (Berg).
4. Rolfe to Maquay, Broadstairs, 3 December 1904 (Berg).
5. Rolfe to Maquay, Broadstairs, 3 December 1904 (Berg).
6. Rolfe to Maquay, Broadstairs, 3 December 1904 (Berg). Cf. Rolfe to Walsh, Broadstairs, 3 November 1904 in *Letters to Walsh*, p. 28.
7. Rolfe to Maquay, Broadstairs, 9 December 1904 (Berg).

8. In Symons, *Quest*, p. 171.
9. Cf. Rolfe to Beauclerk, n.p., 27 March 1905 (Martyr Worthy).
10. Rolfe to Maquay, Broadstairs, 16 December 1904. Cf. Rolfe to Maquay, Broadstairs, 9 December 1904 (Berg); Weeks, p. 244; Cecil Woolf and Brocard Sewell, 'The Clerk Without a Benefice', in *Corvo, 1860–1960*, eds. Cecil Woolf and Brocard Sewell, Aylesford, 1961, pp. 40–2.
11. (Berg).
12. Rolfe to Maquay, Broadstairs, 26 December 1904 (Berg).
13. Rolfe to Maquay, Broadstairs, 3, 9 and 26 December and 20 November 1904 (Berg).

[ii]

1. Rolfe to Beauclerk, n.p., 1 March 1905 (Martyr Worthy).
2. Cf. Rolfe to Beauclerk, n.p., 27 March 1905 (Martyr Worthy).
3. Robert Hugh Benson to Frederick Rolfe, Cambridge, February 1905 in Weeks, p. 249. Cf. Shane Leslie, 'The Cambridge Apostolate', in *Memorials of Robert Hugh Benson*, London, 1915, pp. 47–71; E. F. Benson, *Final Edition*, London, 1940, pp. 34–35; C. C. Martindale, *The Life of Monsignor Robert Hugh Benson*, 2 vols., London, 1916, II, 94, 95, 96.
4. (Bodleian).
5. Rolfe to Herbert Rolfe, Broadstairs, 15 March 1905 in Symons, *Quest*, pp. 171–2.
6. Cf. Martindale, II, 95–6.
7. Rolfe to Dawkins, Poundstock, Bude, 16 March 1908 in *Letters to Dawkins*, p. 85.
8. Rolfe to Dawkins, Poundstock, Bude, 16 April 1908 in *Letters to Dawkins*, p. 109.
9. E. V. de Fontmell, *Life at a Venture*, London, [1929–30], p. 166.
10. Martindale, II, 55.
11. Cf. Martindale, II, 96–7; below, p. 185–6.
12. Cf. Martindale, II; 96, Weeks, p. 249.
13. Martindale, II, 111; cf. II, 6.
14. Martindale, II, 112.
15. Martindale, II, 52 *n*. 1.
16. Cf. Rolfe, *Desire and Pursuit*, p. 37.
17. Cf. Benson, *Final Edition*, p. 41; Martindale, II, 97.
18. Cf. Benson to Rolfe, Buntingford, 25 November [1908] (Bodleian); Martindale, II, 6; Leslie, 'Cambridge Apostolate', in *Memorials*, p. 60.
19. 'Notes', in *Memorials*, pp. 86–7.
20. Rolfe, *Desire and Pursuit*, p. 36.
21. Rolfe, 'The Armed Hands' (Martyr Worthy).
22. de Fontmell, p. 167.
23. Benson, *Final Edition*, p. 24. Cf. William Frederick Rolfe to Hubert Bland, n.p., n.d., [1906] in Doris Langley Moore, *E. Nesbit A Biography*, Philadelphia, 1966, pp. 181 182; below, pp. 187–8.
24. Benson, *Final Edition*, p. 35.
25. Cf. Frederick Rolfe, 'Regarding Benson' in Letter Book (Martyr Worthy).
26. Cf. de Fontmell, pp. 166–78.
27. Weeks, p. 253.
28. Cf. 13, 16 and 18 October 1905, p. 1.
29. Rolfe to Barnard & Taylor, Oxford, 6 December 1905 (Bodleian); Weeks, p. 253. Cf. above, p. 173.
30. Rolfe to Barnard & Taylor, Oxford, 8 December 1905 (Bodleian).
31. Cf. G. E. Hardy, *Studies in Roman History*, London, 1906, p. viii.
32. Rolfe to Bland, n.p., n.d. [1906] in Doris Langley Moore, *E. Nesbit*, pp. 181, 182; cf. above, p. 170; below, pp. 231, 244, 247, 256.
33. Rolfe, *Desire and Pursuit*, p. 38.
34. Martindale, II, 99.
35. Martindale, II, 99.

310

[iii]

1. This account of the meeting between Pirie-Gordon and Rolfe differs somewhat from Symons's account (cf. *Quest*, p. 176) and considerably from Weeks's (cf. p. 254) and Woolfe's (cf. 'Introduction', in *Letters to Pirie-Gordon*, pp. 12–13). It depends on Harry Pirie-Gordon's AM, three and one-half pages sent from London in 1955 with an accompanying ALS to an unnamed correspondent. The letter runs in part 'I enclose a bit about Rolfe—which I think is not covered by anything in the "Quest for Corvo".' (Z. Smith Reynolds Library Wake Forest College). Cf. Rolfe, *Desire and Pursuit*, p. 38.
2. Frederick Rolfe to Mrs. Edward Pirie-Gordon, Oxford, [Autumn 1906] in *Letters to Pirie-Gordon*, pp. 41–2.
3. Cf. Woolf, *Bibliography*, p. 103.
4. (Bodleian); cf. Rolfe, *Desire and Pursuit*, p. 39.
5. [Harry Pirie-Gordon], 'Epilogue' in *Letters to Pirie-Gordon*, p. 144; AM (Wake Forest).
6. Pirie-Gordon, AM (Wake Forest).
7. Rolfe, AM, 1 page (Benkovitz). Cf. Woolf, *Bibliography*, p. 105; Rolfe to Pirie-Gordon, Oxford, 30 September 1906 in *Letters to Pirie-Gordon*, p. 33. *Innocent the Great* was first published by Longmans, Green, and Co. on 1 October 1907.
8. Cf. Pirie-Gordon, AM (Wake Forest); Woolf, *Bibliography*, p. 105.
9. Cf. Rolfe, *Desire and Pursuit*, p. 40.
10. Cf. Rolfe, *Desire and Pursuit*, p. 40; Woolf, *Bibliography*, p. 112. Pirie-Gordon stated that the name Caliban for himself was not used during Rolfe's several visits to Gwernvale but was originated for the title-page of *The Weird of the Wanderer* when it was accepted for publication. Cf. Pirie-Gordon, 'Epilogue' in *Letters to Pirie-Gordon*, p. 144.
11. Cf. Rolfe, 'The Armed Hands' (Martyr Worthy); above, pp. 1, 185; Pirie-Gordon, AM (Wake Forest); Woolf, 'Introduction', in *Letters to Pirie-Gordon*, p. 15.
12. Rolfe, *Desire and Pursuit*, p. 41.
13. Cf. A. J. A. Symons, 'Introduction' in *Hubert's Arthur*, p. 2.

[iv]

1. Rolfe to Pirie-Gordon, Oxford, Monday [1906] in *Letters to Pirie-Gordon*, p. 35.
2. Rolfe to Mrs. Pirie-Gordon, Oxford, [Autumn 1906] in *Letters to Pirie-Gordon*, p. 41.
3. Rolfe to Barnard & Taylor [Oxford], 22 November 1906 (Bodleian); Rolfe to Pirie-Gordon, Oxford, 22 November 1906 in *Letters to Pirie-Gordon*, p. 43.
4. Cf. Rolfe to Barnard & Taylor, [Oxford], 3 and 5 December 1906 (Bodleian).
5. Rolfe to Barnard & Taylor, [Oxford], 3 and 5 December 1906 (Bodleian). Cf. Rolfe to Pirie-Gordon, Oxford, [December 1906] in *Letters to Pirie-Gordon*, p. 44.
6. Rolfe to Barnard & Taylor, [Oxford], 15 November 1906; cf. Rolfe to Barnard & Taylor, [Oxford], 6 March, 25 November 1906 (Bodleian).
7. Rolfe to Barnard & Taylor, [Oxford], 16 December 1906; cf. Rolfe to Barnard & Taylor, [Oxford], 5 December 1906 (Bodleian).

[v]

1. Rolfe to Pirie-Gordon, Oxford, [19 January 1907] in *Letters to Pirie-Gordon*, p. 45.
2. Rolfe to Pirie-Gordon, Crickhowell, 20 December 1907 in *Letters to Pirie-Gordon*, p. 71.
3. Cf. Rolfe to Pirie-Gordon, Crickhowell, 10, 26 and 29 June 1907 in *Letters to Pirie-Gordon*, pp. 50, 56 and 57.
4. Cf. Rolfe to Pirie-Gordon, Crickhowell, 10 February, 10 April 1907 and n.d. [1907] in *Letters to Pirie-Gordon*, pp. 46, 48–9, 47–8.
5. Rolfe to Dawkins, Crickhowell, 21 December 1907 in *Letters to Dawkins*, p. 70.

6. Cf. Rolfe to Pirie-Gordon, Crickhowell, 31 May, 10 and 26 June 1907 in *Letters to Pirie-Gordon*, pp. 49, 50, 56.
7. Cf. Rolfe to Mrs. Pirie-Gordon, Crickhowell, 4 January 1908; Robert Hugh Benson to Edward Pirie-Gordon, Horsted Keynes, Sussex, 25 December 1907 in *Letters to Pirie-Gordon*, pp. 67, 75; below, p. 230.
8. Martindale, II, 99.
9. Cf. Martindale, II, 100–1.
10. Martindale, II, 104; cf. II, 103.
11. Martindale, II, 104.
12. Rolfe to Mrs. Pirie-Gordon, Crickhowell, 4 January 1908 in *Letters to Pirie Gordon*, p. 75; cf. Benson to unnamed correspondent, Horsted, Keynes, Sussex, 5 September 1907 (Berg).
13. Martindale, II, 106.
14. Martindale, II, 105.
15. In Robert Hugh Benson, *Poems*, London, 1914, p. 60. For the opinion that 'Hero Worship' is Benson's apology or expression of regret for his treatment of Rolfe, cf. Weeks, pp. 263–4; d'Arch Smith, pp. 7–8.
16. Cf. Rolfe, *Desire and Pursuit*, pp. 36–7.
17. Cf. Symons, *Quest*, p. 197; Benson, *Final Edition*, p. 36.
18. Benson to Edward Pirie-Gordon, Horsted Keynes, Sussex, 25 December 1907; cf. Benson to Edward Pirie-Gordon, Cambridge, 18 December [1907] in *Letters to Pirie-Gordon*, pp. 67–8, 65.
19. Rolfe to Pirie-Gordon, Crickhowell, 10 June 1907 in *Letters to Pirie-Gordon*, pp. 50–51.
20. Rolfe to Mrs. Pirie-Gordon, Crickhowell, 2 December 1907 in *Letters to Pirie-Gordon*, p. 60.
21. Cf. Rolfe to Mrs. Pirie-Gordon, Crickhowell, 2 December 1907; Rolfe to Pirie-Gordon, Crickhowell, 20 December 1907 in *Letters to Pirie-Gordon*, pp. 59–61, 68; Rolfe to Dawkins, Crickhowell, [2 December 1907] in *Letters to Dawkins*, p. 66.
22. Cf. Rolfe to Pirie-Gordon, Poundstock, Bude, [March 1908] in *Letters to Pirie-Gordon*, p. 82; Rolfe to Dawkins, Poundstock, Bude, 16 April 1908 in *Letters to Dawkins*, p. 99.
23. Rolfe to Mrs. Pirie-Gordon, Crickhowell, 4 January 1908 in *Letters to Pirie-Gordon*, pp. 75–6; cf. p. 74. Benson's account of this transaction, sent to Edward Pirie-Gordon, is a far more genial one than Rolfe's; cf. Benson to Edward Pirie-Gordon, Cambridge, 14 December [1907] in *Letters to Pirie-Gordon*, p. 63.
24. Rolfe to Mrs. Pirie-Gordon, Crickhowell, 4 January 1908; cf. Benson to Edward Pirie-Gordon, Cambridge, 14 and 20 December 1907 in *Letters to Pirie-Gordon*, pp. 76, 63, 66.
25. Cf. Rolfe to Mrs. Pirie-Gordon, Crickhowell, 24 January 1908; Benson to Edward Pirie-Gordon Horsted Keynes, Sussex, 25 December 1907 in *Letters to Pirie-Gordon*, pp. 81, 67–8; Rolfe to Dawkins, Crickhowell, 9 January 1908, in *Letters to Dawkins*, p. 75.
26. Rolfe to Pirie-Gordon, Crickhowell, 20 December 1907 in *Letters to Pirie-Gordon*, p. 69.
27. Cf. Rolfe to Dawkins, Poundstock, Bude, 20 February 1908 in *Letters to Dawkins*, p. 80; Rolfe to Mrs. Pirie-Gordon, Crickhowell, 2 December 1907 in *Letters to Pirie-Gordon*, p. 60.
28. In *Letters to Dawkins*, p. 75; cf. p. 74.
29. Rolfe to Mrs. Pirie-Gordon, Crickhowell, 4 January 1908 in *Letters to Pirie-Gordon*, p. 76.
30. Cf. *Letters to Dawkins*, pp. 75–6; cf. pp. 67, 69, 70, 77; Rolfe to Pirie-Gordon, Crickhowell, 20 December 1907 in *Letters to Pirie-Gordon*, p. 68.
31. Rolfe to Pirie-Gordon, Crickhowell, 20 and 2 December 1907; Rolfe to Mrs. Pirie-Gordon, Crickhowell, 24 January 1908 in *Letters to Pirie-Gordon*, pp. 71, 82, 61.

1. Rolfe to Dawkins, Poundstock, Bude, 16 March 1908, in *Letters to Dawkins*, p. 92.
2. Rolfe to Charlotte Handly, Poundstock, Bude, 28 March 1908 in *Letters to Pirie-Gordon*, p. 84.
3. Cf. Rolfe to Dawkins, Poundstock, Bude, 12 May and 16 April 1908 in *Letters to Dawkins*, pp. 116, 99.
4. Rolfe to Dawkins, Poundstock, Bude, 12 May 1908; cf. Rolfe to Dawkins, Poundstock, Bude, 9 January, 16 March, 16 April 1908 *et passim* in *Letters to Dawkins*, pp. 116, 73, 91–2, 99 *et passim*.
5. Rolfe to Dawkins, Crickhowell, 29 July 1908 in *Letters to Dawkins*, p. 127. Cf. p. 126 *n.* 3; pp. 128–9; Rolfe to Pirie-Gordon, Poundstock, Bude, 28 March 1908 in *Letters to Pirie-Gordon*, p. 83.

PART V

[i]

1. Rolfe, *Desire and Pursuit*, p. 85.
2. Rolfe, *Desire and Pursuit*, p. 185; Frederick Rolfe to The Lord Archbishop of Westminster, Venice, 5 January 1910 in Letter Book (Martyr Worthy).
3. Rolfe, *Desire and Pursuit*, pp. 149, 221–2.
4. Rolfe, *Desire and Pursuit*, p. 131.
5. Rolfe, *Desire and Pursuit*, pp. 42, 221, 101.
6. Rolfe to Dawkins, Poundstock, Bude, 16 April 1908 in *Letters to Dawkins*, p. 201. Cf. Rolfe, *Desire and Pursuit*, p. 225; Rolfe to Mrs. Pirie-Gordon, Crickhowell, 4 January 1908 in *Letters to Pirie-Gordon*, pp. 77–8.
7. Frederick Rolfe, 'An Ossuary of the North Lagoon', in *Three Tales of Venice*, London, n.d., p. 50; cf. p. 48.
8. Cf. Rolfe to Dawkins, Gwernvale, 29 [July] 1908 in *Letters to Dawkins*, p. 128; above, p. 2.
9. Cf. Rolfe to Dawkins, Venice, 22 July 1910 in *Letters to Dawkins*, p. 155.
10. Rolfe, 'Ossuary', in *Three Tales of Venice*, p. 47. Cf. Symons, *Quest*, p. 208; Rolfe to Dawkins, Gwernvale, 29 [July] 1908; Poundstock, Bude, 16 April, 3 June 1908 in *Letters to Dawkins*, pp. 127, 102, 124.
11. Cf. Rolfe to Pirie-Gordon, Venice, 27 December 1908 in *Letters to Pirie-Gordon*, p. 94.
12. Rolfe, 'Ossuary', in *Three Tales of Venice*, pp. 50–1.
13. Rolfe to Dawkins, Venice, 28 January, 1909, 6 September 1911, 16 October 1908 in *Letters to Dawkins*, pp. 140, 158, 135; Rolfe, 'Ossuary', in *Three Tales of Venice*, p. 51.

[ii]

1. Rolfe, 'Ossuary', in *Three Tales of Venice*, p. 52.
2. Rolfe, 'Ossuary', in *Three Tales of Venice*, pp. 52–6.
3. Rolfe, 'Venetian Courtesy', in *Three Tales of Venice*, p. 10.
4. Rolfe to Dawkins, Venice, 6 and 16 October 1908 in *Letters to Dawkins*, pp. 130–1, 135.
5. Rolfe to Dawkins, Venice, [14 October 1908] in *Letters to Dawkins*, p. 133.
6. Rolfe to Pirie-Gordon, Venice, [2 November 1908] in *Letters to Pirie-Gordon*, p. 86; cf. Woolf, 'Introduction', in *Letters to Pirie-Gordon*, pp. 20–1; Woolf, 'Introduction', in *Letters to Dawkins*, pp. 25–6.
7. Cf. Benson to Rolfe, Edinburgh, [1 October 1908] (Bodleian); cf. Rolfe to Pirie-Gordon, Venice, 18 November 1908 in *Letters to Pirie-Gordon*, p. 88.
8. Rolfe to Pirie-Gordon, Venice, [18 November 1908] in *Letters to Pirie-Gordon*, p. 88; cf. Rolfe to Dawkins, Venice, 27 October [1908] in *Letters to Dawkins*, p. 138.

9. Rolfe to Pirie-Gordon, Venice, [18 November 1908] in *Letters to Pirie-Gordon*, p. 88.
10. Cf. Rolfe to Pirie-Gordon, Venice, 19 December 1908 in *Letters to Pirie-Gordon*, pp. 89–90; Woolf, 'Introduction', in *Letters to Dawkins*, p. 28.
11. Rolfe to Pirie-Gordon, Crickhowell, 15 June 1907, in *Letters to Pirie-Gordon*, p. 52; Rolfe to Dawkins, Venice, 26 November 1908, in *Letters to Dawkins*, p. 139.
12. Frederick Rolfe, 'The Bull Against the Enemy of the Anglican Race', in *The Quest for Corvo* by A. J. A. Symons, London, 1955, pp. 251, 255. *The Bull Against the Enemy of the Anglican Race* was first printed separately in 1929 for the Corvine Society.
13. Cf. Ivy Van Someren, 'Baron Corvo's Quarrels,' in *The Listener*, February 1947, p. 108.
14. Laura M. Ragg, 'Epilogue', in *Letters to R. M. Dawkins*, ed. Cecil Woolf, London, 1962, p. 179; Laura M. Ragg, 'Venice When The Century Began', *Cornhill Magazine*, January 1936, pp. 2–16. For Mrs. Ragg's letters telling Rolfe to refrain from writing to Canon Ragg cf. her letters in Rolfe's holograph in his Letter Book (Martyr Worthy).
15. Rolfe to Pirie-Gordon, Venice, 19 December 1908, in *Letters to Pirie-Gordon*, p. 90. Cf. Ragg, 'Epilogue', in *Letters to Dawkins*, p. 171; Frederick Rolfe to Lonsdale Ragg, n.d., n.p. (Berg).
16. Rolfe, *Desire and Pursuit*, p. 93; cf. p. 80 *et passim*; Rolfe to Pirie-Gordon, Venice, 19 December 1908 in *Letters to Pirie-Gordon*, p. 90.
17. (Berg); cf. Rolfe to Ragg, [Venice], 11 May 1909 (Berg), where Rolfe reminds Ragg of the letters of warning sent first to Lady Layard and then to him.
18. Woolf, 'Introduction', in *Letters to Dawkins*, p. 27; cf. Rolfe to Pirie-Gordon, Venice, [18 November 1908] in *Letters to Pirie-Gordon*, p. 87.
19. Rolfe to Pirie-Gordon, Venice, 19 December 1908, in *Letters to Pirie-Gordon*, p. 89; cf. p. 88; Woolf, 'Introduction', in *Letters to Dawkins*, p. 27.
20. Cf. Woolf, 'Introduction', in *Letters to Dawkins*, p. 29; cf. p. 28; Rolfe to Dawkins, Venice, [early December 1908] in *Letters to Dawkins*, p. 139.
21. Woolf, 'Introduction', in *Letters to Dawkins*, p. 38.
22. Rolfe to Pirie-Gordon, Venice, 19 December 1908 in *Letters to Pirie-Gordon*, p. 90.
23. Rolfe to Ragg, [Venice], 11 May 1909 (Berg); Rolfe, *Desire and Pursuit*, p. 162.
24. Van Someren, 'Baron Corvo's Quarrels', in *The Listener*, February 1947, p. 106; Rolfe, *Desire and Pursuit*, p. 163; Ragg, 'Venice When the Century Began', in *Cornhill*, January 1936, pp. 4–5.
25. Rolfe to Pirie-Gordon, Venice, 27 December 1908; cf. Rolfe to Pirie-Gordon, Venice, 19 December 1903; Rolfe to Edward Pirie-Gordon, Venice, 26 December 1908 in *Letters to Pirie-Gordon*, pp. 92, 93, 89, 91–2.
26. Rolfe, *Desire and Pursuit*, p. 154.
27. Rolfe to Pirie-Gordon, Venice, 27 December 1908; cf. Rolfe to Pirie-Gordon, Venice, 19 December 1908 and [January] 1909 in *Letters to Pirie-Gordon*, pp. 94, 90, 93, 96.
28. Cf. Woolf, 'Introduction', in *Letters to Dawkins*, pp. 29–35; Rolfe to Dawkins, Venice, 28 January [1909] in *Letters to Dawkins*, p. 141; Rolfe to Pirie-Gordon, Venice, [January 1909] in *Letters to Pirie-Gordon*, pp. 95–7; above, p. 219.
29. Cf. R. M. Dawkins, to Frederick Rolfe, Athens, 8 March 1909 in *Letters to Dawkins*, p. 42; Rolfe to Pirie-Gordon, Venice, [8 May 1909] in *Letters to Pirie-Gordon*, p. 102; below, pp. 227, 229.
30. Rolfe's holograph statement prepared for Hardcastle (Bodleian); cf. Rolfe, *Desire and Pursuit*, p. 203.
31. Cf. Rolfe, *Desire and Pursuit*, pp. 205–10; Woolf, 'Introduction', in *Letters to Dawkins*, pp. 44–6.

[iii]

1. Rolfe to Pirie-Gordon, Venice, [April 1909] in *Letters to Pirie-Gordon*, p. 10; cf. Ragg, 'Epilogue', in *Letters to Dawkins*, p. 175.

2. Rolfe, *Desire and Pursuit*, p. 212; cf. Ragg, 'Epilogue', in *Letters to Dawkins*, pp. 175–6.
3. Rolfe, *Desire and Pursuit*, p. 212.
4. Rolfe, *Desire and Pursuit*, p. 231.
5. Nicholson to Keynes Jackson, n.p., n.d. in Bartholomew (Texas).
6. Rolfe to Miss Sholl, [Venice], 15 May [1909] in Letter Book (Martyr Worthy); cf. Rolfe, *Desire and Pursuit*, pp. 214, 228–9.
7. Rolfe, *Desire and Pursuit*, p. 169.
8. Robert Hugh Benson to Harry Pirie-Gordon, Buntingford, [1909] in *Letters to Pirie-Gordon*, p. 99; cf. Rolfe, *Desire and Pursuit*, pp. 225, 235.
9. Rolfe to Benson, [Venice, 1909] in Letter Book (Martyr Worthy); cf. Rolfe to Pirie-Gordon, Venice, [8 May 1909] in *Letters to Pirie-Gordon*, p. 102.
10. In *Letters to Pirie-Gordon*, p. 102.
11. Cf. Rolfe to Ragg, [Venice], 23 May 1909 in Letter Book (Martyr Worthy). In *Desire and Pursuit*, p. 237, Rolfe speaks of four days and nights.
12. Rolfe to Ragg, [Venice], 11 May 1909 (Berg); cf. Rolfe, *Desire and Pursuit*, p. 228.
13. Rolfe to Ragg, [Venice], 11 May 1909 (Berg). This is the second of two letters of that date.
14. Rolfe, *Desire and Pursuit*, p. 224. The sequence of events above differs from Rolfe's account in *Desire and Pursuit*. Either the letter dated 'Saturday', above, was written on a Saturday other than 8 May 1909 or the actual events have been changed for fictional purposes—not the only change—in *Desire and Pursuit*. To establish precise dates as to when Rolfe went to the Raggs' flat in the Palazzo Contarini-Corfu or when he left it is impossible. He spoke of fifteen days, seventeen days, eighteen, and three weeks there. Mrs. Ragg wrote of three weeks. Rolfe's forty-eight hours in the open, Ragg's remark about co-religionists in association with Rolfe's return to England and the offer to have Rolfe's clothes washed (without doubt they needed it since he slept in them throughout the stay in Ragg's flat) are all attested to by letters. Cf. Rolfe to Ragg, [Venice], 11 May 1909 (two letters; Berg); Rolfe to Ragg, [Venice], 23 May [1909]; Rolfe to Barbieri, [Venice], 17 May 1909; Rolfe to Captain D., [Venice], n.d., *et al.*, in Letter Book (Martyr Worthy). The account given here is in keeping with the letters.
15. Rolfe to Ragg, [Venice, 23 May 1909] in Letter Book (Martyr Worthy).
16. (Berg).
17. Rolfe, *Desire and Pursuit*, p. 228.
18. Rolfe to Ragg, [Venice], 11 May 1909 (Berg; second letter of that date); cf. Rolfe, *Desire and Pursuit*, p. 228.
19. Rolfe to Ragg, [Venice], Saturday [15 May 1909] (Berg).
20. In Letter Book (Martyr Worthy).
21. Benson to Ragg, [Buntingford], 11 May 1909 (Berg).
22. Cf. Woolf, 'Introduction', in *Letters to Dawkins*, pp. 56–7.
23. In *Letters to Pirie-Gordon*, pp. 103–6.
24. In *Letters to Pirie-Gordon*, pp. 107–9; cf. p. 106.
25. In *Desire and Pursuit*, Rolfe says that he went to the Trattoria agli' Alboretti four days and nights after leaving the Raggs' flat. For the statement that the period in question was two days and nights, cf. his letter to Ragg, above, p. 224.
26. Rolfe, *Desire and Pursuit*, pp. 237–8.
27. In *Letters to Pirie-Gordon*, p. 104.
28. Rolfe to Dawkins, Poundstock, Bude, 12 May 1908 in *Letters to Dawkins*, p. 118.
29. Rolfe, *Desire and Pursuit*, p. 238.
30. In *Letters to Pirie-Gordon*, p. 54.
31. Cf. Rolfe to Pirie-Gordon, Crickhowell, 19 June [1907], in *Letters to Pirie-Gordon*, p. 54; above, p. 133.
32. Rolfe, *Nicholas Crabbe*, pp. 146–7.
33. Rolfe, *Desire and Pursuit*, p. 238. *Desire and Pursuit* is the only authority for the composition of *Toward Aristocracy*.

1. Frederick Rolfe to Lord Alfred Douglas, [Venice, 4 June 1909]; cf. Rolfe to Douglas, [Venice, 18 and 29 May 1909] in Letter Book (Martyr Worthy); Rolfe, *Desire and Pursuit*, p. 238.
2. Cf. Benson to Rolfe, Buntingford, n.d. (Bodleian); Rolfe to Pirie-Gordon, Venice, 15 June 1909 in *Letters to Pirie-Gordon*, p. 111; Rolfe to T. H. Crosland, [Venice, 15 June 1909]; Rolfe to Benson, [Venice, 15 June 1909] in Letter Book (Martyr Worthy); Lord Alfred Douglas to A. J. A. Symons, Hove, 9 February 1934 (Texas).
3. Rolfe to Benson, [Venice, c. 4 June 1909]; cf. Rolfe, 'Regarding Benson', in Letter Book (Martyr Worthy).
4. Rolfe, 'Regarding Benson', in Letter Book (Martyr Worthy); cf. Rolfe to Eustace Virgo, [Venice], 14 June 1909 (the fragment of a letter containing the first sentence and part of the second of 'Regarding Benson'); Rolfe to Stuart Reid, [Venice], 14 June 1909; Rolfe to T. H. Crosland, Venice, 28 June [1909] in Letter Book (Martyr Worthy).
5. Rolfe to Pirie-Gordon, [Venice, 15 June 1909] in Letter Book (Martyr Worthy). The threat is not included in the printed letter of that date; cf. *Letters to Pirie-Gordon*, p. 111. Cf. Rolfe to Benson, [Venice, c. 4 June 1909] in Letter Book (Martyr Worthy); Rolfe to Pirie-Gordon, Venice, 18 May 1909 in *Letters to Pirie-Gordon*, p. 106.
6. Cf. Rolfe to Pirie-Gordon, [Venice], 30 June 1909 in Letter Book (Martyr Worthy); Symons, *Quest*, p. 232; Benson to Pirie-Gordon, Buntingford, n.d. (Bodleian); Benson to Pirie-Gordon, Buntingford, [1909] in *Letters to Pirie-Gordon*, p. 113.
7. Rolfe to Pirie-Gordon, Venice, 18 May 1909; cf. Rolfe to Pirie-Gordon, Venice, [8 May 1909] in *Letters to Pirie-Gordon*, pp. 104, 103.
8. In *Letters to Pirie-Gordon*, p. 110.
9. In Letter Book (Martyr Worthy).
10. Frederick Rolfe to Francis Griffiths, [Venice, c. 6 June] and 18 June 1909 in Letter Book (Martyr Worthy).
11. Rolfe to Barnard & Taylor [Venice], 11 June 1909; cf. Rolfe to Barnard & Taylor [Venice], 27 and 28 May, 4 June 1909 in Letter Book (Martyr Worthy).
12. In Letter Book (Martyr Worthy).
13. Cf. Rolfe to President, The Law Society, Venice, 22 and 27 June, 8 July 1909 in Letter Book (Martyr Worthy).
14. Rolfe to Captain D., [Venice], n.d. in Letter Book (Martyr Worthy); Rolfe to Dawkins, [Venice], 29 May 1909 in *Letters to Dawkins*, pp. 144–7.
15. Rolfe to Barbieri, [Venice], 17 May 1909; cf. Rolfe to Barbieri, [Venice, 15 May 1909] in Letter Book (Martyr Worthy).
16. Rolfe to Barbieri, [Venice], 22 May 1909; cf. Rolfe to Barbieri, [Venice, 18 May 1909] in Letter Book (Martyr Worthy); Rolfe, *Desire and Pursuit*, pp. 241–2.
17. Rolfe to Brown, [Venice], n.d., [22 and 24 May 1909] in Letter Book (Martyr Worthy).
18. Rolfe to Brown, [Venice, 29 May 1909]; cf. Rolfe to Brown, [Venice, 24 May 1909] and n.d. in Letter Book (Martyr Worthy).
19. (Bodleian). cf. below, p. 252.
20. In *Letters to Pirie-Gordon*, p. 89.
21. In Letter Book (Martyr Worthy).
22. Cf. Rolfe to Barbieri, [Venice, 31 May 1909]; Frederick Rolfe to Edward de Zuccato, [Venice, 6 June 1909] in Letter Book (Martyr Worthy).
23. Evaristo Barbieri to C. H. C. Pirie-Gordon, Venice, 9 June 1909 in Woolf, 'Introduction', in *Letters to Dawkins*, p. 56.
24. Cf. Rolfe's form letter in Letter Book (Martyr Worthy); Symons, *Quest*, p. 228; Rolfe, *Desire and Pursuit*, p. 244.

25. Cf. above, p. 234; Woolf, 'Introduction', in *Letters to Dawkins*.
26. Rolfe to de Zuccato, [Venice, 31 May 1909] in Letter Book (Martyr Worthy).
27. Cf. Rolfe to de Zuccato, [Venice, 11 June 1909] in Letter Book (Martyr Worthy).
28. Cf. Rolfe to Ragg, [Venice, c. 13 June 1909] and 1 July 1909; Rolfe to Lady Layard [Venice], 1 July 1909; Rolfe to Hardcastle, [Venice], 1 July 1909; Frederick Rolfe to Giovanni Zandinoni, Venice, 23 June and [1 July 1909] in Letter Book (Martyr Worthy); Rolfe to Pirie-Gordon, Venice, 15 June 1909 in *Letters to Pirie-Gordon*, p. 111.
29. Cf. Rolfe to de Zuccato, [Venice], 24 June 1909; Frederick Rolfe to Dr. Ernest Van Someren, [Venice, 1 June 1909] in Letter Book (Martyr Worthy).
30. Rolfe to Van Someren, [Venice, c. 18 June 1909]; cf. Rolfe to Van Someren, [Venice], c. 4 June 1909] in Letter Book (Martyr Worthy).
31. Rolfe wrote two letters to de Zuccato, both undated, to the same effect. Both are in his Letter Book (Martyr Worthy). Weeks, p. 292, states that the Foreign Office denied Rolfe's request for repatriation. For evidence that Rolfe refused repatriation cf. 'Notes from the F.O. File on Rolfe', Bartholomew (Texas).
32. In Letter Book (Martyr Worthy).
33. Frederick Rolfe to Lord Rosebery, [Venice, 25 June 1909]; cf. Rolfe to Rosebery, [Venice, 31 May 1909] in Letter Book (Martyr Worthy).

[v]

1. Rolfe, *Desire and Pursuit*, p. 245.
2. Rolfe, *Desire and Pursuit*, p. 263.
3. In Letter Book (Martyr Worthy).
4. Cf. Rolfe to de Zuccato, Venice, 9 and 10 August; Frederick Rolfe to George Demain Cooke, [Venice, 29 July 1909] in Letter Book (Martyr Worthy); Rolfe, *Desire and Pursuit*, p. 255.
5. Rolfe to de Zuccato, [Venice, 1 July 1909] in Letter Book (Martyr Worthy).
6. Cf. Frederick Rolfe to Eliot, Venice, 5 July 1909; Rolfe to G. S. Davidson, [Venice, 5 July 1909) in Letter Book (Martyr Worthy).
7. Cf. Rolfe to Cooke, [Venice, 29 July 1909] in Letter Book (Martyr Worthy).
8. Rolfe to Cooke, [Venice, 29 July 1909] in Letter Book (Martyr Worthy); Rolfe, *Desire and Pursuit*, p. 268.
9. In Letter Book (Martyr Worthy).

[vi]

1. Rolfe to Van Someren, [Venice, 30 June 1909] in Letter Book (Martyr Worthy).
2. Cf. Victor Hall, 'The Last Years: Some Memories of Rolfe Venice, Recalled by Mrs. Ivy Van Someren, in an Interview' in *Corvo, 1860–1960*, eds. Cecil Woolf and Brocard Sewell, Aylesford, pp. 63–4.
3. Rolfe to Barnard & Taylor, Venice, 3 January 1910 in Letter Book (Martyr Worthy). The text of the letter is scored with a single line. Thus, it may not have been sent. Facchino means a messenger boy.
4. Frederick Rolfe to Masson Fox, Venice, 25 October 1909 (Texas); cf. below, p. 254.
5. Cf. Rolfe to Barnard & Taylor, [Venice], 28 May and 11 June 1909; Rolfe, 'Regarding Benson'; Rolfe to Pirie-Gordon, [Venice, c. 12 June 1909]; Frederick Rolfe to R. L. H. Curteis, [Venice], 25 July 1909; Rolfe to Brown, [Venice, c. 28 May 1909]; Rolfe to Barbieri, 29 May 1909 *et passim* in Letter Book (Martyr Worthy); Rolfe to Pirie-Gordon, Venice, 4 June, 15 July, 22 August 1909 in *Letters to Pirie-Gordon*, pp. 110–11, 114, 116 *et passim*.
6. In *Letters to Moore*, pp. 58–9. Cf. Frederick Rolfe, Holograph Document marked 'Private & Confidential', c. 1902, 5 pp. (Bodleian).

7. London, 1950.
8. Cf. Frederick Rolfe to Charles Francis Cazenove, Venice, [27 September 1909] in Letter Book (Martyr Worthy). This biographer is unfamiliar with 'An Open Confession'. 'Daughter of a Doge' exists in two ten page holograph manuscripts. One is dated 1 October and the other 6 October 1909. Both are at Harvard. Cf. below, p. 253.
9. Cf. Frederick Rolfe to Thomas Cook & Son, Venice, 28 July 1909; Rolfe to Cooke, Venice, 28 July 1909; Rolfe to Brown, [Venice, c. 8 September 1909] in Letter Book (Martyr Worthy).
10. Rolfe, Desire and Pursuit, p. 252.
11. Ivy Van Someren, 'Baron Corvo's Quarrels', in Life and Letters, February 1947, p. 109.
12. William Butler Yeats, Memoirs, ed. Denis Donoghue, New York, 1973, p. 224.
13. Frederick Rolfe, 'On Cascading into the Canal', in Three Tales, p. 33.
14. Cf. above, p. 115.
15. Rolfe to Nicholson, [Venice, c. 8 September 1909] et passim in Letter Book (Martyr Worthy); Rolfe to Walsh, Hampstead, 23 January 1903, in Letters to Walsh, p. [9].

[vii]

1. Cf. Rolfe to de Zuccato, Venice, 7 August 1909; Rolfe to Cooke, Venice, 31 July 1909; Rolfe to unknown correspondent, Venice, 22 July 1909 in Letter Book (Martyr Worthy).
2. Rolfe to Ragg, Venice, 17 July 1909 in Letter Book (Martyr Worthy); cf. Rolfe to Masson Fox, [Venice], 6 June 1910 (Texas).
3. Rolfe to Cazenove, Venice, 27 September 1909 in Letter Book (Martyr Worthy); cf. Rolfe, Nicholas Crabbe, p. 13.
4. In Letter Book (Martyr Worthy).
5. Rolfe, Desire and Pursuit, p. 4.
6. Rolfe, Desire and Pursuit, pp. 8–9.
7. Cf. Rolfe to Cazenove, Venice, 14 October [1909] in Letter Book (Martyr Worthy); Rolfe to Fox, Venice, 25 October 1909 (Texas); above, p. 244, below, p. 253.
8. Rolfe, Desire and Pursuit, pp. 44, 46.
9. Rolfe to Nicholson, [Venice, c. 15 September 1909] in Letter Book (Martyr Worthy); Rolfe to Fox, Venice [c. 13 January 1910] (Texas).
10. Rolfe to Nicholson, [Venice, c. 15 September 1909] in Letter Book (Martyr Worthy).
11. Cf. Rolfe to Fox, Venice, 11 December 1909 (Texas); Symons, Quest, pp. 12–14; Weeks, pp. 318–29.
12. Cf. Rolfe to Fox, Venice, 11 December 1909 (Texas).
13. Cf. Rolfe to Fox, Venice, 8 November and 9 December 1909 (Texas).
14. Rolfe to Fox, Venice, 10 February [1910]: cf. Rolfe to Fox, Venice, [c. 12 October 1909], 25 October, 9 December 1909 (Texas).
15. Rolfe to Fox, [Venice], 28 December 1909; cf. Rolfe to Fox, [Venice], 9 December 1909 and 10 February [1910] (Texas).
16. Rolfe to Fox [Venice], 11 December 1909 (Texas).
17. Rolfe to Fox, [Venice], 20 January 1910 (Texas).
18. Seventeen letters, five postcards, and two telegrams to Fox are extant.
19. Rolfe to Fox, Venice, Thursday, n.d. (Texas).
20. Rolfe to Fox, [Venice], 11 December 1909; cf. Rolfe to Fox, [Venice], Thursday (Texas).
21. Rolfe to Fox, [Venice, October 1909] (Texas). Cf. above, p. 250.
22. Rolfe to Fox, Venice, 25 October 1909, (Texas).
23. Rolfe to Fox, [Venice], 20 January [1910] (Texas). This letter was written in

three parts under the dates 20, 25 and 27 January. The quotation is from the part dated 25 January 1910.
24. Cf. Rolfe, *Desire and Pursuit*, pp. 46–8, 299; above, p. 167.
25. Rolfe, *Desire and Pursuit*, p. 14.
26. Cf. Rolfe, *Desire and Pursuit*, p. 45.
27. Rolfe to Cazenove, Venice, [27 September 1909] in Letter Book (Martyr Worthy).

[viii]

1. Cf. Hall, in *Corvo 1860–1960*, p. 64.
2. Rolfe to Fox, Venice, 25 October 1909 (Texas).
3. Rolfe to Fox, Venice, 8 November [1909] (Texas); cf. Rolfe, *Desire and Pursuit*, pp. 281–4; Rolfe to Chaffey, Venice, 1 November [1909] in Letter Book (Martyr Worthy).
4. Rolfe to Fox, [Venice, November 1909] (Texas).
5. Rolfe to Pirie-Gordon, [Venice, 25 September 1909] in *Letters to Pirie-Gordon*, p. 120. The MS (13 pp.) of 'Arrested As A Spy', is part of the Martyr Worthy Collection.
6. Rolfe to Benson, [Venice, 25 September 1909] in Letter Book (Martyr Worthy).
7. Cf. above, p. 243.
8. Cf. Rolfe to Fox, Venice, 8 November [1909] (Texas).
9. Cf. Rolfe to Mrs. Eram, [Venice], 22 July, 25 and 31 October 1909 in Letter Book (Martyr Worthy).
10. Rolfe to Fox, [Venice, November 1909] (Texas); cf. Rolfe to Pirie-Gordon, Venice, 22 November 1909 in *Letters to Pirie-Gordon*, p. 122; Rolfe to Dawkins, Venice, 1 November 1909 in *Letters to Dawkins*, p. 150.
11. Rolfe to Cazenove, Venice, [27 September 1909] in Letter Book (Martyr Worthy); cf. Rolfe to Moore, Venice, 18 and 26 June 1909 in *Letters to Moore*, pp. 58–9.
12. Cf. above, pp. 244, 247.
13. Cf. Rolfe to Cazenove, [Venice], 14 October 1909 and n.d. in Letter Book (Martyr Worthy).
14. Rolfe to Fox, Venice, 25 October 1909 (Texas); cf. Rolfe to Cazenove, [Venice], 14 October 1909 in Letter Book (Martyr Worthy).
15. Rolfe to Mrs. Eram, [Venice], 25 October 1909 in Letter Book (Martyr Worthy); cf. Rolfe to Fox, Venice, [November 1909], 9 and 28 December 1909, 27 January [1910] *et passim* (Texas).
16. (Martyr Worthy).
17. Frederick Rolfe to E. M. Knapp, Venice, 2 September 1909; cf. Rolfe to Knapp, Venice, 29 July 1909 in Letter Book (Martyr Worthy).
18. Cf. Rolfe to Fox, Venice, 8 November [1909] (Texas).
19. Rolfe to Pirie-Gordon, Venice, 7 November 1909; cf. Rolfe to Pirie-Gordon, Venice, 1 November 1909 in *Letters to Pirie-Gordon*, pp. 121, 120; Rolfe to the Archbishop of Westminster, Venice, 19 October [1909]; Rolfe to Benson, [Venice], 1 November [1909] in Letter Book (Martyr Worthy).
20. Cf. Rolfe to Barnard & Taylor, Venice, 7 November [1909] in Letter Book (Martyr Worthy).
21. Rolfe to President of the Law Society, [Venice, 19 November 1909]; cf. Rolfe to Barnard & Taylor, Venice, 19 November [1909] in Letter Book (Martyr Worthy); above, p. 257.
22. In Letter Book (Martyr Worthy).
23. Rolfe to Pirie-Gordon, Venice, 20 November 1909 in *Letters to Pirie-Gordon*, p. 122.
24. In Letter Book (Martyr Worthy); *Letters to Pirie-Gordon*, p. 126.
25. Rolfe to Knapp, Venice, 10 December [1909] in Letter Book (Martyr Worthy).
26. In Letter Book (Martyr Worthy).

27. In Letter Book (Martyr Worthy).
28. In Letter Book (Martyr Worthy).
29. Rolfe to Mrs. Eram, Venice, 25 October 1909 in Letter Book (Martyr Worthy); Rolfe to Fox, Venice, 25 October 1909 (Texas).
30. Rolfe to Fox, Venice, Thursday (Texas). Internal evidence dates this letter as following one of 8 November 1909; the earliest letter of December is 9 December with two letters intervening.
31. Rolfe to Fox, [Venice], 9 December 1909 (Texas).
32. Cf. Rolfe to Barbieri, Venice, 24 February 1910; Rolfe to Knapp, [Venice], 24 [February 1910] in Letter Book (Martyr Worthy).
33. Rolfe to Curteis, Venice, [1 August 1909] in Letter Book (Martyr Worthy); cf. above, p. 241.
34. Rolfe to Dawkins, [Venice, 31 January 1909] in Letter Book (Martyr Worthy).
35. Cf. Rolfe to Mrs. Eram, Venice, 25 October 1909 in Letter Book (Martyr Worthy); above, pp. 225, 259.
36. P. x; cf. Rolfe to Ragg, [Venice], 11 May 1909 (Berg); above, pp. 216–7.
37. In Letter Book (Martyr Worthy). Cf. Lonsdale Ragg to Rolfe, Stamford, 3 August 1909 (Berg).
38. Cf. Rolfe to Brown, Venice, 5 January 1910, 2 November [1909]; Rolfe to Eden, [Venice], 25 December 1909; Frederick Rolfe to Augustus Montalba [Venice, c. 28 December 1909], 5 January 1910 in Letter Book (Martyr Worthy).
39. In Letters to Pirie-Gordon, p. 126; Letter Book (Martyr Worthy).
40. Rolfe to Ragg, Venice, 25 July 1910 (Berg); Rolfe to Fox, [Venice], 28 December 1909 (Texas).
41. In Letter Book (Martyr Worthy).
42. Rolfe to Rivingtons, Venice, 9 February 1910 in Letter Book (Martyr Worthy). No record of publication has been found.
43. Rolfe to Dawkins, [Venice, c. 1 February 1910] in Letter Book (Martyr Worthy).
44. Rolfe to Fox, [Venice], Thursday [1909]. Cf. Rolfe to Fox, Venice, 8 November 1909 (Texas); Frederick Rolfe to Mr. Seely, Venice, [6 November 1909]; Rolfe to de Zuccato, Venice, 13 October 1909; Rolfe to Cazenove, Venice, [27 September 1909] in Letter Book (Martyr Worthy).
45. (Texas); cf. Rolfe to Barnard & Taylor, Venice, 3 January 1910; Rolfe to Knapp, Venice, 10 December 1909 in Letter Book (Martyr Worthy); Rolfe to Fox, Venice, 9 and 11 December 1909 and n.d. (Texas).
46. Rolfe to Fox, Venice, 20, 25 and 27 January 1910 (Texas).
47. In Letter Book (Martyr Worthy).

[ix]

1. Cf. Rolfe, Desire and Pursuit, pp. 1–6; Rolfe to Knapp, [Venice], 15 April [1910]; Rolfe to Pirie-Gordon, [Venice, 15 April 1910] in Letter Book (Martyr Worthy); Rolfe to Pirie-Gordon, Venice, 15 April 1910 in Letters to Pirie-Gordon, p. 130; Rolfe to Fox, [Venice] 6 June 1910 (Texas).
2. Cf. Hall in Corvo 1860–1960, p. 65.
3. Frederick Rolfe to Horace Fletcher, [Venice], 16 March [1910]. Cf. Frederick Rolfe to Vail, Venice, [3 April 1910]; Rolfe to Van Someren, [Venice, 26 March, 1910] et passim in Letter Book (Martyr Worthy); Hall in Corvo 1860–1960, p. 65.
4. Rolfe to Horace Fletcher, [Venice], 16 March [1910]; cf. Rolfe to Vail, Venice [3 April 1910]; Rolfe to de Zuccato, [Venice, 5 March 1910] in Letter Book (Martyr Worthy).
5. (Texas); cf. Rolfe to de Zuccato, [Venice, 5 March 1910] in Letter Book (Martyr Worthy).
6. Rolfe to Fox, Venice, 5 April 1910 (Texas).
7. Cf. Rolfe to Van Someren, [Venice, 17 March 1910] in Letter Book (Martyr Worthy).

8. In Letter Book (Martyr Worthy).
9. In Letter Book (Martyr Worthy).
10. In Letter Book (Martyr Worthy). Cf. Rolfe to Van Someren, [Venice, 17 March 1910] in Letter Book (Martyr Worthy).
11. In Letter Book (Martyr Worthy).
12. Cf. Frederick Rolfe to David Garnett, [Venice, 19 March 1910], 1 April [1910]; Rolfe to Horatio Brown, [Venice, 3 April 1910] (copies were sent to Frederick Eden, August Montalba, Canon Ragg, and Lady Layard); Rolfe to Chaffey, [Venice, 20 March 1910]; Rolfe to Ivy Van Someren, [Venice, 20 March and 3 April 1910] in Letter Book (Martyr Worthy).
13. Cf. Rolfe to Fletcher, [Venice], 16 March [1910]; Rolfe to Knapp, [Venice], 16 March [1910]; Rolfe to Van Someren, [Venice, 17 March 1910] in Letter Book (Martyr Worthy).
14. (Texas).
15. Cf. Rolfe to Pirie-Gordon, [Venice, 19 March 1910]; Rolfe to Barnard & Taylor, [Venice], 19 March [1910]; Rolfe to Knapp, [Venice], 16 March [1910] in Letter Book (Martyr Worthy); [William Rider & Son, Limited] to Frederick Rolfe, [London], 9 March 1910 in *Letters to Pirie-Gordon*, p. 137.
16. Rolfe to Knapp, [Venice], 27 March 1910 in Letter Book (Martyr Worthy).
17. Cf. Laura Ragg, 'Epilogue', in *Letters to Dawkins*, p. 178; Laura Ragg, 'Note' (Berg); Rolfe to Fox, [Venice], 6 June 1910; copy of telegram to Fox, London, 22 April 1910 (Texas); Rolfe to Dawkins, [Venice, 28 May 1910] in *Letters to Dawkins*, p. 153; Rolfe to Walsh, Venice, 21 February 1910 in *Letters to Walsh*, p. 30; Rolfe to Moore, Venice, 26 June 1909 in *Letters to Moore*, p. 59.
18. In Hall, in *Corvo 1860–1960*, pp. 67–8.
19. In *Letters to Pirie-Gordon*, p. 131; *Letters to Dawkins*, p. 152; Rolfe to Ragg, [Venice, 12 May 1910] (Berg). Cf. Rolfe to Walsh, Venice, 18 May 1910 in *Letters to Walsh* p. [31]; Rolfe to Fox, [Venice], 12 May 1910 (Texas); Laura Ragg 'Note' (Berg).
20. In *Letters to Walsh*, pp. [31]–2; Donald Weeks, 'Notes', in *Letters to Walsh*, p. 55; Rolfe to Fox, Venice, 12 May 1910 (Texas).
21. Cf. Ralph Shirley to Frederick Rolfe, [London], 26 July 1910 in *Letters to Pirie-Gordon*, p. 138; Rolfe to Fox, [Venice], 30 June and 11 July 1910 (Texas); Rolfe to Walsh, Venice, 18 May 1910 in *Letters to Walsh*, p. [31].
22. Rolfe to Walsh, Venice, 18 May 1910; cf. Rolfe to Walsh, Venice, 21 February 1910 in *Letters to Walsh*, pp. 33, 30.
23. Cf. Rolfe to Walsh, Venice, 28 August 1910 in *Letters to Walsh*, p. 33. *Nicholas Crabbe* was published (London, 1934) with the sub-title *Or The One And The Many*. A typescript in two volumes of *Nicholas Crabbe*, now at the Bodleian, is preceded by three and a half pages, holograph, on which the title is written as published. Yet, repeatedly, Rolfe referred to *Nicholas Crabbe* as one book and 'The One And The Many' as another. No satisfactory reason for that fact has been established. It can only be conjectured that he once planned a book, even started it, meant to be called 'The One And The Many' or that he was careless or that he deliberately lied. That last was hardly the case with Walsh inasmuch as Rolfe had every expectation that Walsh would receive his typescript and attempt to place it.
24. Rolfe to Fox, [Venice], 5 April 1910 (Texas); Rolfe to Dawkins, [Venice], 19 March 1911 in *Letters to Dawkins*, p. 165. Cf. Rolfe to Fox, [Venice], 6 June 1910 (Texas).
25. Rolfe to Fox, [Venice], 11 July and 6 June 1910 (Texas).
26. Rolfe to Fox, [Venice] 11 July 1910 (Texas).
27. Rolfe to Walsh, Venice, 18 May 1910 in *Letters to Walsh*, p. 33.
28. Cf. Rolfe to Walsh, Venice, 28 August 1910 in *Letters to Walsh*, p. 34; Rolfe to Fox, [Venice], 1 and 21 August, 11 July 1910 (Texas); Ivy Van Someren, 'Corvo's Quarrels', *Life and Letters*, February 1947, p. 109.
29. Walsh to Rolfe, New York, 16 August 1910 in *Letters to Walsh*, p. 35.

30. In *Letters to Walsh*, p. 36.
31. Rolfe to Pirie-Gordon, Venice, 6 September 1910 in *Letters to Pirie-Gordon*, p. 138; cf. Rolfe to Fox, [Venice], 21 August 1910 (Texas).
32. Cf. Rolfe to Moore, Venice, 22 August 1913; Weeks, pp. 353–4; Symons, *Quest*, pp. 236–7.
33. Cf. Rolfe to Dawkins, 6 September 1910 in *Letters to Dawkins*, p. 158.

[x]

1. In *Letters to Dawkins*, p. 161; cf. p. 165. The proverb in Rolfe's translation reads, 'Love is for him who knows how to make it'. Cf. Rolfe, *Desire and Pursuit*, p. 297.
2. (Berg).
3. Cf. Rolfe to Dawkins, Venice, 19 March 1911 in *Letters to Dawkins*, p. 165; Rolfe to Walsh, Venice, 16 March 1911 in *Letters to Walsh*, p. [37].
4. Rolfe to Dawkins, Venice, 19 March 1911 in *Letters to Dawkins*, p. 65; Rolfe to Walsh, Venice, 16 March 1911 in *Letters to Walsh*, p. [37].
5. In *Letters to Dawkins*, p. 162.
6. Cf. 'Notes from the Foreign Office File on Rolfe', in Bartholomew (Texas).
7. In *Letters to Walsh*, p. 38; *Letters to Dawkins*, pp. 165–6; cf. pp. 162–4.
8. In *Letters to Dawkins*, p. 167; cf. Rolfe to Walsh, Venice, 19 May 1911 in *Letters to Walsh*, p. 39.
9. Cf. Letter Book (Martyr Worthy).
10. (Martyr Worthy).
11. Rolfe, 'Arrested As A Spy' (Martyr Worthy).
12. Cf. unnamed article on the Venetians (Martyr Worthy); Frederick Rolfe to J. S. Serjeant, [Venice] n.d. (Bodleian); Frederick Rolfe to William Rider & Son Ltd., [Venice], 12 March [1913] (Bodleian); Ellen E. Rolfe to Mrs. Pirie-Gordon, Broadstairs, 5 and 15 April 1911 in *Letters to Pirie-Gordon*, pp. 139–40; above, pp. 192, 213, 218; below, pp. 276–7.
13. (Bodleian).
14. Rolfe to Serjeant, [Venice], n.d. (Bodleian).
15. Cf. Rolfe to Ragg, Venice, 20 December 1911 (Berg); Rolfe to Pirie-Gordon, Venice, 20 December 1911 in *Letters to Pirie-Gordon*, pp. 140–1.
16. Cf. Frederick Rolfe to William Shirley, Venice, 7 June [1912] (Bodleian).

[xi]

1. Cf. Rolfe to Dawkins, Venice, [2 April 1912] in *Letters to Dawkins*, p. 168.
2. Cf. Hall in *Corvo, 1860–1960*, p. 70; interview with Antonio Arban, June 1970.
3. Rolfe to William Rider & Son Ltd., [Venice], 12 March 1913; Rolfe to W. Marris, [Venice], 16 August [1912] (Bodleian); cf. Rolfe to Moore, Venice, 22 August 1913 in *Letters to Moore*, p. 67.
4. John Cowper Powys, *Autobiography*, London, 1934, p. 411.
5. Cf. Rolfe to Shirley, Venice, 7 June [1912] (Bodleian).
6. Cf. Rolfe to Shirley, Venice, 7 June [1912] (Bodleian).
7. Cf. [Mrs. Morgan Akin Jones], 'Encounter with Corvo', reprinted from *Desiderata*, 5 August 1915 in 'Introduction', by Cecil Woolf and Bertram W. Korn in *Letters to Moore*, pp. 18–20; cf. Rolfe to Shirley, [Venice], 28 June 1912 (Bodleian).
8. Cf. Frederick Baron Corvo, *Amico de Sandro . . .*, Privately printed, 1951.
9. [Frederick Rolfe], Holograph MS. (Bodleian).
10. (Bodleian).
11. Holograph MS. (Martyr Worthy); cf. Frederick Rolfe, 'Venetian Courtesy', *Blackwood's Magazine*, September 1913, pp. 360–6; Frederick Rolfe (Baron Corvo), 'Venetian Courtesy', in *Three Tales of Venice*, pp. 9–24.

12. Rolfe to Shirley, [Venice], 16 August 1912; Rolfe to Marris, [Venice], 16 August 1912; cf. Rolfe to Shirley, [Venice], 28 June 1912; Rolfe to Smith Elder, Venice, 31 May 1912 (Bodleian).
13. (Bodleian).
14. Cf. Frederick Rolfe to Macmillan, Venice, 31 May 1912; Rolfe to Smith Elder, Venice, 31 May 1912 (Bodleian).
15. Cf. above, pp. 256–7.
16. In *Letters to Moore*, p. 63. Cf. *Blackwood's Magazine*, June 1913, pp. 815–22; July 1913, pp. 54–62; September 1913, pp. 360–2.
17. Rolfe to Moore, Venice, 3 October 1913; cf. Rolfe to Moore, Venice, [c. 2 September 1913], 12 July 1913, [c. 20 June 1913], [c. April 1913] in *Letters to Moore*, pp. 60–70.
18. Cf. Rolfe to Moore, Venice [c. April], 12 July, 5 and 22 August, [c. 2 September], 3 October 1913 in *Letters to Moore*, pp. 60, 64, 65, 66, 67, 68.
19. Norman Douglas, *Looking Back*, London, 1933, p. 309; cf. p. 312.
20. (Bodleian).
21. Rolfe to William Rider & Son Ltd., [Venice], 12 March [1913] (Bodleian).
22. (Bodleian).
23. Interview with Arban, 1970. Cf. Rolfe to Dawkins, Poundstock, Bude, 16 May 1908 in *Letters to Dawkins*, p. 102; above, p. 2.
24. Covelli had the portrait in England in 1915, when he attempted to sell it. Cf. Robert Cust to A. T. Bartholomew, Hampstead, 12 May 1919 in Bartholomew (Texas).
25. Interview with Arban, 1970.

[xii]

1. Cf. Laura Ragg, 'Epilogue', in *Letters to Dawkins*, p. 179; Rolfe to Moore, Venice, [c. April 1913] in *Letters to Moore*, p. 60.
2. Cf. above, p. 281; Rolfe to Moore, Venice, [c. 20 June], 15 July, 5 and 22 August, [c. 2 September], 3 October 1913 in *Letters to Moore*, pp. 62–3, 64–5, 66, 67, 68–9.
3. Herbert Rolfe to A. T. Bartholomew, London, 21 May 1926 in Bartholomew (Texas).
4. Cf. Rolfe to Moore, Venice, 3 October 1913 in *Letters to Moore*, p. 68.
5. Herbert Rolfe to Ellen E. Rolfe, Venice, 30 October 1913 in Bartholomew (Texas); cf. Weeks, pp. 371–2.
6. Cf. Herbert Rolfe to Bartholomew, London, 21 May 1926 in Bartholomew (Texas). Weeks, p. 397, says that through the intervention of Sir Shane Leslie, whose article 'Frederick Baron Corvo', had appeared in *The London Mercury* for September 1923 (pp. 507–18), John Quinn, the New York lawyer, bibliophile and patron of the arts, actually paid for the niche on the Cemetery Island of San Michele purchased in perpetuity. Quinn may have done so. Herbert Rolfe clearly stated that he held the receipts for the arrangements made for his brother's 'decent Christian burial', on 30 October 1913. He is less precise in his reference to the second, permanent burial niche. He says only that he 'was allowed after much negotiation, to buy a permanent resting place'.

323

Index

Bonds, 217
Borgia, Cesare, 141, 169
Borgia, Count Cesare, 2, 120, 139–40, 148, 149, 285
Borgia, Count Francesco, 2, 285
Borgia, Lucrezia, 169
Borgiada, 140–1, 143, 147–8, 150, 156, 158, 172, 173, 174, 181, 185, 186, 187, 194, 220, 233, 258, 284
Borgias, 112, 117
Botticelli, Sandro, 280
Bourne, Archbishop, 201
Bowen, Elizabeth, 10
'Boy Martyr of Norwich, The' (Rolfe), 27
Bracht, Franz Wilhelm V. (*pseud.*), 92
'Breastplate of St. Patrick, The' (Rolfe), 87
Brown, Horatio, 214, 217, 223, 224, 235–236, 243, 246, 248, 256, 259, 262, 270
Bull Against the Enemy of the Anglican Race, The (Rolfe), 213, 228, 229
Bullen, Arthur Henry, 142–3, 149, 156, 280
Burke, 195
Burnett, Robin, 60
Burney, Fanny, 20
'Burrowers, The' (Rolfe), 243, 258
Bute, John Patrick Crichton, Marquis of, 17–18, 20, 26

Caenazzo, Carlo, 208–9, 210, 248–9, 250, 253, 254, 281
Campbell, Monsignor James A., 29, 31, 32, 33–4, 35, 37–8, 286
'Canzonata' (Rolfe), 49
Caracalla, 130
Caradoc, 76
'Cardinal Prefect of Propaganda, The' (Rolfe), 127, 137
Carlo; see Caenazzo, Carlo
Carmont, Canon Robert, 32, 35, 36, 38
Carpenter, Edward, 68, 228, 248
Castle, Cecil, 26, 46, 48, 50, 54
Catherwood, E. J., 90
'Catholic Criticism' (? Rolfe), 69
Cazenove, Charles Francis, 256–7, 282
Cellini, Benvenuto, 80
Chaffey, Edith A., 217, 223, 246, 254, 259, 260, 261–3, 267, 270
Champion, Henry Hyde, 61, 66–70, 71, 78, 161, 162
Chapman, Frederic, 95, 96, 98, 116, 117, 133, 158
Charles II, 67
Charles III, 54

Chaucer, Geoffrey, 80
'Chaunte Royal in Honour of the Most Pure Mother of God, A' (Rolfe), 23, 26, 31
Chester, May (*pseud.*), 92
'Christ Bearer, The' (Rolfe), 26
Chronicles of the House of Borgia (Rolfe), 113, 119–20, 133, 135, 138, 139–40, 141, 143, 149, 158, 169
'Cicero's Oration for Joan of Arc' (Rolfe and Douglas), 177
Clarke, Father, 20
Cockerton, 248, 249, 252
Colles, 71, 78
'Commercial Future of Rhodesia, The' (Rolfe and Thomas), 172
Commodus, 130
Comper, John, 64
'Concerning Benson' (Rolfe), 237
'Concerning England and Germany' (Rolfe), 162, 229
Conder, Charles, 113
Conrad, Joseph, 138
Cooke, George Demain, 238, 239–41, 243, 244, 245–6, 278
Cooke, Mrs. George Demain, 240–1
Corrigan, Thomas, 90
Corrigan, Mrs. Thomas, 90
Corvo, Baron (*pseud.*), 45, 47, 49–51, 52, 56, 67, 74, 77, 86, 87, 120, 156–7, 207 *et passim*
Coulton, G. G., 15
Courtney, 141
Covelli, 283, 285
Crabbe, Nicholas (*pseud.*), 2, 123–4, 157, 163–5, 167, 244–5, 269 *et passim*
Crabmaid (*pseud.*), 165
Crackanthorpe, Hubert, 79, 113
Creighton, Mandell, 119
Crosland, T. H., 229–30, 258
Crowley, Aleister, 164
Curtis, Mrs. Daniel, 214, 220
Curzon, Sophia Caroline, 39
Custance, Olive, 79

D., Captain, 234
Dalrymple, Sir Walter, 65
Daly, 55
D'Annunzio, Gabriel, 218
d'Anvers, N.; see Bell, Mrs. George Arthur
d'Arcy, Ella, 1, 79, 108, 113, 170
'Daughter of a Doge' (Rolfe), 244, 247, 253
David, Saint, 76
Davis, William Henry, 108, 112

Dawkins, John, 196
Dawkins, Richard, 1–3, 106, 200, 203, 204, 208–10, 211–12, 216, 219, 228, 234, 236, 245, 263, 270, 274–5, 276, 278, 283
'De Academia' (Rolfe), 256
d'Este, Cardinal Ippolito, 169
de Fontmell, E. V.; see Virgo, Eustace
'Deinon to Thely' (Rolfe), 220, 227, 229, 230, 235
Deira, Vincenza, Duchess of (*pseud.*), 87, 92, 97
Delli, Matilde, 273, 275, 282
de la Gard Grissel, Hartwell, 38
de Maricourt, René, Conte, 117
'De Presbytero' (Rolfe), 256
Desire and Pursuit of the Whole, The (Rolfe), 35, 78, 123–4, 165, 225, 243, 245–7, 253, 254, 260, 264–7, 269, 270–2, 275, 282
Dey, Monsignor James, 22–4, 101, 160
de Zucatto, Edward, 236, 237, 245, 265, 272, 275
Dickens, Charles, 177
Dole, Nathan Haskell, 135
'Dom Gheraldo' (Rolfe), 96, 125: see *Don Renato*
'Don Ghirlando's Diarium' (Rolfe), 158: see *Don Renato*
Don Renato (Rolfe), 38, 47, 96–7, 111, 115, 117, 134, 193, 197, 200, 203, 212, 216 227, 232, 243, 258, 282
Don Tarquinio (Rolfe), 125, 127, 137, 158, 165, 168–70, 178, 180, 183, 186, 188, 192, 193
Doré, Gustave, 58
Douglas, Lord Alfred, 79, 110, 229–30
Douglas, Canon Archibald, 29
Douglas, Norman, 283
Douglas, Sholto, 128–32, 138, 145, 158, 167–8, 188
Doyle, John, 209
du Cane, Olivia, 217
'Duchess Attendolo' (Rolfe), 178
Duhamel, 18–19
Dunbar, William, 47

Eden, Frederick, 217, 236, 259
Edmund, Saint, 49
Edward VII, 15, 228
Egerton, George, 79
Eliot, George, 177
Ellwanger, George Herman, 52
English, Frank (*pseud.*), 138–9, 140, 141, 142 *et passim*
Ephoros, Toto, 40–2; see *In His Own Image: Stories Toto Told Me*; Toto
Eram, Mrs., 255–7, 260, 266

Esher, Lord, 185
'Esoteric Jewelry' (Rolfe), 155
Evans, J. Y. B., 31
Evans, P. M., 100
Ewing, Mrs. Juliana Horatia, 22
'Excommunicate' (Rolfe), 142

Faliero, Marino, 253
Fausto, 237, 248, 250
Felici, Lieutenant Italo, 218
Firbank, Ronald, 177, 184, 214
Fisher, W. J., 114
Fletcher, Horace, 242, 266
Flynn, Father, 86, 90, 93
Fox, Charles Masson, 248–50, 251–2, 254, 257, 260, 262, 264, 265–6, 267–8, 269, 270, 271
Frederick of Venice (*pseud.*), 281

Galsworthy, John, 138
Gardner, Charles Carrington, 46, 54–6, 99, 118
Garnett, David, 267
Garnett, Richard, 79, 119, 139, 140–1, 147, 160
'General Election of 1890 in Italy, The' (Rolfe), 47
George III, 7
Gerrie, Father Alexander, 61
Geering, 62
'Ghost or Fancy' (Rolfe), 31
Giamini, Luigi, 31
Gigio, 237
Gilder, Joseph, 141
Gildo; see Vianello, Ermengildo
Gleeson White, Cecily, 51
Gleeson White, Eric, 48, 51, 52
Gleeson White, Joseph William, 25–6, 28, 45, 46, 48, 49, 50, 52, 54–6, 58, 63, 64, 80, 111
Gleeson White, Mrs. Joseph William (Nancy), 25, 45, 46, 50–2, 53, 56, 67, 99, 111, 161, 184
'Goat in Priest's Clothing, A' (Rolfe and Douglas), 129, 142, 167
Gosse, Sir Edmund, 146, 147, 150
Graham, Arthur Smith, 129, 168
Grahame, Kenneth, 79, 110, 115, 118, 158, 169
Gray, John, 113
Green, Father Patrick, 99
Greene, Graham, 163
Gregory, Lady, 244
Gregory, Saint, 76
Griffiths, Francis, 232, 237, 258, 282
Griffiths, Mrs. Isabelle, 108, 118, 138,

Griffiths, Mrs. Isabelle (*contd.*) 144–5, 151–2, 153, 154–5, 157, 158, 159, 172, 174, 177, 219

Haddon, Trevor, 124–8, 129, 132, 159, 166
Hadrian The Seventh (Rolfe), 14, 36, 38, 68, 72, 78, 123, 144, 158–64, 166, 168, 169 170, 171, 172–3, 178, 179, 180–3, 189, 193, 229
Haggard, H. Rider, 192
Hamner, N. J., 76, 88, 94
Handly, Charlotte, 190
Hannay, Arnold, 233
Hannay, James, 114, 122, 128
Hannay, Mrs. James (Margaret), 114, 122
Hardcastle, Edward, 220–1, 223, 225–6, 234
Hardie, Keir, 68, 69, 161
Hardy, E. G., 14, 16, 103–4, 114, 117, 136–137, 138, 139, 147, 160, 171, 172, 180, 187, 189, 192–3, 196
Hardy, Mrs. E. G., 16
Hardy, Thomas, 22, 123
Harland, Henry, 78, 79–80, 85, 109–10, 113–14, 122, 128, 129, 136–7, 157, 166, 170–1, 188
Harland, Mrs. Henry (Aline), 113–14, 122, 170–1
Hart, Horace, 141
Haves, Father, 17
Hay, Cuthbert, 60, 78, 98, 99
Hay, Georgina, 60–1, 99
Hay, James Gordon, 60
Hay, Malcolm, 60, 78, 98, 99
Heliogobalus, 129
Henderson, James, 63
Henley, W. E., 22
Henry IX, 54
Herford, Vernon, 179
Hewlett, Maurice, 136, 137–8, 147
Hilliers, Ashton, 231; see Wallis, Henry Marriage
Hocheimer, Frank W., 87, 90–5
Hocheimer, Mrs. Frank W., 92–4
Hohenlohe, Prince, 217, 223, 236
Holden, John, 72, 79–80, 81, 82, 83–5, 86, 89, 92, 97, 102, 124, 127, 128, 158, 159, 188
Holland, Vyvyan, 184
Holmfield, Frank (? *pseud.*), 127
Hopkins, Gerard Manley, 162
'How Christians Love One Another' (Rolfe), 89
'How I Was Buried Alive' (Rolfe), 97–8, 107, 162

Howes, George, 11
Hubert's Arthur (Rolfe and Pirie-Gordon), 1, 34, 123, 192, 197, 200, 203, 209, 212, 213, 218–20, 227, 231–2, 234, 243, 258, 260, 276–8, 280, 282
Hunter Blair, Father David, 19, 99, 120, 173
Hulton, William, 217
Huntly, Marquis of, 65

'Ideal Content, An' (Rolfe), 125, 128, 129, 133, 138, 140, 142, 143, 168, 183, 192; see *Don Renato*
Ignatius Loyola, Saint, 76
In His Own Image (Rolfe), 41, 78, 121, 122, 124, 128, 132, 134, 136, 140, 158, 166, 178; see Ephoros, Toto; *Stories Toto Told Me*; Toto
'In re Lead Fume' (Rolfe), 137
Innocent III, Pope, 191
Innocent The Great (Rolfe and Pirie-Gordon), 192, 197
Isaacs, Isaac Henry Solomon, 111, 115, 169; see Scott, Temple
'Ivory, Apes, and Peacocks' (Rolfe), 178, 180, 185

James III, 54
James, Henry, 79, 109, 138, 214
Jenkins, 8, 146
Jerome, Jerome K., 69, 78
Jerrold, Blanchard, 58
Jesurum, Aldo, 241
Johnson, Brimley, 149
Johnstone, Humphreys, 218
Jones, F. Llewellyn, 88
Jones, Mrs. Morgan Akin, 280
Jones, Parry, 80

Kains Jackson, Charles, 26, 28, 40, 45, 46, 47–50, 51, 53–4, 58, 113, 156, 157, 223
Kerr, Philip, 184, 195
'King of the Wood, The' (Rolfe), 178, 243, 258
Knapp, E. M., 257–8, 259, 264, 267, 268
Knill, Sir Stuart, 65
Kitchener, Lord, 195

Labouchere, Henry, 179
Lamb, Mr. and Mrs., 61, 65–6, 99, 118
Lampridius, 130
Lane, John, 78, 85, 91, 95, 96, 97, 108–12, 113–15, 118, 121, 127, 132, 134–5, 137, 138, 144, 145, 146–7, 158, 159, 166, 170–171, 174
Laurie, Werner, 170

329

330